EVERYBODY'S BUSINESS

EVERYBODY'S BUSINESS

THE UNLIKELY STORY OF HOW BIG BUSINESS CAN FIX THE WORLD

JON MILLER & LUCY PARKER

First published in Great Britain in 2013 by
Biteback Publishing Ltd
Westminster Tower
3 Albert Embankment
London SE1 7SP

ISBN 978-1-84954-608-9

10 9 8 7 6 5 4 3 2 1

A CIP catalogue record for this book is available from the British Library.

Set in Chronicle and Neutra Text

Printed and bound in Great Britain by
CPI Group (UK) Ltd, Croydon CR0 4YY

CONTENTS

INTRODUCTION

Start a conversation about the role of big business in the world and, even before you reach the end of your first sentence, you'll often find you've unleashed a furious response. It's as if you tap into a well of anger, an instinctive animosity. You hit a nerve, a sharp sense of injustice. The very subject meets with a narrow-eyed mistrust. To many, it feels as though business has become detached from society. So, for lots of people trying to imagine how to make the future a better place, it's hard to see how to put business in that picture. That's a great problem for the world: we're facing global challenges of unprecedented magnitude, and business has the scale, resources and expertise to make a positive difference. So if you want to fix the world, you might find you're better off harnessing the power of business, rather than fighting it.

It's easy to see why the standing of big business in public opinion has been on a relentless downward slide over the years. For many, the business world has an ignominious recent history. Back in the 1970s and 1980s, a series of devastating leaks and spills in the oil and chemical industries gave credence to the view that corporates were growing rich at the expense of others and at great cost to the natural world. At that time, the dark arts of the tobacco industry and the dubious practices of the pharmaceutical companies began to hit the headlines. In the 1990s, the world was shocked that much-loved consumer brands were manufactured in terrible sweatshop conditions. As the 2000s started and obesity levels soared in the developed world, the food and drink industry stood accused of making vast profits at the expense of their customers' health. The extractive industries – mining, oil, gas – were seen to plunder the resources of the developing world, leaving environmental destruction in their wake. All of this while corporate fraud on a massive scale brought down a string of well-respected companies. Most recently, the financial crisis and a succession of major banking scandals have rocked public confidence further. And a steady supply of stories about tax dodging and sky-high bonuses reinforces a widespread perception about big business: that it exists for the enrichment of a small elite, at the expense of everyone else.

From this perspective, it looks as if the relationship between the business world and the rest of society has broken down completely. Big businesses are the bad guys, the faceless megacorps, unaccountable and out of control. On that logic, the only reasonable conclusion is to rein them in, to subdue the beast.

We want to turn the argument on its head, to come at it from a different angle. Today's big companies are powerful actors in the world and it's our view that we need to mobilise that power, not try to take it down. Of course, power, any power, has the potential for great harm. While there is much in the record of business which is unacceptable by any lights, business is also a powerful engine of progress and social change. It's time to get beyond the cartoonish storyline of 'good' in a noble fight against 'evil', because to demonise big business is to waste a huge opportunity. Big companies have many of the essential capabilities we need to tackle many of the most challenging problems we all face. It's not an act of faith or a theoretical construct. There are many real-life examples of how it can work in practice. In *Everybody's Business* we take a journey through the world of business to look at some of those companies that demonstrate such potential.

Our journey begins in the smallholder farms of Africa, where it's possible to see in vivid relief the difference a big business can make when it engages directly in the struggle of rural communities to lift themselves out of poverty. We travel to Silicon Valley and meet some of the businesses that are shaping the world we live in, driven by a sense of purpose and a restless desire to innovate. Although they're worlds apart, the village cooperatives of Uganda and the high-tech corporations of the Valley both illustrate how businesses grow up to create the fabric of the local economy that people live and work in.

We visit corporates in many different sectors, operating all over the world: telecoms, manufacturing, mining, technology, pharmaceuticals, apparel, engineering and others. We look at how some of the angriest of fault lines in the relationship between business and society have become fertile ground for collaboration. We hear how working in partnership is the new front-line of doing business in a way which works for everyone. Some of the companies we meet have had their own dark night of the soul: today's heroes are sometimes yesterday's villains, and their stories have much to teach us.

Even as we wrote, some of the companies we feature in this book found parts of their operations challenged for bad practice, accused of corruption or in the firing line of the debate on hot issues, such as tax. We are not arguing – and, by the way, neither are the companies themselves – that everything in the garden is always rosy. There is no steady state of equilibrium to be arrived at. What matters is how a company chooses to face the challenges as they arise: the authenticity of the response, and their readiness to engage with the problem.

The territory we're in is big business, because these are the kinds of businesses that people are worried about. These corporates have tens of thousands, sometimes hundreds of thousands, of employees. Their products reach millions, sometimes billions, of people. As big beasts in the corporate ecosystem, they have a symbiotic relationship with tens of thousands of smaller companies, for whom they provide a route to market and a source of opportunity. When they work out how to create a positive impact for society at large, they have the influence to move the others in their sector and set the pace for change. That's why how they act is everybody's business.

BIG BUSINESS IS IN EVERYBODY'S LIFE

Every time we send an email, feed our families, charge our mobile phones, take a painkiller, pay a bill, have a shower, make a journey, watch a movie or enjoy a beer, we can be sure that a number of big companies are at work. Big business is an organising force: bringing together the ideas with the investment, building the infrastructure and production capability, running the systems, delivering the products and services. Our modern lifestyles are underpinned by these enormous companies. Wherever we live in the world, it's a reality that business is playing an important part in our lives. Big business is an integral part of society, not separate from it.

BIG BUSINESS IS EVERYBODY'S RESPONSIBILITY

Today's large companies have become significant players on the global stage. Nobody runs the internet, but around seven large corporates provide its physical backbone. A handful of major mining companies extract most of the world's copper – an essential building block of our electronic age. For example, it's thought that around ten corporates run the global food system. These companies, and others like them, are all important actors in our world, and we are all affected by what they do and how they do it. So big business really is everybody's concern.

Society gets the businesses it deserves: if we're unhappy

about a company's behaviour, we need to do something about it. Most of the smartest businesses we meet know this. They register criticism – even the harshest, most uncomfortable criticism – as a signal, and they use it as an opportunity to question old practices and a spur to innovation. Social censure can be highly effective: some of the leading companies in this book have responded to such pressure by using it as a catalyst for change. Businesses are big problem-solving machines: identifying flaws in the operation today in order to make it work better tomorrow. That's why, on occasion, facing the negative social consequences of their actions can become the basis of the plan to create a more positive impact.

BIG BUSINESS NEEDS TO WORK FOR EVERYBODY

Every business is made up of myriad choices – some big strategic decisions and countless small tactical ones. The impact that a business has on the world depends on how it makes choices: where to source raw materials from, how to design its manufacturing processes, how to transport goods, how to pay employees, how to cut costs, when to close a factory, where to open a shop, how to price its products, how to market them, where to invest time and money. When there has been a breakdown of trust between business and society, it has been when those decisions are made with little consideration of the likely impact on the outside world.

In the past few decades the rise of shareholder interests has often served to push to the margins a more balanced consideration of the interests of others: everyone else seemed to be of secondary importance. But the business world is on a journey. Most corporates are aware now that the way they do business needs to take account of their social and environmental impact. There's hardly a big business in the Western world that doesn't have a large corporate and social responsibility department busy measuring the consequences of its actions and charged with helping the management to make better decisions. Yet today's more progressive businesses are taking this one step further. They're not content with just minimising harm; they want to have a positive impact on the world. The stories we tell in this book are of businesses that aim to deliver financial value hand in hand with social value.

BIG BUSINESS CAN HELP FIX THE WORLD

A big company can be thought of as an intense concentration of resources, skills and expertise. Major corporates today have complex networks of operations, suppliers, distributors and partners stretching across the globe. Some leading companies are waking up to their own potential to use this power to have a broader benefit. The conventional assumption would be that businesses provide social benefit through philanthropic donations to good causes, and it ends there. Philanthropy is a valuable contribution in itself, but it's not what we're talking about here. *Everybody's Business* is about how a business can add value to the world around it *by being a business* – in other words, through its core activities and not through philanthropy on the side. And our journey through the world of business gives us reasons for hope. In this book, we look at a number of examples of companies which are growing their business by joining the global effort to take on some of today's toughest challenges. Drawing on the resources and capabilities at their disposal, they're asking a powerful question: *how can we help?*

This means we're seeing a new stance from some quarters of the business world, companies that are deliberating aligning their strategies to respond to global challenges. It's a big shift in attitude from the bastion mentality associated with the old days. The traditional big corporate seems like a citadel: a well-defended fortress, built to keep the world out. From inside, if the issues that concern the world appear on the horizon, they're to be treated as threats and wrestled into submission. But today's most forward-looking business leaders have stepped out over the drawbridge with the aim of engaging with the wider world.

There's no shortage of places to start. We're living in the Age of Conversation: the world is noisy with an ever-expanding sprawl of conversations about the things that worry us all. Fuelled by unprecedented access to information and ubiquitous communications devices, the tone seems increasingly intense, growing in urgency. Everyone's got a say. It's unsurprising then that some corporates, historically more comfortable in situations where they can control the conversation, stay out of the fray. It's hard to hear their own thoughts above the racket and they don't know where to join or how.

This is why we crystallised *The 11 Conversations* – a way of giving shape to the big debates in the public information space. Just as it's said that there are only seven basic plots in drama, so we think there are only eleven big conversations. These are enduring themes in the global debate, such as energy and climate change, education and skills, health and human rights. People are drawn into these conversations because they're concerned about the challenges facing the world right now: on conference platforms, on media channels and in social networks, people worry away at the issues, try to understand the realities more clearly, to tangle out new ways of coming at the problems.

In *Everybody's Business* we're making the case that today's big corporates are relevant to these big conversations. They need to be involved – and society needs them involved. By the very nature of what they do, they are protagonists, not bystanders, in the big debates of our time. Whatever sector they operate in, their experience and skills mean they have a meaningful contribution to make, and they know how to act to scale. And, of course, the role of business in society is a hot topic in itself. Often it boils down to the question: is big business part of the problem or part of the solution? Our hope is that this book can make a contribution to that debate.

PART I

THE PLACE OF BUSINESS

1

A WHOLE SOCIETY, RISING UP

NYAKOI VILLAGE

We had set off early, but already the Kampala traffic was heavy: cars and minibuses jostled along the city streets, while pedestrians and motorcycles swarmed their way perilously between the trucks and taxis. According to the World Bank there are only seven vehicles for every 1,000 people in Uganda, and it felt as if all of them were jammed onto the roads of the capital city. Eventually we made it onto the highway that curves around Lake Victoria and on towards Nairobi in Kenya. But that wasn't our destination: we were bound for Nyakoi, a small village in the foothills of Mount Elgon, one of East Africa's highest mountains.

Nyakoi is a five-hour drive from Kampala. It's slow going: the highway is single-lane and riddled with murderous potholes. After some four hours, we turn off the tarmacked highway and onto a broad red road leading to the town of Mbale, and every turn we take brings us onto a smaller, rougher road – until they can hardly be called roads at all. The trucks and the traffic are far behind us; we pass farmers with large sacks slung over their shoulders, or piles of bananas balanced improbably on the backs of their bicycles.

It's an archetypal African journey: a sweeping sky with soaring white-domed clouds, a rough road carved into the red earth, flanked by lush vegetation and ragged-leaved banana trees. But the physical beauty of Uganda's countryside belies the suffering it contains. According to the Ministry of Finance Planning and Economic Development, almost 25 per cent of people – 7.5 million men, women and children – still live in absolute poverty. Uganda has made great progress in bringing down poverty levels, which were at over 50 per cent in the early 1990s, but it remains one of the poorest countries on earth. There can be few places where it's possible to see so dramatically the positive impact that business can make on society – and that's why we've made the journey from Kampala to the village of Nyakoi.

The village is surrounded by large old mango trees and, like much of rural Uganda, it clearly benefits from fertile land and plenty of rainfall. Uganda's cities are growing, and the middle-class is gaining strength – but farming remains the biggest source of work for Ugandans, employing 80 per cent of workers. Most farmers work on small plots of only a few acres: they are one step up from peasant farmers, and the crops they produce often aren't good quality. The urban demand for their produce may be growing, but farmers are often unable even to reach their local market. We've come to Nyakoi to meet a group of farmers who are overcoming these barriers, through their own hard work, and with the help of an unlikely ally: the Coca-Cola Company.

Coca-Cola is, of course, the world's biggest brand – the swirling Spencerian script of its logo and the smooth curves of its bottle have become international icons. The company has long been a poster child of multinational corporate capitalism: as long ago as 1930 you could buy a cola in nearly eighty different countries, and Coca-Cola was calling itself 'the International Beverage'.[1] Today, people inside Coca-Cola talk about 'the system' – and indeed it has become an immense system, operating in over 200 countries. And it isn't just the big red signature brand: the system markets and distributes more than 500 brands, fifteen of which are billion-dollar brands, including Diet Coke, Fanta, Sprite, Vitamin Water, Powerade, and Minute Maid. It seems strange, as we arrive in the village of Nyakoi, that such a vast corporation could possibly be interested in the smallholder farmers of this remote part of eastern Uganda. Nyakoi feels a long way from the towering edifice of the company's global headquarters in Atlanta: a few simple mud-brick buildings, surrounded by clusters of round, grass-thatched huts.

But the Coca-Cola Company has a problem. Around the world, obesity is reaching epidemic proportions – and as the world's biggest sugary soda, Coca-Cola is first in the firing line. At the same time, consumer demand is changing: more people are seeking healthier lifestyles, and healthier drinks. In the USA, soda sales have been on the slide since 2005, and the decline in consumption is accelerating. Coca-Cola has responded to this with a big goal: to triple the size of its juice business by 2020. This presents the company with a new challenge: today, there simply isn't enough fruit being grown to provide a secure supply of juice ingredients at the right cost and quality. Coke has launched a number of projects to tackle this, looking for innovative new ways of sourcing good-quality fruit.

One such initiative is Project Nurture, which aims to develop a good source of local mangoes and passion fruit for the company's Minute Maid drinks. The project sets out to achieve this by working with smallholder farmers in parts of Uganda and Kenya – and the hope is that it will serve as a model for the company as it grows its juice business around the world. It's an ambitious programme: more than 50,000 small fruit farmers are taking part, and the plan was to increase the farmers' productivity and double their incomes by 2014. For Coca-Cola, this is about a reliable supply of quality raw materials for its juice drinks, but it also has a significant positive impact on the local communities, helping them to create sustainable livelihoods for themselves.

We learnt about Project Nurture from Afzaal Malik, who at the time was the VP of International Public Affairs for the Coca-Cola Company, charged with managing relationships with the company's main stakeholders around the world, from governments and regulators to NGOs and campaign groups. This put him on the front-line, dealing with the company's harshest critics, so you might expect him to be a battle-hardened and cynical corporate operator. But Afzaal is a soft-spoken man from Birmingham, and he has a quiet optimism about him. We begin by asking him about his job title, and he laughs. 'I have difficulty explaining it to my kids,' he says. 'Really it's about being able to engage in a meaningful way with people who care about a range of issues, and being able to talk about what we're doing and to learn from others.'

Speaking to us by phone from Coca-Cola Plaza in Atlanta, Afzaal explains the company is on unfamiliar territory with Project Nurture: training smallholder farmers in Africa how to improve their crop yields isn't exactly core business for a company like Coca-Cola, so working in partnership has been the key to making it happen. 'If we're going to have a profitable product that's going to end up on the shelves, and we don't have the quality and the specification and the sustainable source of product, mango or passion fruit, then we're not going to get very far,' he tells us. Coca-Cola needs a sustainable supply of fruit, and shares an objective with the government: agricultural development and the alleviation of poverty. 'That's when you start opening up a conversation around the common interests that all parties have on a social objective.'

As well as a shared objective, you need to assemble the right mix of capabilities, Afzaal tells us. 'It's hard work, doubling the revenues of thousands of farmers in Uganda and Kenya. You need the right partners.' Working directly with the farmers is one of the most crucial aspects of the project, and so Coca-Cola chose to partner with an NGO called TechnoServe, which trains the farmers in basic business skills and agricultural techniques. As well as TechnoServe, Coca-Cola brought on board the Bill & Melinda Gates Foundation and the Ugandan Ministry of Agriculture. Afzaal describes how the partnership works:

> It happens through a common pooling of interests. The Bill & Melinda Gates Foundation said, 'We'll assume some of the risk and the cost of training those farmers to be better farmers'; the Coca-Cola Company and our bottlers have said, 'We'll guarantee that a certain amount of product is bought and we'll work with the farmers to ensure that the quality of the raw materials is high enough to be used in our products.' Then the Ministry of Agriculture comes in and says, 'Well, we'll put some emphasis here behind the infrastructure to allow you to better bring those crops together, making sure that basic roads are built or improved.' And in the process you also help the agricultural market to develop, so that mango and passion fruit is becoming more available on shelves in stores locally.

Well, the Ugandan Ministry of Agriculture's road improvements had clearly not reached Nyakoi by the time of our visit, but there is plenty of evidence that Project Nurture is having a real impact here. As we arrive in Nyakoi, it seems as if the entire village has gathered to greet us. The mood is very upbeat: a group of men are playing marimbas and shakers, and singing, while some of the women dance around them. It feels like a celebration and, in a sense, it is: 'A few years ago we could never have imagined that one day we would have visitors such as you, who come to tell our story,' says one of the farmers, Okiring Moses, as we are led into the shade of the meeting shed. Of course, we aren't visitors of particular importance, but our visit is a reflection of the progress they have made: 'It shows us how far we have come, and how quickly,' says Okiring.

We have come to meet the Nyakoi Stores Farmers Group, one of 1,300 groups across Uganda and Kenya taking part in Project Nurture. Rather than attempting to work with thousands of individual farmers, the project begins by forming smallholder farmer collectives. On the ground this work is done by TechnoServe, an international NGO specialising in reducing poverty through business solutions. In total, 50,000 farmers are taking part in Project Nurture. The Nyakoi group started in 2009 with eighteen farmers, and now has 275 members – ninety-five of whom are women. A few dozen members have come to meet us today – so many in fact that the meeting spills out of the cool, dark room and into the sunlight.

Inside, one wall is covered with flipchart pages, outlining the objectives, rules and methods of the group. Written in careful capital letters, in thick marker pen, is information on how to use manure, how to protect the trees from pests, how to prune them, and how to sort, grade and pack the mangoes. Another wall is covered with a bookshelf, containing big binders with titles such as *Cashbook & Accountability, Hygiene & Sanitation, Workplan* and *Finance & Oversight*. Directly opposite the entrance is a page proudly displaying the group's mission and vision, and its motto: 'We gain from our sweat'. The people sitting on the benches around us look as though they understand the meaning of this motto, their hands and faces weathered by work. They are keen to tell us their story.

'Before, mango was a wild tree, a community tree,' we're told. 'Sometimes our fathers would plant a tree for the family. And when the mangoes fell, there were too many to eat, and many would rot where they fell. There were so many mangoes and we never knew there was a market for them.' Meanwhile, life was becoming increasingly difficult for the villagers. 'Problem number one was poverty – which was biting. There was malnutrition, because households lacked a balanced diet. And we could not educate our children, because of the biting poverty.'

In many ways, their problem was isolation. Nyakoi is such a remote community that they had no idea that their mangoes had any value, or how to get them to market. 'We are hardworking people,' they tell us, 'what we lacked was a *link*.' That link arrived in the form of a visit from Nathan Emuron, a young business adviser working in TechnoServe's Mbale office. Nathan's task was to show the villagers that their mangoes had a commercial value, and help them to organise themselves so that they could realise this value. He worked with them to formalise their group into a collective with structures and governance, so that they could begin to access the markets, and deal with financial institutions. One of the biggest challenges, Nathan tells us, is bringing about a new, commercial attitude in the farmers.

To demonstrate that their mangoes had value, Nathan organised for a few of the farmers to polish and pack their fruit, and take it to the market. 'When I supplied my ten bags,' one of the assembled farmers tells us, 'I got school fees, I got clothes for my children.' In such a small community, this soon got people's attention. Farmers are very cautious: all they have is their land, and changing the way they use this land is always a risk. But once people saw that the mangoes had commercial value, the group started to grow. 'At first the other farmers couldn't believe we were harvesting the mangoes – they couldn't believe it. Then they saw the trucks coming to pick up the mangoes and they wanted to join the group.'

By joining the group, the farmers get access to training in modern farming methods and cultivation techniques, as well as basic bookkeeping skills. As a group, they have more confidence to deal with the local market. The nearest market is in the town of Pallisa, which is only around 25 kilometres away, but that's a day's journey if you're pushing a heavy-laden bicycle along these roads. 'The farmers think that the market is a hostile place – everybody is out to make a profit,' Nathan explains. 'Maybe the farmers go to the market once, and then never again – they take their crops to the market and can't take them back because the mangoes are perishable and so they take a low price. The farmers are risk averse and they don't know how to negotiate in this environment, and so they stay in the village and the agents come and offer a low price.'

The farmers agree. Everybody has a story to tell about being cheated at the market: 'You bicycle to Pallisa and leave your produce, and they reduce your price, or even steal it,' they say. 'Cheated in broad daylight! They know you have to sell or the fruit will rot and so they can give you a low price, because you can't take the fruit home.' Being part of a group gives them some extra bargaining power, they tell us. It's like many farmers acting as one large farm: 'You get a bigger voice to bargain for higher prices – and every individual benefits from the higher prices.'

The farmers group has set certain conditions that individuals must meet if they wish to join. They must have at least five mango trees, and their houses must have a latrine, a drying rack to keep their cooking implements off the ground, and a separate place for a rubbish tip. These simple conditions have made a big impact in the village: there have been no cases of dysentery since the group began, and it's been years since cholera was known in the village. The farmers are feeling the benefits of their increased incomes – and educating their children seems to be the number one priority. Look on a Google Maps satellite image of the area, and only one building is labelled for kilometres around: *Nyakoi Primary School.* By this time in our meeting, the day's classes are over, and the children have gathered around the entrance, peering into the dark room with curiosity. They are wearing clean, bright pink and blue uniforms. It is a source of immense pride in the village. When we ask the group about it, one of the farmers exclaims '*We* employ the teachers!' and spontaneous applause breaks out.

It's a touching moment. This village has come a long way in a short time: only a few years ago there was not enough food to go around, and now they are able to educate their children. And they want us to know that all of this has been achieved through their own hard work: 'Nobody has given us anything,' says Okiring. 'Since the beginning we haven't received any help or money of any kind, other than advice and information.'

Although the farmers are now selling mangoes to the local market, they have yet to start selling to Coca-Cola. Sample bags of fruit are regularly sent to the company's Global Juice Centre in Belgium for testing. Mangoes are like apples: there are dozens of different varieties, and formulating a juice drink that can be mass produced and marketed is an exact science, as there needs to be a consistent taste, sweetness, texture and colour. The mangoes from Uganda have proved quite fibrous, which means that they only produce 30 per cent juice, and machines tend to get clogged. Coke's product developers are working on blending them with mangoes from other areas. The farmers understand this process. In fact, they seem to relish it, Okiring tells us: 'Coca-Cola has very demanding quality standards – and this is very encouraging.' TechnoServe has also enabled the Nyakoi farmers group to start working with Britania, a Ugandan juice company that produces a local brand called *Splash*. Britania currently imports mangoes from overseas, in pulp form – a crazy state of affairs, given the prevalence of mango trees across this region of Uganda. The farmers are immensely encouraged to be working with companies such as Coca-Cola and Britania, says Okiring: 'These big companies upgrade us; they make us go to a new level. They give skills – we have devoted members and we want to learn.'

The most important thing the farmers are learning, we are told, is an *attitude*. 'We try to inculcate the *spirit of business* in the farmers,' Nathan says. 'How much does it cost to till this land, to create a kilo of mangoes? We get them to look at it as a business. They've been farming since they were adults, but they haven't known how much they made. Was it a profit or a loss? And if it's a loss, what can we do to remove that loss? What do we have to do to make your enterprise profitable?' Nathan spends much of his time running training sessions for the farmers, introducing them to bookkeeping techniques, showing them the basics of running a business. The farmers are eager to learn, but this is a very new way of looking at the world, as Okiring tells us: 'Before we didn't even know our income, we'd just sell and buy things.'

Not long ago, the Nyakoi farmers didn't even know their mangoes had any value; now, they have a business plan which includes investing in a pulping machine, so they can get even more value from their fruit. They are very optimistic about their future: 'We have higher hopes because we have been able to achieve this much with so little capacity,' says Mr Ojolong, who is the village Reverend and clearly a leader of the community. Everybody looks to him as he speaks, using his hands to show the climbing of a ladder: 'Our hope is, if at one time we were at this level, now we've moved to this level; then we were here; we now have a hope that one day soon we will be on the rooftop!'

Further up into the foothills of Mount Elgon, we visit another farmers group in the village of Bumwangu. This one is smaller, with only sixty-five members, and it focuses on passion fruit – but their story is very similar. As in Nyakoi, they seem pleased with our visit: 'When we see visitors such as you, we are impressed that we are moving forward,' they tell us, before introducing the group's management: the Chairman, the Secretary, the Treasurer, the respective committee Chairpersons – the Sorting Committee, the Investment Committee, the Finance and Oversight Committee, the Marketing Committee – and a youth representative. The group calls itself BUSACA – the Bumwangu Savings and Credit Association. Managing cash is important for the group: each member contributes 5,000 shillings a year, which is used to pay for members to attend training, as well as looking after each other's social needs, such as supporting a member during illness. Access to credit is also important: the farmers need to buy poles to support the trees, and wire to train the branches. Like the Nyakoi group, it is redolent of the agricultural cooperatives and credit unions that spread across Europe and North America in the nineteenth century. Those were started by the reformers of the age; these groups have been catalysed by a global corporate, Coca-Cola, with the help of an international NGO, TechnoServe.

Across Uganda and Kenya, there are 54,000 farmers taking part in this project – and as we've seen, it's detailed, complex work. It made us wonder: surely, for a company of the scale and resources of Coca-Cola, there must be an easier way to source fruit? What's really going on? We asked Bob Okello, one of Coke's executives in the region:

> Right now we import pulp from Brazil and India. Africa has so much undeveloped agricultural land. There is a commercial reason for doing this: if we can get these foods locally it's cheaper, it's more reliable, you deepen your footprint in the country, you reduce your exposure to fluctuating global food prices – and at the same time you help people improve their lot, increase their income, educate their children. It makes economic sense, and it makes social sense.

Bob is always on the road, travelling between Coke's operations in Kenya, Uganda, Tanzania and Ethiopia. We speak to him on a faint mobile line, but his perspective is crystal clear, and goes to the heart of this book's theme: 'We can achieve our commercial aims whilst in the same breath achieving a social good,' he tells us. He feels strongly that Coke has a role to play in the continent:

> Here in Africa, Coca-Cola is one of the longest investors, first coming in eighty-three years ago. We've been investing in Africa for a long time. We employ many people. Our contribution to GDP is bigger than any other company. Our value-chain footprint is huge, both upstream and downstream. *Of course* we have a responsibility to Africa.

TechnoServe is Coca-Cola's partner on the ground and none of this would happen without them. Erastus Kibugu is the director for TechnoServe in Uganda. We spoke to him at their headquarters in Kampala, and he was keen to emphasise that initiatives like Project Nurture depend upon the hard work of the farmers, not on any form of aid. 'Handouts haven't worked for Africa,' he says. 'The future of Africa is going to be partnerships, where global companies like Coca-Cola can develop the sort of supply chain solutions that make sense for them.' And the work of an NGO such as TechnoServe is vital to getting the system up and running:

> As Coca-Cola you can't partner with each individual smallholder farmer. They're too small. You need some sort of social action – building social capital, organising farmers into viable production groups, teaching them the tools of business, helping them to increase their productivity. That's where we come in, that's why TechnoServe is also an important partner.

And it's not just mango and passion fruit: TechnoServe works in this way with more than 100,000 farmers, across a number of different crops, including cotton, maize, peas and milk. 'We ask them, how can you become a large farm if you only have one acre?' says Erastus. 'If a thousand of you have one acre, you have a thousand acres. If each of us has one acre of mangoes, or two cows that produce a bucket of milk, then there's a thousand buckets of milk.' At the heart of TechnoServe's approach, he stresses, is *business*: 'It happens through social action, but it has to be driven by business. If they're not competitive, if they don't make a profit, then they're not going to last.'

Erastus gives us an example from his dairy farmers – it's a simple story, almost a parable of economic development:

> You need to chill the milk within two hours of milking or it goes bad, so we got together maybe a thousand farmers and arranged for a cooling plant, a large tank that cools the milk. Each farmer brings their milk to the plant, and every morning a large Kampala company comes and collects up to 5,000 litres. Now there's a lot of revenue going back to the farmers, and this creates incremental businesses like artificial insemination and feed systems for the cows. And now there's an opportunity to grow that community. People want light, they want power, so guys who sell solar panels start setting up. People want doctors, so clinics set up. People want credit, so bank microfinance institutions come along – and then it goes beyond dairy: lo and behold, now they have maize, because they can afford proper maize seed. And the parents want new uniforms for their kids, clothes for themselves, and shoes – and so sellers come and set up. And so now they're even thinking of chickens, and cattle. And so you begin to see a whole society rising up. That's what we do. And this is the whole plan for Project Nurture.

A whole society rising up. It's a powerful description. Back at Coca-Cola, Afzaal Malik tells us that the benefits of Project Nurture extend beyond securing a sustainable supply of raw ingredients. 'It's also about the character of the company,' he tells us. 'I think for us, for Coca-Cola, we're one of the most visible brands in the world; and this visibility makes us a prime target for activists. If someone wants to launch a campaign of advocacy on – you name it, pick a cause – we are very vulnerable to that.' Afzaal believes that consumers are taking a harder look at the brands they spend money on: 'People will increasingly buy products not only based upon what they constitute but upon what they stand for. So it's about character: we believe that putting the character of the company behind our products will be increasingly important.'

When it comes to questions of character, many people will raise an eyebrow at the prospect of big corporates playing a role in countries like Uganda. There remains a perception that corporate involvement in the developing world is exploitative, and causes more harm than good for the local communities. This mistrust has deep roots, and Dr Rajiv Shah, who heads the US Government's development agency USAID, explained why: 'The early experience of corporate investment in the developing world was characterised by activity that notoriously caused great harm. Sweatshops, infant formula, Bhopal – all words that conjure images of corporations taking advantage of bad regulations, enriching elites and exploiting the poor.' But things are starting to change, according to Dr Shah, and the time has come to take a more constructive view of the corporate world. Speaking at a forum on public-private partnerships in Washington DC, he argued that the world of international development should 'step out of its comfort zone and imagine new linkages with private sector firms'.

Increasingly, business is seen as playing a potentially positive role in lifting people out of poverty. In 2000, the UN launched its ambitious *Millennium Development Goals* aimed at improving life for the world's poorest, but the private sector got hardly a mention. The focus was almost entirely on commitments by the G8 finance ministers, and the role of organisations such as the World Bank and the International Monetary Fund. By 2010 the role of business had moved centre stage: as world leaders gathered to review the progress made on the goals, Secretary-General Ban Ki-moon told them,

> Government leadership will be crucial. But more than ever before, we depend on the resources and capacities of the private sector to make things happen. Business is a primary driver of innovation, investment and job creation. There is no longer any doubt that business plays an integral role in delivering economic and social progress.

The UN General Assembly issued a resolution, titled 'Keeping the promise: united to achieve the Millennium Development Goals', which issued a powerful plea to the business world: 'We call upon the private sector to further contribute to poverty eradication, including by adapting its business models to the needs and possibilities of the poor.'

'POLITICS BY ANOTHER MEANS'

Back in Kampala, we meet a man with an unrivalled perspective on how business can fight poverty. Not many people have such broad experience of life in Uganda as Onapito Ekomoloit: he began his career as a journalist, rising to become editor of *The Crusader*, one of the country's main newspapers. He then served as a Member of Parliament, before becoming Press

Secretary to the President. Now the scribe-cum–politician-cum-presidential adviser has taken his talents to the business world: he is Corporate Affairs Director for the brewer SABMiller in Uganda. To find out why, we met Onapito at the company's depot on the outskirts of the city, with Lake Victoria shimmering in the distance.

'Business is about *doing*,' he tells us (after introducing himself with a warm smile and an effusive handshake: 'Onapito Ekomoloit – difficult for you to say isn't it? Call me Ona.'). It's the biggest difference between life in the public sector and working for a public company:

> We say things and *do* them. Government says it will but it won't: they lack resources, they lack accountability. That's why it's great to be in a private company. OK, so our main business is making and selling beer, we've done many more things for Uganda – empowering farmers, commercial agriculture and alleviating poverty... It may be on a small scale but it is actually happening – can be touched, can be counted, can be seen.

It might not be immediately obvious how making beer might help contribute to alleviating poverty, but SABMiller's operations in Uganda show how a successful business can bring real social and economic benefits: creating employment; supporting livelihoods in the supply chain; bringing in new skills and global standards; developing new products to meet local needs; innovating new ways of working for local conditions; and also playing a role in the community through social investment and philanthropy. It's quite a list, but Ona assures us that each of these elements comes to life vividly in Uganda. 'As someone in politics I was motivated by development, by making a change,' he tells us. 'By coming here I am basically doing politics by another means.'

Politics by another means: this sounds like an activist's view of business, rather than the perspective of a corporate affairs director in a major multinational company. It's the central thought of this book: if you want to change the world, business is a good place from which to do it – even a beer business like SABMiller. It's a great African success story, in fact: SABMiller came out of South Africa after apartheid, and is now a global player with 200 brands, including Grolsch, Peroni, and Miller Genuine Draft. In Uganda, the company's main product, Eagle Lager, is a great example of how a business can grow by adapting its business model to the needs of the poor. Eagle is a crystal clear golden lager that looks as good as any standard European lager. Introduced in 2002, it quickly became a hit with local consumers: before, most Ugandans were unable to afford a quality beer, and so many people would drink crude home brews, strong in alcohol and sometimes containing dangerous ingredients. Indeed, the World Health Organization (WHO) has said that as much as 50 per cent of the alcohol drunk in Africa is unlicensed, often with harmful impurities and adulterants.

The problem was that the quality of local ingredients was not reliable enough for commercial brewing, and imported ingredients were expensive and pushed up the price of local beer brands. SABMiller set out to develop an affordable local brand made out of a widely available local grain crop, sorghum. Many people were sceptical at first: existing sorghum brews were cloudy and thick, like drinking bitter, watery porridge. SABMiller spent two years working with local scientists, experimenting with different types of sorghum, and developing the business model for an affordable beer. For the company, the result was a winning formula: Eagle now accounts for more than half of the company's 55 per cent market share. For some of the lowest income consumers, Eagle transformed the experience of having a beer: home brew drinkers sit around a pot of cloudy beer with bamboo straws, whereas Eagle offers the chance to enjoy a clear, filtered bottle of lager with no impurities. Eagle has also had a development impact, according to Ona: more than 9,000 local smallholder farmers are now involved in supplying sorghum to the brewery. 'We give them a market, buy their crop,' he tells us. 'It makes such a difference to them. Poor education, poor health, low income – farmers suffer from every social problem you can think of.'

Tukei William Wilberforce is Chairman of the Bukedea district, and many of the sorghum farmers live in his area. He is tall and smartly dressed, and has something of the presence you might expect from a man bearing such a name (which he adopted at the age of thirteen). 'William Wilberforce was very instrumental in making progress,' he tells us. 'I thought, why not me?' He describes the impact that having a guaranteed buyer for sorghum has had on the local farmers. 'It was bad here, the farmers were worse off. They used to grow enough for staple diet but not enough to sell,' he says. 'Now the income from sorghum brings food, school, school books, small houses – brick and corrugated iron instead of thatch – and some of them now have electricity. You can *see* how life is improving.'

Wilberforce is right – you can see the improvements. We went for a stroll around the plots of land, and met some of the farmers. 'I used to live here,' says Alfred Omoding, pointing to a traditional round grass-thatched hut. 'And now I live here,' he says, pointing to a simple brick-built house: one room, a door and two small windows. Inside, he and his family now sleep on mattresses, instead of on the floor. Some of the houses now have small solar-powered generators, which provide some light after sunset. Alfred tells us that he can now afford to send his children to school, which means they need books and new clothes. He proudly adopts the air of a long-suffering family man when he says, 'my job now is *paying for things*.'

SABMiller buys a guaranteed amount of sorghum from the farmers at a guaranteed price. It's difficult to over-state how important this is to the farmers, but the programme is a lot more involved than this. It begins with advancing the farmers money to buy the seeds, and subsidising the price; helping them to invest in a seed-planter so that the seeds are correctly spaced and planted; making fertiliser available and training them in cultivation techniques and pest control methods. None of this is the kind of routine commercial activity you might expect from a brewer. But there is one piece of hardware, above all else, that gets the farmers excited: the tractor. 'It used to take two days and two oxen to plough one acre,' Alfred tells us. 'Now, the tractor can do twelve acres in a day.' And make no mistake, ploughing is back-breaking work, and everybody has to lend a hand: 'Before the tractor service, a lot of time was spent by the family on ploughing. Everybody had to help. Now the tractor services leaves the women and children free to do something else; now the children can go to school.'

It's nothing less than an agricultural revolution. Now the farmers are able to cultivate more land and increase their yield. Wilberforce gives us a politician's view of this. 'For me, it's economics: when someone has an excess of sorghum, he sells it. Then he has some resources, and he can put some of those resources to good use – for himself, his household, his family and eventually his community.' This, for Wilberforce, is the goal: the good of the community. When enough people in a community progress in this way, everybody benefits: 'If 70 to 80 per cent of people in the community become empowered, the others can fit in, can find a place, can find some support,' he says. It echoes the picture painted for us by Erastus from TechnoServe: a whole society rising up.

SABMiller wanted to understand better the effect its operations are having in countries like Uganda, and so commissioned a socio-economic impact study. It's an increasingly common endeavour, as companies seek to get a grip on their relationship to society; Nike, Unilever, Standard Chartered and Vodafone have all commissioned similar studies. For SABMiller, the study was done by Professor Ethan Kapstein of INSEAD.[2] He looked at the company's impact on household income, employment and government revenue, as well as its broader social and environmental impacts. One of the company's main contributions, the report concludes, is jobs: for every person directly employed by the brewery, 200 jobs are supported in the Ugandan economy – farmers, drivers, retailers, bar workers etc. – that's a total of over 44,000 jobs. This is significant in a country where unemployment is at crisis point, as Ona points out: 'Jobs mean everything here,' he says. 'You have to remember, we have 80 per cent jobless among the youth.'

The jobs at the brewery are skilled jobs, Ona tells us: 'There is robust training, because people don't have relevant skills when they come into the business.' SABMiller employees can become qualified as master brewers, and there is training on general management topics such as problem solving and performance management. For Uganda, it means that new skills and global standards are entering the economy – a process of *human capital formation,* in the jargon of the socio-economic impact study. 'You have the same level of skills here as anywhere in the SABMiller group around the world,' Ona says. 'These are world-class skills, our people here can hold their own against anyone in the US, or anywhere.'

The brewery itself is like an enclave of global operational excellence: gleaming vats and cylinders connected by a maze of pipes, tubes, ducts and channels. Workers in bright blue overalls check the flickering gauges and watch the blinking monitors. Everywhere you look there are charts and graphs showing the brewery's performance: energy, water, quality, efficiency, safety – all of them benchmarked against other

SABMiller breweries. Everybody here wants this brewery to be a truly world-class operation. It feels like you could be in any SABMiller brewery, anywhere in the world; only the sweet smell of the hops mixing with the thick tropical air reminds us we are in Africa.

Water use has been a major area of focus for the operation in recent years. Uganda is not yet a water-stressed area: it is a lush country with plenty of rainfall, interlaced with rivers and freshwater lakes. But the population is growing rapidly – from 10 million to approaching 40 million in the last forty years – and water availability is expected to become a big issue. It's a similar story in many parts of the world, and 'making more beer using less water' is a global priority for SABMiller: it aims to cut the water used per hectolitre of lager to 3.45 between 2008 and 2015 – a drop of 25 per cent. At the time of writing, the group average is 4 hectolitres, and the group best is 2.7. The Uganda brewery still has a way to go: it uses 4.65. Even this number represents significant progress: it once took over 12 hectolitres for the brewery to make a single hectolitre of beer.

Everyone we meet in the brewery is enthusiastic to show us the latest operational advances they've made. It's a ceaseless quest for incremental improvement, pushing forward the brewery's performance – a litre here, a percentage point there. It's clearly a very engaged workforce, as Ethan Kapstein notes in his socio-economic impact study: the brewery has a very low level of staff turnover, and it is consistently referred to as one of Uganda's best employers. All of the staff are unionised at the shop-floor level, and they receive a range of benefits – most strikingly, free health care. We visit the brewery's health clinic, where employees and their families can receive treatments, and even stay overnight for more serious conditions. The clinic is run by Dr Moses, who introduces himself emphatically: 'I am the company doctor.'

Dr Moses has the natural, affable authority you might expect to find in a trusted community physician. He is clearly an important figure in the life of the brewery – and also in the *business* of the brewery. 'Health is a key determinant of productivity,' he explains. 'Our model is to provide healthcare ourselves so we are able to make decisions fast and make medical interventions fast, through our clinic here.' The publicly available health services can be very slow, he tells us. 'It's better to treat people here rather than at a local hospital where people have to wait, and then it takes them longer to recover and longer to return to work.' Of course, Uganda was hit extremely hard by the epidemic of HIV/AIDS: in the 1990s infection levels approached 30 per cent, according to Dr Moses. Infection levels fell down to 6.4 per cent, he tells us, but are on the rise again (7.3 per cent at the time of writing). It's top of the agenda for Dr Moses: 'We look at HIV/AIDS as a risk to the business,' he says. 'We have a highly trained and experienced staff and we risk losing them. Skills are hard to come by in Uganda. If you lose a skilled person your efficiencies will slide, delays will occur, you will need to invest in more training – your business will suffer.'

Testing is at the heart of the brewery's efforts to combat HIV/AIDS. Each year, around 80 per cent of employees are tested – voluntarily, and confidentially. 'There is still a lot of stigma and fear around it,' Dr Moses tells us. 'So we inculcate a culture of testing. The leadership all get tested, the MD and his wife, the Finance Director, the Human Resources Director – it's good to see the leaders leading by example.' Every quarter the clinic runs a testing day, with entertainment, drummers, videos, refreshments, and freebies such as T-shirts and condoms. The clinic also organises home-based testing to increase coverage. It means a lot to the local people, and Dr Moses tells us they are always trying to reach further. 'You get to the spouses and the family. And you can educate them on other issues – sanitation and hygiene, child health, malaria...'

Alcohol abuse is another major health issue in Uganda, and one of obvious concern to a brewer such as SABMiller. In 2010, hundreds of people across Uganda died after drinking a methanol-laced batch of *waragi*, a strong home-made gin. Illegally produced alcohol is easy to make, and regularly causes blindness and even death. Bananas, sugar molasses, millet and maize are all fermented and distilled into hard liquor, and sold on the informal market. SABMiller hopes that its Eagle Lager will help to alleviate this by providing an affordable alternative. Even so, alcohol abuse is a particularly acute problem in Uganda: studies by the World Health Organization have shown it to have the world's highest alcohol consumption per person, with adults consuming the equivalent of 19.5 litres of pure alcohol a year. As Chairman of a local government district, it's a problem that Wilberforce is acutely aware of. For him, the answer is economic growth, of the kind we saw with the sorghum farmers:

> The more you get empowered, the more money you have, the more your priorities change. Those who are drunk are living from hand to mouth, but if you've sold your sorghum, and you're putting up your house, your priorities change. You don't have time to sit and drink. You get more resources, you interact more with the community around you. The negative tends to lose strength.

Back at SABMiller's offices, Ona echoes this sentiment. 'Alcohol abuse is a problem,' he says, 'And that's very closely linked to the broader problem of poverty, which leads to despondency, to instability and conflict. Alcohol abuse hits low income people hardest.' Most alcohol abuse is in the informal sector, Ona tells us – cheap home-brew, which Eagle

Lager provides a safe, affordable alternative to. Still, there's no doubt that alcohol abuse has a devastating effect in Uganda, and in many other parts of Africa: it's associated with violence and crime, and lost productivity. Money spent on alcohol is money that isn't being spent on the family's well-being. But isn't it counter-intuitive that making beer more affordable is a way to tackle alcohol abuse? Surely a brewer like SABMiller wants people to spend as much money as possible on beer? These are points Ona hears a lot. 'Even our bar workers sometimes say that this is a contradiction: you want us to sell as much as we can. We tell them, your challenge is to attract as many drinkers as you can, who each have a few drinks.' Ultimately, it's about good business, Ona explains: 'We don't want drinkers who drink two crates each – who will get ill, or get fired, or die – because that's not an investment in your customers.'

Whether it's Coca-Cola's work with mango and passion fruit farmers, or SABMiller's work with sorghum farmers, these projects require a new approach to doing business: new commercial models, new product formulations, and new skill sets. In London, we talked to Andy Wales, who is head of Sustainable Development at SABMiller. Andy and his team have a growing number of projects like this running across Africa and Latin America. To make them work, he tells us, you need an 'open business mindset':

> From the business side, we need people who have the capabilities to manage what are essentially more open ways of doing business – people who understand that our success depends on the success of society around us, and so they are prepared to invest the time and the

> relationships with government, with communities, with NGOs, and to understand the way they think, their time frames, the language they use. We need business people who can set up value chains, who have that external engagement skill set, who can work with an open business mindset.

Back at Coca-Cola, this is a sentiment echoed by Afzaal Malik: 'Our business does not exist in a vacuum,' he says. 'You're not going to have a business if the community that you're operating in doesn't have a reliable supply chain, or doesn't have a viable source of water, or isn't able to provide you with employees who are able to do the job.' And, like Andy Wales, he sees that this is changing the capabilities inside the business: 'There are parts of our business that are being forced to think more like development agencies.'

This approach to business is welcomed by some of those development agencies, which are on the front-line of fighting poverty. Both SABMiller and Coca-Cola are the focus of a study by Oxfam, called 'Exploring the Links Between International Business and Poverty Reduction'. The report looks specifically at the operations of these two companies in Zambia and El Salvador, and concludes:

> ... as companies gain a deeper understanding of their impact on poverty reduction, they recognise that their own success is often directly linked to the success of the communities in which they operate. This recognition has driven some companies to take a more strategic approach to development. Many are investigating how to transfer knowledge and skills to low-income people along their value chains in a more inclusive manner. Small enterprises and large multinationals alike are creating innovative new products and services that simultaneously satisfy the needs of people at the base of

> the pyramid, achieve a development impact, and create new consumer markets.[3]

NGOs have frequently been strident critics of the role of corporates in the developing world, so it's striking to read this from Oxfam. But it's even more striking to hear it on the ground, from Wilberforce: 'I'll tell you what it means,' he says. 'It means, from thatched roof to corrugated iron, from a mattress to a bed, from no electricity to solar-powered generators. That's what it means – *that's* development.'

2

SHAPING THE FUTURE

SILICON VALLEY

The train between San Jose and San Francisco is a fairly ordinary commuter service. The steel exterior gleams in the California sunshine, but there are trains like this all over the United States. However, as you pass through the extended, flat suburbs filled with low-level buildings and parking lots, you can't help thinking there is something special about this journey. This is Silicon Valley, and from the train window you can glimpse some of the places that have changed history: Mountain View, birthplace of the silicon chip and now home to the sprawling Google campus; Menlo Park, home to Facebook; Palo Alto, origin of Hewlett-Packard, the company that established this region as the home of the computer industry. To the west, towards the redwood-covered hills, is Cupertino – the home of Apple. And clustered around these giants are thousands of small and medium-sized businesses, all playing their part in the Valley's ecosystem, and some of them may become the next Amazon, Airbnb, eBay, Intel, Autodesk, Dropbox, Salesforce, Cisco, Adobe, LinkedIn, Twitter, Electronic Arts, Netflix, Yelp... It's hard to think of anywhere with a greater concentration of businesses that are shaping the world we live in. If you want to understand the role that business plays in shaping the future, you have to come to Silicon Valley.

There has been a train service running on this route for 150 years. Back then, the area was known as the Valley of Heart's Delights because of its abundance of fruit orchards, made possible by the unbroken blue skies, the moderate temperatures and the rich soil. Today, there's little evidence that this was once the largest fruit production region in the world, full of orchards growing cherries, oranges, apricots and apples. As the computer industry grew, the fruit trees slowly made way for the manufacturing plants of companies making microprocessors, and by the 1980s the area had acquired its moniker as Silicon Valley. Still, according to valley lore, an apple orchard called All One Farm was a regular hangout for a young Steve Jobs. As its name might suggest, this wasn't a typical farm: it was more of a commune that gave Jobs the chance to explore fruitarian diets and psychedelic drugs – and, ultimately, provided the inspiration for the name of the company he would build with his partner, Steve Wozniak. Today, Apple is earning more money in any given quarter than all but a handful of companies in history – and there aren't many businesses that have done more to shape the everyday lives and aspirations of people around the world.

Apple made its first imprint on the public imagination a full three decades ago. It happened during the 1984 Super Bowl. Few people will recall that the Los Angeles Raiders beat the Washington Redskins in an uneventful game. Fewer people still would be able to recall the commercials that played during the breaks: one ad featured the Incredible Hulk flogging PCs from Radio Shack; another showed off a new Atari computer. The ads that played that day, like the products they featured, are all long since forgotten. All, that is, but one. That Super Bowl ad break ran the only airing of Apple's famous '1984' commercial, announcing one of the most significant product launches in history: the *Macintosh*. It has become an advertising legend – named by *Advertising Age* as the greatest commercial of all time – and it laid the cornerstone for Apple's enduring brand position.

The ad is set in a dystopian industrial blue-grey world. Lines of blank-eyed mind-controlled workers shuffle towards a large screen. On the screen is Big Brother, droning on about 'information purification directives'. It's a depressing, totalitarian scene. Suddenly we see a young woman running towards the screen, chased by storm-trooper riot police. She flings a sledgehammer into the face of Big Brother, smashing the screen and freeing the minds of the audience. A portentous voice declares: 'On January 24th, Apple Computer will introduce Macintosh. And you'll see why 1984 won't be like *1984*.'

It had an instant impact: as soon as the ad was aired, controversy erupted. A wave of media coverage followed, and the ad was replayed on all three national US networks – worth millions in free publicity. Unlike other computer company commercials, the ad didn't sell the computer – it sold a *story*. And the story was simple: an upstart tech company with a cool new product was insinuating that IBM, pillar of the American corporate establishment, was like Big Brother. As Steve Jobs said in an Apple keynote speech:

> It is now 1984. It appears IBM wants it all. Apple is perceived to be the only hope to offer IBM a run for its money. Dealers initially welcoming IBM with open arms now fear an IBM-dominated and -controlled future. They are increasingly turning back to Apple as the only force that can ensure their future freedom. IBM wants it all and is aiming its guns on its last obstacle to industry control: Apple. Will *Big Blue* dominate the entire computer industry? The entire information age? Was George Orwell right?

And this was how Apple gained its first real foothold in the public imagination: 'the only hope', a force from freedom, fighting against a dominant corporate culture – a business self-consciously being 'everybody's business'. A few years later, the famous *Think Different* campaign – dedicated 'to the crazy ones' – would push this anti-establishment position. From the beginning, everything about the brand was *un-corporate* – from its iconoclastic founder to the original colourful logo. And what kind of company was called *Apple*?

There's something of a paradox about Apple's rise: the upstart challenger is now the dominant global megacorp. In 2011, Apple Inc. became the world's most valuable company by market capitalisation, regularly swapping the top spot with ExxonMobil. A decade ago, Apple was a $10 billion company; now it's worth over $400 billion. We live in an age of growing suspicion and hostility towards the corporate world, and yet people can't get enough of Apple. It's one of the most loved brands, regularly named by *Fortune* magazine as the World's Most Admired Company. When Steve Jobs died in 2011, thousands of fans left flowers and candles outside Apple stores around the world, from Beijing to Cupertino. In a climate of anti-corporate angst, it was extraordinary to see such an outpouring of affection for the leader of a major multinational company.

In the haze of adulation that now surrounds Steve Jobs, it's hard to remember that there was a time when he had some vocal critics. As the business grew and grew up, some people increasingly expected it to take on the mantle of traditional corporates, and part of that was support for good causes. In 2006, *Wired* magazine published an article called 'Great Wealth Does Not Make A Great Man', comparing the philanthropic activities of Steve Jobs and Bill Gates. The article concluded that Jobs is 'nothing more than a greedy capitalist who's amassed an obscene fortune'. Jobs didn't see it that way: he had opened a foundation but closed it after fifteen months, saying he didn't have time to do it properly. Friends told the *New York Times* that Jobs felt he 'could do more good focusing his energy on continuing to expand Apple than on philanthropy'.[4] Judging by the good fortunes of Apple, most people agreed with him. As Frank Zappa said, 'Without music to decorate it, time is just a bunch of boring production deadlines or dates by which bills must be paid.' And the arrival of iTunes transformed the experience of music for people more than anything since the gramophone. Then everybody fell in love with their iPhones and iPads, and the new possibilities that they opened up. For most, these innovative products were gift enough.

That's before you get to the use of the products explicitly for the public good. More philanthropy dollars are spent on education than anything else, and the iPad has a contribution to make there. Health care is another of the priority causes for corporate foundations, and the iPhone and its apps have been playing a big role in the health sector in poor communities everywhere. And as big businesses do, Apple became a landmark in the landscape of Silicon Valley, generating employment and wealth, with an energy that draws an entire ecosystem of developers and distributors into its orbit. And let's not forget the app economy which has spun out of it. With 850,000 apps and 45 billion downloads in just five years, the App Store has spawned a whole new industry, paying billions in royalties to app developers in all corners of the world.

Few Silicon Valley businesses are household names like Apple. Most are low profile, behind-the-scenes companies – but in many ways their impact on the world is no less profound. Take Autodesk, for example – the world's leading maker of design software. This may sound niche – but our modern world would look quite different without computer-aided design, or CAD. Bike wheels, perfume bottles, drilling bits, running shoes, train carriages, crankshafts, thermos flasks, suspension bridges, wind turbines, aircraft engines – much of our world has been digitally designed, and when it comes to design software, Autodesk is the major player. The company was founded in 1982 – the year that the computer was named *Time* magazine's 'Man of the Year', and Apple became the first personal computer company in history to hit $1 billion in revenue. Today's architects, engineers, product designers, and manufacturers might have grown up with Autodesk, and they might find it hard to imagine life before CAD: drafting and redrafting in 2D, by hand – it was painstaking and often uninspiring work. Digital design tools changed all that. Designers could enjoy the creativity, given the freedom to experiment without requiring endless redrawing. It became possible to design more sophisticated objects in 3D. Designers could now visualise their designs using 3D models, allowing customers and end-users to contribute to the process. To ask designers to return to the pre-Autodesk age would be like asking the rest of us to go back to the world of typewriters and Tipp-Ex.

In an imposing building on San Francisco's harbour front, Autodesk has a gallery that showcases projects that use its software. Large arched windows overlook the ferries scuttling across the bay, but the view inside is even more captivating. The first thing you see is a model of the new 'supertall' Shanghai Tower – at 121 storeys high China's tallest building. It has a skin of glass that twists and tapers, which makes it look impossibly ephemeral. It's an incredibly complex structure, designed with Autodesk tools by Gensler, a German architectural firm. Then there's a mesmeric Mercedes-Benz concept car, the Biome, designed on Autodesk software to mimic the structural cavities of a mammalian skull – making it very light. The gallery is packed with such wonders; it really is the most extraordinary corporate space. 'We created this space so we could show off the work of our customers,' says Autodesk's CEO, Carl Bass – and when he says 'customers', he's talking about the millions of individuals using Autodesk tools to push the limits of design. 'What we wanted to do was go behind the scenes and show all the decisions and all the thoughts and the inspiration that allows these creative people to bring these things to life.'

That's what design really means to Carl and his colleagues: making decisions. For most people, *design* brings to mind graphic design, or font design, or interior design – in other words, *aesthetic* design. But this isn't really what Autodesk is about, as Jeff Kowalski, their Chief Technology Officer, tells us: 'The designer is not the person in the black turtleneck, the person making the beautiful objects; it's the person understanding the paths that follow from various decisions' – such as the decision to use a different material, or change a dimension, or alter the structure. Here's where Autodesk comes in, Jeff explains. 'Through simulation, analysis and visualisation, our tools literally let people see the consequences of their decisions before they hit the material world. It's safer, it's more exploratory, and it's potentially more innovative. Our tools let you select the future you'd like to bring into the present.'

In common with much of Silicon Valley, conversations at Autodesk tend to be about the future – and of course, any conversation about the future leads rapidly towards some of the urgent concerns facing the world, as the global population soars towards 9 billion. 'The demand for innovation has never been greater,' Carl told students at Silicon Valley's Singularity University, 'We have these grand challenges – how do we supply people with ample food, with clean water, with sustainable energy sources?' There is reason for optimism, he thinks. 'The tools we have to solve these challenges have never been better.' Smarter design and systems thinking is at the heart of tackling these challenges, and Autodesk sets out to build the tools that make this possible – for example, by modelling the energy use of a building, squeezing waste out of a factory, or planning more sustainable infrastructure. Using these tools, Carl thinks that we can change our approach to using resources and manufacturing objects. 'There are things we do now that are crazy – the idea of chopping a tree down in Oregon and shipping it to Asia to be turned into plywood to be incorporated in a house in Kansas. That doesn't make any sense. Those things are going to change,' he says.

At the far end of the Autodesk Gallery is arguably the most significant exhibit of them all. In a glass box about a metre square, a small robotic nozzle glides silently but purposefully, making small repetitive movements. It's a 3D printer: it looks innocuous, but according to Carl and Jeff, this industrious little machine will change the world. Carl explains how it works.

'Think of an inkjet printer, which lays down a thin layer of ink. A 3D printer lays down a thin layer of plastic – it's mostly plastic – and then it just goes up a little bit, a fraction of an inch, and prints another layer and another layer, until you have a 3D object. It's kind of science-fiction-like, because it gives you the ability to take a file and send it halfway around the world and I can print the exact same object sitting 5,000 miles away.'

Just like an inkjet printer, a 3D printer prints from a digital file – and Autodesk develops the software that makes these files. In a sense, it's the Microsoft Word of 3D printing – along with a number of other 3D software makers, such as Blender and SketchUp. Many people think it could change the way products are made and sold. If you need a spare part for your bike, you don't need to order one from the manufacturer, you can print one off. If a coat-hook snaps, print a new one. Bored of your iPhone cover? Design and print your own.

And already there's a proliferation of innovative alternatives springing up in the industry. Companies like Solidoodle and MakerBot are racing to produce the first breakthrough 3D printer for the consumer market. Dreambox is a 3D printing vending machine, allowing consumers to upload a 3D design from a USB stick and print it out. Shapeways is an online marketplace for 3D designs, and their marketing director Carine Carmy told PBS's *Off Book* how 3D printing changes the product development process:

> You can essentially bring a product to market with no risk. You don't have inventory any more. You don't have to make sure there's a market ready for your product. If you sell one, that's awesome; if you sell 10,000 then all of a sudden you have a passive income model. Usually to bring a product to market takes a year, and then you have to find the manufacturer, and the investor, and so it's going to force us to change the way we think about not only buying products but how they're made.

Autodesk's Carl and Jeff are both gripped by the scale of change that 3D printing will bring about in the world of manufacturing. 'Once we got out of the craft stage during the industrial revolution, ordinary people had a lot less involvement in design,' Jeff tells us. Just as digital technology allows anyone to make music or edit video, now we can design and create products. 'It's the undoing of the industrial revolution. It literally gives them the tools to design things they would previously have had to buy.' Carl also describes the impact of 3D printing in terms of 'reversing the industrial revolution':

> What I think's going on here with digital manufacturing is that we're fundamentally rewriting the economic laws of the industrial revolution. That was where we needed

> mass production. You needed to be able to produce things in high volume to get high quality and low cost. The fundamental economics are changing. I can now produce things in small quantities at really high qualities and reasonable price – so that changes the equation of making stuff.

As with any new technology, it's bound to have both positive and negative impacts. A shift away from the economics of mass production would be welcome by those worried about our use and abuse of the environment and its resources. At the same time, people are worried about the possible effects on jobs under this new, more efficient manufacturing paradigm. The US Congress is concerned about the open-source production of firearms using 3D printing. In a world where manufacturing power shifts to people's living rooms, others worry about protection of intellectual property and copyright enforcement. Jeff is philosophical about these anxieties: areas of genuine concern like these are inevitable as society adapts to a new technology.

'Our tools have changed the way we *think*,' he says. 'In fact, in many ways we literally see the world through our tools, because often it's the arrival of a new tool that opens our minds to new possibilities that we would never have imagined before.' As the developer of software used by designers, architects, engineers and amateur 3D makers, Autodesk is essentially a toolmaker. 'Everything needs to be designed,' Jeff tells us. 'And therefore everything needs a tool for design. That creates an opportunity and a responsibility to do that in a lasting way for the benefit of a broader number of people.' He shrugs his shoulders, as though it's obvious. 'That's why I come to work.'

Speaking to people in and around Silicon Valley, you get the impression that everyone feels a sense that they are part of shaping the future. And with such a history of producing successful, world-changing companies, it's hardly surprising that many other cities and countries have tried to foster a Silicon Valley of their own. Scotland has Silicon Glen and Cambridge has Silicon Fen, while London has the quintessentially British Silicon Roundabout. Africa is home to Silicon Lagoon in Lagos, Nigeria, as well as Silicon Savannah near Nairobi, Kenya. One of the largest tech clusters outside of Silicon Valley is Bangalore, known by locals as the Silicon Valley of India. It's the centre of an IT services and outsourcing industry that's worth over $100 billion to the Indian economy each year, and like Silicon Valley it grew up around a small number of IT giants – in this case Infosys, HCL and Wipro. Helsinki is home to Silicon Suomi – the Finnish word for Finland, where a vibrant cluster of wireless businesses has grown up around the mobile giant Nokia. Interestingly, in December 2012 a BBC report suggested that Nokia's steady decline was stimulating a strong start-up culture in Finland: 'Now that Nokia is doing worse the ecosystem around it is developing,' one interviewee remarked. It brings to mind the image of a reef, established around some long-since washed away volcano; the ring of coral which surrounded it teems with a huge variety of colourful life forms.

COTTONOPOLIS

The energy emanating from Silicon Valley shapes our lives today – but the pattern is not new. In a different time and in a different place Cottonopolis was the 'phenomenon of the age'. Two hundred years ago, Cottonopolis was the popular name given to the English city of Manchester, which became the centre of the cotton trade – the booming global industry of the time. People knew then that something special was happening there. Visitors came from all over to see and understand it. Countries around the world, from the USA to Germany to India, attempted to replicate the model. Leon Faucher, a French economist who travelled to Manchester in the 1840s, was astonished at the prolific capacity for innovation that suddenly came up out of that one location: '... the effect of which has been to revolutionise the whole of British society and to influence, in a marked degree, the progress of civilisation in every quarter of the globe.'

That's the reason it's worth us stopping to visit Cottonopolis. Like Silicon Valley, the spark that brought technologies and businesses into being there changed how millions of people worked and lived. But Cottonopolis conjures up a very different atmosphere. Unlike the sunny orchards out of which Silicon Valley grew, Manchester in the north west of England is surrounded by the rainy Pennine hills. The rushing rivers and streams were ideal for driving the water wheels used by spinners in hundreds of villages around Lancashire to spin cotton yarn. And until the 1760s all yarn spun anywhere in the world was spun by hand.

At that time, British spinners couldn't compete with the fine muslins that came from India. The yarn they produced was coarse and not strong enough for weaving into pure cotton textiles, so it was destined to make fustian, the rough cotton-linen mix worn by working men and labourers. The country produced only three million pounds of cotton thread a year – an insignificant quantity in comparison to Bengal's 85 million. Then 'in a short period of feverish invention'[5] the cotton industry was revolutionised – and eventually all industry was revolutionised. The sheer speed at which it took off is evident in the numbers. In the 1780s, the nation's cotton exports were worth just £350,000; just twenty years later that figure had risen to £5.4 million, and in another twenty years it had increased fivefold again. The industry came to represent 8 per cent of GDP and 16 per cent of jobs. As a cotton manufacturer at the time, William Radcliffe said 'cotton, cotton, cotton was become the most universal material for employment.' Manchester was the epicentre of that activity, and the population of the city almost doubled between the 1780s and the time of the first census in 1801, from less than 40,000 to 70,000 – and by the 1830s it had more than doubled again.

If Manchester was at the centre of cotton, Richard Arkwright was at the centre of Manchester. He was the Bill Gates of his era, developing the intellectual property that would underpin an industry. The popular commentator of the time, Thomas Carlyle, called him a 'historical phenomenon'. His early career gave little sign of what was to come: he began as a travelling wigmaker, turned innkeeper, and only later switched his attention to cotton. Arkwright's business empire was built on a combination of manufacturing and licensing his patented technologies to others. The most important of those patents was the water frame. It took several years, significant investment and lots of trial and error to arrive at. Arkwright was not an inventor himself: his brand of originality was in pulling together the right elements to make the many moving parts work together. The ingenuity of the water frame was to take the mechanical rolling processes developed for other industries, such as metal and glass production, and adapt them to cotton. The speed of the rollers, the spacing between them, the arrangement of the gears, the materials from which to make them, the pressure they exerted in order to spin fine high-quality thread were all engineering problems waiting to be solved. And Arkwright brought together the people with the right skills to find solutions.

He made an extraordinary imaginative leap: he employed watchmakers to develop the gears. The watch industry had grown out of Galileo's discoveries in astronomy. Centuries before, marine navigation had been transformed by ships' clocks, which could keep time with great accuracy for years.

Arkwright's inspiration was to bring the technology and skills from the shipping industry to use in devising precision parts which would revolutionise the production of cotton. His team took five years to develop the finely tuned gears and precision parts for the water frame, which he patented in 1769. Over time, hundreds of local watchmakers became a source of highly skilled labour for the cotton industry. And by 1785 around 30,000 people were employed on machines that ran on Arkwright patents.

But just as Bill Gates faced resentment over Microsoft's grip on the growing personal computer industry, so Arkwright's stranglehold over the booming cotton trade made him the subject of antipathy. In 1785, a group of Lincolnshire cotton manufacturers took him to court to challenge his patent for the water frame. It was a celebrated case, going on late into the night – and Arkwright eventually lost. His power had made him a particular target and there was evident glee among his competitors when they wounded him. But he was already hugely wealthy and ultimately the verdict did not overturn his business success. Though it was high profile, it was not really such an unusual occurrence. A continuous stream of innovations leading to new patent registrations, accompanied by continuous and expensive IP battles, was a common feature of the emerging technology-led businesses of that time – as it is in ours.

The water frame was by no means the only, or even the most important, innovation of the time. Just five years before in 1764, a Lancashire weaver, James Hargreaves, had invented the spinning jenny. Before that, the economics of spinning had been based on one pair of hands operating one spindle. Hargreaves's invention allowed twelve spindles to be worked at the same time, still by one pair of hands. It instantly improved productivity so, even in the cottage industry of the villages, it had quick take-up. By 1788 there were 20,000 in use in

Britain. And with continual incremental improvement on the original design, the numbers of spindles that could be worked simultaneously kept rising and rising – from twelve up to twenty-four and, by the 1780s, up to 100.

In 1779 Samuel Crompton succeeded in putting together the two inventions of the spinning jenny and the water frame. He had learnt to spin as a boy in the Lancashire villages and grew up determined to improve how it was done. Crompton's spinning mule combined the merits of both of its predecessors. It had taken him ten years to do it and, with a local farmer providing the finance, it was a homespun version of the modern R&D process, but he achieved something remarkable. For the first time ever, cotton textiles could be manufactured finer and stronger at the same time, and at a fraction of the cost. Like Hargreaves though, Crompton was a weaver, not a businessman. He failed in his efforts to patent or commercialise his invention and died penniless in the 1820s. But it was his work that established the basis for the country to compete with India's finest muslins.

The spinning jenny, then the water frame and then the spinning mule: each of them was a breakthrough piece of equipment and moved the industry on. Soon, every aspect of the spinning process, and eventually weaving, became mechanised. Yet, for all their ingenuity, they were all just pieces of kit. What made Manchester Manchester was the cotton mill. Arkwright built the first one. The world had never seen anything like it. Powered by steam, five storeys high, 60 metres long, it worked through the day and night. As when he had developed his water frame, the revolution Arkwright led was about the orchestration of the many moving parts: the organisation of the machines involved, how they worked together, the flow of the materials through them and the management of the power required to drive that level of production. Arkwright had invented not just the next advance in equipment, but the entire factory system. As firms like Hewlett Packard would do later in Silicon Valley, it acted as a catalyst to others. By 1800 there were thirty-two cotton mills in the city; and by 1816, eighty-six. These were big businesses, the largest employing 1,500 people on site. Their tall chimneys shot up like skyscrapers and gave Manchester its distinctive silhouette.

The mills were powered by the 'all-purpose steam engine', the invention of James Watt. Trained as a tool maker in Scotland, he set off to make his mark on the world. One of the workers in his father's business recognised the young man's talents with the prophetic words, 'Jamie has got a future at his fingers' ends.' Back at the start of the eighteenth century, the early steam engines had been developed by engineers to solve a pressing problem – which is familiar in the mining industry even today – that vital sources of fuel were proving ever harder to access. Drilling deeper to reach the next seams of coal would require pumping out the water that collected in the bottom of the mines. While repairing a Newcomen steam engine, which was typically used to do that job, Watt saw what others hadn't: the enormous waste of energy caused by having just one condenser to provide both the heat and the cooling in the process. By introducing a separate condenser, Watt transformed the efficiency of steam engines – and so the mining industry. It also removed the need for a mill to be located near a water source, and so made it possible for Arkwright to build that first Manchester mill.

Watt was certainly an extraordinary engineering talent but he was lucky too in his business partner, Matthew Boulton. Boulton, who already ran a sizeable business employing 600 skilled men on a site powered by a water wheel, immediately saw the potential of Watt's design. He put together plans to invest in a manufacturing plant to take the engine to market. Initially cautious, Watt wanted to hang on to control of his hard-won new patent for the all-purpose steam engine and offered Boulton a licence to produce it in just three English counties. Boulton rejected the suggestion, and his response to it gives a feel for the man and captures the spirit of the time: 'It would not be worth my while to make it for three counties only, but I find it very worthwhile to make it for all the world.'[6]

The two men came to an understanding, and together applied for an extension to the terms and length of the patent. That secured, James Watt and Matthew Boulton became a long-lasting partnership, in the vein of Steve Jobs and Steve Wozniak. Like Wozniak, Watt didn't have much interest in running the business, and was later to write of himself, 'What I can promise to perform is to make an accurate survey & a faithful report of anything in the engineer way ... [but] I can on no account have anything to do with workmen, cash, or workmen's accts.' Meanwhile, Boulton was clear from the outset, 'I do not intend turning engineer': he saw building the business as his province. It was a dynamic combination and the business took off.

Boulton spotted the opportunity in the textile industry. At the start of the 1780s, he observed that people had become 'steam mill mad' and in his estimation 'the most likely line for our engines is the application of them to mills which is certainly an extensive field.' Originally, Watt's engine had been designed for the Cornish tin and copper mines but that market was getting saturated. Boulton was proved right. By 1795, they had built 150 engines, most of them to drive the cotton mills. Manchester knew what it owed to this man and a statue honouring his memory stands in Piccadilly Gardens, in the centre of the city, today. Watt's design is commonly acknowledged as the most important of all the innovations of the era because it was, as its name suggested, 'all purpose': it had so many applications. His was the technology which enabled the transformation of every other industry: it turned out that Jamie Watt did indeed have the future at his fingertips.

With large-scale mills came large-scale warehousing. By the start of the nineteenth century, there were over 1,100 warehouses in Manchester and the number climbed from there as production ramped up. Workers employed directly by the mills were almost matched by the numbers of warehouse men, clerks and porters who earned their living supporting commercial transactions in the city.

On market days, every Tuesday and Friday, 11,000 merchants travelled in from 280 textile towns and villages of Lancashire to do business at the Manchester Exchange. First established in 1792, it became the clearing-house for 80 per cent of the global trade in finished cotton – and by the end of the nineteenth century it was the largest trading room in the world. All this commercial activity required servicing. Financiers came into the city to provide capital and, as trade grew, accountancy and law firms grew up to advise the businessmen.

Whole new industries sprang up in support of cotton. In the days when spinning was a cottage industry, sour milk had been used in bleaching; cow dung had served to help fix dyes. As cotton boomed, bleaching became a bottleneck for the manufacturers. So demand spurred work in the new branches of chemistry and, as soda, chlorine, alum and other newly discovered chemicals turned out to offer new bleaching solutions, businesses emerged to mass-produce them – and that was the start of the modern chemical industry. Textile manufacture transformed the paper industry as well, as soft bleached cotton rags, a waste product from the mills, created a great, new source of raw material for paper manufacturing. And soon Manchester became a centre for paper production, from the strongest paper needed for packaging to the finest for letter writing, and from bankers' bills to newspapers.

Cottonopolis was a city full of people passionate about technology – the geeks of their day. The mills, and the machines in them, spun and whirred because of the ingenuity of toolmakers. Countless specialised businesses materialised, skilled in the production of rules, scales, lathes, planes, drills, bores and other precision instruments which got the factories up and running and kept them going. The city's workshops were inventing tools to make tools, and designing machines that made parts for other machines.

And the products themselves were part of the revolution they wrought. For people who could never have aspired to buying imported muslins, cotton brought colour and lightness to everyday clothes. Ordinary girls wore colour prints for the first time. The world looked a brighter place. In her book about the period, *The Lunar Men*, Jenny Uglow writes, 'I now marvel at the way the history of technology underpins the simplest things in our lives – the coins in our pocket, the plate on the breakfast table, the newspaper beside it.' These were all products of the businesses in Manchester and the Midlands at that time – along with cutlery, carpets, glass and clocks, soap, matches and other consumer goods snapped up by the new 'middling classes'. Ubiquitous and ordinary to most of us today, they were transformative to the lifestyles of millions of people then. Everyone wanted these products, as today we want what's designed in California, and owning them gave people a new and modern lifestyle.

A complex ecosystem built up in and around Manchester, in a pattern that can be seen in Silicon Valley today. The great mills and warehouses stood out in the landscape, while in between and all around them clusters of smaller businesses grew up to supply and service them. One innovation acted as a catalyst to the next; the emergence of one business opened up the opportunity for the next new one to appear. The place acted as a magnet for talent and became home to a highly skilled workforce. Big businesses invested continuously in research and development and grew on the back of the intellectual property they generated. These elements came together to make up the fabric of the economy, locally and even nationally – producing products the world didn't know it needed but which, once they existed, quickly found a global market. In Cottonopolis, as in Silicon Valley, invention built upon invention, business upon business, and industry upon industry. And so the industrial revolution was born, and the modern world began to take shape.

A SENSE OF PURPOSE

At 367 Addison Ave stands a double-storey redbrick Californian bungalow. It has a low-pitched roof with deep overhanging eaves and a spacious porch. To the side, set back a little, is a simple wooden garage – much like many other garages in the neighbourhood, except that this one is on the US National Register of Historic Places. It is, of course, the birthplace of Hewlett Packard. It has become the stuff of business legend: two guys in a Palo Alto garage who start a global tech company with nothing more than a few hundred dollars and some electronics parts. Founded in 1939, the company's success played a central role in establishing Silicon Valley. As we saw with the rise of the first mills in industrial Manchester, an entire ecosystem grew up around the company: a cadre of talented tech professionals, engineering suppliers, electronics manufacturers, financial services companies, specialist attorneys and eventually the venture capital firms – all of which created fertile ground for new start-ups. Large businesses create an environment for broader economic activity. Bill Miller, the former provost of Stanford University, likes to call Silicon Valley a 'habitat' because it is not just about the genius of individual entrepreneurs, but about a complex system of interdependency between the big companies and many small players.

In the Valley, you can see too how some of today's giants grew up out of the clusters which formed around the earlier generation of big beasts. For example, whilst Steve Jobs was finding himself on a fruit farm, Steve Wozniak was finding his inspiration at Hewlett-Packard. By the 1980s, HP had become a large company and an anchor for a growing constellation of smaller businesses. Wozniak was working there, and to this day talks passionately about the company. On an unusually warm English summer's evening, Wozniak gave a talk as part of Oxford University's series called 'Silicon Valley Comes To Oxford',[7] and describes his response in 1974 when he was offered a job by another firm:

> I said no: I work for Hewlett-Packard. Hewlett-Packard is an engineering company. They make products that engineers use: oscilloscopes, calculators, test equipment, signal generators, power supplies. This is an engineer's company, started by engineers, full of engineers throughout the entire org chart. Ideas for new products can come from the lowest levels of the org chart on up. The engineers working on products can also direct where the company's next products will go. It's not a top-down-run company... I love that company. I believed engineers were the best people in the world. When I did a calculation for an engineering solution, the answer was right or it was wrong. It was testable. It was truth in its purest form. And the engineers always had to live with things that could be proven or disproven, they had to be true or false, and I just believed that these were the most special perfect people in the world and I wanted to be among them forever. I made up my mind to be an engineer for the rest of my life. Never to move up the org chart in a company. And Hewlett-Packard was the place for me.

Nostalgia isn't an emotion you associate with Silicon Valley, but people often talk about Hewlett Packard with a kind of wistful affection. In its heyday, the company was admired for its culture of innovation and progressive management practices. Dissent was actively encouraged, and a 'Medal of Defiance' was awarded annually 'in recognition of extraordinary contempt and defiance beyond the normal call of engineering duty'. The labs were left unlocked at night so that engineers could work on pet projects in their own time, using company equipment – and it was in one of these labs that Steve Wozniak designed the first Apple computer. Hewlett Packard also played a formative role in the life of Steve Jobs: when he was only thirteen years old, Jobs decided to build a frequency counter for a school project, and needed parts. This was a time when you could still find the home phone number of the boss of a major corporation in the local phone directory, and so the young eighth-grader decided to call Bill Hewlett and ask for some electronics components. Hewlett said yes, and Jobs later landed a summer job with the company.

David Packard gave a speech in 1960, shortly before his death, thinking about the future of the company he founded, by then nearly a quarter of a century old:

> I want to discuss why a company exists in the first place. In other words, why are we here? I think many people assume, wrongly, that a company exists simply to make money. While this is an important result of a company's existence, we have to go deeper and find the real reasons for our being. As we investigate this, we inevitably come to the conclusion that a group of people get together and exist as an institution that we call a company so they are able to accomplish something collectively which they could not accomplish separately. They are able to do

> something worthwhile – they make a contribution to society (a phrase which sounds trite but is fundamental).

This may sound like the unworldly musings of an old hippy, but it represents an ethos that has driven success in Silicon Valley for decades.

Craig Newman, founder of Craigslist, likes to tell interviewers that his motivations are *nerd values*: 'First I need to earn an okay living, then change the world.' Craig's nerd credentials are beyond question: he describes himself in high-school wearing thick black taped-together glasses, with a plastic pocket protector and marginal social skills. Two computer science degrees later and, after a spell at IBM, Craig found himself working at a bank, and started Craigslist as a hobby. He didn't set out to disrupt an entire industry, but Craigslist has diverted billions away from the newspaper business by providing an easy alternative to classified advertising. When asked about the secret of his success, Craig says you have to start with the right attitude: 'First, run and persist running a site that's a genuine community service, without specifically intending to get rich at it.'

Craig had planned to call his listing service 'sf-events', but friends persuaded him to call it Craigslist to emphasise the personal, un-corporate nature of the service. It's a common pattern in the land of tech giants and billion-dollar valuations: as we saw with Apple's early brand campaigns, many of the Valley's most successful companies have consciously positioned themselves as distinctly *anti-corporate*. It's as though they're trying to emphasise that they have a sense of purpose in the world, that the purpose of the business is not profit.

For a place that's so forward-looking, Silicon Valley is full of echoes of the past. And for a place so young, there are already many stages in its evolution. In Mountain View lie a pair of unremarkable college-campus style buildings that were once home to Netscape, the company that introduced the world to the web browser. It was Netscape's phenomenally successful Initial Public Offering in 1995 – when the company was just sixteen months old – that sparked the dotcom boom. Within eight years the company would be history, unable to compete with the rise of Microsoft's Internet Explorer. Along the swampy shore at the bottom of San Francisco Bay is a vast campus of 100,000 square metres that housed Sun Microsystems, which once outstripped IBM and HP in its sales of workstations and powerful servers, and which invented the Java programming language. For two decades Sun was a giant of Silicon Valley, but its business faded as competitors gained ground, and in 2010 it became part of Oracle. The company's expansive campus is now home to one of today's Silicon Valley colossi: Facebook. A little further down the valley, on a great stretch of land by US freeway 101, was the estate of Silicon Graphics International, or SGI, famous for bringing the world the powerful graphics tools used to make movies such as *Jurassic Park, Lord of the Rings* and *Titanic*. Slowly SGI was outpaced by lower-cost technology, and another powerhouse passed into history.

Today, SGI's old campus is the realm of Google, refashioned as a kind of corporate playground called the Googleplex. It's a painstakingly un-office environment: parasols, lava lamps, pool tables, inflatable furniture and liberal splurges of the insignia green, blue, red and yellow. But behind the infantilisation of the workplace is a business that has done much to shape the world we live in. Google's Android operating system has fuelled the global growth of smartphones: today, three-quarters of all new smartphones run Android. Gmail is the world's most widely used web-based email service, and many of us would be lost without Google Maps.

And of course the company is synonymous with its founding product: search. It's worth remembering that back when the web was a primordial swamp of links, finding information was very hit-and-miss. In 1994, a couple of Stanford students, David Filo and Jerry Yang, founded a multi-billion-dollar business when they started building a web directory called Yahoo!. However, digging through a list of lists was still a laborious way of finding your way around the web, and there were no really effective search tools. Better navigation was needed if the internet was really going to take off. In 1998 another couple of Stanford graduates, Sergey Brin and Larry Page, launched a search engine based on a breakthrough idea – and like all truly breakthrough ideas, it seems obvious in hindsight: a web page is likely to be more relevant to a particular search if lots of other relevant web pages link to it. They wrote an algorithm that ranked pages on this basis, and so Google was born.

Google is now the world's most visited website. The site's appearance has remained almost unchanged since its launch, but behind the familiar front-end is a perpetual cycle of incremental improvement. Since those early days, the company's engineers have reportedly spent more than 1,000 'person-years' perfecting this algorithm. There is constant tweaking going on: in 2011, Google launched 520 improvements and ran over 58,000 experiments – many of them in real time, on live searches. Although you may not realise it, each time you do a Google search, you are probably a 'lab rat' for their engineers. Hundreds of different criteria define each set of results. Google keeps many of these secret, but some will reflect individual interests: Google collects data on people's search histories, web use and location, and these all feed into the calculation. According to Google, it's estimated that more calculations go into a single set of search results than it took to put man on the moon.

All of this activity is given meaning in Google's clear statement of purpose: *to organise the world's information and make it universally accessible and useful* – and becoming a listed company wouldn't alter this. As CEO Eric Schmidt told *Time* magazine, 'The company isn't run for the long-term value of our shareholders but for the long-term value of our end users.' When, in 2004, Google made its IPO, hundreds of employees became instant paper millionaires. It was an unconventional IPO, done through an auction to make it easy for the public to participate. It was also an unconventional prospectus, containing the following proclamation:

> Don't be evil. We believe strongly that in the long-term, we will be better served – as shareholders and in all other ways – by a company that does good things for the world even if we forgo some short-term gains.[8]

As a corporate maxim, 'Don't be evil' doesn't seem very *corporate* – and, of course, that's the point. It's another one of the great Silicon Valley businesses growing up wanting to be one of the good guys. Too often, a sort of moral sclerosis sets in as companies reach a certain scale – and the young founders were keen that their company avoided this. 'Search engines play a really important role in people's lives, determining what information they get to look at. You really want to trust the people that are doing that for you,' Page said in a 1999 interview.[9]

However, as Google has reached into more areas of our lives, it has found itself in the middle of many of the world's big conversations and controversies. People use Google to find information about their health, to make decisions about their finances, to learn about the world. It's even been described as a reality interface[10] – for many people, Google has become the gateway to the entire internet.

All big companies face their own versions of this: as they grow, their relationships with society become more complex.

Inevitably, there are areas of real friction, as there are now for Google. Many people question the integrity of their search results. Others point out the potential conflict of interest that comes from a business model based on advertising revenues. Google is accruing people's personal information at a phenomenal rate – 'vast pools of data about its users', as the *Wall Street Journal* puts it[11] – and many people question whether Google (or any other company, for that matter) can be trusted not to misuse this data, and to keep it safe from being stolen for criminal purposes. A Microsoft spokesman said that privacy was 'Google's kryptonite'[12]. The company has also been criticised in the past for being too friendly with governments: sharing data on individuals and censoring search results at the request of governments.

As you would expect, Google has robust responses to all of these criticisms but that in itself won't do away with the challenges which come to the corporate sector from the wider world, whatever the reality of the situation. Sergey Brin said in an interview that because Google deals with so many different types of information, many of the decisions they take will inevitably upset some people. Rather than engage in endless debates, they have to get on and make decisions, he said. Sometimes the issues are straightforward; but when they're more complex, with conflicting points of view, Google is sometimes forced to 'break a tie'. They're reconciled to the reality that because their increasing scale makes them powerful actors in the world, controversy is bound to seek them out.

But the simple exhortation 'don't be evil' offers a hostage to fortune for a mature company. Margaret Hodge, Member of Parliament and Chair of the UK's Public Accounts Committee investigating Google's tax payments, used their words against them when she rounded on one of the company's senior executives with the words: 'You are a company that says you do no evil. But I think you *do* do evil.' The journal *First*

Monday published a thought-provoking essay on 'Don't be evil', which concludes: 'In the modern era, saying that one is not evil is meaningless. It suggests an unexamined morality; one that finds virtue in good intentions, rather than in good social practice.'[13]

The question of whether big business is good or evil is a live issue right now, but it's not new. Two centuries ago, as the industrial revolution gained pace, Manchester became, as the historian Asa Briggs said, the 'shock city of the age'. Its inventiveness and energy was stunning, and people came to marvel and participate. It was a wonderful city, but it was a terrible city at the same time. Commentators described the smoke-filled skies and the dye-stained rivers. Alexis de Tocqueville, one of the most famous of the visitors to Manchester, wrote about its contrasts. Here, he said: 'Humanity attains its most complete development and its most brutish; here civilisation works its miracles, and civilised man is turned back almost into a savage.'

As thousands of people poured in from the rural areas to find work, the slums expanded. The infrastructure couldn't cope and, for those at the bottom of the heap, living conditions were appalling. Working conditions in the mills were harsh, typically with twelve-hour days. Children had been part of the family workforce in the villages and child labour was considered normal in the factories. As young as six, children worked long and hard shifts, with little food. Many were maimed, or even killed, operating the machinery. Health was poor and people became trapped in a vicious cycle of illness and poverty. The gap between the rich and the barely-surviving grew. There were those who found their place in it and profited from it, and those who became its victims. It led to protests and even riots.

In nineteenth-century Manchester, the dichotomy was highly visible, and right on the doorstep. For today's big corporates the front-line of the problem is often the other side of the world. The realities are brought to light on digital cameras, in NGO reports or employee blogs. It's a sign of our times that one of Tim Cook's first acts as CEO of Apple, just months after Steve Jobs's death, was to fly to Beijing to meet head-on the challenges of working conditions at the far end of the global supply chain. It was the start of a long process for Apple, and led to a commitment to audit and improve labour conditions among the half a million people working for its suppliers.[14] Increasingly, labour conditions in the emerging markets have risen up the corporate agenda. And it remains to be seen how Apple and the relatively young big businesses in Silicon Valley will respond to the acute social challenges of our times.

When Manchester was faced with the social problems that resulted from rapid industrialisation, it drew on the very spirit that had helped to build it. There was a free-thinking, radical strain in the culture of the city. There were strong Methodist and Baptist communities. Manchester's Dissenters, who were barred from attending Oxford and Cambridge Universities and from holding public office, took pride in succeeding outside the paradigms of the old establishment. And, while some factory owners held a hard line on what they saw as the limits of their responsibilities, others chose to step out and take a leading role in turning the situation around. Robert Owen, for example, only twenty-one years old when he was made a manager at one of the city's largest mills, became an ardent voice for social change. Manchester was the birthplace of the Trade Union Congress, female suffrage and the cooperative movement – and eventually it became well known for social progress as well as for business progress.

And Cottonopolis established something that was much more than the sum of its products: it brought in 'a system of society constructed according to entirely new principles,' as the historian Asa Briggs said: 'It seemed to be creating a new order of businessmen, energetic, tough, proud, contemptuous of the old aristocracy – and yet, in some sense, constituting an aristocracy themselves.'[15] They sound very like some of the famous names of Silicon Valley.

For most people, though, the greatest sign of progress was literally the shirt on their back: gone were the rough fustian smocks, as the steam engines and mills of Cottonopolis made comfortable fabric affordable to all. Gone was the tinder box which for centuries had been the primary means of making fire, as the invention of matches made it accessible to all. These were disruptive innovations. It's in the nature of progress that not everything moves forward in step. Imaginative leaps in remarkable technologies, everyday benefits in ordinary products, new opportunities for people to improve their lives and fresh potential for suffering and ugliness.

Yet public debate, even today, about the role of business in society is so often framed within a lazy narrative of *good versus evil*: enlightened consumer-champions versus destructive profit-seekers. The storyline of a good guy turned bad is especially compelling, and Silicon Valley offers candidates for the role of upstart challenger morphed into unaccountable megacorp. Our argument is that these archetypes are not useful: they generate heat but very little light. If we want to reconnect business with society, we need to get beyond good and evil. We need to recognise more clearly what business is as an engine in society and put its energy to useful purpose.

A few kilometres along the Bay from the Googleplex is the headquarters of Facebook, a densely packed campus with the word *HACK* tiled in huge letters across the central courtyard. The company moved in over a year ago but it still feels like a new home, not quite lived-in. Unlike Google's multicolour playground, this definitely has the air of a workspace, with wooden benches and fluorescent tubes, and stencilled posters imploring 'Stay Focused and Keep Shipping'. The liberal application of spray-cans on the newly whitewashed walls prevents the space from feeling too *corporate*. The large open-plan floors are quiet and studious, and people walk purposefully, but it doesn't feel like the pulsating epicentre of a global communications revolution – which is, in effect, what Facebook has been since Mark Zuckerberg launched the site from his university dorm room in 2004.

'It feels like an honor,' Zuckerberg said when Facebook passed the billion user mark. 'We get the honor of building things that a billion people use. I mean, there's no core need. It isn't a core human need to use Facebook. It's a core human need to stay connected with the people you care about. The need to open up and connect is such a deep part of what makes us human. Being in a position where we are the company – or one of the companies – that can play a role in delivering that service is just this ... it's an honor.'[16] One billion users, but Facebook isn't resting back just yet. 'We have this ethos where we want to be a culture of builders, right?' Zuckerberg says, explaining to journalists why there was no huge celebration to mark the billionth user. 'Everyone came together and counted down. Then we all went back to work.'[17] As the posters put it: stay focused, keep shipping.

Zuckerberg talks of creating 'a more open and connected world' – a phrase that feels full of the zeitgeist. Social media has clearly had a major impact across the globe – primarily Facebook, but also Twitter and YouTube. It's plain to see that in the communications landscape we now live in, the power structures have changed. Those who would try to control the flow of information find it increasingly difficult to do so: the old top-down, broadcast model has been superseded by very fluid, horizontal networks of communication. It is, indeed, a revolution, and offers a bright vision of a world in which consumers are more empowered, communities have become a force to be reckoned with, and people can collaborate and share in ways we haven't even imagined yet. It's a *nowhere-to-hide* world in which political leaders and corporate management will be more accountable. And, simply, it's a world in which we can all keep in touch with those we care about – even across vast distances. One of the most enthusiastic proponents of this new world is the author Don Tapscott, whom we spoke to on his way to talk at TED Global, and asked him why he is so excited by the possibilities of social media:

> It's a sort of social tsunami. There are more than a billion people on Facebook, and social media is now becoming a new means of production. In the private sector, it is changing the way that we orchestrate the capability to innovate, to create goods and services. In the public sector, it is changing the way we create public value – and the nature of democracy itself. Just as the internet lowers the cost of transacting and collaborating, it also lowers the cost of dissent. So you put all of that together and what you've got is a revolution.

Of course, the technologies that underpin this new age of communications have been developed by many different businesses: companies like Cisco have built the physical infrastructure that makes the internet run, and companies like Intel and ARM have developed processors that are cheaper, faster and more energy-efficient. Thousands of companies are involved in designing, manufacturing and distributing the devices through which we all connect to the internet. Still, no single company is more associated with this new, connected world than Facebook. During the Arab Spring, Facebook became an emblem of freedom and progress for the demonstrators, as people sprayed the word on walls across the region, and someone even named their child after the company. Little wonder that, when Zuckerberg took his business into an IPO in 2012, it was the company's role in society that he most wanted to highlight. Just as Google's founders had written an idealistic letter to potential investors ahead of their own IPO, so Zuckerberg wrote a letter that sets out his vision for Facebook's social purpose. It conjures David Packard's philosophy of business when he spoke in Silicon Valley fifty years before about 'why a company exists in the first place':

> Facebook was not originally created to be a company. It was built to accomplish a *social mission* – to make the world more open and connected...
>
> Today, our society has reached another tipping point. We live at a moment when the majority of people in the world have access to the internet or mobile phones – the raw tools necessary to start sharing what they're thinking, feeling, and doing with whomever they want. Facebook aspires to build the services that give people the power to share and help them once again transform many of our core institutions and industries...
>
> Most great people care primarily about building and being a part of great things, but they also want to make money. Through the process of building a team – and also building *a developer community, advertising market and investor base* – I've developed a deep appreciation for how building a strong company with a strong economic engine and strong growth can be the best way to align many people to solve important problems. Simply put: we don't build services to make money; we make money to build better services...
>
> By focusing on our mission and building great services, we believe we will create the most value for our

> shareholders and partners *over the long-term* – and this in turn will enable us to *keep attracting the best people* and building more great services. We don't wake up in the morning with the primary goal of making money, but we understand that the best way to achieve our mission is to build a strong and valuable company.

When this letter was published, there were many who questioned whether it was a cynical attempt to avoid Facebook appearing to be another profit-hungry big corporate, cashing in and selling out with a multi-billion IPO. *Wired* magazine wrote, 'Sometimes companies get so large, ubiquitous, and profitable that they need to have a social mission to legitimise their activity and give them something to work towards beyond cashing checks.'[18] Only Zuckerberg can really know how much of his social mission was genuinely present at the inception of Facebook, and how he's grown into it as the potential power of the platform became more evident as the company grew. And in a sense, does it matter? The important thing, surely, is that, as one of the world's leading corporate entities, Facebook has put a clear stake in the ground about the role it wants to play in the world: something to work towards and something to be accountable for.

Leaving Facebook's HQ and heading back out onto the Bayfront Expressway, you notice the road that loops around the campus has been named *Hacker Way*. It's a neat, nerdy joke, and relates to a section of Zuckerberg's IPO letter:

> The Hacker Way is an approach to building that involves *continuous improvement and iteration.* Hackers believe that something can always be better, and that nothing is ever complete. They just have to go fix it – often in the face of people who say it's impossible or are content with the status quo [italics ours].

Continuous improvement and iteration – more than anything else, this describes the success of Silicon Valley: endlessly adapting to an ever-changing environment, responding to shifting user needs, recalibrating to new forms of behaviour. This is how business works: it's a restless cycle of invention and reinvention, a continuous search for better processes, better products, better services. The results of this surround us: a steady tide of progress, continually upgrading our everyday lives, wherever we live in the world. For example, in 2012, the number of mobile phones exceeded the number of people on the planet – yet a couple of decades ago the world's first commercially available cellular telephone was the size of a brick and would cost you nearly $10,000 in today's money. This is business in action – the relentless push to improve and innovate – and when it works, we all benefit.

Silicon Valley is home to some of the world's most successful and iconic businesses. Many of them have become profit generators on a phenomenal scale, making vast fortunes for their shareholders. But, by and large, these companies are more than mechanisms for money making: they are driven by a desire to reinvent the world. Social impact is at the heart of what they do. As Larry Page told *Time* magazine, 'If we were motivated by money, we would have sold the company a long time ago and ended up on a beach.'[19] Mark Zuckerberg agrees, arguing there's no need to choose between making money and having a social impact: 'Building a mission and building a business goes hand in hand,' he says. 'We are about doing both.' Of course, as they grow, all of these companies become enmeshed in difficult social and environmental issues. As they become big economic agents, they must take care not to abuse their power. Still, spend time in Silicon Valley and it's easy to see how businesses can thrive when they make a positive impact on the world.

It's not surprising that Silicon Valley companies attract the brightest talent from the worlds of business and technology.

Google, for example, regularly tops lists of employers that graduates want to work for. Of course talented people want to make money, but they also want to feel they are making a difference. They're attracted by both the size of the paycheck and the scale of the challenge – and the world has plenty of challenges on offer, despite the great progress made in recent decades. Hundreds of millions have been lifted out of poverty, but the gap between rich and poor continues to grow. Many diseases have been beaten back or eradicated; others threaten to become epidemics. Economic growth and technological progress have transformed life for billions of people, but our demands on the earth's finite resources are unsustainable. In this book, we look at some of the big companies around the world that are working to tackle some of these big complex problems by applying their creative energies and their ability to execute at scale. One thing's for sure: if we want to fix the world, we're going to need to harness the full power of business, and the full-hearted endeavour of the people making businesses work.

PART II

A JOURNEY THROUGH THE WORLD OF BUSINESS

3

A HARD PATH TO LEADERSHIP

It was a busy afternoon at the height of the pre-Christmas shopping season and TV crews gathered outside a department store in midtown Manhattan. They were there to capture some good prime-time news footage: a man dressed as Santa Claus being dragged into a police car, arrested for civil disobedience. Over in Sacramento, in the full glare of the national media, dozens of Girls Club members occupied a Disney Store dressed as the Seven Dwarfs.[20] These two stunts were part of a campaign drawing attention to the use of sweatshops by companies manufacturing clothes and toys. This was 1996, a year that had seen a flood of exposés on big brands with unethical offshore working practices. Undercover journalists using hidden cameras had brought back shocking images of people working in terrible conditions in factories across the world: in Haiti, Vietnam, El Salvador and Burma. People were appalled to discover the toys they were buying for their own children were made by other children in Indonesia and China, forced to work behind barbed wire in hazardous factories. Some of the best-loved and most iconic brands were found to have an ugly side, including Mattel, Gap and Walmart. These companies were hit hard by the revelations, which fuelled a growing anti-corporate movement. But one brand more than any other became the focus of public anger over sweatshops: Nike.

In the 1990s, Nike was a global phenomenon. Nike-sponsored athletes were cultural icons worldwide, among them Michael Jordan, Bo Jackson, Andre Agassi, and Pete Sampras. The company had signed the entire Brazilian football team in a headline-grabbing $200 million deal. Nike had become a powerful force in sports and one of the most desired brands in the world. *Forbes* magazine regularly marked it as America's most profitable company and its founder, Phil Knight, was one of America's richest men. It had been one of the great success stories of the time: a company named for the goddess of victory, championing the spirit of endeavour, soaring high in the public imagination, and also on the public stock market. Knight would often account for this achievement by explaining that Nike was driven by a higher purpose. Its mission wasn't simply to sell sportswear, but to 'enhance people's lives through sports and fitness' and to keep 'the magic of sports alive'. Nike's athletes, together with its aspirational 'Just Do It' advertising, sent a positive message to many young people around the world: with the right attitude, with the right vision, you can do anything. For many, especially those in poor urban areas, a pair of Nike Air Jordans became a symbol of rising above a drab reality. For a while, it seemed, the world had fallen in love with Nike.

In many ways, Nike had become the archetypal US corporate, fuelled by the edgy creativity of American urban culture. And yet almost none of its products were manufactured in the USA. From the outset, Phil Knight's big idea was that shoes could be made in Asia that would compete with established brands such as Adidas. This was the subject of a paper he wrote while studying for his MBA at Stanford University. It was to become a powerful formula for Nike: cut the product costs by manufacturing overseas, thereby generating large cash surpluses which could be invested in building a powerful brand. 'There's no value in making things any more,' said Knight.[21] And so, in 1971, with a business plan and a freshly designed swoosh, Nike began by placing orders with factories in Taiwan and South Korea. As demand grew, the company did open its own shoe factories in Maine and New Hampshire, but by the mid-1980s these were closed and production had moved to China, Thailand and Indonesia. By the mid-1990s, Nike had built a substantial network of suppliers stretching across Asia. Few of Nike's enthusiastic consumers had any idea that the trainers they loved were being made in some of the world's poorest countries.

As many as 500,000 people were working in factories making Nike products, but not a single one of them was a Nike employee, and Nike didn't own any of the factories that manufactured its gear. From Nike's point of view, the operation of these factories was entirely a matter for their owners – and this included the treatment of the people who worked in them. But from the outset, stories of poor treatment filtered back from these production outposts: people were working long hours for low wages, and some of the factories were said to be run like military camps, with corporal punishment. Workers might be allowed only two toilet breaks in a twelve-hour shift, and water was rationed. Many of the workers were women, and there were reports of sexual harassment. As demand for Nike products grew, so did the intensity of production in these factories – and accounts of poor treatment became more widespread. Human Rights Watch raised the issues in 1989, and reports started appearing in the media. Nike's response at the time is a good indicator of how times have changed: essentially, 'these aren't our factories, it's not our problem'. After a series of disturbances at factories in Indonesia, a Nike manager in the country was reported as saying, 'It's not within our scope to investigate.' He was aware that there were problems, but didn't know what they were about: 'I don't know that I need to know.' [22]

Today, it's difficult to imagine any well-run company taking such a cavalier attitude. Nike, in particular, has been on a long journey from the days of 'I don't know that I need to know'. As we shall see, the company is now widely recognised as a pioneer in managing supply chains responsibly. Back in the mid-1990s, unease about the treatment of workers in Nike factories was becoming a public outcry. Phil Knight was greeted by jeering students when he was invited back to Stanford University Business School as a guest lecturer. Media reports filled the newspapers with headlines like 'Worked to Death' and 'Wages of Shame'. Dozens of activist groups sprang up with names such as 'No Sweat' and 'As You Sow'. The sloganeering possibilities were immense, and included 'Do It Just', 'Just Boycott It', 'Just Don't', 'Ich Kaufe Es Nicht!' (German for 'I Don't Buy It') and 'Just Duit' (French for 'Just Products'). Many of these voices were part of a growing anti-globalisation movement, and they were easy to dismiss as fringe groups. But there were also signs of rising anger in many inner-city communities, which were essential to the brand's image, and its mainstream consumer appeal – and this really did start to rattle Nike. Up to this point, people living in poor urban areas had been Nike's core devotees, wearing the swoosh like a talisman against the grim realities of the ghetto. But many were starting to question this, especially given the high prices paid for Nike products by people on very low incomes. Naomi Klein talks to a sports store owner from New Jersey in her book *No Logo*:

> I do get weary and worn down with it all. I'm always forced to face the fact that I make my money from poor people. A lot of them are on welfare. Sometimes a mother will come in here with a kid, and the kid is dirty and poorly dressed. But the kid wants a hundred-twenty-buck pair of shoes and that stupid mother buys them for him. I can feel that kid's inner need – this desire to own these things and have the feelings that go with them – but it hurts me that this is the way things are.[23]

Stories were appearing of kids being assaulted – and even murdered – for their sneakers, and many people began to wonder whether the Nike brand was becoming a monster. When Nike's core customers watched TV news reports of how the company was making vast profits by using sweatshop labour in poverty-stricken countries, it felt like a betrayal. Nike's own figures showed that from a $70 pair of shoes less than $3 would go into workers' hands. Klein recounts how customers sent hundreds of letters to Phil Knight, telling him how much they had spent on Nike products over the years. 'I just bought a pair of Nikes for $100,' one kid wrote, according to Klein. 'It's not right what you've been doing. A fair price would have been $30. Could you send me back $70?' By the late 1990s, a fully-fledged consumer backlash was under way, with protestors picketing Nike stores, and activists working hard to make the swoosh a symbol of sweatshops. As the backlash grew, profits began to shrink, and so did Nike's stock price. Nike's gleaming brand had lost its lustre.

'One of the biggest mistakes we made was to think "we don't own the factories, so that's their problem",' says Nelson Farris, Nike's longest tenured employee and now Global Head of Talent Development. 'That's when we recognised we were more powerful than we realised and as a consequence, people expected more of us. Employees were embarrassed and disenchanted and confused. The media had sweatshops and child labour in every sentence.'[24]

Todd Maclean, who was a director at Nike at the time, agrees that the company failed to get a grip on the issue: 'Quite frankly, that was a sort of irresponsible way to approach this. We had people there every day looking at quality. Clearly, we had leverage and responsibility with certain parts of the business, so why not others?'[25]

In 1998 Nike publicly recognised the severity of the

situation. On 12 May, Phil Knight stood before the National Press Club in Washington DC and had a *nostra culpa* moment:

> It has been said that Nike has single-handedly lowered the human rights standards for the sole purpose of maximising profits. The Nike product has become synonymous with slave wages, forced overtime and arbitrary abuse. I truly believe that the American consumer does not want to buy products made in abusive conditions.

With this, he declared that the minimum age of footwear factory workers would be raised to eighteen years of age, in response to numerous reports of factory workers as young as twelve years old. He committed to allowing independent monitors from some of Nike's harshest critics to inspect the factories. Finally, he announced that Nike would impose US standard working conditions in areas such as air quality. Nike's adversaries offered a cautious welcome to these announcements. For some of them, it was the culmination of more than two decades of campaigning. Many people were taken aback at the sudden ardour of Knight's tone: 'We believe that these are the practices that the conscientious, good companies will follow in the twenty-first century,' he told a surprised audience. 'These moves do more than just set the industry standards. They reflect who we are as a company.' It was the beginning of a series of contrite media appearances by Knight. 'You can make a lot of mistakes around here, but the brand is sacred,' he explained to the *New York Times*. For a company like Nike, the brand represents what it stands for in society. 'I messed that up,' he said.[26]

Not everybody gave Nike's announcements a wholehearted welcome. Harvard economist Jeffrey D. Sachs saw things differently. 'My concern is not that there are too many sweatshops but that there are too few.'[27] In his view, low-wage factory jobs were an essential stepping-stone for a developing economy. After all, the 'Asian tigers' of the 1990s – Singapore, Hong Kong, South Korea and Taiwan – had high-tech manufacturing industries and booming financial sectors, although each had started by making clothes, shoes and toys. A Unicef report had highlighted the unintended consequences of increasing the minimum age of labour: often child workers are forced into alternative jobs 'more hazardous and exploitative than garment production'.[28] There are even reported cases of factories being closed and the child workers subsequently being found in the sex industry. Nobody was arguing that child workers, forced labour or abusive conditions were acceptable, but it was far less clear how to deal with these realities. In a provocatively titled article 'In Praise of Cheap Labor' Paul Krugman argued that the anti-sweatshop campaigners had 'a policy of good jobs in principle, but no jobs in practice'.[29] They didn't live in the real world, according to Krugman: 'You may say that the wretched of the earth should not be forced to serve as hewers of wood, drawers of water, and sewers of sneakers for the affluent. But what is the alternative?' And so Nike, a company whose core business was making trainers, found itself at the centre of a global debate on economic development in the Third World.

Into the maelstrom stepped Hannah Jones, who joined Nike in 1998 at the height of the company's difficulties. Hannah is now the Vice President of Sustainable Business & Innovation at Nike, and she looks back on that time as a formative period for Nike. 'It was one of the single best things to have ever happened to this company, because frankly it gave us a very early wake-up call,' she told students studying corporate responsibility at Duke University.[30] Nike's nadir, in her view, helped to prepare the company for the 'tidal wave of change' that was heading towards the business community. Over the next decade, society's expectations of corporate behaviour would shift substantially, and not just in the area of workers' rights, but across the full range of social and environmental impacts. In many ways, Nike's journey since Hannah joined the company is representative of the transformations that still continue to shape the business world. For Nike, it began by setting up a distinct internal function to address these issues. 'You have to remember, when I joined in 1998 the words "corporate responsibility" didn't exist. They didn't exist,' she tells her audience of corporate responsibility majors. 'We were the world's first corporate responsibility team, my boss was the first ever vice president of corporate responsibility. It was utterly unheard of.'

Hannah hadn't planned a corporate career. 'Nobody in my family ever worked in business, and I never believed I would ever work in business,' she says. As a teenager, Hannah wanted to fight for social justice – and like many people eager to change the world, she thought corporates were the bad guys. 'I had a completely different career path set out for myself. In my fantasy, when I was thirteen, I was somewhere between war journalist and campaigning activist, probably scaling buildings with Greenpeace.' Today, Hannah heads a team based in Nike's global headquarters in Beaverton, Oregon. It's an expansive, leafy campus arranged around a lake, and criss-crossed by running tracks. Sports fields separate the low-rise office buildings, which have names like the Tiger Woods Center and the John McEnroe Building (the main gym was once known as the Lance Armstrong Center, and has been discreetly renamed the Fitness Center). It's everything you might imagine of Nike's HQ – modern, corporate, and embracing the outdoors. Still, it's not the kind of bucolic habitat in which you might expect to find a campaigning activist, but Hannah Jones feels like a woman on a mission: 'At some stage in your life, you have to figure out whether you are more effective shouting from the outside, or whether you can effect change from the inside.'

Effecting change from the inside is no less challenging. For Nike to really deal with the issues facing it a significant internal shift was required, says Hannah. 'Those first early years we did everything wrong. We didn't understand what was going on, we didn't accept it, and we simply added fuel to the fire.' The journey begins with some self-examination, she says. 'There comes a time when the company has to delve back into themselves, and learn the art of conflict resolution, of listening, of looking back into oneself and of taking responsibility. That in itself is a massive transformation culturally for a company to go through.' For Nike, this led to an inevitable conclusion: you can't change in a vacuum. In order to understand properly what was going on in the factories across Asia, Nike would need to work with a range of partners. To ensure the welfare of those who were working in those factories would need full collaboration with civil society: community groups, local authorities and NGOs. To resolve issues such as minimum wages and minimum working ages – without causing bad unintended side-effects – would need the participation of local governments. It was a big challenge, given the complexity of the supply chain, as Naomi Klein explains:

> The only way to understand how rich and supposedly law-abiding multinational corporations could regress to nineteenth-century levels of exploitation (and get caught repeatedly) is through the mechanics of subcontracting itself: at every layer of contracting, subcontracting and homework, the manufacturers bid against each other to drive down the price, and at every level the contractor and subcontractor exact their small profit. At the end of

> this bid-down, contract-out chain is the worker – often three or four times removed from the company that placed the original order – with a pay check that has been trimmed at every turn.

It was a complex network of suppliers, and Nike had been running it like a distant empire, issuing edicts for lower prices, faster productivity and higher quality – and it was the workers who suffered. As a report in *Asian Monitor* put it, 'When the multinationals squeeze the subcontractors, the subcontractors squeeze the workers.' But Nike still needed low prices, fast production and high quality. The challenge was how to deliver this in a way that could benefit everyone involved, including the dyers, machinists and gluers in the factories of its Asian subcontractors. To do this, an entirely new approach was needed – a more collaborative approach, as Hannah explains. 'Once you begin to understand your full footprint, it becomes pretty clear that one is going to consider how to work in partnership with civil society, and also how to start looking internally, to changing the business processes and systems. And I call that the business integration phase.'

Collaboration has become a watchword for Nike, as it has for many companies on a similar journey. As the CEO Mark Parker writes in the company's Corporate Responsibility Report, 'We learned that the path to change ... is paved by collaboration with multiple stakeholders.' Listening to external voices isn't always a comfortable experience, but Nike's mauling by its critics taught an important lesson: that sometimes the harshest voices are the ones that can prompt positive change. As Nike configured a new approach to running its network of suppliers, it became clear that a dependable critic was needed – one that was politically neutral, credible and with the ability to access workers in their own communities. They would need to be sensitive to local cultural issues and able to talk to local people in their own languages – across the many countries from which Nike sourced its products. The trouble was, no such NGO existed at that time. And so Nike took an unusual step for a corporate: it created one. In 1999, the Global Alliance for Workers and Communities was launched, in partnership with Gap, Inc. and the International Youth Foundation.

Over time, the work of the Global Alliance was superseded by organisations like the Fair Labor Association (FLA). At the height of public clamour over sweatshops, President Clinton had summoned leading footwear and apparel companies to meet with human rights campaigners and representatives from consumer and religious groups. It was a very public banging together of heads by the President, and those assembled agreed to establish an ongoing working group. President Clinton gave them a clear task: to give consumers 'confidence that the clothes they buy are made under decent and humane working conditions'. It was out of these beginnings that the FLA was born. It was incorporated in 1999 as a collaboration between corporations and various civil society bodies, as well as colleges and universities. Today, the FLA remains a powerful force for workers' rights around the world, whether for farmers growing coffee or factory workers making smartphones.

For Nike, cleaning up such a large and complex supply chain proved a real challenge. As one of the first major multinationals to grapple seriously with this issue, there were few precedents they could draw upon. Their initial instinct was to treat it as a compliance problem: develop a strict set of criteria that suppliers must adhere to, covering all the major areas of concern (such as working conditions, wages, hours and minimum age). However, it soon became clear that simply imposing new, stringent requirements wasn't enough: suppliers needed help to meet these conditions – such as access to examples of best practice and support to change their processes. This had to be done by working in detail with the suppliers, together with the relevant unions and local community groups. And then, once suppliers met the conditions, the Nike team found that the next challenge was keeping them there: very often, improvements in performance could slip backwards. It's a continual process and is much more demanding than simply publishing a code of conduct: it requires a full-time team of people dedicated to making it work. It was a protracted journey for Nike, and one that many other companies have since followed.

Even as Nike was beginning to get to grips with its sweatshop problem, a new front had opened up. Nike's most famed product innovation is its Air Cushioning Technology, introduced in 1987. High-pressure air pockets were put into the soles of shoes, allowing greater cushioning and comfort – and, it was claimed, greater athletic performance. The shoes were immensely popular with athletes, and when the Nike Air Max was launched in 1987 – with distinctive, visible air pockets – they became iconic, must-have footwear. But there was a problem: the technology was an environmental nightmare. The air in a Nike Air was SF6 – a super-potent greenhouse gas, with a global warming potential 22,800 times greater than CO2. Nike's newly formed corporate responsibility team could have been forgiven for thinking that the small pockets of air in their trainers were relatively harmless, but by 1997, Nike Air shoes carried a greenhouse impact equal to a staggering 7 million metric tons of CO2 – about the same as the exhaust from 1 million cars. This time, the company was much faster to respond – perhaps sensing the risk of another image meltdown. And so, just as Nike had embarked on a journey to improve the conditions of workers, a new journey had begun – and one which would prove no less transformative for the company.

It proved a far greater technical challenge than anyone had imagined. Pressurised air was the perfect shock absorber: it could handle the repeated impact of a heal pounding a pavement far better than foam, and kept its springiness far longer. And it was lighter, too – a big advantage for runners. SF6 was the perfect gas: it didn't leak at high pressure, unlike every other gas that had been tried. After several years of experimentation the breakthrough came: the answer was not in the product itself, but in the production process. The company hit upon a new technique called 'thermo-moulding', which created a much tighter seal than the conventional blow-moulding techniques. In fact, it was so strong that it allowed the air pockets to extend the entire length of the shoe. The result was a better-designed shoe, from both perspectives – performance and environmental impact. It could be filled with a harmless gas, and the shoe was lighter and more comfortable. 'It was a moment of clarity that showed us a risk could turn into an innovation,' says CEO Mark Parker, who was the designer of the iconic Nike Air Max a decade earlier. 'It launched us on a continual search for similar advances in sustainable technology and performance.'

Hannah Jones agrees that it was a turning point in the way Nike approached issues of environmental impact. 'We found that if you start to look at product design through the lens of sustainability, you could start to deliver different types of innovation to the market that weren't just about green innovation, they were about performance innovation as well,' she told her audience at Duke's. Hannah has a show-and-tell style of giving talks – her stories are often brought to life through a colourful assortment of products and materials, which get lobbed into the audience for closer inspection. One of her favourites is the Air Jordan XX3, one of the first shoes that scored highly with pro basketball players as well as green observers. It was designed by Tinker Hatfield, messiah to the sneaker-heads, and showed how performance and sustainability can work together. The shoe's stitching provides the geometry that holds the shoe together, reducing the materials and glues needed, and resulting in a lighter, more flexible shoe. 'It broke the myth that you can't do both,' says Hannah. '[People thought that] you can't win an All-Star game in a crunchy hippy-dippy tree-hugging shoe. And this shoe showed you are wrong.'

Another show-and-tell favourite is the Nike Trash Talk, which is 100 per cent made of waste from the factory floor. The shoe's upper is pieced together from scraps of leather and synthetic leather waste using chunky zigzag stitching. The mid-sole uses scrap-ground foam from factory production. The outsole uses 'Nike Grind' material, made from recycled footwear from any brand. It was designed with Phoenix Sun player Steve Nash, and he wore it in his All-Star games. The shoe made a powerful point to the business: there were materials worth tens of millions lying as waste on factory floors. Hannah explains, 'Suddenly waste got really sexy at Nike. It's a basic story of efficiencies, which is a basic story of common sense. And guess what, the gross margins on this were just unbelievable because it was just made of waste.' It was another product that made a point, says Hannah. 'The point is, look how waste can be turned into gold.'

Products like the Air Jordan XX3 and the Nike Trash Talk were part of a new approach to sustainability at Nike. Previously, environmental impacts were evaluated as the products were shipping – clearly too late to have any influence. To many of the designers, sustainability felt like carping from the sidelines. Corporate responsibility seemed like a mindset of fault-finding and limitation, not a constructive part of the design process. Hannah changed this: 'We picked up the environment team and we put them right up in the innovation and design place, and we said "now go make it easy for designers real-time, as they're sitting at their sketchbooks and at their computers, to design products that will deliver performance and lower the environmental impact".' The result was a new type of corporate responsibility department, with responsibility for developing new design processes and new business models. Nike calls it Sustainable Business and Innovation (SB&I), and Hannah explains why: 'We threw away the words "corporate responsibility" and introduced the words "sustainable business and innovation" because we needed to move out of being police, and move into being the architects and designers of the future growth strategy for Nike.'

It's been a real shot in the arm for Nike's product designers, forcing them to look at the product in a new way. Traditionally, shoes are made from multiple layers of material, all stitched together, providing shape and support. Nike's designers developed a way to make a shoe using polyester thread and cable, woven into the shoe's upper section and joined to a moulded sole. Essentially, the shoe is knitted, a bit like a sock. The result is the Flyknit Racer – the most striking new shoe to come out of Nike for many years. It weighs half what you expect when you pick it up – making it an instant hit with runners. The production process is faster, more efficient and produces less waste – bringing both economic and environmental benefits. It seems like more than just a new product, but a whole new manufacturing paradigm for the business: Hannah says it will 'turn the industry on its head'. Understandably, the Flyknit has attracted a lot of interest: it was listed as one of *Time* magazine's Best Inventions, and helped push Nike to the top slot on Fast Company's list of most innovative companies in 2013. It also had the rather surprising effect of generating Nike product reviews in a number of knitting publications.

Fusing product design with sustainability has clearly unlocked innovation for Nike – but of course there were barriers to overcome, the most significant of which was a dearth of information: Nike's designers had very little data on the environmental impacts of their products. It's a complex picture: for a start, there are hundreds of different materials to choose from – ranging from hemp, wool and leather to advanced new materials such as bio-based thermoplastics. On top of this, more than 900 different vendors supply these raw materials – each with their own environmental strengths and weaknesses. Clearly, a product's environmental impact will be largely determined by decisions about which materials to use, and where to get them from – but there were no comprehensive and reliable sources of data available to help make these decisions. And so Nike embarked on years of research and analysis of hundreds of different materials, evaluating their environmental impacts, including energy use, greenhouse gas emissions, water use, land use, waste and chemical use. The result is the Nike Materials Sustainability Index (Nike MSI), launched in 2012, and one of the most comprehensive databases of its kind. In a move that won widespread praise, the company has made Nike MSI an open index, available for anyone to use and even contribute to.

This follows Nike's decision to place more than 400 patents in the public domain, in an effort to promote sustainability through open innovation. The announcement was made as Nike launched the GreenXchange (GX), a web-based marketplace where companies can share intellectual property. It's a simple but powerful idea: for example, Nike's 'Environmentally Preferred Rubber' contains 96 per cent fewer toxins than the original formulation, and so Nike has placed the patent for this on GX so that other companies can pick it up and use it. Hypothetically, it could end up being used to make environmentally-friendly wellington boots or bicycle tyres by companies that wouldn't have the R&D capability to develop such a material for themselves. GX was launched in 2010 at Davos by CEO Mark Parker, who explained that the company's lawyers had initially opposed the idea. It's not surprising: sharing intellectual property goes against a deeply engrained corporate instinct to keep everything locked down and under wraps.

This spirit of openness has become a driving force for SB&I, and 'transparency is an asset, not a risk' is a core precept for the company. Nike was the first major corporate to announce full supply chain transparency – complete disclosure of every factory used to make Nike products. Today, anyone can go on Nike's website and use an interactive map to view details of more than 800 factories: the address, products made and profile of workers.[31] It was a bold move; for years, Nike had stuck to its position that this was commercially sensitive information, and many within the company had argued that publishing a full list of factories would be a competitive risk for Nike. In the end, the company decided that it was one worth taking. Collaboration was a central part of Nike's response to the sweatshop issue, and this proved difficult without being open about factory locations. Transparency signalled that Nike was serious about collaborating, and sent a confident 'nothing to hide' message to critics.

Of course Nike has still got plenty of detractors, but the company has come a long way from the days when it denied that workers' rights in its suppliers' factories were any of its concern. It has become far swifter to respond to criticism: in 2011 it was targeted by Greenpeace in their 'Detox Fashion' campaign, which aimed to stop the use of toxic chemicals in the apparel industry. Within weeks, Nike had produced detailed plans to eliminate all hazardous chemicals across its entire supply chain and across the entire lifecycle of its products by 2020. 'Nike sets a new pace', read the Greenpeace headline, but Nike wasn't alone in this: the campaign also named other leading sportswear brands such as Adidas, Puma, Reebok and Timberland – all of which have fallen into line. This kind of fleet-footed corporate response would have been very unlikely only a decade ago. Across the sector, companies have become more aware of the need to account for their impacts on society. Puma in particular has worked hard to understand the company's environmental impact, introducing an accounting framework called Environmental Profit & Loss (EP&L). It was a particular passion for Jochen Zeitz, who was the chairman and CEO of Puma. Jochen became the youngest chairman and CEO in German history, taking the role at the age of thirty. When he took the helm in 1993, the company's share price was €8.6, and Jochen took it to an all-time high of €350. So when Jochen began something of a crusade on environmental accountability, people listened. He began by asking some interesting questions:

> I wanted to know how much we would need to pay for the services nature provides so that Puma can produce, market and distribute footwear, apparel and accessories made of leather, cotton, rubber or plastic for the long run. I also wanted to know how much compensation we would have to provide if nature was asking to be paid for the impact done through Puma's manufacturing process and operations. While nature is much more to us as humans than a mere 'business', the simple question I put forward was – if our planet was a business, how much would it ask to be paid for the services it provides to a company in order to operate?[32]

This line of questioning took Puma to the EP&L – or, as Jochen likes to call it, 'environmental calories'. The idea is simple: in the same way that you can see the calorie content on the side of a box of cereal, so Jochen wanted to display the 'eco-cost' of Puma products. And they've made a good start: you can see, for example, that the environmental cost of a pair of InCycle Basket shoes comes in at £2.74. Greenhouse gas emissions make up the biggest chunk of this (£1.41). Air pollution (£0.84) and water (£0.49) comprise most of the rest.[33] Add that up across all of Puma's products and you can calculate a total cost of the company's environmental impact – £115 million in the most recent report.[34] Of course, putting a price on nature is not an exact science, and lots of big assumptions are required, but Jochen believes that measuring a company's environmental impact is an important first step towards reducing it – and he thinks this will become common practice. 'Even those concerned only about bottom lines – and not the fate of nature – must now begin to realise that the sustainability of business itself depends on the long-term availability of natural capital.'

Putting an environmental cost against each product means that Puma is able to understand which materials and processes work together to generate the lowest cost – in the same way that Nike's Materials Sustainability Index allows designers to make more sustainable shoes. Certain things become clear very quickly: for example, products that use a lot of leather are a lot more damaging overall. However, leather is a cheaper option for Puma because of government agricultural subsidies – labelled as 'perverse subsidies' by environmentalists. In addition, import duties are placed on more sustainable synthetic materials, and Puma points out that shifting from leather would cost an additional €3.4 million each year in duties. Here's where we start to see a business move from addressing its internal processes to campaigning for external change: 'I call upon governments to start supporting companies to use more sustainable materials in their products instead of continuing with antiquated incentives,' Jochen told *The Guardian* newspaper.[35] Once, corporates were dragged by regulators into facing their environmental responsibilities. Now, some corporates are leading the calls for change:

> Governments have a unique opportunity to incentivise corporations so that they can accelerate their evolution to a more sustainable economy through more sustainable practices and products.

Back at Nike, Hannah Jones shares the frustration with governments. 'The political systems of the world are geared to solving short-term national issues, and these are long-term global issues,' she says. Characters like Hannah and Jochen have brought a fresh energy into the debates about the role of business in society. By fusing sustainability with innovation, Hannah has shown that it can be more than a drag on performance or a cost to business. She's become a chief proselyte for the idea that sustainability can drive business performance. 'That's the key: how do you reposition sustainability as a design concept, as an innovation concept, as a business concept? Let's just jettison the language of *it's about less* or *it's about doing the right thing*. Let's talk about how you redefine business.'

For Hannah, 'redefining business' isn't just about lessening the negative impacts. 'Doing less bad is not the same as doing well,' she says. 'To do well we need to create products that can be continuously recycled, reused, that are decoupled from the use of water, that are decoupled from fossil fuels, and that will take innovation. And so the story of innovation today needs to be a story of radical and fast-scaled innovation.' As she speaks, you can hear a sense of urgency in her voice. Words like 'radical', 'fast-scaled' and 'innovation' aren't empty buzzwords – they carry an undertone of insistence, and even apprehension. 'We need to get to a place where growth is decoupled from scarce natural resources, and has far more equity built into the fabric of how wealth is dispersed,' she says. You might think that the journey Nike has been on in the past two decades gives Hannah cause for optimism – but she is anxious about the path to a sustainable future. 'I am deeply concerned that we are going to have to be shocked into getting there. I had hoped that we would walk in a more planned way, as a collective, into that new future. I no longer believe that that is going to happen,' she says. 'The world is going to enter into a time of great stress and forced change. And so I believe that our role collectively is to be there to enable that change, when people are ready to make the wholesale transformation that will be needed.'

4

PURPOSEFUL BUSINESS

On 14 August 1947, Jawaharlal Nehru told the Indian people: 'At the stroke of the midnight hour, when the world sleeps, India will awake to life and freedom.' It was the eve of independence, and the country was delirious. Crowds ran riot, and police lost control as they stormed government buildings – not in anger, but in elation. After years of struggle, it was a moment of joy and optimism for India. But Nehru, about to become the country's first Prime Minister, cautioned that independence was 'but a step, an opening of opportunity, to the greater triumphs and achievements that await us'. He put a question to his countrymen: 'Are we brave enough and wise enough to grasp this opportunity and accept the challenge of the future?'

Listening to this speech was Jagdish Chandra Mahindra, who until recently had been a sales manager at Tata Steel, one of the country's biggest steel companies. It was good, secure employment – but JC was gripped with a sense of new opportunities for India, and he had left to become an entrepreneur. Working in the steel industry, he had witnessed first-hand the important role that big business had played during the Second World War. Now, the newborn nation needed new infrastructure, as well as a strong manufacturing sector to reduce its reliance on imports, and to create jobs – and so, together with his brother Kailash, JC founded the company that would become today's Mahindra. It was a brave move, made at a time of great hope but also enormous uncertainty.

Anand Mahindra, the grandson of JC and current chairman of Mahindra, explains this bravery: 'He realised that it was a moment of opportunity: an opportunity to do well both for himself, and an opportunity to make a difference for his country, and to the lives of his countrymen. That, in a sense, is what I believe we have been doing ever since.'

Today, Mahindra is one of India's biggest companies – a vast multinational conglomerate spanning a range of different industries. Across India, Mahindra is never far away: it is the country's leading manufacturer of utility vehicles and the world's largest tractor maker. On top of this, Tech Mahindra is one of India's largest IT companies. The Mahindra Group covers an array of businesses that seems sprawling when you first encounter it, including aerospace, energy, finance and steel. But there is a logic behind this, explains Karthik Balakrishnan, who is in charge of the company's brand. We met him at the corporate HQ – Mahindra Towers, an enclave of calm amidst the hustle of Mumbai's Worli district. 'When you look at the mix of businesses at Mahindra, you'll notice we always have been aligned to the needs of the nation,' he says, before launching into a speed-history of India and Mahindra:

> Newly independent India had pressing needs of infrastructure and transportation, and so we went into steel and automotive. Fast-forward to the sixties and India badly needed food. The call of the nation was to increase food productivity. We identified farm mechanisation, as opposed to human labour, as the solution – and in the seventies we became self-sufficient in food. Fast-forward to the eighties and early nineties. We looked at rural India and realised that most people don't have access to financial services – the formal sector bypasses them. We said, can we make a profitable business by lending

> to these people? And this has expanded into financing homes in rural India. And all of this with the expectation that we make a profitable return – but the red thread that connects these businesses is the contribution they make to society.

It's an enthralling story – a corporation and a country, both pushing forward, solving the next problem, a symbiotic advance. Anand Mahindra reflected on this in a speech he made when he was named Businessman of the Year 2007:

> The history of Mahindra is a microcosm of the history of India. We share the same horoscope. After all, our company was born in 1945, infused with the ideals and aspirations of an imminently independent India. And our path closely tracked India's path, from initial entrepreneurship, through paralysis imposed by socialism to a painstaking reinvention motivated by economic reform. At every step of this journey, we knew that if we could survive and win, then India certainly would, and conversely, we delighted in every victory for the country, because we knew that if India won, we too would win.

Mahindra's story is deeply entwined with the history and prospects of India – but even so, the company has expanded into many different geographies: today it operates in over 100 countries across the globe. As the group grew into disparate business areas, across many different countries, it became clear that there were no clearly articulated principles unifying these diverse activities. When the company was founded, Mahindra's brand purpose was 'to demonstrate that Indians are second to none', and although this was a galvanising thought in the years following independence, its relevance had waned. Each of the operating companies had subsequently filled the void by developing its own brand positions, and so there was little sense of an overall Mahindra brand. So the senior management decided to revisit its brand positioning, and in 2011 they launched *Rise*, a statement of their core purpose, in keeping with the spirit of India's development and its own global ambitions. Although everybody in the company is keen to emphasise that *Rise* is more than a slogan. Anand Mahindra talks about *Rise* as a philosophy of enlightened self-interest: 'Mahindra helps you rise, because when you rise your community rises, and we rise with all of you.'

We spent time with a number of Mahindra's businesses, to see how this comes alive on the ground. Agriculture is a major part of the Indian economy – more than half the workforce are farmers – and so we started with Mahindra's ever-expanding agricultural business. This part of the company isn't run from the calm sanctuary of Mahindra Towers but from a large manufacturing plant to the north of Mumbai. We travelled there to hear about the company's work with farmers. Our conversation is punctuated by sirens marking out the shifts. In 2005, we're told, the company had set itself the ambitious goal of becoming the world's largest tractor manufacturer – and by 2007 it was clear that they would reach this goal within a couple of years. This left them with an interesting conundrum: *what next?* 'As a vision, "continuing to be the world's number one" isn't that motivating to come to work every day,' jokes Sanjeev Goyle, one of the company's senior vice presidents. Saurabh Vatsa, a manager, agrees: 'We used to think it would be a proud moment to be part of the biggest tractor company in the world. And then it happened, and we thought, "Wouldn't it be a proud moment to be part of a company making a positive contribution to the world?"'

It was a period of soul-searching for the company, reflecting on the purpose of the business, as Sanjeev tells us:

> We realised we had a very 'inside out' kind of vision. We asked ourselves, why not try to have a vision that is 'outside in', and so we started to focus on something more than selling more tractors. We made our ultimate aim to bring prosperity to our end customer – which is an individual farmer.

This change of focus unlocked a new approach to business. Sanjeev is in charge of marketing for the company, and describes the shift in terms of marketing strategy. 'As a marketer I was always thinking about grabbing market share – 29 per cent, 30 per cent, 31 per cent – it's dog eat dog. But then I thought, shouldn't it be *market expansion* ... delivering mechanisation to people who can afford tractors? Suddenly things started to fall into place.'

Mahindra's tractors had been an important part of the 'green revolution' that swept India in the 1960s – the powerful combination of mechanisation, fertiliser and irrigation that had made the country self-sufficient in food. Now, the company started to talk about a second 'green revolution'. The majority of farmers in India work on small plots of only a few acres, and it's hard toil – relying on the strength of their own backs and the slow, hefty bullocks that drag the tillers through the fields. It can take days to plough a field, and days to seed it, and days to take in the harvest under the hot sun. Often, it takes an entire family to work a farm. As part of the company's new 'outside in' approach, 150 of the company's most senior managers were asked to spend days on these small farms, finding out about life for the farmers. It was a real wake-up call. 'Although I'd worked in a tractor company, I realised what an urbanite I was,' Sanjeev recalls. He saw how farmers lacked information about irrigation techniques, or access to basic equipment, or a supply of good seeds. 'I learnt that it's all about the knowledge, the technology and the right inputs.' One thing became obvious: the machines rolling off of Mahindra's assembly lines were too big and too expensive for these farmers – and so this seemed like a good place to start. It led to the launch of the Mahindra Yuvraj – the *Prince* – a one-cylinder 15-horsepower tractor that was compact enough to be useful in small fields, and far less expensive. The Yuvraj has become an indispensible part of life for many farmers, Saurabh tells us: 'A tractor is part of a farmer's family; a business partner and an earning partner.'

The Yuvraj tractor was a success, but it wasn't sufficient. Spending time on the farms had given the team an appreciation of the challenges facing their customers. 'We were knowing the customer as a tractor user, not as a farmer,' said Saurabh. 'This was important for moving from a transactional relationship to an emotional bond.' The new, smaller tractors were proving popular, but Mahindra would need to do more if it was to deliver against the new vision of delivering prosperity to farmers. 'Just having a tractor is not going to deliver prosperity because it's just a small part of it,' says Sanjeev. 'So we started to think very differently: is there something more we can do to deliver prosperity?' Armed with a fresh understanding of the realities of life for the farmers, the team set about answering this question. In the process, they began the transformation of Mahindra's tractor business into a broad-based agribusiness, covering everything from seeds and irrigation to warehousing and exporting.

They began with an asset right under their noses. Mahindra had hundreds of tractor service centres, spread out across India. They were only used for maintaining customers' vehicles, but the team realised that these centres could play a much wider role: they could be an access point for a wide range of information, advice, products and services for farmers. And so the Samriddhi Centres were born – or, in English, Prosperity Centres. As well as selling and maintaining tractors and implements, these centres now offer soil and irrigation-water testing facilities. They deliver the latest information on weather, crops, eradication of pests and diseases, and mandi (agricultural markets) locations and prices. Sometimes, the centres provide health screenings for farmers coming in to get their tractors serviced – a check-up for the tractor, a check-up for the family. They also run demo farms, showing techniques for increasing productivity. 'The communities are very risk averse – their land is all they have,' says Abhijit Page, who runs the Samriddhi programme. 'The farmer would like to have a tried and tested formula. He needs to see it with his own eyes.'

The centres run local awards, recognising the farmers who have the best ideas for increasing productivity. This proved to be a successful way of spreading best practice, and led to an annual national event – the Samriddhi India Agri Awards, which has become an effective way of promoting innovation. Winners have included simple and ingenious ways of boosting productivity – such as the woman who realised that termites were attracted to eucalyptus wood, and so placed strips of it around her crops, to lure the pests away. Simple ideas like this can make a world of difference, and Abhijit thinks it's appropriate to recognise the farmers who are finding new ways to do things. He shows us a photograph of the award ceremony: farmers from small, rural communities standing centre stage alongside the Indian Minister of Agriculture and leading farming academics, beneath the headline 'The Heroes of Agriculture'. It's a touching image. 'In India, we have ten awards for the Bollywood industry but only this one award for the people who feed us every day,' he says.

The Samriddhi programme springs from a strong sense of enlightened self-interest at Mahindra: helping the farmers to *Rise* is a good long-term business bet. 'There's a space between philanthropy and business,' says Abhijit. 'Today we're not getting anything out of it. But the farmers are getting better lives, improved prosperity. They will one day rise above their current situation and maybe they will buy a Mahindra tractor.' Or, indeed, Mahindra has a growing range of farm equipment that the farmers may invest in, such as irrigation systems. Having spent time on the farms, the team had seen the highly inefficient 'flood irrigation' system commonly used: literally, flooding the field with water. In an increasingly water-stressed country, this is a problem: 80 per cent of available water is used in agriculture. It's a problem for the farmers too: flood irrigation uses more electricity, it feeds the weeds and pests, it's more labour intensive, and in some places it means there's not enough water for everyone. Yet, aside from rice, most crops require a relatively small amount of water to survive. Through the Samriddhi Centres, Mahindra introduced the farmers to 'micro-irrigation', a system that drips just enough water directly onto the plant roots. Using this system, according to Mahindra, a farmer can achieve a 20 to 30 per cent reduction in the cost of cultivation with an accompanying 10 to 20 per cent increase in productivity.

Today, Mahindra has a promising end-to-end agriculture business, extending from provision of seeds and equipment to buying and selling the produce. The banks of the Godavari River in the western state of Maharashtra have long provided ideal conditions for growing grapes, and the region is the biggest producer of grapes in India. The farmers were accustomed to an average yield of around four tonnes per acre, but have increased this by 50 per cent using Mahindra's agriculture services. The company is now buying grapes from this region and selling them on export markets. Bananas and apples are next, then pulses and oilseed. It's a big journey for a tractor company. 'We realised we had really no knowledge of agribusiness,' said Sanjeev. 'Our agronomy knowledge was low. We are an engineering company, a manufacturing behemoth, so we had to develop a new vertical business line for agriculture.'

This doesn't sound like anybody's idea of an easy life. 'We knowingly took up the challenge,' says Sanjeev. 'The transformational journey was far more arduous than we thought: let's accept that. But now we have gained momentum.'

Growing a new agriculture business by bringing prosperity to farmers illustrates what Mahindra's *Rise* brand position means in reality. Sanjeev warms to this theme, when we ask him about *Rise*:

> Removing the drudgery from the farmer's life, stopping the women from bending in the fields, *that is Rise*. If I'm creating a tractor for the life of a farmer at the bottom of the pyramid, elevating his social status and prosperity, *that is Rise*. If I am developing an award to show the success and inspire others, then what it is it? *It is Rise*. Mahindra helps you *Rise*, and we *Rise* with you.

His words carry the emotional charge you might expect from a conviction politician, not the marketing director at a tractor company. It's clear that Saurabh and Abhijit also find the business deeply rewarding. 'It gives you immense satisfaction when a farmer says, 'Thank you – this is changing my life,' Saurabh tells us, with a modesty that counterweighs the grandness of his words. 'They say, "this is my dreams come true" – and this is what touches us'. Abhijit reminds us that *Rise* is not a charity initiative, but a platform for Mahindra's future: 'The most important thing is the thought of inclusive growth. I grow, the farmer grows, my channel grows, my company grows – and India grows. It's a satisfying journey for me.'

A natural complement to Mahindra's agricultural business is finance – loans and insurance. Back at the corporate headquarters in Mumbai, we meet R. Balaji, a Vice President at Mahindra Finance – one of India's leading non-banking financial companies: 'Nearly one in ten of all new cars, utility vehicles, tractors and commercial vehicles are financed by Mahindra Finance,' he informs us. Balaji is fast-talking and full of energy. We sit in his office drinking strong, sweet chai, and he gives us a quick-fire explanation of why the company's growth lies in raising people out of poverty in rural India:

> In rural areas there are no documents. It's all cash. You buy fuel for cash. You buy agricultural inputs for cash. You transfer your produce from A to B, and exchange it for cash. This leaves no documentation, no credit assessment. And yet you need credit – to buy inputs, to buy tools. Money lenders are accessible but extortionate. Banks have affordable interest rates but are reluctant to lend. Banks assess you for what you *are* worth – they don't account for what you *could* be worth. We are in between banks and money lenders: more accessible than banks, more affordable than money lenders. We see what you *could* be worth.

In a low-income economy like this, lending is about enabling people to secure their livelihoods, Balaji explains:

> Many people confuse this with sub-prime, but it's not. It's not just a loan; it's a loan to increase your productivity. And so our growth will come from rural areas: increased productivity for the farmers, increased prosperity for them and their communities, and a customer base for us.

It's a crisp and compelling logic – but it raises an obvious question: why aren't the banks doing this? Balaji explains that banking structures are too inflexible to effectively manage the risk involved.

> The banks require the paperwork: fill out the forms, send them to head office for a decision to be processed. You can't evaluate a farmer like that. You need to know them, their circumstances. It's a judgement. We empower our staff to make decisions on the ground. They know the farmers; it's their call. We have 12,000 people across the country. We recruit them from local colleges, so they know the region.

Working in this way, Mahindra Finance has built up 2.5 million customers in 170,000 villages. At the heart of this model is the personal relationship between Mahindra staff and their customers. When someone applies for a loan, the Mahindra manager will get to know them, and talk to the locals to assess their reliability. They sit down with the applicant and work out the cash flows and repayments. Then they decide whether to approve the loan. It's a model of retail banking that has long since vanished in the West. It's a labour-intensive approach, but it allows Mahindra Finance to make loans that would not be possible otherwise. It also becomes possible to make better decisions when things go wrong, Balaji tells us:

> If the rain fails, if the crop fails, then they default on payment. But it's not their fault. We can see this, and so we don't foreclose. We don't take back the tractor. This would make matters worse, and is of no benefit to us. But if a customer is intentionally defaulting, we can see this too and we take action, we take back the tractor. We can distinguish between *circumstantial default* and *intentional default.*

Mahindra Finance is working with customers in highly volatile circumstances. People living in poverty are disproportionately affected when things go wrong, whether that's a flood, a doubt, a crash in prices, an illness, or a tractor breakdown. We asked Balaji whether this means that Mahindra Finance has to work with higher levels of risk, and he gave us a snappy account of the approach to risk:

> We de-risk across different types of customers. We de-risk across geography: the monsoon is unlikely to fail everywhere. We de-risk across products: car loans, tractor loans, and now home loans. We de-risk across customer segment: different types of farmer, or the idli-maker selling idli on the roadside, or the potter, the artisan, the craftsman. Many types of loan, many types of circumstances, this is our approach to risk.

Something is clearly working for Mahindra Finance. In 2000, the company had 7 billion rupees in assets; by 2013 this number had grown by more than forty times to 300 billion. When you hear the human stories behind these numbers, you understand what's driving Mahindra's *Rise* brand position. Take Sudam Bhaurao Shinde, a farmer in a small village in Nasik. Until 2006 he farmed his land with bullocks, using traditional equipment. It was slow and arduous work, and his output was low. He lived with his entire family in a small wooden hut. 'Like every common man, I too dreamed of having a big house, advanced agricultural land and a vehicle of my own. I wanted to become a modern equipped farmer,' says Sudam. He decided to buy one of Mahindra's new, compact Yuvraj tractors. 'But who would give me a loan? I approached the banks, the cooperative societies, the credit unions, but no one would give me a loan.' He visited a Mahindra tractor showroom, and a salesman introduced him to Mahindra Finance. A manager from Mahindra came to meet Sudam on his land, and worked through cash flow forecasts. The officer gave him an on-the-spot loan approval – an event he remembers as a life-changing moment. Today, Sudam has not one but two tractors, and a new brick house stands next to his old wooden hut. 'The company saw my determination and my hard work,' says Sudam, 'and I really thank them for it.'

Farmers like Sudam live precariously close to poverty, with few safety nets if things go wrong. A family can be quickly pushed back into destitution if they lose a productive asset – a tractor, say – or their home, or their sole income earner. This is the real nightmare of poverty: many years of hard graft can be wiped out in a single day. Imagine the persistent anxiety of knowing that your family could lose everything at any moment, and that it might take many years – generations, even – to climb back out of poverty. Little wonder that insurance is such a fast growing area for Mahindra Finance, which frequently sells cover alongside loans. Customers can buy life insurance or general cover, and the company is on track to reach its ambition of becoming India's biggest insurance broker. For those living near poverty, insurance is enormously liberating. It's more than protection, it gives them the security to make different decisions: plant a new crop, try a new technique, or make a long-term investment. It's a natural move for Mahindra's *Rise* agenda: insurance can give people the confidence to take a leap, to accelerate their rise from poverty.

Mention the name Mahindra to most people in India and it isn't loans and insurance that springs to mind, or seeds and irrigation systems; Mahindra is most closely associated with cars. In the 1950s, the company established itself as a major automotive manufacturer when it seized the opportunity to make and sell the iconic Willys Jeep in India. From there the company expanded into a range of different commercial and utility vehicles, and eventually passenger cars. On the road in India, sometimes it seems as though every other car is the company's flagship Mahindra Scorpio. Today, Mahindra is one of the country's leading automotive companies – and in a rapidly growing country like India, that's a significant place to be. In August 2012, Anand Mahindra reflected on the 'future of mobility', as he inaugurated a new car plant on the outskirts of Bangalore:

> On the eve of Indian independence Mahatma Gandhi was asked by a British journalist whether independent India would follow the British model of industrial development, and he famously retorted that, well, it took Britain half the resources of the planet to achieve its prosperity – how many planets will a country like India require? And it's a no-brainer today that no country can afford to plunder half the planet for the cost of its development. The future of mobility has to be clean.

He was speaking at the opening of a state-of-the-art facility set up to manufacture electric cars. It's a big bet on the future of green automotive technology, with a capacity to manufacture 30,000 vehicles a year. The factory belongs to Mahindra Reva, named by *Fast Company* magazine as one of the world's fifty most innovative companies in 2013. When we met the company, it was still buzzing from the recent launch of its latest model – the e2o, which can clock 100km on a fully charged battery. It had clearly caught the attention of India's media, and the State Bank of India was offering cheap seven-year loans to buy the car. In Delhi, the city government had decided to subsidise the car, bringing down the price by nearly a third, and there were rumours that other local governments were considering doing the same. We spoke to the company's Chief of Operations, R. Chandramouli, to see what all the fuss was about.

'It's more important for India to have EVs [electronic vehicles],' he says, explaining that the market dynamics are very different from those in a developed country. In the USA, or in Germany, there are between 300 to 500 cars for every 1,000 people. The market is fully developed: every new car sold replaces an old car – it doesn't add a new car to the road. In India, he tells us, the picture is very different: there are only around forty cars for every 1,000 people. 'Every new car sold adds to the number of cars on the road,' he says. 'The impact is far higher in India. It's a disaster waiting to happen, so we need to look differently.'

In a world that is worried about soaring demand for energy, the prospect of millions of additional cars on the road in India is disturbing. The International Energy Agency expects that 75 per cent of growth in demand for oil will come from the transport sector. Globally, the transport sector today already accounts for nearly 30 per cent of energy consumption – and three quarters of this comes from road vehicles. Almost all of this energy comes from oil. This is a particular anxiety for India, which imports 80 per cent of its oil. The Indian government is so alarmed at this state of affairs that it launched the National Electric Vehicle Mission in 2013, focusing on energy-efficient public transport, and working with industry to promote private ownership of electric vehicles. It puts Mahindra Reva in a great position. 'Not long ago, the entire world was cynical about EV,' says Chandramouli. 'Now we have the most affordable electric car in the world.'

Already, Mahindra Reva operates in twenty-four countries around the world. Still, many people will find it hard to shake off the impression that EVs have all the style of an electric toaster. This may change, as prototypes like the BMW i8 and the Mercedes-Benz SLS AMG E-Cell start competing for the interest of car enthusiasts. Still, the likely price bracket of these cars means they won't make much impact on energy-efficient car ownership on a mass scale. The Tesla Roadster, made in California, is well liked in the USA, but it carries a six-figure price tag. It may look good cruising down Santa Monica Boulevard, but it's unlikely to appear on the Baharagora Junction any time soon. Tesla's new Model S is half this price, but that still puts it out of reach for the vast majority of the world's aspiring car owners. For Mahindra, there's simply no point in being clean if you're not also affordable.

There's an obvious question that occurs to anyone thinking about an electric vehicle: *what if I run out of juice?* It seems like an inconvenient prospect: finding somewhere to plug in and then waiting hours for the battery to charge. 'It's a non-issue,' Chandramouli tells us cheerfully, but it's clear from his tone of voice that this is a recurring question. 'I've been driving an electric car for five years, and I charge it at night like I charge my mobile, and then I use it all day. I know where I'm going. I never run out.' He takes this as a cue to knock down a few other misconceptions. 'People say India is a power-starved country – already we don't have enough electricity, they say, why do you want to add to the demand? In reality you charge it at night when demand is low and electricity is cheaper,' he explains. A related criticism is that electric vehicles still require electricity generation, most of which relies on fossil fuels. 'People say, aren't you just shifting the pollution to another place?' – and Mahindra Reva has the perfect answer to this question: the new e2o comes with a solar charging system. They call it 'sun-to-car technology', and it means there is no emission associated with charging the car, no fossil fuel use. It also means that owners are fuel-independent: once they've bought the car, the only cost will be to replace the battery every few years. In fact, solar power is another big bet for the group, which is investing heavily in Mahindra Solar – an ambitious venture to build large grid-connected solar power plants across India.

Chandramouli speaks with the zeal of someone who clearly feels that they are on the frontier. 'I joined because of the challenge,' he says. 'It wasn't about going from 17 per cent to 18 per cent market share, but about creating a market.' Many of the people we speak to in various different Mahindra companies share a similar sense of excitement about the significance of their work. Back in the peaceful sanctuary of Mahindra Towers in Mumbai we caught up with Karthik, who sits at the helm of the company's *Rise* brand position. He has an interesting job title, responsible for 'Corporate Brand Management and Business Transformation' – two things that aren't usually united. We ask him what this means. 'If you go out to the outside world and say "this is who I am today, and this is what I aspire to be tomorrow", then the gap between those two has to be bridged through a set of business actions,' he tells us. 'As custodian of the brand, part of my role is delivering on what we say that we are, and if there are gaps, to work with the business and fill those gaps. That's why brand building is also business building.' The very existence of such a role is an indication of how seriously Mahindra is taking the *Rise* philosophy. It's a great example of a purpose-driven brand position: 'It began as an exercise to sharply define what Mahindra stands for,' he says, suggesting that it's everyone's responsibility to ask, 'Are we positively impacting people's lives in a way that is beyond a slogan, but comes alive on the ground?'

From what we've seen in our time with Mahindra, people seem to have taken *Rise* to heart. '*Rise* is actually an attitude,' Karthik tells us, 'an attitude towards life that rests on an optimistic outlook, tenacity and perseverance to build a better future for oneself, and in the process also create a situation, an ambience for other people to *Rise* along with you as well...' It's a rousing vision, and Karthik is in full flow: 'So it's an ambition, an ambition to build a better future. So *Rise*, to that extent, is an exaltation, it's a rallying cry to egg people on, to create a better world.' It's contagious – and for a moment the thought flickers across your mind that Mahindra Towers is the nerve centre of a growing global happy-cult. But Mahindra Group is a US$16 billion Indian multinational, run by some highly respected business people. As if to reinforce this, Mahindra Towers is also home to the Mumbai bureau of Harvard Business School. *Rise* seems to be more than gushing brand rhetoric – it's playing an important strategic role for the company.

Rise was developed by US agency Strawberry Frog, one of the few creative agencies these days still actually based on Madison Avenue. Their offices once housed Hillary Clinton and her staff, when she was a New York State Senator. It's a generous space, spread across the penthouse floor, looking directly down on Madison Square Park – which, at the time of our visit, was covered in a thick blanket of snow. It feels a long way from the hot, humid streets of Mumbai. A different kind of hustle. Scott Goodson, the agency's founder, describes *Rise* as a movement: 'It's a different way of doing brands,' he tells us. 'Forget about the brand pyramids and brand onions, this is about mobilising people behind a shared purpose – customers, consumers, employees – all of your audiences.' It rings true: you do get a sense that people at Mahindra are 'mobilised' by *Rise,* and several senior managers used the word 'movement' when talking about it. First and foremost, it seems to be a powerful internal tool. The thinking behind *Rise* was developed by Ilana Bryant, who at the time was Chief Strategy Officer at the agency. 'We did extensive cultural analysis and we discovered an internal cultural challenge for Mahindra, that could be a drag on their innovation,' she tells us. 'In the company there was a leading edge that was very forward-thinking, but you've also got a generation of people who were never taught to raise their hand. There was a civil service mentality in the mainstream of the business. And then you've got this very visionary leader, Anand Mahindra, who wanted to encourage people to question – not necessarily question authority, but question the status quo.'

Anand Mahindra likes to recall an event that took place when he was studying in the USA. He was attending a philosophy seminar taught jointly by the famous philosopher Robert Nozick and an elderly and venerable Bengali professor (who Anand declines to name). Nozick liked to encourage the rough-and-tumble of a debate, but the Indian academic didn't respond well to this:

> At one point, after the Indian professor had expounded on a topic, an American student questioned his premise. The professor shifted uncomfortably and gave a perfunctory and unsatisfactory answer. The student, quite understandably, persisted and wanted to debate the issue. All of a sudden, taking us by surprise, the Indian professor erupted with anger and shouted at the American student: 'This is no way to treat a teacher. I have never experienced such rude behaviour. You have no *right* to question me!' There was a stunned silence all around. It was embarrassing. The idea of being *questioned*, being *challenged*, was totally foreign to the Indian professor. I remember wondering how and when had we become so fossilised. After all, the Vedas, the Upanishads, the principles of mathematics were certainly not the products of fossilised minds – and to my young eyes, everything about India in the seventies and eighties seemed to be frozen in time and intolerant of questioning.

Breaking down these old, ingrained cultural patterns was part of the task facing Ilana and the team at Strawberry Frog as they developed a strategy for the brand. 'We wanted a call to action, to raise your hand, to challenge the status quo,' says Ilana. When the copywriters came up with *Rise*, she knew they had nailed it. 'I knew it could be appealing on a national level as well as on a personal level,' she recalls. 'It could give the brand a tone of voice that could inspire employees as well as customers to realise their full potential.'

Today, you can see the *Rise* brand emblazoned proudly across the world of Mahindra – from business cards to banners on the factory walls, which proclaim 'Accepting no limits, Driving positive change, Alternative thinking. We call it *Rise*.' Aside from advancing an internal cultural change, the *Rise* philosophy is also attracting attention in the outside world, on a global stage: Mahindra is now on the *Forbes* list of Most Reputable Companies, and in 2013 it won the FT Boldness In Business Award. As the senior manager who looks after *Rise*, Karthik has a very firm view of how to communicate the brand externally: 'In terms of taking the whole philosophy, the idea of *Rise*, to the outside world, we have avoided a uni-directional broadcast strategy of using mass media,' he says. 'We considered doing a national advertising campaign but instead we wanted to find a way to give people an experience of the Mahindra brand idea.'

Instead of a national brand campaign, the team launched an initiative intended to be emblematic of the *Rise* philosophy. They called it 'Spark the Rise' – which aims to put the energy of Mahindra behind aspiring entrepreneurs who are trying to make a positive social impact. At its heart is an online open innovation platform for entrepreneurs to connect with each other, collaborate and exchange ideas. Now in its third year, Spark the Rise has almost 300,000 users, who can compete for grants from Mahindra. We were fortunate to be in Mumbai as the finalists were flown in from across India, for the Grand Finale – a two-day series of workshops and collaboration sessions, including a talk from Anand Mahindra himself. We caught up with a group of them on a shady terrace at Mahindra Towers. They had come fresh from a session honing their elevator pitches – and so we appeared as fresh quarry for practising on. The ideas were all ardently presented, and included 'Mentor Together' (matching poor children in school to professionals who act as mentors) and 'India Open Your Eyes' (a programme to prevent street harassment of women by getting commuters to wear wristbands indicating they will join in and intervene if there is an incident; many assaults take place in public places because bystanders are afraid to intervene). The latter is the brainchild of Manwinder Singh, who is enthusiastic about the Spark the Rise initiative: 'I'm inspired that Mahindra has made this a brand-building exercise, not a CSR exercise,' he says. 'Instead of taking a Bollywood star to do branding, they are investing in making a social impact.' Indeed, it's people like Manwinder who are the stars of the show, according to Karthik: 'We spent our corporate advertising budgets making heroes of these people, rather than only extolling the virtues of Mahindra,' he tells us.

It all adds up. The story of Mahindra *Rise* resonates across the business. The history of the company, entwined with the rise of modern India, has given it a strong sense that its success is part of a larger story, as Karthik tells us:

> You function as part of society, you're not distinct from society. Just as there are public institutions and different types of organisations that make up society, so do businesses. It's every business's responsibility – just as it is every individual's responsibility – to make a contribution to society.

Indeed, Mahindra isn't alone in this; there are a handful of large Indian conglomerates with a similar instinct. Tata is another huge Indian business working across many sectors. It too has a long history of community engagement, and is now investing in a number of initiatives aimed at poorer consumers. In 2008 Tata launched the Nano – the world's cheapest car at 100,000 rupees (about US$2,000). Although this was widely seen to be a market failure – sales didn't take off, and production was beset with technical issues – Tata has clearly embraced a drive to innovate for very low income consumers. They've launched the flat-pack house, which takes a week to put up and costs $700. Then they formed a joint venture with PepsiCo – NourishCo – that sets out to market cheap beverages that contain added nutrients. 'Of course you have businesses that are good and bad in India,' says Karthik, 'but some of the large business groups have always been at the forefront of doing business in the right way, discharging their social obligations in a quiet and not-so-loud manner.'

But where's the rub? As we approached the end of our time with Mahindra, we began to wonder whether it was an implausibly sunlit picture. Most of the businesses we meet in this book have had to manage stormy areas of contention: difficulties in the supply chain, fraught dealings with local communities, concerns over privacy, or some other troubled issue. Where is the friction in this story? We asked Karthik for his comments on this. One area of concern for Mahindra is the carbon emissions associated with their automotive business. 'Of course, Mahindra is a major manufacturer of SUVs, and we are worried about the associated carbon emissions, and so we work hard to ensure they are best-in-class in terms of sustainability.' Similarly, Mahindra's tractors are the most energy-efficient in the world. Karthik also reminds us of Mahindra's investments in alternative energy and electric vehicles. 'It would be stupid to avoid these friction points,' he says. Recognising these friction points, and innovating towards them, is what will create the future growth of the company. 'It would be stupid to ignore alternative energy. Companies that try to slow down the rate of change are shooting themselves in the foot. There has to be a race to get to better solutions.'

Where are the risks? What could go wrong? 'The risks are on the business side,' Karthik tells us. 'The business bets that you place are based on certain scenarios – political, economic, etc. These are normal business risks. What we don't want is a shift in who we are: we may be wrong about our business choices, but it doesn't change who we are.' This is what worries Karthik: 'As the company grows into different territories, into different categories, there may be times when the values and philosophy may not be fully expressed.' That's why *Rise* is so important to Mahindra – it's a 'unifying force' for the company, a clear expression of ambition for the business: to grow by making a purposeful contribution to the wider world. When he was named Indian Businessman of the Year, Anand Mahindra finished his acceptance speech with a quote from T. S. Eliot:

> There will be time to wonder,
> Do I dare, Do I dare?
> Time to turn back and descend the stair...
> Do I dare
> Disturb the Universe?

Reflecting on this, Anand captures the essence of *Rise*: 'there will be no turning back,' he says. 'India and Indian companies, including Mahindra, will continue ascending the staircase and continue aspiring – to disturb the universe.'

5

RECONNECTING BUSINESS TO SOCIETY

On 11 March 2011, Colin Harrison was waiting for his flight home from Tokyo's Narita airport, when the terminal buildings started to shake. It was 14.46, and Colin was about to experience the most powerful earthquake ever to strike Japan. Tokyo was some 400 kilometres from the epicentre, but still the ground shook. 'It was like being in an airplane going through severe turbulence,' he tells us, 'but without any seatbelts.'

Soon after, Colin toured the worst affected areas, some 300 kilometres north of Tokyo, where the earthquake was most violent. He saw for himself the debris and devastation, and the struggle to deal with the effects of the powerful tsunami set off by the shocks. People were living in refugee camps set up in schools and sports centres. Families and communities had been broken up in the chaos. There was hardly enough food and water to go around. Lorries would offload supplies – clothes, soap, medical supplies, batteries – but they were stacked in makeshift stores with no attempt to keep an inventory. The service stations had plenty of gasoline, but there was no electricity to drive the pumps. There was no lighting, so all activity came to a halt when the sun went down. The enormity of the challenge was staggering: 'it is difficult to convey the feeling of a world in which systems have simply ceased to exist,' he says.

Colin resolved to spend some time in Japan to do what he

could to help. He is a softly spoken scientist from Scarborough in the north of England. He began his career as an engineer at the CERN nuclear physics lab in Geneva, and later led the development of the world's first MRI scanner (indeed, the first ever MRI brain scan was done on Colin's head). He was then recruited by IBM, where he now works as a technologist. An impressive résumé, no doubt, but not an obvious asset in a disaster zone. How does this qualify Colin to help with a major national catastrophe? Today, he's based in the USA, leading IBM's *Smarter Cities* initiative, part of the company's overall *Smarter Planet* agenda. The initiative is about finding the best ways for a city's systems and infrastructures to work, and so Colin felt there was lots the company could do to help in the aftermath of the earthquake.

'IBM wanted to bring to bear the resources of the company to help Japan recover and rebuild,' Colin tells us, 'and so we ran a workshop to try and think of what capabilities would be relevant.' Several initiatives came out of it, such as putting in place systems to track supplies. An emergency task force was established to help in recovering local computer systems. What struck Colin was that, aside from the destruction of the region's physical infrastructure – buildings, roads, power, water – the entire information infrastructure had also been lost. This made it even more difficult to respond to the disaster, let alone start planning for recovery. Administrative data was gone: residents' records, land registers, vehicle ownership and medical records. There had often been backups, but these were wiped out as well. The collective memory residing in the area's local governments was hard hit: up to 40 per cent of municipal staff had been killed, and the rest had just lost their homes and loved ones.

Colin spent three months living in the city of Sendai, helping to understand and respond to the challenges presented by the obliteration of a society's systems. It was a tragically dramatic demonstration of how our modern world is dependent on its information infrastructure – what Colin calls 'our system of systems'. The corporate sector recognised this dependency more than a decade ago, Colin reckons, citing the backup systems in New Jersey that whirred into life on 9/11, enabling businesses to survive the destruction in lower Manhattan. Just as we now have resilient businesses, so we now need resilient societies, he argues. This throws up plenty of demanding dilemmas. For example, greater use of cloud computing would have made local government in east Japan less vulnerable to the destruction of their data centres, but would have increased their dependence on network infrastructure – which struggled to maintain service. He would later write an academic paper on his experiences, concluding that the real question was 'how do we put society back together after an event of this kind in the age of information and globalisation?'[36]

This is the kind of question you might expect to come from a global NGO, or perhaps the UN; it's not what many people would expect from a multinational company. But this is exactly the kind of question that IBM's *Smarter Planet* agenda sets out to answer. *Smarter Planet* is about capturing the potential of smarter systems to address some of the world's big challenges – anything from efficient water use to smart grids and traffic congestion. The basic idea is that these challenges can be tackled by collecting the right information, and analysing it in the right way. Data is being generated at a ferocious rate, much of it as a by-product of everyday life: car journeys, phone calls, web searches, shopping trips – Colin calls it 'data exhaust'. Add to this the billions of sensors embedded in everything from washing machines to traffic lights, and you have a flood of data. 'We live on a planet with enormous amounts of information available, if only we could make sense of it,' says Colin. '*Smarter Planet* is making sense of it.'

Smarter Planet originated in the dark times of 2008. As the financial crisis loomed on the horizon, IBM looked sluggish. The company's intellectual firepower was as immense as ever: it has the world's largest corporate research department, and IBM's employees have been awarded five Nobel Prizes. No company holds more patents than IBM, and its lead continues to grow with each passing year. Yet despite the immense intellectual capital, IBM seemed more like a lumbering giant than an innovation powerhouse. The world of business had been thoroughly redefined by the internet, and a new generation of energetic young companies had become established. By comparison, the colour had drained away from IBM: it seemed dull and grey, out of ideas and out of touch. And then the storm hit: IBM's steady customers pulled back their budgets, and suddenly the future looked unclear. Sam Palmisano, the company's CEO at the time, saw the need to act. As he said at the time, 'Despite the dark skies we are seeing today, I believe there is enormous upside and opportunity. Many are going to hunker down and try to ride it out. But the leaders who emerge will be those who see the opportunities for growth and societal progress, make the tough choices ... and go on the offence.'

And so, as most companies were battening down the hatches, IBM looked to the outside world, and embarked on a search for 'opportunities for growth and societal progress'. In October 2008 – in the midst of the financial debacle and global economic turmoil – Palmisano called an *Innovation Jam*: a four-day online brainstorm, including employees from over 1,000 companies in twenty industries. In some ways, it seemed the worst possible time for a global innovation workshop – but that was the point: 'May you Jam in interesting times', read the invitation. The result of the Innovation Jam laid the foundations for what would become known as *Smarter Planet*. It's since been codified into a clear definition. 'We call it the three I's,' explains Colin: the first 'i' is *Instrumented* – there have to be sensors in place to collect real-time data, monitor the system; next comes *Intelligent* – taking that data and doing analysis, finding the patterns, making the predictions; finally there's *Interconnected* – joining up all the parts of the system to make it smarter. It's a simple formula for how to apply IBM's core skills to some big issues in the world: *Smarter Planet* programmes include Smarter Education, Smarter Energy, Smarter Food, Smarter Health care, Smarter Water – and of course Colin's own area, Smarter Cities.

These are all challenging areas, and using smart systems to try to tackle challenges in areas like education, energy, and water sounds like it might be an innovative philanthropic venture, separate from the everyday business of making money. Not at all, according to Steve Hamm, a journalist who has written extensively about IBM. '*Smarter Planet* is IBM's core long-term business strategy,' he tells us. Steve thinks that *Smarter Planet* is an example of a new type of engagement between business and society. 'It's much more powerful than mere altruism; it's about how the company creates value – for itself and its customers, and for the world.' Steve has written an essay on IBM called 'Transforming the Modern Corporation' – part science, part business theory, seen through the lens of history. In it he quotes Sam Palmisano, reflecting on *Smarter Planet*:

> Addressing the issues facing the world now – from clean water, better health care, green energy and better schools, to sustainable and vibrant cities, and an empowered workforce and citizenry – does not pose a choice between business strategy and citizenship strategy. Rather, it represents a fusion of the two.[37]

The concept that the corporate plays a key role in society isn't new to IBM – what's new is the idea that this can be fused with the company's core business strategy. In a lecture delivered in the 1920s another former CEO, Thomas J. Watson Sr, told his audience,

> Business leaders are not just 'doing business'. They're knitting together the whole fabric of civilisation. Its harmony, pattern, design and mechanisms are due to their clear thinking, ingenuity, progressiveness, imagination and character.

It's interesting to imagine how the world must have looked to Watson, as a new era of American capitalism was transforming society – the railroads, the steel companies, the merchants and traders – all using IBM machines to increase their productivity, to scale their operations, and to invent new markets. Throughout its history IBM has made significant contributions by just 'doing business' – take the invention of the hard drive or the floppy disk, for example, or even the humble barcode – an item so commonplace it's easy to forget what a transformative innovation it was. The barcode is about more than just the convenience of self-checkout at the grocery store: modern retail, with its tens of thousands of product lines, simply wouldn't exist without the barcode. It's essential to the safe movement of medicines through the health system. It is used to track everything from express mail to airline luggage and nuclear waste. Developed at IBM in the 1970s, the barcode is a very visible example of how the company has made an impact on the world.

Smarter Planet is an embodiment of this idea that making a valuable societal contribution can be a powerful way of 'doing business' – and for IBM, it seems to have opened up new horizons for doing business. As Steve says, 'it means the company is engaging with clients in new ways, and finding it has to build bridges between existing fields, and even invent new disciplines.' Colin echoes this: '*Smarter Planet* has caused us to make a lot of new friends, and also to get to know existing customers in new ways,' he says. *Smarter Planet* is connecting IBM to the outside world in new ways, and you get the sense that this is energising the business. It no longer feels like the lumbering, out-of-touch corporate. 'Now we're working with engineering consulting companies, architects, urban planners, infrastructure service companies – we've built many new types of partnerships. And we're working in new IT areas – sensing systems, building management systems. This is how *Smarter Planet* is driving the business.'

Innovation, it's said, is the ability to turn ideas into invoices. This is the ultimate pay-off of *Smarter Planet*: it has accelerated innovation for the company, bringing together different areas of R&D, and identifying new fields for commercial exploration. We spoke to Francoise Legoues, who is VP of Innovation Initiatives, reporting to the Chief Information Officer. It is potentially a daunting position to hold in a company with such a long legacy of innovation: it has, for example, been the number one recipient of US patents for nineteen consecutive years. So what exactly does a VP of Innovation Initiatives do? Francoise explains:

> IBM has more than 400,000 employees. My job is to help them be as innovative and collaborative as possible. We do this with social network tools, with mobile working, and through allowing people to use their own preferred devices. All of this is about creating the right environment for innovation – but still, people need to have something

> to innovate *for*, something to collaborate *for*. This is what *Smarter Planet* can do.

Francoise has done much to create an 'agile' working environment for IBM – earning her a place on the HackWorking website's list of 'Disruptive Heroes'. In their introduction of Francoise, they describe her as 'helping the elephant to dance'. To labour the metaphor, Francoise may provide the dance-floor – the platforms and systems – but *Smarter Planet* is the beat to which the elephant is dancing.

In a sense, *Smarter Planet* is the ultimate employee engagement programme, a way of motivating staff and aligning their efforts behind a shared endeavour. This represents a new attitude to management, and one that was articulated to the *Harvard Business Review* by Sam Palmisano in 2004:

> How do you channel this diverse and constantly changing array of talent and experience into a common purpose? How do you get people to *passionately* pursue that purpose? You could employ all kinds of traditional top-down management processes, but they wouldn't work at IBM – or, I would argue, at an increasing number of 21st-century companies. You just can't impose command-and-control mechanisms on a large, highly professional workforce.[38]

The *Smarter Cities* work led by Colin Harrison shows this philosophy in action: channelling the company's talents into solving some very specific challenges. It's a hot subject in the world: rapid urbanisation continues apace, placing strain on city infrastructures. Companies and citizens are increasingly mobile, forcing cities to think about their competitiveness – both commercially and in terms of quality of life. Austere fiscal environments make it imperative to run a city efficiently.

And underpinning all of this is the need to plan for long-term sustainability. City leaders have never before been under such pressure. However, most cities are a complex tangle of systems – transport, energy, water, waste, law and order... These systems are rarely designed to deal with rapid growth – or even to work with each other. The infrastructure issues are very dense, but most of us only experience this at a basic level, as Colin explains: 'On any given day a water utility might dig up a road to put down a pipe. Then some two weeks later an energy company will come along and dig it up again to lay down some cable. If we connect up these systems we can avoid this kind of thing – and connecting up systems is what Smarter Cities is about.'

So far this thinking has led to over 2,000 consulting engagements in cities around the world. Rio de Janeiro is a great example: the city is more than 400 years old, and home to over 6 million people, although this is expected to rise to 11 million. It has an ageing infrastructure and a difficult, mountainous geography. Getting around the city is a challenge: the roads are frequently crippled by congestion and there is a lack of public transport. Severe tropical storms cause chaos and even loss of life: on 5 April 2010 seventy people died as the result of a mudslide caused by heavy rain – and the city's response to this event highlighted the lack of coordination between Rio's thirty or more agencies. All of this prompted Mayor Eduardo Paes to look for a new approach to running his city – and so he engaged IBM's Smarter Cities programme. And the pressure is on: Rio de Janeiro is host to both the 2014 FIFA World Cup and the 2016 Summer Olympic Games.

The result is the Centro De Operações Prefeitura Do Rio, or City Operations Centre: sun-lovers on Copacabana Beach are probably unaware that they are a short distance from a NASA-style nerve-centre, monitoring the city's systems in real time. A few blocks from the sparkling waters and gleaming white buildings on the waterfront, a cavernous space with black-painted walls houses an 80-square-metre screen, which stretches across one entire side of the room. It is watched by dozens of city operatives, tracking weather, traffic, police and emergency services – and making sure that the city runs smoothly. Social media is used to keep the local people informed of what is going on as it happens. It's a model of data-driven city management.

Rio de Janeiro's state-of-the-art system shows what's possible when a company like IBM focuses its expertise on solving complex real-world problems. Steve Hamm calls it 'an operating system for cities', and it is already rolling out to other cities around the world. For Rio, it has transformed the way the city works, making truly joined-up planning possible. Response times of the city's emergency agencies increased 30 per cent, according to IBM. Carlos Osorio, the local government official responsible for the operations centre, told the *Smarter Planet* blog that 'better cooperation and practical integration activities are the greatest by-product of the centre'. He said that the centre was 'Like a mobile phone ... before you have one you don't see the need. After, you can't understand how you lived without it.'

Smarter Cities is answering one of the most important challenges facing the world right now. Cities are the powerhouses of the global economy, responsible for driving much of the world's economic growth. Each week, an estimated one million people are moving into cities, and the urban population is expected to hit 6.4 billion by 2050 – that's 70 per cent of the predicted world population. Cities are resource hungry: already 75 per cent of the world's energy is used in cities, and they produce 80 per cent of the world's greenhouse gases. The decisions taken by today's city leaders will have a major impact on the economic, environmental and social issues faced by the next generation.

Within IBM, Smarter Cities has created a lot of enthusiasm,

and it has become something of a flagship for the *Smarter Planet* programme. In 2010, IBM launched the Smarter Cities Challenge, a philanthropic initiative in which cities compete for free time from IBM systems experts, to help them address some of the issues they face on the ground. Teams are assembled from different IBM business units, and they spend time on the ground working with city leaders to understand their problems. The result is a report containing detailed recommendations. To win a place on the programme: they're expected to show how they will match IBM's commitment of time and resources, how they could collect and access data, and what kind of track record they have on innovation. Winning cities so far come from all corners of the globe, from Malaga to Chicago, from Chengdu to Milwaukee, from Helsinki to Ho Chi Min City.

In Philadelphia, for example, the Smarter Cities Challenge team worked to bridge the city's growing 'digital divide', which was gradually creating a city of two communities. The problem wasn't a lack of activity: the team found hundreds of local organisations tackling low digital literacy, and working on development of the city's workforce. 'They all have their own silos of data, and none of them are talking to each other,' explained Martha Vernon, one of the Challenge team. 'So one of the things we're working on is building an aggregated view of the citizen.' The result is a technology platform that enables different organisations, working in different sectors, to coordinate their activities. It seems straightforward in principle, but integrating the many different systems and sources of data was a painstaking task. Lisa Nutter, who runs a local non-profit called Philadelphia Academies Inc., says the Smarter Cities Challenge team has made a valuable contribution: 'I feel like this kind of support, from a team of people who have really done this kind of system building work before, we certainly could not have purchased.'

With an investment of $50 million, the Smarter Cities Challenge is IBM's largest single philanthropic initiative. It's a very visible demonstration of the *Smarter Planet* agenda, emblematic of the core strengths of the IBM business. It has also provided a wealth of insight for IBM: few organisations now have such a breadth and depth of understanding about the issues facing city leaders, whether it's about economic pressures, infrastructure issues, or even civic engagement. In 2013 IBM published a report, 'How to reinvent a city', summarising its insights to date. It's clear that city leaders face growing pressure to squeeze austerity budgets, cut bureaucracy and get stuff done – or 'GSD', as Philadelphia's mayor Michael Nutter likes to call it. Mayor Nutter describes Philadelphia as a 'business enterprise'. He's aware that Philadelphia must compete in an economy where companies and citizens are increasingly mobile. At times he sounds more like a CEO than a mayor: 'I'm fighting for market share every day, and if I don't deliver my product more efficiently and effectively and cheaply, my customer base will find somebody else,' he says.

The Smarter Cities Challenge also plays a valuable role with IBM employees. 'These projects are development opportunities for our professionals, to look at challenges they've never seen before in a city.' says Colin. People also enjoy the chance to travel, and experience new environments – but Colin is keen to point out that it's challenging work. 'It's not a holiday. People go there and work hard, long hours, but they love it. They get exposed to the local culture, and it's part of making sure we're a globally integrated company. IBM people need to be able to work anywhere in the world, to develop cultural sensitivity.'

On the banks of the Winooski River in Vermont, IBM has a facility that offers a glimpse of the future of energy efficiency.

Smarter Energy is another of IBM's focus areas: population growth, urbanisation, rising living standards and climate change have put pressure on finding more efficient ways to generate and distribute energy. It's become one of the big global challenges. One of the main areas of research is *smart grids*: in much of the world, electricity grids use twentieth century technology, built in a time when cost or environmental impact weren't major considerations. According to a Smarter Energy paper, existing grids are so inefficient that enough electricity is lost annually to power India, Germany and Canada for an entire year. If the US grid alone were just 5 per cent more efficient, it would be like permanently eliminating the fuel and greenhouse gas emissions from 53 million cars. That's why energy is an important part of the *Smarter Planet* agenda.

Flanked by Lake Champlain to the west and the forests of Mount Mansfield to the east is an advanced semiconductor manufacturing plant that has become a pioneer of smart grid technology. Janette Bombardier is Director of Site Operations, and she has spent more than a decade developing a system to make energy use as efficient as possible. There are now 6,000 sensors across the plant, monitoring in real time the activity of the tools, chillers, machines, computers, furnaces and lights. This information is analysed and relationships are established with other variables such as the weather, so that electricity demand can be predicted. 'At eight o'clock this morning I could tell you what my peak power was going to be for the day, and if I can reduce that peak power use by switching some things off I can make big cost savings,' says Janette. There's also a big environmental benefit, she explains: 'If you can reduce your peak power, you're really stopping your utilities from turning on that last dirty bit of power.'

The results are impressive. 'We've reduced our energy use by 20 per cent over the last ten years and upped our output in the meantime – the number of products we get out the door is up 40 per cent,' Janette tells us. Of course, this has a positive impact on the bottom line. 'It's been cost avoidance: if electricity rates had stayed flat, my electricity bill would be down by $7.5 million a year, but electricity rates have gone up by 17 per cent so our bill is still around $36 million a year.' Of course, this hasn't happened overnight. 'We tell people it's a journey. Every year you've got to come down a couple of per cent, a couple of per cent, a couple of per cent.' It's a painstaking process of incremental improvement – and over time it gets increasingly difficult to find those improvements: 'The more you're into this process, the more you need your *Smarter Planet* principles – more information, more analytics, more ways to mine the data,' says Janette.

Of course, the smart grid in IBM's Burlington facility sits within the larger state electricity grid, and the more Janette learnt from running the facility's grid, the more she started to think about electricity use beyond the facility's perimeter fence. 'We are a very large user, and our energy use affects the grid for Vermont as a whole,' she says. 'When we reduce our peak load in Vermont, we actually impact the state.' This prompted a new question for Janette: how could IBM help the state run a more efficient grid?

Janette began having conversations with local electricity companies. At first there was some scepticism that a technique developed at an advanced manufacturing facility could be made to work in more everyday environments. 'People said, well of course you can do it, you're IBM, you have the resources and expertise, but it'll never work anywhere else,' Janette recalls. 'So we said, OK we'll show you it can work. We're going to demonstrate it in a hospital and a college, because they're both about as different as you can get from running a facility like ours. We're going to get it working, teach people the method, and prove they can get results.' So Janette and her team started *Smart Vermont,* working with Green Mountain Energy, a local energy provider, and some of their top customers – including Central Vermont Hospital, Vermont Technical College and a handful of local businesses. 'It was like jump-starting the Smart Grid, faking it out,' says Janette. 'They agreed to share all their data – we call it their *power profile,* it's completely unique, like a personal signature – so we could analyse it, and figure out how they could reduce energy. We had to use some old-school ways at first, like putting data on a disk and bringing it over, but we got it working.'

The project soon got the attention of the local press: 'Could a smarter grid work for Vermont? It already does, at IBM', read the headline of an article in the *Burlington Free Press.* This didn't escape the notice of the state's two senators, Senator Leahy and Senator Sanders, who seized on the ambition of making Vermont the country's first Smart Grid state. Together with the state's utility companies, they put forward a successful proposal to the federal government for a $69 million grant to develop a state-level Smart Grid. As part of this programme, IBM is collaborating with the Vermont Electric Power Company (VELCO), the state's transmission utility, to build a network that will deliver a more than 6,000 times increase in capacity. 'We were in a good position as a state to say, "hey we're ready to do this, we're going to execute it, we have all the ducks lined up,"' says Janette, who relishes the thought that the energy management system developed at Vermont is proving itself to be a model of how it's done. 'We're enormously proud of what we've been able to do here,' she says.

The potential of Smart Grids featured heavily in IBM's initial *Smarter Planet* advertising campaign – but the ad's creators weren't aware of the progress made by Janette and her team. 'We saw the first *Smarter Planet* ad on TV, we all laughed and said, "They're talking about what is possible in the future, and we already do that today!"' She instantly recognised *Smarter Planet*'s '3 i's' formula: 'To me it all comes down to that – instrumented, interconnected and intelligent. I saw it and thought, yeah, that's what it's all about. I'm an engineer first and foremost, but also I'm a proud IBM-er, and it was great to see what we already do branded up so well. It makes perfect sense.'

The *Smarter Planet* brand and campaign were created by IBM's advertising agency, Ogilvy, building on the groundwork laid by the Innovation Jam in 2008. *Smarter Planet* is a hard-working idea: as well as being a tagline and ad campaign for IBM, it's the basis for all their social media and digital communications, as well as employee communications. Most importantly, it's a way of framing what IBM actually does, and dramatising what it can offer customers. After all, it's a complicated company, with a very broad base of activities: there isn't an industry sector or government department that IBM doesn't operate in. What links all of this is the same highly specialised, highly technical skill set. And yet most of IBM's customers are not technical people: city majors, police chiefs, hospital administrators. And there's no hero product that IBM can point to – such as GE's jet engines, or Microsoft's Office software – so it isn't easy to explain what the company actually *does*. There are no easy labels: media and financial analysts use shorthand such as 'software and services' and 'information technology' – but these phrases hardly capture the ingenuity of Vermont's Smart Grid or the 'operating system' for Rio de Janeiro. *Smarter Planet* offers a new definition of the company, as Steve Hamm explains:

> IBM realises it shouldn't think of itself as being in the computer services business, or the software business, but

> in the business of innovation, on a global scale – innovating to make the world work better. That informs the *Smarter Planet* strategy.

As you might expect, IBM takes a data-driven approach to evaluating *Smarter Planet*. Two years after it launched, IBM analysts estimated that the *Smarter Planet* strategy has expanded their 'market potential' by as much as 40 per cent globally, or $2.3 billion. IBM's own survey data showed an increase in 'consideration' in worldwide business prospects of 48 per cent. In the USA, 'preference' among business decision makers increased by an astonishing 156 per cent. All the indications are that *Smarter Planet* works for IBM, and in 2010 it won advertising's prestigious Gold Global Effie in recognition of its effectiveness. The paper, written by Ogilvy, contains some other significant measures of success: according to Interbrand, IBM's brand value increased 2 per cent, in an economic climate in which most brand values dropped. This was reflected in IBM's share price: the Dow had started to recover the crash losses, climbing by 14 per cent; IBM's stock, meanwhile, grew 64 per cent. IBM is the biggest supplier of information technology – hardware, software and services – to companies and governments around the world, and so the company is highly exposed to the continued drag in the global economy. Maintaining growth will be a struggle, but today's IBM seems like a better bet than the drab, out-of-touch company that preceded *Smarter Planet*.

At the heart of *Smarter Planet* is a really clear sense of purpose, a statement about IBM's role in the world: innovating to make the world work better. It's a purpose that gives IBM a voice in the world's big conversations and places the company firmly on a global stage. In his essay on the company Steve Hamm describes IBM's transition from a traditional multinational company (with structures fixed by geography) to a 'globally integrated enterprise' (with flexible structures organised around customers' problems). It's an idea introduced by former CEO Sam Palmisano in a manifesto-like article published in the journal *Foreign Affairs,* in which he writes:

> The emerging globally integrated enterprise is a company that fashions its strategy, its management, and its operations in pursuit of a new goal: the integration of production and value delivery worldwide. State borders define less and less the boundaries of corporate thinking or practice.[39]

This has become a strong trend in recent years: with national governments preoccupied with internal fiscal issues or focused on managing the strains of rapid growth, it is increasingly corporates who really have the ability to think and act globally. It's one of the central contentions of this book: if you want to address the world's big problems, you really need the corporates involved. As Palmisano went on to say:

> Government leaders will find in business willing partners to reform health care and education, secure the world's trade lanes and electronic commerce, train and enable the displaced and dispossessed, grapple with environmental problems and infectious diseases, and tackle the myriad other challenges... Issues that are too big for business alone or governments alone to solve.

Some will read such a statement with cynicism, viewing corporates firmly as part of the problem, not part of the solution. Of course, many corporates have exacerbated the world's social and environmental problems, but increasingly we're seeing how forward-looking businesses are aligning their commercial interests with the broader interests of society

– and that *Smarter Planet* is a big step in this direction for IBM. It is the antithesis of the popular archetype of the corporation as a malign megacorp that will do anything in the pursuit of profit. IBM was once a model of the faceless corporate, mocked by Apple as a grey army of drones in their famous Macintosh TV commercial. For old Big Blue, Colin Harrison tells us, the strategy has 'reconnected us to society':

> In 1995, after IBM sold its laptop division, it was cut off from society. The company practically lived in its data centres. The wonderful thing about *Smarter Planet* is that it has reconnected us to society, simply by asking, 'what are the problems that a company like IBM ought to focus on?'

6

MAKING THE BUSINESS CASE

A long time ago William Lever, son of a grocer in the north of England, set up a company to sell soap. It was 1884 and Lever was an unusual businessman. Dancing was the great passion in his life, that and art. He was a social reformer, and became an MP, before joining the House of Lords as Lord Leverhulme. He believed that the key to well-being was sleeping outdoors, whatever the weather. He also believed that hygiene was essential to health, and so went about building his soap business with an evangelical zeal. His first soap was called Sunlight – the first ever packaged laundry soap for the household, a bright brand for the grey, soot-filled world of Victorian Britain. Made with glycerine and vegetable oil, instead of animal fat, it lathered well and was easier to use than anything that had gone before. Soon Lever & Co. was producing hundreds of tons a year of Sunlight.

Lever's next product was a disinfectant soap for personal hygiene. He called it Lifebuoy, because it was literally a life-saver: cholera epidemics had ravaged the cities, claiming tens of thousands of lives. Deadly outbreaks of typhoid and dysentery were common. The poor were especially hard hit, living in overcrowded, unsanitary slums. For many people even basic sanitation was unachievable; there was no easy way to keep yourself, your hair, your clothes or your home clean. Lifebuoy's message was straightforward: this was a soap 'for the preservation of health and the prevention of sickness.' Lever was on a mission to make it possible for everyone to live free of the squalor that was causing so much misery. Lifebuoy was a simple product with a big ambition: 'to make cleanliness commonplace'.

Within four years Lifebuoy was being shipped around the world, to the USA, across Europe and into India – where its rapid growth was the basis of what later became the Indian business of Unilever. The grocer's son made good got his peerage and became one of the most celebrated businessmen of his generation. And in 1930 his business merged with the Dutch business Margarine Unie to form Unilever. The company today is one of the giant consumer goods companies of our era. It sells many household brand names: Dove personal care, Sure deodorant, Sunsilk shampoo, Signal toothpaste, Persil laundry liquid, Cif household cleaner, Domestos bleach, Flora margarine, Hellmann's mayonnaise, Knorr stock cubes, Wall's ice cream and PG Tips tea, to mention just a dozen of the best known – and still Lifebuoy soap. Every single day, somewhere in the world, two billion people buy a Unilever product. That makes it one of those big businesses many of us interact with regularly, without really realising it.

In the developed world, where consumers have unprecedented choice of what to spend their money on, soap is a humble product. It's understood to be necessary but it's a pretty basic purchase. Luxury shower gels and scented liquids compete for consumer attention, but the more medicinal, carbolic Lifebuoy bar has had its day. In India, however, Lifebuoy is still the leading soap brand by volume. And true to its original purpose, it can be a life saver.

'Everybody in India has grown up with the Lifebuoy jingle, it's instantly recognisable,' Sudir Sitapati tells us. Sudir is head of the skin cleansing business, which is a billion-dollar turnover business for Hindustan Unilever. 'It's been visually consistent; it's been red and chunky; it's been talking about health always. It's a very well loved brand in India and that gives Lifebuoy permission to do a lot of good things.' Hindustan Unilever is one of India's oldest companies and 'Doing Well by Doing Good' has been its motto for decades. Although part of the international Unilever group, the company's operations in India have been run by local Indian management since the 1950s, which has played a big part in its good fortune in the 1970s. When other foreign-owned companies were forced to reduce to a minority shareholding, Hindustan Unilever had the feel of a naturalised Indian company and was able to argue successfully to hold on to a 51 per cent stake, setting it up well for a decade of rapid growth after liberalisation at the start of the 1990s. These days it's rated as India's 'Dream Employer No. 1' by management graduates in the country's top business schools.

Arriving at Unilever House in Mumbai is something of an occasion. The imposing building is designed to curve around the huge century-old cashew tree which throws shade across the courtyard. It's a famous campus on the corporate scene in India and we're offered lunch on what's called The Street, the walkway that runs through the centre of the atrium, where you can sit down for a sandwich, grab a coffee or an ice cream, buy flowers, have your hair cut or do your household shopping at the U Shop. We've come to learn more from Sudir about the genesis of Swasthya Chetna, Lifebuoy's well-known hand washing programme. 'I was looking after sales in a very backward part of India when we first came up with the programme in 2002. This was an area which we call "media dark", meaning no TV, or radio or even magazines reach there. And yet we had to come up with a way to increase soap consumption,' Sudir tells us. 'We knew that people were not using soap adequately and that a potential way to grow the business was to educate people on hand washing. But as we continued on the journey we realised what we were doing was more than just selling soap.'

Three thousand children a day die from diarrhoea in the world, one thousand of them in India. As the NGO water.org proclaims, that's the equivalent of crashing a jumbo jet full of children every four hours, every day. Diarrhoea is the second leading killer of children under five in the world. And lack of hygiene is a basic and preventable cause. Some of the remedies are very basic: Unicef and the WHO recommend the 'promotion of hand washing with soap' as part of the prevention package. Swasthya Chetna – 'Health Awakening' – was Unilever's education campaign to get the message out to thousands of villages. It was based on the central insight that most people believed that if something looks clean, it is clean. So the aim was to communicate the existence of invisible germs. The Lifebuoy team dreamt up the 'Glo-germ': an ultra-violet lamp which produced a glow on a powder which stayed on hands washed only with water, and not on hands washed with soap. This simple but neat device caught children's imagination with the idea of soap's ability to get rid of what the eyes may not see – and got the children to tell their parents. The campaign took off nationally. On World Health Day 2006, the Indian Post Office issued a special postal cover for letters in honour of 'the phenomenal work done by Lifebuoy' and the Post Master General said:

> I urge all my brothers and sisters to take personal hygiene habits like washing hands with soap seriously. I congratulate Lifebuoy and Hindustan Lever for initiating and assiduously implementing this socially beneficial movement.

According to the UN, washing hands with soap can reduce the risk of diarrhoea by around 45 per cent. Put in that context, hand washing remains quite simply one of the cheapest and most effective ways of preventing disease – as it was when

William Lever first launched his soaps. 'It's not a small thing this, it's such a powerful thing to communicate about washing your hands,' Sudir tells us. 'We were making a big impact on health and as a by-product of that soap consumption was going up. A lot of us got very motivated about the power of the brand.' They were discovering that it was possible to *do well* and *do good* at the same time.

The team worked away at building up the programme over the years and by the end of the decade it had reached some 120 million people in rural India. And, since 2010, they've got the message out directly to 50 million more people – while seeing double-digit growth in sales, and over 1,000 employees volunteer their time to run sessions in schools and villages in their communities. But, of course, children dying every day of diarrhoea isn't only an India problem and the step change for the programme came when it went global.

In 2001 Unilever partnered with a cluster of public and private sector organisations to launch Global Handwashing Day, an annual flagship event for the campaign. Though the day does not register on news screens in developed countries, 200 million people participate in 100 countries around the world from Brazil to Saudi Arabia to Rwanda to Mongolia. This commitment to scale has given the movement fresh life. It makes it possible to deliver business results because it drives an increase in the use of soap in the long-term and, at the same time, it reduces disease. As Sudir explains, it provides common ground with the goals of governments and global funding bodies focused on health, who are interested in partnering with Unilever to make it happen, 'If you have a programme like this that provides both a business good and a social good, then other people are willing to bear the cost of the social good with us.'

Sudir is charged with creating a viable business model and a payback over a three- to five-year period, as any investment would be expected to do. The company has always been clear that this was a marketing campaign with a social purpose, not a philanthropic programme – and his experience is that it works best that way:

> If you separate the two, then the 'doing good' tends to become a bit niche, some small things that live somewhere on the side of the organisation. But if it gets integrated into the heart of the business, as this is now, the kind of organisational resource and management focus it gets is of a different order, which makes this a very exciting opportunity for the future.

Continuously pushing further into rural India is characteristic of Hindustan Unilever. In fact, the business is credited with pioneering a business model for reaching people at 'the bottom of the pyramid' – the world's very lowest income consumers. It started up in 2000, at a time when women's self-help groups were springing up all over India and Unilever was tapping into that energy. They made the crucial decision to recruit village women as their rural sales force and today the Shakti Ammas, as these women are known, embody the spirit of the idea. The word 'shakti' literally means power, or empowerment, but in Hindu culture it also refers to the divine female creative energy; the word Ammas simply means mother. The name has travelled with the network as it spread across fifteen states in India.

There are 48,000 Shakti Ammas today, in a network covering 100,000 villages and reaching three million households every month. Ashish Rai heads up rural business for the company and feels lucky to have responsibility for the Shakti network: 'I think I've inherited a brilliant legacy. I'm very, very fortunate because the thinking is so good; it's that pristine thinking that's taken us to the scale we have now.'

The whole thing started with the conviction that there was a real demand for these products among people at the bottom of the income scale: soap to wash their hands, shampoo to wash their hair, detergent to clean their clothes. But the problem was that these people are living on a dollar a day, and the small sums of money they have are held as cash in their pockets. They couldn't possibly afford the products as they appear on the shelves in the city supermarkets. So the first and critical innovation was to create very small pack sizes. The business produced single-use sachets, costing just one or two rupees. That one move is what brought products like shampoo or detergent within the reach of these consumers. Ashish impresses on us, though, that for many rural women a sachet of shampoo is still a luxury for a special occasion, a wedding maybe, and the rest of the time she will use bath soap or the traditional solution of mud from the river.

But the next problem was that there are 600,000 villages in India, many of them very remote, with no roads linking them up. So, as Ashish explains, it was a challenge to see how to develop a distribution system that can work in those circumstances. To build up a full time conventional sales force at the scale needed would be prohibitively expensive and, anyway, having men selling household products to women face-to-face, door-to-door would be unacceptable in the villages. So, the idea of the Shakti Amma was born.

Unilever approaches women to join the network through self-help groups or the Panchayati Raj, the elders of the village. They are looking for someone who would like to supplement the family income earned by her husband or brother, probably through farming. They provide her with micro-financing to get started, training in administration and bookkeeping, and a portfolio of Unilever products.

Lifebuoy, of course, is a mainstay of the Shakti Amma's basic portfolio, along with maybe one other soap, such as Lux, a shampoo, a laundry detergent and Lipton's tea. These are aspirational brands that people in the villages want to be associated with, Ashish explains, but the vital advantage Unilever has is the breadth of products it can provide for the Shakti entrepreneur. Where other consumer goods companies might be able to provide, say, toothpaste or a laundry bar, Unilever can provide the full range of products that any basic household is likely to need. So the Shakti Amma has enough variety and volume to make it worth her while to get out and about and sell.

Yet, while Ashish clearly admires the detail of the operating model, what lights up the way he describes it is his consciousness of the impact it has on the life of the Shakti Amma:

> You cannot imagine the change in the social order it brings about. Now she's able to contribute to the family by earning income. It's a huge boost to her self-esteem, she was a marginalised woman who would just cook and take care of the kids and never leave the house. Now she has a voice in the family and in the community.

Part of her training is about family hygiene and she's equipped with visual materials in her own language and posters which illustrate the principles clearly. So a Shakti Amma becomes a local source of knowledge as well as products. 'They get respect. They make decisions. They handle money. You can see their confidence grow. She becomes almost an institution in these villages and an aspirational figure for the women around.' The words paint a simple and practical picture of what is contained in the often abstract-seeming term 'empowerment'. Now it exists, the model seems so obvious, but it was a revolution in thinking at the time. There was resistance initially from men not keen for their wives to go out of the home selling door-to-door, and from local shopkeepers fearful of losing trade. But the additional money is persuasive, often doubling the household income. And the pride the women feel in their own success carried the project forward.

Sunita Bhandwalkar became a Shakti Amma when her husband died and she was left all alone to fend for her children. She had to find a way to live and to earn. It was a terrible time, she tells us, 'At first, it took a lot of courage to be able to go out and do this. I didn't know if I would ever be able to manage it.' But the income was all important for her and she persevered. Sunita agrees with Ashish that her role has earned her status in the village. Most of all, it matters that both her daughters are going to engineering college: something she would not even have dreamt of when they were born. 'It was through interaction with the Hindustan Unilever representatives I first realised the importance of education,' she says. 'Now my neighbours talk about how well I've done and they praise me for educating my children.'

'You see, it's not just the money,' Ashish insists. 'Equally important is that she becomes elevated in the society. But let me put it very clearly, it's a mutual benefit, good for us as well as them.' For Unilever, Project Shakti is a business proposition to get to the places they could not reach before. The network reaches 100,000 villages today but there are still plenty more it doesn't get to. So they've been working out how to get further out into the enormous hinterland of rural India. 'We need to get to a place where a vehicle can't go, where there are no roads. People don't have fixed addresses; they don't even have registered shops. To get to the next village, people walk through the paths or maybe go on bicycles.'

As a way of expanding the network further, in 2010, Unilever introduced the idea of the Shaktimaan. Now the Shakti Amma's husband or brother can work alongside his wife or sister to expand the family income. Unilever provides him with a bicycle so he can cover five or six villages further afield and reach deeper still into the rural areas.

We travelled out of Bangalore, past the modern tech giants of India's Silicon Valley, through small towns into the rural areas to visit the village of Krishnagiri where a Shaktimaan meets us, smiling but apologetic – because his wife has just gone into labour and been rushed off to hospital. But he welcomes us into their home to see their products all laid out neatly on the table. Perhaps most surprising is the variety: five different types of soap, including Pears and Dove; several shampoos and toothpaste. Sachets of Comfort sit on the table alongside small packets of tea and jam. Arvind Ramchandran, Unilever's Sales Manager for the area, points to the TV in the corner to explain that, these days, as mass media reaches the villages so does the appetite for higher quality products. As we walk down the road, we pass the tiny mud brick shops – which the Shakti Amma now supplies – which are festooned with long strings of sachets hanging up to make eye-catching displays. Children often buy the jam sachets or Kissan ketchup as an after-school treat, Arvind tells us. It turns out this Shaktimaan used to work in the local town but came back to Krishnagiri and when we asked why, he answered simply, 'This is where I belong.' Being a Shakti family gives him and his wife a real role in the life of the village.

While the essence of the idea is unchanged since it began, how the network operates is evolving. These days the Shakti Amma carries a mobile phone provided by Unilever, loaded with details of the entire product portfolio available to her. She can place her orders over the phone and take care of her accounts at the same time. New developments are coming through now which build on the established strength of the network. For example, Unilever has gone into partnership with Tata DoCoMO, a telecoms operator with the strategy of reaching the rural market, so many of the women can now provide mobile connectivity to their customers. And the potential keeps growing.

The Shakti Amma is now stepping up to the role of banker in the village. Supporting the government's policy of extending banking facilities to the poor, the State Bank of India has gone into partnership with Unilever to reach the villages. Because the Shakti Amma is already known and trusted in the local community, she is in an ideal position to act as a correspondent for the bank in the village. 'Because a lot of people in rural India can't write, the State Bank provides her with a biometric device to capture fingerprints which establish identity,' Ashish tells us. 'So she's able to open bank accounts for people; they can make deposits and do transactions.' To Ashish, it's an important acknowledgement of the fact that Unilever's distribution system goes wider and deeper than even some of the government agencies. When incomes rise even a little, typically, it's consumer products which reach the villages first because these are everyday basic necessities of life. So the reality is that, while it's not viable for the State Bank to establish branches across rural India, it does makes sense for them to piggy-back the Unilever network to reach that 'last mile'.

These days the global business community talks a lot about reaching the bottom of the pyramid. Professor C. K. Prahalad's book *The Fortune at the Bottom of the Pyramid* put it on the agenda in 2004 and profiled Project Shakti.[40] Since then companies, business schools and strategy consultants have been discussing what it takes to make it work effectively and economically. Working through micro-entrepreneurs, especially women, designing systems which offer mutual benefits, and adapting products to make them accessible to very low income consumers has caught on. Whether it's mobile operators with air time, pharmaceutical companies with medicines, beverage companies with drinks or energy companies with solar panels, there's a lot of experimenting going on all over the world. But the Shakti Amma led the way.

Many companies, of course, are avidly pursuing the opportunity presented by the rising wealth of the middle classes in the world's fastest growing economies. City streets in India are crammed with luxury brands trying to attract the attention of the upwardly mobile, urban consumer. But those countries are also wrestling with how to lift up their large rural and poorer populations who want to share in the improving living standards. For them, these basic products represent a better quality of life and a step away from the subsistence, hand-to-mouth existence that is the reality in so much of rural India. Ashish talks about what that means to him in the context of the society he lives in:

> It's about accepting that people are trying to make ends meet. People are struggling to grow. If you have an arrogance in your attitude, I don't think you can run a Shakti programme because you have to have a very, very strong linkage to the culture of this country and culture of the company – because it's all about holding hands with people: the people who are at the bottom of the spectrum.

Project Shakti and Lifebuoy are deeply rooted in the history of Unilever, and both now are encompassed with the over-arching framework of Unilever's Sustainable Living Plan. Launched in 2010, the Plan committed the business to an ambitious new goal: to double the size of the business by 2020 *while* halving its environmental footprint.[41] Each side of that equation is challenging enough alone: doubling in size is no mean feat for a big business with an enormous customer reach already. Halving negative environmental impact is something most businesses don't even try to commit to. It's the combination, though, which caught people's imagination. Bringing the two imperatives together goes to the heart of one of today's great questions: is it really possible to keep growing and to minimise the harm our activities have on our natural environment?

We went to ask Keith Weed, one of the core Unilever team who devised the Sustainable Living Plan, why they decided to pit themselves against such a great challenge. Keith, who very unusually in the business world holds the dual role of Chief Marketing Officer for Unilever and Head of Sustainability, dives straight into the answer, 'We did it because we believe the industry needs to reinvent itself. To be more sustainable environmentally and more sustainable socially for the future.' It's an argument he and the team have taken to public platforms around the world and he wants us to understand that the point of the dual goal is to weave the aspiration to become sustainable into the core of the business operations, rather than have it as a separate strand:

> Business is at a crossroads right now and I would argue that there are some choices to make. According to the WWF, we're living on 1.5 planets worth of natural resources already. If the whole world lived like Europeans we'd need three planets; if the whole world lived like America we'd need five. Unfortunately, we only have one. You know, Unilever is the largest tea company in the world, the largest ice cream company, the largest deodorant company... If we want to serve the next two billion people arriving on the planet between now and 2050, we have to change our approach to agricultural raw materials and natural resources.

Unilever believes that having this clear sense of purpose acts as a spur to innovation: people invent new products and new ways of operating because of it. Keith directs us towards the story of Pureit as a live example of innovation responding to social need. The need is obvious: one billion people worldwide don't have access to safe drinking water. In developing countries, 80 per cent of diseases are waterborne and three and a half million young children die every year from diarrhoea or acute respiratory infections as a result of that. Just as they recommended hand washing with soap, so Unicef and the WHO include the treatment and storage of safe drinking water in their package for prevention. Pureit is the water purifier Unilever developed in India to tackle the problem in that market.

When we speak to Deepak Saxena, who leads the effort to get Pureit out to people at the bottom of the pyramid in India, he begins by describing the search for a solution, 'For a long time we were looking for something that could answer the need of getting safe water to people. Then we thought, rather than supplying the water, let's supply the device that will purify the water.' The team had free rein to create a product that would work for the target market, he tells us, but with one essential condition – there should be no compromise on the water quality. So there would be different models for different price points and types of customer, but all must provide the same level of water safety. 'Previously in India the quality of your drinking water depended on whether you were rich or poor!' he exclaims:

> If you're rich you're living in an area where the municipality provides good quality water anyway, so you'd just be purifying pure water. If you're poor, there is no water supply or it's very bad quality and dangerous, but you can't afford to purify. What we did is demonstrate that safe water is possible for everybody.

Safe water for everybody means it has to work without

access to electricity or running water – which is essential for the system to be any use in rural or slum communities. A kit of chlorine tablets and carbon filters removes all harmful viruses, bacteria, parasites or pesticides from the water. An independent study carried out in 2006 in the Chennai slums confirmed its effectiveness in reducing sickness.[42] But, however good the product, low income households cannot pay upfront. So Unilever had to work out how to get the product into the hands of the people who need it most. They tied up with the vibrant movement of micro-finance institutions around the country and set up a number of partnerships. The Integrated Village Development Project (IVDP), made up of around 8,000 self-help groups of women across Tamil Nadu in Southern India, is one of those.

Through IVDP, women are organised into groups of twenty and, based on their track record of savings, get micro-loans direct from the bank. We joined two groups of women to listen to a presentation from the Unilever team about using Pureit. Vividly identified in their two groups by pink and blue saris, they sit barefoot on a tarpaulin on the ground, with long-legged chickens scratching in the sand around them, to hear about the threats of waterborne diseases, the benefits of Pureit and the offer of a twenty-month loan arranged by IVDP. We're invited into a home nearby to see one in action. Selvi's kitchen is about a metre square, with one ring to cook on, a few shelves with a few pans lined up and a Pureit. While she talks about how it cuts down sickness in her family and her pleasure at paying back the loan in only ten months, her children peer in from the doorway.

Kulandei Francis is the founder of IVDP and its inspiration. His early experience was shaped by extreme poverty and the suffering his parents endured to enable him to be educated – and his life has been dedicated to the single-minded goal of enabling people in villages to transform their lives. Twenty-five years on, the network has grown to a membership of 160,000 women. It's a source of deep pride to the network that in 2012 Mr Francis – as they all respectfully call him – was presented with the Ramon Magsaysay Award, often described as South East Asia's equivalent of the Nobel Prize. We visited him to understand better the link between a front-line community not-for-profit like IVDP and the big multinational that Unilever is. His gentle self-effacing manner belies, momentarily, the fierce determination of his energy. He wants to connect with anyone and anything that he believes will genuinely help the women improve their lives. He agrees that part of the challenge is that many of them don't even realise that contaminated water is causing the sickness; there are so many other things it could be. Boiling water is costly and dirty, and it's quickly re-contaminated. When Unilever first came to him with Pureit, he gave it first to his staff – who are also members of the network – to use for a few months to see if they found it worked before he introduced it to the network. It passed the test.

Having seen his members hand over their precious notes to pay back loans, we ask if he would prefer – if it were only possible – that Pureit was given free to the women. His answer is emphatic: 'Our people are very strong and very capable of paying. If they have to depend on people giving it to them, then it's not sustainable and it's not empowerment.'

So then what more can big companies do to support development? 'Create products that are relevant to poor people, develop technologies which solve the problems they have. And make it possible for them to buy them,' he responds. 'Then they will come out of their problems themselves.' Already 90,000 of his network have taken out a loan to buy Pureit.

Back at head office, Deepak puts it forcefully when he describes why the women want to enter into the purchase. 'It's the woman who bears the brunt of disease in the household, and she feels guilty. She's the one who sees how her children are getting sick with diarrhoea and she must do the cleaning up. So her burden of guilt increases and her burden of work increases. So when you explain the benefits it provides, the women understand very quickly. Then it takes about a year to fully appreciate it: one rainy season round, so what would have been six or eight bouts of diarrhoea has fallen to one or two.'

One of the most important things they've learnt along the way, he tells us, is that aspiration is an important driver for everybody – and certainly for the poor, maybe especially for the poor. The fact that Pureit appears on the shelves at supermarkets and in advertising helps to drive demand, even in the rural market. Upmarket consumers buy fancier models from urban stores, with additional features, such as bigger containers which need filling less often or fixtures to hang them on the wall. Meanwhile, for people in especially vulnerable situations, such as refugees caught up in war or natural disasters, there are donations programmes through charities. But, Deepak reminds us, they all share the same standard of safe water.

Deepak remembers in the early days listening to a colleague present Pureit to a women's group, as we had been doing, though this time in the setting of an urban slum. He tells us how, when it was finished, one woman raised her hand to ask timidly how much it cost. Hearing the answer, all eyes went to the ground: nice, but not for us. Their NGO partner explained the financial arrangement that created the option of a 51-week loan. 'I can't describe the visual change I saw come over them in the next thirty seconds,' says Deepak, 'It was the first time I saw it, but I've seen it time and time again since. There was a barrage of questions: how to clean it, how to maintain it, what the colour options are... What we'd call 'after-sale questions' – they'd already decided to buy it. It made me think of my wife: her self-confidence when she goes into a store because she can afford almost anything in there. Suddenly they were as confident as my wife because everything was within their reach. That was all the proof I needed that this was going to work.'

At the local level for the rural consumer, NGOs and micro-finance institutions are an essential link in the chain for Unilever. Yet, as Keith Weed sees it, the key contribution that multinational companies can make is to scale solutions that work:

> It would be tough for NGOs to take on a task of such scale. That's what we can bring. Pureit's reaching 30 million people in India already. We're launching in Brazil, Mexico, Indonesia, Sri Lanka, Bangladesh and more will follow. We're aiming to reach 500 million people.

The commitment to act at scale is built into the Sustainable Living Plan. Halving the environmental footprint of Unilever's products is the other side of the original dual goal. And flowing from that is the target to source 100 per cent of their agricultural raw materials sustainably by 2020. Once again, in practice, the over-arching corporate goal requires the business to deliver at the micro level on the ground all over the world. One and a half million smallholder farmers supply raw materials to Unilever – and the company's ability to achieve their goal of sustainable sourcing is dependent on enabling those farmers to work differently.

So back in India, we hear from Vijay Sachdeva how that's going for tomato farmers in southern India. To put it in context, Unilever buys 3 per cent of the world's production volume of processed tomatoes, and India contributes some 40,000 tonnes to that annually, for products such as their popular Kissan Ketchup. In 2011 Hindustan Unilever entered into a partnership with the Maharashtra Government to develop a sustainable model for local tomato farming. Vijay has responsibility for supply and development of agricultural raw materials across the whole of South East Asia, so all the fruits, vegetables and spices in that region fall into his span of control – and he explains to us what he's aiming to achieve with the tomato project in Nasik: 'We need everybody to win. The win for the farmers is improved productivity – that means increasing their yield and reducing their cost of cultivation – which leads to increased income.'

Typically, the farmers participating in the programme have a smallholding of around five hectares each and achieving increased productivity requires a significant step up in agricultural practices. As Vijay explains, 'Until now the farmers basically have been growing their crops without even getting their soil looked at. They don't even know what nutrients they have or lack.' So there's a long way to go. But improving farming techniques is not Unilever's area of expertise, which is why they've gone into partnership with Syngenta, a global agricultural business which can help them deliver the training programme on the farms. With 27,000 people working in ninety countries, this is another of the major corporates working on the front line of the world's food supply. Syngenta's Kavita Prakash picks up the story: 'When a big manufacturer like Unilever asks for different and higher standards, how does the small farmer do that? They turn to us to help them manage it.'

The process starts by working out with the farmers how to identify what fertilisers and nutrients their particular soil needs and a lot of detailed implementation follows from that: showing them how to use their own green waste for composting, introducing drip irrigation in place of flooding their fields, staking their seedlings to protect them from fungus on the ground. What gives the farmers the greatest confidence to adopt new techniques is a farm-based demonstration, she tells us, and that's why it matters to have a field force on the ground: 'It's amazing to see that in just a few seasons, you can transform people's lives.' The Syngenta teams work with a farmer on a piece of his land to show him and his community what's possible, right through the cycle from planting to harvesting.

Training to use pesticides in a more controlled way is a big part of the programme. 'What you spray, how you spray and how you store it are all part of our demonstrations because, you have to remember, many of these smallholder farmers can't read the instructions on the pack,' she explains. Pesticides are an important and often controversial part of the mix of agricultural techniques. These are hazardous chemicals and, used to excess, they cause harm. So the industry's become increasingly heavily regulated and the big players, like Syngenta, have been progressively changing their portfolio to replace old products with a new wave of more advanced products. A huge amount of scientific research has gone into controlling every detail of how they're administered: droplet size and spray technology have become specialisms in their own right. But, as Kavita tells us, the problems arise when the farmers themselves don't know how to use the products safely – which is why the business is so keen to get out into the fields and train people. One of the ever-present environmental threats these days comes from low quality, unregulated, local generic products used indiscriminately. But, we ask her, why would a farmer pay more for their products and why would the business encourage farmers to use less of it? The answer she gives is that their business model is based on effectiveness not volume, which means using less of an advanced product in a more targeted, less indiscriminate way – and they want a chance to demonstrate to farmers why paying more for their product is worth it.

Kavita is a recent arrival into the corporate arena, coming from the World Resources Institute, a not-for-profit policy research unit based in Washington DC, and she carries an extraordinary job title: Head of the Global Food Security Agenda. But what got her involved with Syngenta was exactly that: her concern about how to feed the world's fast-growing population. And she has a mandate from Syngenta to identify how the business can make a meaningful contribution to the challenge of global food security. In practice, that means getting more initiatives like the Nasik tomato project happening all over the world: 'Most of the problems we're all trying to deal with in the global food system today start on the farms and, in Syngenta, that's where we are – out on the farms. We have a unique opportunity to make a huge difference at the base of the pyramid because we have the expertise and a big presence on the ground,' she says.

At first, her NGO friends were sceptical about her move into an industry that has been the subject of so much controversy, but she has her answer: 'Smallholder farmers are responsible for growing a quarter of the world's food now. We need to work out how to increase their productivity. And if we don't, the world's simply not going to be able to feed nine billion people.'

More resilient, drought-resistant, higher-yielding seed varieties are increasingly being seen by policymakers around the world as an essential part of the solution to the global challenge of food security and that puts Syngenta, and other life science companies, in the centre of the action. 'There's a lot of precision agriculture going on these days,' Kavita tells us. Yet as well as developing more advanced products, the business is adapting how it goes to market to make it more effective, she explains. 'This business used to be just two divisions selling our wares separately – a seed business and a crop protection business – and we thought predominantly about *the products we sold*. These days we focus on fixing the farmers' problems.

We look at *what the farmers need* and we wrap all our products and services around that. It's switching our whole mindset around.' And there's a business rationale:

> Smallholders are the businesses of tomorrow. Around the world a significant part of agricultural growth will come from this level of farmers. It's our job to bring these farmers up to the level where they know they can be productive and profitable. What they want is their farm land to be sustainable as a business, and that's what will fundamentally change their lives. We can help them do that and, in the long run, if these farmers aren't profitable, we don't have a business – so our interests are aligned with theirs.

For the tomato farmers in Nasik, yields have jumped from around forty tonnes per hectare to eighty or even ninety tonnes – and both Unilever and Syngenta can claim part of that victory, along with the farmers. 'Because farmers are getting double the yield, their confidence level has gone up,' Vijay tells us, and goes on to explain that his strategy is more than the increase in yield. Unilever has also set up a tomato processing facility, in partnership with a local company Varun Agro, as an outlet for the product coming from the farms. 'So by working with us, now the farmers are getting the assurance that their product will get lifted directly from the farm and go to the facility.' Otherwise, the farmers would have to take their chances with the daily market price and typically around 20 per cent of what they grow goes to waste before it ever gets to market, he tells us. 'Now nothing is going to waste. The fresh produce is taken directly from the fields to the factory and, you know, they are very happy for that. And they know that when they deliver today, they get paid tomorrow – no waiting.'

So far 1,200 farmers have participated in the programme

and, after the first year, 5,000 more put themselves forward to join. Vijay takes that as a vote of confidence that it's working for the farmers. The real win for the government is a more resilient agricultural system. As more people move off the fields and into the cities – just at the time when there are more mouths to feed – improved agricultural productivity and smarter agribusiness is a strategic priority for India. The programme supports the government's push to get private enterprise involved in raising standards in farming. Meanwhile, Unilever in India used to import 100 per cent of its tomatoes all the way from China and that's fallen to zero. And the company has established a much stronger supply chain for one of its top agricultural raw materials – and progress towards their goal of sustainable sourcing. By 2011, 60 per cent of tomatoes for Kissan Ketchup in India were sourced sustainably, giving Vijay heart that Unilever will reach their goal of 100 per cent by 2015. Everybody wins.

Unilever is one of the world's biggest food businesses, and so one of the biggest buyers of tomatoes, palm oil, tea and many other agricultural materials. As Keith Weed reminds us, their objective is to source all raw materials sustainably across their whole range, and in all countries. So the real opportunity for Unilever is to learn from these imaginative and pioneering – but still relatively small – projects, and roll them out across the entire business.

Some dismiss Unilever's goal as unachievable or not credible because the route towards it can't be mapped out in full. Refreshingly, Keith laughs at the idea that it could be: 'It was impossible when we started three years ago. When I say something's *impossible* I mean that the way of doing it doesn't exist right now. It doesn't mean it can't be cracked.' He adds:

> Three years ago it was impossible to source 3 per cent of the world's palm oil sustainably. Absolutely impossible. There was no way you could do it; you could throw money at it and it wouldn't make any difference. Last year we did it – several years ahead of plan. But that's what business is about – setting an objective, setting off on a path, learning along the way and adjusting the business to hit that target. When I say, it's impossible, it's impossible at this moment.

Palm oil is one of the most controversial of raw materials and Unilever is the world's biggest purchaser of palm oil. Used in a wide range of products from shampoo to margarine, much of it is grown in countries such as Indonesia and Malaysia and rainforest is being cut down to produce it. So, given that context, sustainable production means the palm oil must come from plantations that are not causing further destruction of the forest.

In 2008 Greenpeace's campaign on palm oil turned its sights on Unilever's flagship Dove brand. Unilever had focused its marketing nous into establishing a connection between Dove and 'real beauty', seeking to raise awareness about the importance of self-esteem in young women. A beautifully shot, fast cut, arresting film of plastic surgery and crash diets, all undertaken in the name of the beauty industry, led up to an exhortation to 'talk to your daughter before it's too late'. Greenpeace counterpointed this with a message on the rainforest: an equally beautifully shot, fast cut, arresting film with images of Indonesian forest hacked down and orang-utans dying, all prosecuted in pursuit of palm oil, leading up to a demand to 'talk to Dove before it's too late'. Unilever took the challenge head-on and, having done its own investigations, joined the call for a moratorium on further deforestation in Indonesia. The business committed to have traceable supply chains in place by 2012.

Greenpeace, a number of other NGOs and environmental campaigners are keeping the pressure up on the industry for further action. Their argument is that certification schemes are set by the lowest common denominator and their fear is that the standards set are too weak to save the forest. The accusation is that the system of buying GreenPalm certificates creates a false comfort while masking the reality that genuinely certified product is mixed with uncertified product in an untrackable way. There's growing consensus that the current system has to be only a transition stage to a more transparent way of operating right through the chain. But doing that will be a monstrously difficult undertaking. Unilever acknowledges that although their certification is progress, 'this is just the beginning'.

In 2012 they set a new target, this time to purchase palm oil entirely from traceable certified sources by 2020, meaning each tonne can be tracked back to the plantation where it was grown. The business is making a €69 million investment in a new processing plant in Indonesia to help them get closer to the source. It's another of those goals which Keith would say seems impossible to do only because 'the way of doing it doesn't exist right now'.

To make it happen, Unilever will need to continue to use the influence they have over the companies who supply them as a way to accelerate change, as many big businesses are doing these days. Put baldly, says Keith, 'We're the largest palm oil purchaser in the world and we've said that, come 2020, we're not going to buy any *unsustainable* palm oil. So, by definition, if you don't sort out your plantations, you ain't selling to us.'

One of the reasons the business has become increasingly vocal about all these issues, Keith tells us, is that they cannot achieve their goals alone:

> For instance, we wouldn't have been able to get this far

> if the Roundtable on Sustainable Palm Oil hadn't been set up. And if we didn't have collaboration with NGOs, competitors, suppliers, the Indonesian government and others. Although Unilever is a big company, it's a drop in the ocean in actually changing the way the world works. We need everyone to help.

The Consumer Goods Forum is a coalition of around 400 corporate members: retailers, manufacturers and others, whose combined turnover adds up to over $3.2 trillion. At Rio+20 the Consumer Goods Forum, in alliance with the US government, made a commitment that by 2020 their activities would cause no further net deforestation. Unilever, unsurprisingly, was one of the champions of the cause. 'Soy is one big driver of deforestation, beef is another, timber and paper are a big driver, as is palm oil. So I think the world's biggest chance of stopping deforestation right now just might be the Consumer Goods Forum. Isn't that bizarre?' It's a rhetorical question from Keith but a pointed challenge about how new ways of operating are going to be achieved in practice. He sees the momentum in the hands of the big corporates and wants to keep pressing for their collective power to be used to make a positive difference.

He tells us that – drawing inspiration from the spirit of William Lever's original mission 'to make cleanliness commonplace' – Unilever has articulated a new mission: 'to make sustainability commonplace'. He says it brings to mind the Chinese proverb: the best time to plant a tree is thirty years ago or now. 'So our view is, let's start to do this now.' There are 150 commitments in the Unilever plan to 2020 and they're some way down the road, with some way further to go. Then, probably, there'll be a new destination ahead.

'We know the Unilever Sustainable Living Plan is still a plan. We've still got to deliver it,' cautions Keith, but he's determined about the goal. There are supporters cheering from on the sidelines and there are detractors who doubt its feasibility:

> Some people challenge what we're doing. Some say, 'What's the business case for sustainability?' I'd love to see the business case for the alternative.

7

ENGINES OF WEALTH CREATION

When you fasten your seat belt and settle in for your flight, as you glance out of the window and down the length of the wing, you might notice in passing that the engine carries the Rolls-Royce name and, because it's one of the great engineering brand names of the world, it adds to your sense of reassurance on take-off. At any one time, around 400,000 people are in the air on planes powered by a Rolls-Royce engine. Airborne, you're probably flicking through the movie listings and only half listening to the announcement: 'We'll be travelling today at a cruising speed of 567 miles an hour and flying at an altitude of 37,000 feet', because as passengers we've learnt to take that astonishing fact in our stride.

What you're looking at when you look at that engine consists of thousands of individual components and advanced materials, from hundreds of suppliers, finely calibrated, meticulously assembled, continuously tracked and monitored – and the result is a piece of kit which generates enormous power over long periods of time under extreme conditions, and does it safely.

Making that happen is the business of high value engineering companies like Rolls-Royce, GE and Pratt & Whitney. These companies are home to some of the world's most talented engineers and scientists, whose great passion in life is pushing the boundaries of what's possible. And these businesses, and others like them, are the engines of wealth creation for the societies in which they operate.

We travel to Derby to get a view from the inside and are met by Dr Steven Halliday, a no-nonsense, modest, long-serving Rolls-Royce engineer, who's going to show us around the plant to see how the Trent 1000 engine is put together. Looking down on the place from above as we enter, the floor gleams with the bright lights bouncing off it, the open space is marked out by hubs of activity around different stages of the assembly process and teams work quietly on their piece of the process, before it gets passed on in the continuous flow to the next stage. Nothing is out of place. The finished engine is a sight to behold: walking round the shining silver casing and looking up into the cone at the centre of the great circle of blades at the front, Steven tells us that when it gets handed over to the customer there's not a fingerprint on it. But the main event of the day for the engineers is the testing which is scheduled on a new engine design. They're going to take an operating engine and push it to its limits: under controlled conditions, they explode one of the massive fan blades to prove that the engine is capable of landing a plane even in a worst-case scenario. A fully assembled engine is sacrificed to the extreme testing. It seems a crying shame to destroy such a beautiful object, especially when you see the obvious pride in the team who made it. But it's an essential part of the process which provides the assurance of performance and safety that their customers, the airlines, pay them for.

Although the engine itself has a natural glamour, so much of the story of what makes high value manufacturing high value lies in the detail. To help us understand, Steven hands us one tiny component which sits at the core of an aero engine. It's called the 'single crystal turbine blade'; its job is to help provide thrust in the engine, it weighs only a few ounces and you can hold it in the palm of your hand. Yet it has to withstand the most extraordinary demands placed upon it: it has to be able to operate in the high pressure turbine where gas temperatures can reach 1,600°C – which is 200°C hotter than the melting point of the metal it's made of. 'You can look at it like this: take an ice cube out of the freezer and put it in an oven heated to 200°C, then give yourself the engineering challenge to stop it from melting,' says Steven. Because it's locked into a disc that's spinning at 12,000 rotations a minute to create the thrust that's needed to power the aircraft, the centrifugal force generates up to eighteen tonnes of load pulling on the blade – equal to suspending a train carriage from its tip; a colossal weight to hang from something so small you can hold it in your hand.

'Any normal material will simply disintegrate under those conditions,' Steven tells us, 'So we knew we had to use something new which could cope with those demands.' They make the component from a highly advanced nickel-based superalloy, which has the necessary qualities of both strength and flexibility. The next problem came with the realisation that, if they were to employ standard casting methods, the final component would be made up of many thousands of microscopic crystals, which can move slightly in relation to one another thus creating a potential weakness under the extreme loads that the component has to bear. 'So we realised we needed a process that would result in significantly higher performance than any traditional techniques,' he continues. So they developed advanced ceramic moulds that enabled them to *grow* the blade from a single crystal of the superalloy. In the metallic environment of an assembly plant, it's incongruous even to hear the idea that the blade is grown. Steven explains that it starts with a very small crystal and through precisely controlled furnace temperatures and cooling techniques that one crystal is expanded in the vacuum mould to become the entire component that we're holding. Hence its name: the single crystal turbine blade. Unsurprisingly, that process has become part of Rolls-Royce's portfolio of intellectual property. And it's hard to imagine a better example of how engineers just love to solve problems most of us don't know exist.

So the blade is strong enough but it has to stay cool enough, as well. Steven points out the solution to that problem: hundreds of tiny holes in the structure which allow cool air to flow across the surface of the blade in flight. Every one of the holes requires its own size, direction and geometry, which have taken thousands of hours of computational analysis and modelling to design. Because no conventional drill bit can produce such holes, they used sparks of electricity to melt the material away from the surface of the blade in exactly the orientation required. The surface is layered with a ceramic coating similar to the material used to protect the space shuttle on re-entry to the Earth's atmosphere. The dimensions of the blade must be accurate to the tolerance of 15 microns – about one seventh the width of a human hair.

When you see the huge amount of advanced technology and complex processes that go into making a component capable of such high performance you understand what makes it high value. The blade is worth many times its weight in silver. There are sixty-six of them in one Trent 1000 engine alone and the company produces hundreds of thousands of them a year for a wide variety of engines.

But however impressive any single component he's describing, as Steven walks us through the assembly plant, what he's showing us is that the real challenge is how it's all brought together. Eighteen thousand components come together to produce a Trent 1000. 'The assembly and testing of each engine is the culmination of the activity of a truly globalised supply chain, inside and outside the business. Everything has to be brought together in its place and every component has to be correct in lead time, quality and cost,' he tells us:

> In the global aerospace market, competitiveness is delivering an engine that's lighter than the competition's, burns less fuel, has lower emissions, and can remain on wing for longer, so that the cost of ownership of the engine over the long-term is less.

We pause again on our journey through the site, this time to notice an unprepossessing small black box attached to the hundreds of wires which are winding round and through an engine frame. Steven tells us that this is 'the engine's brain'. It's called the Engine's Electronic Controller, the EEC, and it houses the sophisticated software which detects changes in operating conditions, anything from a new instruction coming from the cockpit to sudden rain. 'It modifies the engine's behaviour in less than a fortieth of a second,' he says. 'It's designed to survive lightning, fire and cosmic radiation, but it has a service life of around thirty years, compared to the three to five years expected of your laptop.' And looking at the EEC stuck limpet-like to the side of the great engine casing illustrates how highly sophisticated software is incorporated into the production of high performance hardware: they're no longer two separate industries, they are two facets of any advanced manufacturing business today.

We finish up with Rolls-Royce at the Operations Centre where banks of screens monitor the engines in flight, 24 hours a day, 365 days a year, anywhere in the world. The Engine Health Monitoring Unit takes signals from dozens of sensors around the engine and transmits the data via satellite live into the Operations Centre on the ground in Derby. John Brown, the Services Operations Executive who greets us, has been with Rolls-Royce for many years – as so many of them have. He explains that on a Trent engine, like the one we've just seen being assembled, they're measuring around twenty performance parameters while the engine is in flight:

vibration levels, oil pressure, temperature and so on. It allows them to alert the airline to any potential problems in advance and, if repairs are necessary, they have field teams on standby on the ground for when the plane lands.

Like the manufacturing side of the business, these are high-tech activities, generating their own intellectual property. Rolls-Royce has patented miniaturised repair processes which inspect inside an engine using a fibre-optic cable equipped with a camera, as doctors might do a non-invasive medical inspection. Relaying pictures from a runway the other side of the world, it allows engineers in Derby to diagnose the problem and plan for rapid response repairs which can now be done on the wing – massively cutting down delays and saving costs for the airline and time for the passengers.

These engines are in service for twenty years or more and, as John explains, 'We no longer sell just an engine. These days our customers are asking us to deliver the engine and the services to look after that engine on the wing.' The services side of the business, he tells us, is built on the intelligent use of data: 'masses and masses of data'. Every day, about nine gigabytes stream into their operations centre from the skies. That information means that for many of their customers today, Rolls-Royce can plan and manage the maintenance, repair and overhaul of their engines; they take on the logistics of spare parts around the world, and manage field repair teams wherever they're needed. Their aim is to keep every engine on the wing for seven million miles between overhauls – that's to the moon and back fourteen times. It's probably not what most people associate with a big manufacturing business, but services now account for more than half of global revenues for Rolls-Royce.

In reality, though, these services provide a lot more than revenues. They generate an enormous amount of information about how the engines perform in the real world, over time

– which is fed into the development process to improve the design of the next engine. So for Rolls-Royce, it creates a virtuous circle: long life-cycle products, long-term relationships, long running secure contracts. It's what investors call 'quality of earnings'. For the airlines, it's all about lowering the overall cost of owning the engine throughout its life. For everyone who flies, it's what keeps the world's air routes flowing pretty smoothly even as they get busier – and it's more reasons to feel secure when you see the engine on the wing at take-off.

There's no doubt about it, holding in your hands the single crystal turbine blade is something memorable and, in it, you get a glimpse of the world of high value engineering. But walking through the assembly plant demonstrates unequivocally that no component works in isolation: each has to play its part in the whole system, in harmony with thousands of others. And these days, software is integrated into hardware. Internal global supply chains are synchronised with external supply chains. Services grow out of manufacturing. It's really not hard to admire the extraordinary feat of orchestration. As Steven puts it to us very simply, 'This stuff is hard to do.' Few companies have the capability to manage that in its entirety, which is why complex systems integration is one of the defining characteristics of high value businesses like Rolls-Royce.

There are people who'll be thinking it's a pity that all that brain power and ingenuity goes into producing engines for airplanes. Don't we all know that more flying is a bad thing? Aviation, as a whole, already contributes 2 per cent to man-made CO2 emissions globally. And, as millions more people around the world get the chance to travel, demand is expected to grow rapidly in the coming years. So most of us, when we fly, also travel with some guilt, in the knowledge that we're adding to the problem. Assuming that the world's appetite for flying doesn't abate, it's likely that the very people who have the know-how to make these engines also hold the key to developing solutions to one of the great challenges of our time: greater energy efficiency.

According to a recent study of the aerospace industry by Deloitte, 'Fuel efficient jet-propulsion is one of the most significant technological innovations that have come to the commercial aviation market in the last few years.'[43] Rolls-Royce has been at it for a long time. The Trent XWB which powers the enormous Airbus is 15 per cent more fuel efficient than its predecessor, the Trent 700, which first went into service in 1995. Meanwhile, GE – America's largest industrial business and the world's largest aero engine manufacturer – recently announced the arrival of GEnx, their next generation engine for widebody aircraft, and their most fuel efficient engine yet. As we saw at Rolls-Royce, inventing new materials is an essential ingredient of progress and, in this instance, the breakthrough is in carbon composite blades. GEnx claims a 15 per cent improvement on what went before and savings in fuel costs of around $6 million for each aircraft that switches over to the new model. GE estimates that if the entirety of the global fleet which this engine could be applied to were to switch, it could save more than two million tonnes of CO2 emissions a year – equivalent to the emissions of approximately 448,000 cars on US roads.

GEnx is part of GE's broader business strategy of investing in products and services designed to help the world adapt to a more environmentally rational way of living and doing business. Launched in 2005 and called Ecomagination, the strategy was presented to the world in the slick marketing language that was popular with corporates at the time. But unwrapped from the shiny packaging, it emerges as a significant commitment to build revenues and profits by seeking out and backing new environmental solutions. Mark Vachon, who is VP of Ecomagination, has worked in many places around the GE world for about thirty years now and has an energetic sense of purpose about him. He sees the investment in environmental innovation as defying a lazy business assumption:

> We're using innovation to eliminate this concept of a false choice between – pick one – great economics *or* great environmental performance. We think that's absolutely nonsense. Through innovation we can have both – and in the process grow faster. That's what Ecomagination is about, that's how we come to work every day and that's how we think about investment.

So far, GE has been proving the proposition that you can have it both ways. To qualify as part of the Ecomagination portfolio a product has to provide dual benefits: a measurable improvement in environmental performance of at least 15 per cent, plus a performance improvement for the customer's operations. The portfolio now boasts more than 200 products which meet that criterion and has generated more than $100 billion in revenues since it launched. It's made up of an eclectic mix of products and services from different divisions – so alongside the new GEnx aerospace engine, for example, is a technology that enables a power plant to integrate energy from a variety of sources including solar and wind, and smart appliances which can reduce kitchen electricity use by 20 per cent.

'We've never viewed clean energy as ideological,' says Jeff Immelt, one of the world's highest-profile business leaders and GE's CEO since 2000, talking to greentech entrepreneurs who won the Ecomagination Challenge in Australia. He tells them, 'We've always viewed it as problem solving. That means it can take place in a mine, in ports, or in natural gas, or wherever a problem needs to be solved.' He goes on to explain the origins of the Ecomagination concept, coming from 'a 2004 exercise which pitted a "red team" of internal researchers that were asked to prove the science of global warming, against a "blue team" that were tasked with refuting it. In the end, eighteen out of the twenty-strong blue team defected to the red team.' GE's top engineers had tangled with the evidence themselves, argued it out, and were convinced that climate change presents a real challenge for the world and that they should turn the resources and expertise of the business towards tackling it.

Nearly a decade later GE is a big investor in green technologies. As Mark introduces Ecomagination to an audience gathered in the Palm Springs sunshine for a Green Tech Investor Summit, GE's conviction in its own argument comes across loud and clear:

> The strategy came from the belief that climate change is real. Followed quickly by: these are $1.5 trillion markets to get into. Then on top of that, it's what a great and a good company should do.

Encouraged by the success of the first five years, in 2012 GE committed to the next phase of Ecomagination. As Mark tells it: 'Jeff doubled down on the idea.' They doubled the R&D and committed to growing the revenues in the Ecomagination portfolio at double the rate of the rest of the business.

When the UN Investor Summit on Climate Risk and Energy Solutions drew fund managers representing trillions of dollars of investment to New York in early 2012, Mark's point was that, 'Companies that don't get this really risk becoming irrelevant to the marketplace – whether you believe it for climate change or for great economics – it's our responsibility as businesses to be responsive to the design signal the world is giving us. And that is all about: let's do more with less, particularly around natural resources.'

Finding new ways to manage resources more efficiently is central to what high value engineering businesses offer their customers today. Whether they're airlines, railroads, utility companies, city municipalities or manufacturing plants, they're all asking for help with that. Siemens, based in Germany, is another of the global brand names with an impressive portfolio of options for its industrial customers – software monitoring tools to track how energy and water are being used in manufacturing textiles, or a more efficient production environment for a car plant. At the Hanover Fair in 2013 Siemens was the star attraction, showing off *Curiosity*, the Mars Rover which they built in partnership with NASA to explore the surface of another planet in a level of detail never possible before. Hanover Fair is the world's biggest showcase for industrial technologies, attracting over 200,000 visitors from all over the world each year. Opening the Fair, Chancellor Merkel focused on how modern manufacturing is being transformed as the 'options opened up by software are merging with the capabilities of hardware'. She talked about this new integrated model of high value manufacturing as equivalent in significance to the invention of the steam engine during the industrial revolution.

Siemens, like GE, has a broad portfolio across energy, industry, infrastructure and cities, and health, with over 350,000 people working in 190 countries. In many ways GE is the archetypal American corporate; Rolls-Royce is a quintessentially British brand; and Siemens embodies the spirit of German engineering – but today they have all become global giants. Siemens describes the relevance of what they do in terms of 'how our world is changing'. They expressly identify four trends that create the context within which they innovate: climate change – 2012: the highest CO2 concentration in the atmosphere in 800,000 years; urbanisation – 2050: 70 per cent of mankind will live in cities; demographics – 2050: 9.3 billion people; and globalisation – 2030: emerging markets will account for two thirds of the world's economic output. They hone that down to 'four questions that move us':

> How can we ensure health care that is excellent and affordable? How can cities grow and at the same time offer a high quality of life? How can we make industrial production more flexible, efficient and competitive? How can we create economic growth and reduce the consumption of energy and resources at the same time?

These are questions many people are asking and they're why these high value hi-tech businesses matter to global society today. Much of their capacity for innovation is directed at finding answers to those questions. The choices, investments and discoveries they make right now will determine many aspects of our daily life for several decades. More than 150 years ago, Siemens built the first long-distance telegraph line in Europe between Berlin and Frankfurt; only a few years later they went on to to build the Indo-European Telegraph Line – reducing the time it took to get a message from Calcutta to London from thirty days to twenty-eight minutes; then they laid the sub-sea cables from Ireland to the USA for the first ever direct transatlantic telegraph. So it's been a global business from the outset. Werner Von Siemens presented the first ever electric railway at the Berlin Trade Fair in 1875; they built Europe's first electric underground in Budapest and China's first electric tram in Beijing. Before the end of the nineteenth century they were global experts in electrification.

Meanwhile, Siemens Healthcare were pioneers of X-ray technology in the 1930s and the producers of the world's first cardiac pacemaker in the 1950s. And today the Siemens Healthcare research team is still at the front edge of new treatments, exploring the potential of using breath samples from patients for the early diagnosis of lung cancer and tuberculosis. These businesses have a deeply embedded capacity to create a lot of *firsts* and, in an age when the world is looking for new solutions in almost every area of life, they have a lot to contribute.

Siemens may be one of Germany's best known global brand names in engineering, but the country is famous as a champion of manufacturing generally. Thousands of small and medium sized engineering companies are strategically important to the economy; the Mittelstand, as they're called. Often family owned, deeply rooted in their community but export-focused, they are supported by local banks and an educational system that prioritises – and places a high value on – technical skills. Writing in the *Washington Post,* the columnist Harold Meyerson notes that manufacturing accounts for around a quarter of the German economy – as opposed to around just 11 per cent in the USA and the UK. He reflects that Germany got it right: 'Its trade balance – the value of its exports over its imports – is second only to China's, which is all the more remarkable since Germany is home to just 82 million people.'[44] And according to an Asian Development Bank paper, it's not just the amount of manufacturing exports which has been so important to Germany's resilience in Europe, it's the type:

> In the case of the Eurozone, it is not high labour costs in the non-German states that are preventing the countries' economies from growing, it is that they produce goods that are less complex and thus open to more global competition.[45]

That's the key to the economic importance of high value manufacturing businesses: their products are competitive in the global marketplace, providing exports and taxes and a significant contribution to GDP. In the UK, it's possible to track that economic impact in the activities of Rolls-Royce. The company employs 21,000 people in the UK and, because this is a highly skilled workforce, wages are typically 40 per cent higher than the national average. It spends about £2.4 billion with UK suppliers annually, buying goods and services from over 2,000 companies across the country. In 2009 it contributed £4.2 billion in exports – representing 2 per cent of all goods exported. It made a value-added contribution of almost £8 billion to the country's GDP –that's equivalent to the annual pay of 38,000 National Health Service nurses. And because it has operations spread across the country, rather than just in the major metropolitan centres, it contributes hundreds of millions to the GDP of every region in the UK, making it important to the resilience of local economies, as well as the national economy. A similar pattern plays out wherever the company has major operations, for example, in Germany and the USA, and is replicated by other high value engineering businesses.

Behind that string of numbers are people who are highly engaged in the enterprise. Visiting the assembly plant, the research centres and service centres, we met people who share a sense of belonging to a crack team – quick to point out the expertise of others, confident in the relevance of their own contribution, and proud of being part of the whole operation. Nowhere is that more visible than in the apprentices. Some of them have come straight from school to be trained on the job. They're all sporting the logo on their shirts and they wear their hearts on their sleeves: they're bursting to tell you how proud they and their families are of what they do. Some common themes come up. Everyone loves the kit and how clever it is, they get a real kick out of working with the technology. They enjoy the sense that they're learning from highly skilled people and, universally, they're keen to tell you about the future. Amber Lomax, who left school at seventeen and became an assistant in a law firm, tells us that she knew nothing at all about engineering when she started. She found herself in a Rolls-Royce open day and heard about an opportunity to train in computer-aided design. 'I'd always liked art at school and was good at it,' she says. 'My friends were stunned that – as a girl – I wanted to come into this. They thought of engineering as dirty and a man's job. But I think that's because most people haven't seen what it's like.' When we spoke, she was finishing up her apprenticeship, which she was doing alongside studying for a Mechanical Engineering degree, and working on 3D computer modelling for combustion and casings for aerospace engines. 'I can't imagine wanting to do anything else now. I love that I'm working on engines that are taking people on holiday – you can look up into the sky and see them on the wing.' Her enthusiasm is infectious and now, no doubt, next time we're travelling at 30,000 feet and see the engine on the wing, we'll think of her working on the design. But what's most striking is how clearly she sees a path ahead of her. 'You can work your way up and, if you want to, you can go far. In the next ten years I want to be someone who's developing new ideas for engines.'

With a workforce of about 40,000 around the world, the business employs an enormous variety of scientists and engineers: materials technologists, stress technologists, aerodynamics experts, vibration experts, reactor physicists, marine propulsion specialists and naval architects, electrical systems engineers and information engineers, to name only a few. They breathe life into the concept of a company as a concentration of skills. Our guide around the world of Rolls-Royce, Steven Halliday, has worked with them for fourteen years and, when we ask him what keeps him going, he answers, 'It's the breadth of the technologies and the depth we can go into. There's the interest and opportunity for engineers here.' He knows he's only on one piece of the whole, but that small piece commands his attention: 'When you get several millions invested in one piece of equipment you get some very clever academics and some top engineers gathered around it.' Currently, he's captivated by what he describes as the 'super plastic forming techniques' for fan blades. 'There's a lot of firsts here,' he explains, 'You look around you and you know that what people are doing here may be a first for any institution anywhere in the world. That excites us quite a lot.'

It's the advanced technology involved in the products and services of high value businesses which stimulates demand in other businesses and industries. Rolls-Royce spends more than £5.5 billion a year with its suppliers around the world. That means that a significant proportion of the total manufacturing cost of an engine flows out from Rolls-Royce itself into the supply chain – typically as much as 70 per cent – to buy products and services from other companies, big and small. So while the company employs about 40,000 people directly, it also works with around 8,000 suppliers in seventy countries, which means the business supports an additional 250,000 jobs in its global supply chain. For these smaller companies, a big business like Rolls-Royce is their route to market.

So with demand increasing in the fast growing markets of the world, Rolls-Royce has been establishing supplier relationships in new territories. Frisa is one of those, a Mexican company which started in the 1970s as a small forging works selling to local machine shops. Today it operates out of state-of-the-art facilities, and proudly says that it's 'trusted to serve the world's leading OEMs (original engine manufacturers) in aviation'. Stepping up to the requirements of the big high value corporates makes it a global competitor in its own right.

However, it's also a reality that the growing technical skills of the emerging markets have proved a challenge for the established businesses of the developed world. Some have risen to it, growing with the globalisation of their big customers: for example Weston EU, a traditional Midlands engineering firm which has supplied Rolls-Royce with compressor aerofoils for many years. Based on the strength of that relationship, Weston EU set up a factory in Thailand. They replicated some of their own core manufacturing activities and processes in the new plant and trained up a local workforce. The operation earned Rolls-Royce quality approval and has been successfully integrated into their global supply network. That in turn helped lay the foundations for a Rolls-Royce cluster of suppliers in the South East Asia region. And what began as a Lancashire-based family firm has made the leap to being a strategic player for Rolls-Royce in Asia.

Meanwhile, it's vital to the survival of small engineering companies that they continue to invest in innovation at home. We take a trip off the beaten track to Shrub Hill in the sleepy country town of Worcester to get a feel for what that means. It seems an unlikely place to find a company pioneering cutting-edge methods of working with materials. Yet it's the home of Materials Solutions, an entrepreneurial spin-off from Birmingham University that's intent on creating its own intellectual property. It's one of the hundreds of high-tech start-ups working with Rolls-Royce to develop breakthrough manufacturing technologies. The offices of the utilitarian building are brightened up with colourful animal puppets hanging from the rafters, and here the founder Carl Brancher and his team are perfecting an advanced process which builds up solid components from paper-thin layers of nickel superalloy powder.

Carl takes us to watch how it happens in a small cabinet, rather like a microwave, where a laser beam traces out the shape of the component. Wherever the beam hits the powder, sparks fly, it melts and then solidifies. The surface is swept smooth and the laser traces over it again and again, adding layers just 20 microns thick, until the component is complete. Gently, Carl digs it out of the powder and dusts it off to show it to us. With immense satisfaction, he turns it around to be sure we see the inside – as delicately structured as the inside of a cowrie shell. The laser process is capable of building up intricate shapes, with hollows and internal structures designed to serve the exact purpose they're required for.

Components like this are suitable for use on highly complex combustor tiles and heat shields, and the process itself saves a lot of raw material. A conventional production method takes a hunk of metal and shaves away a lot of material to leave behind the shape. But with this new 'additive layer' technique, any excess powder can be reused, reducing waste to a mere 5 per cent. So working with Materials Solutions creates a significant opportunity for Rolls-Royce. And, as the entrepreneur and scientist behind the small business, Carl explains to us why it makes all the difference to him to win the status of approved supplier:

> The reason we want to work with Rolls-Royce is they are a world class company and they pose the most interesting engineering challenges. If we can solve their problems, we do something of very great value that means we can then use it with many other companies in other industries.

In a nutshell, that's why the Rolls-Royce supply chain adds value so far beyond the boundaries of its own business. It's a symbiotic relationship. Because these smaller businesses are essential to their ability to deliver to their customers, in this case the airlines, Rolls-Royce is insistent about the high standards and reliability it requires. So when the smaller companies prove themselves capable of satisfying those demands, they know they've earned their spurs in the global marketplace – and that becomes their platform and the basis of their own growth. And in the three examples from the Rolls-Royce supply chain we've just seen is a microcosm of the dynamics of the global marketplace today. In the rapidly growing economies – as we saw with Frisa in Mexico – being a supplier to the big high value businesses opens up opportunities for the rising aspirations of entrepreneurial small businesses. In the developed world – like Weston EU in the UK – those who succeed jump into the slipstream of the successful global corporates and go international themselves. And the most technologically advanced – like Materials Solutions – dedicate themselves to creating their own intellectual property and producing products which keep pushing the boundaries of what's possible. Rolls-Royce acts as the aggregator of a huge supply network, integrating thousands of smaller players. It sets the bar high and in the process lifts everyone up towards it.

Long term commitment to R&D is what distinguishes all of these big high value businesses. Rolls-Royce, for example, spends almost £1 billion on R&D each year. Steven Halliday, as he took us around the engine assembly plant in Derby, summed it up: 'R&D is the life blood of the company. Everyday we're working to come up with new technologies which make things possible that haven't been possible before.'

It's Rolls-Royce's inventions that differentiate them and make them competitive. So the outcome of successful R&D is intellectual property, which earns the business the licence to use that invention exclusively for a period of time. It's a long game: typically, they approach their technology investment over a twenty-year horizon and expect the development of an idea to take up to a decade to come to fruition. And, as we saw with Steven, the design of an engine, or even any of its complex components, is inevitably accompanied by the design of the processes which will manufacture it in the production environment. You can't have one without the other. So the business builds up value through its patents in equipment *and* software *and* production process, generating more than 450 patent applications a year.

'Invent one, use many times' is the R&D philosophy of the company – and the growth of the business demonstrates that in action. Gas turbine technology, which on a jet engine moves huge volumes of air to push an aircraft through the skies, can be adapted to drive the propulsion system on a ship or the compressor for a gas pipeline. So their equipment is now installed on 30,000 marine vessels of every different type – ferries and cargo ships, offshore oil and gas exploration and fishing fleets. And Rolls-Royce engines are being used to generate electricity, pump oil or compress gas all over the world: on the West-East pipeline in China, for instance, which stretches thousands of kilometres across the harsh landscape of the Gobi desert. Whether the engine is used in the aerospace, marine or energy sector, 80 per cent of the gas turbine technology is the same. So the original investment in intellectual property and the core expertise embedded in the business are constantly being applied to new ends.

To Steven, the victory of the Rolls-Royce system is that it's designed to keep the innovation flowing:

> What our customers are relying on isn't just our ability to invent or manufacture one remarkable component, or one engine even. It's our capability to deliver innovation consistently, on a broad front, throughout the entire system, year after year, continually upping the game.

Universities are essential contributors to that whole process. The world of academia and the world of business come together in R&D. Rolls-Royce has established a global network of relationships with leading research scientists. And the company funds thirty technology centres, in universities from Germany to the USA, Norway to South Korea, including around 350 people working on their doctorates. 'These relationships give us access to some of the best research brains in the world and connect our engineers to what's going on at the forefront of scientific discovery,' Steven tells us. Several universities feed into the research and development phase of any of the core Rolls-Royce technologies. For the universities, the benefit is funding for long-term posts which help them attract top-class talent. And, for the academics, the work leads to publishing papers which help them secure their own position in the competitive educational marketplace.

In the past few years, a radically new collaborative research model has been emerging, in the form of Advanced Manufacturing Research Centres. AMRCs are purpose-built facilities which bring together an academic faculty and a group of high value industrial businesses to find solutions to real problems in the commercial world. Dr Hamid Mughal, Director of Manufacturing for Rolls-Royce and a passionate champion of the Advanced Manufacturing Research Centres, calls it 'a pull model' because there's already an identified need for what comes out of the work. Hamid explains to us why it's breaking new ground:

> It's not a university research lab and it's not a production facility: it's something that stands between the two. Manufacturing development cannot be conducted entirely in a university environment because it needs a different infrastructure: it needs full scale manufacturing equipment and very high tech tools. On the other hand, it

> can't be done in a manufacturing plant either, where the priority must be given to the products being delivered. So in the past, we've struggled with taking academic technology out of laboratories and into production and this gives us a whole new approach which bridges that gap.

The academic research scientists get access to industrial scale tools they would not normally have available to them and a wealth of data about how these technologies work in action. The commercial engineers get an injection of fresh leading-edge thinking on hard problems. This creative interdependency between industry and academia establishes its own ecosystem. And the centres bring alive how the research activities of the big high value businesses help to underpin the science and knowledge base of the countries they operate in.

John Rose, CEO of Rolls-Royce for over ten years, likes to say: 'There are only three ways to create wealth. You grow it, you dig it up or you convert it – adding value to the raw materials when you convert them into products.' Rolls-Royce and other big science-based, technology-based businesses that invest heavily in R&D are definitely in the third category. Wherever they base their operations, they draw other businesses into their orbit and lift the competitiveness of the whole economy.

Singapore has taken that logic as the foundation of its strategy. An island city-state in South East Asia, not quite 50 kilometres across, since the 1960s Singapore has become one of the most advanced and technologically driven economies in the world. In such a densely populated, urbanised, confined space, they have no options to dig up or grow wealth, so they've focused on converting it and aimed at the high end. The government was determined to attract investment from high-tech industries, aerospace included. Much of the future growth in the aviation sector is expected to come from Asia, so Rolls-Royce also made a strategic choice and selected Singapore as the hub for all the company's Asian operations. Seletar Campus, opened in 2012, represents a $700 million investment and the manufacturing facilities are capable of producing the most advanced products in the Rolls-Royce portfolio. Yet it's not just the manufacturing aspect of the aerospace business which factors into the government's plans. The Singapore Economic Development Board calculated that for every dollar of value added to the economy by manufacturing, there's the potential for up to 90 cents more contributed by services.

Meanwhile, the whole enterprise is dependent on having the people with the right skills to take up the new jobs. So the government intends to use the presence of Rolls-Royce to build up a pipeline of relevant skills. The Workforce Development Agency and the Institute of Technical Engineering are partnering with the company to develop courses in the specialist technical skill sets needed – diffusion bonding and laser cutting technology, for example. Seletar Campus itself will also house a Rolls-Royce Advanced Technology Centre, which will act as a research base and a focal point for collaborating with universities. And the campus is large enough to encourage strategic suppliers to relocate to the site – thereby establishing the basis of a local high-tech cluster for the industry to draw on.

You can see the entire ecosystem of a high-value business being brought together – purposefully, from scratch, at speed, and in one place. It makes the factors that lead to economic development very visible. First, aiming to produce products and services that are hard to deliver, and which can provide exports. Second, building the relevant skills, and ever higher levels of skills. Third, developing clusters of suppliers, and plugging them into a global marketplace. At the same time, investing in high tech R&D, and generating IP from it. Finally, supporting universities that can collaborate with industry, and create a productive science base for the country. Just as Rolls-Royce isn't the only high value business to be able to catalyse this effect, Singapore isn't the only Asian country to have gone down this route. No doubt, some people are nostalgic for life as it once was, but this is a recipe that's lifted the fortunes of everyone in Singapore and given them options for the future that they didn't have a generation ago.

Many of the greatest challenges of the twenty-first century demand science-based, technology-based solutions, so high value businesses have an important part to play in that: whether they're developing new medicines, as we will see with GSK; smarter ways of managing cities, as we saw with IBM; or more efficient use of our natural resources, as we saw with GE's investment in new energy solutions.

Looking to expand the Ecomagination portfolio, GE decided to invest in new clean-tech ventures. To help them find the right technologies to invest in they created the Ecomagination Challenge: it's an open invitation for businesses with good ideas in energy or water management to come forward with investment proposals. So one of the world's very largest corporations is seeking out technology entrepreneurs whose ideas might be no more than a twinkle in their eye – what VP Mark Vachon calls pre-revenue companies. As he told *GreenBiz*: 'The real magic is that we need to see these technologies implemented to scale – both for these organisations and for the agenda we're all working on. If you leave it at the interesting ideas stage, that doesn't happen.'[46]

Mark sees it as a great opportunity for both GE and for the

new ventures: 'We bring what they are interested in: management experience, in these spaces, that can help facilitate that. And global distribution to say boom!' To these tiny pre-revenue companies, getting GE behind their ideas represents the potential for explosive growth that can put them on the map. Mark concludes that the greatest contribution his business can make is to scale and commercialise these new technologies to make them viable in the mainstream. And Ecomagination aims to generate billions in revenue – thereby continuing to prove its premise that innovation can deliver great financial performance *and* great environmental performance.

There's no doubt that GE has the scale to make the most of these ideas, but Mark saw scope for greater speed. So he created an 'Innovation Accelerator' – a process to select a few of the ventures which show particular promise and move them through the development phases faster than they could alone. For instance, a common inhibitor to progress for an early stage company is the chance to prove their technology in the real world, so GE might arrange a pilot with a customer to help them test their product. Or it could be that the business has a technology ready to go, but no scalable route to market, and GE can offer them global distribution. The aim is to get these ideas up and out and into the market as quickly as possible. After all, any, or all, of them could be a game-changer in how 'we can do more with less'.

One of the Ecomagination Challenge winners is Richard Williams, co-founder of Xergy Inc., who beams as he holds up his winning device which he says is 'the most efficient, modular, noiseless, cleanest refrigeration device available'. He just happened to see Ecomagination Challenge advertised on the internet and thought, 'That's for us, this is exactly what we should be doing.' His ambition is simple and it's impossible not to wish him well: 'We want to get this into the hands of as many engineers, chemists and scientists as possible... We want to be the clean green future of refrigeration.' And now he has GE behind him to help him do it.

The Clean Tech Investor Summit offered Mark a good opportunity to let some of the entrepreneurial talent know what's on offer. He wanted to get across GE's continued commitment to clean-tech investment, in spite of weakness in the public markets. GE's sense of resolve, he says, comes from 'the realisation that we haven't solved these problems – they haven't gone away – so therefore the innovation and technology that's represented in what all of you do actually gets increasingly more important all the time as the problem gets more intense.'

That's the purpose which guides the investment choices that Mark oversees: aiming to grow a hugely successful business by creating a positive impact for society as a whole. What motivates him is that, in his role, he can direct the resources and know-how of GE towards solving one of the urgent challenges of our time: the ever increasing demand for energy. Between 2010 and 2015, the plan is that GE will spend $10 billion on both energy and water technologies, and with that scale of backing, Mark is ambitious for what Ecomagination can achieve in the world:

> ... it shows we are incredibly committed to rebuilding the energy infrastructure of planet Earth – and that foundation, along with of course other organisations throughout the world, provides somewhat of a base for all of us to innovate around.

8

MOBILE FOR EVERYBODY

MTN is the leading telecoms player across Africa and the Middle East, and Karel Pienaar was its first employee. On the wall of his office is a framed market study, written back in 1994, as South Africa was celebrating the election of Nelson Mandela and a new start for the nation. The market study forecasts that by 2010 the company would have 350,000 subscribers. When 2010 came around, the reality was very different: MTN had 129 million customers, and today it has approaching 170 million. 'It really is laughable, looking back on it,' says Karel, who is now the CEO of MTN in South Africa. 'Today, cell phones are such an important part of life, across the continent.'

MTN's story brings to mind an old business fable in which two consultants are sent to Africa to assess the market opportunity for shoes. The first consultant concludes that there isn't much of a market, saying 'Bad news: people don't wear shoes here.' But the second consultant takes a different view: 'Great news: people don't wear shoes here.' Opportunity, the story suggests, is in the eye of the beholder. It's a neat parable for MTN: two decades ago, Africa was suffering from terrible poverty and the devastating HIV/AIDS epidemic. Few thought of it as a telecoms investment opportunity. MTN took a different view, says Karel: 'We have a different mindset. Maybe it's because we're an African company, coming from South Africa, but we see things differently. What others see as a challenge, we see as an opportunity to build a business.'

Indeed, MTN is now one of Africa's most successful businesses: it has built operations in twenty-two countries, becoming the largest company with a primary listing on the Johannesburg Stock Exchange and the most valuable brand on the continent. It's based in Fairlands, a leafy low-density suburb of the city, in a gleaming new headquarters called the Innovation Centre. Arranged around large open atriums the building is light and spacious, with sleek steel-grey columns and flashes of MTN's trademark yellow. Three-storey walls of sheer glass open onto the rolling hills of Fairlands, and for a moment you might think you were in a Silicon Valley tech campus. But these rarefied surroundings belie the hard graft and guts it took to roll out a telecoms network across some very challenging environments. After establishing itself in South Africa, MTN got the network up and running in difficult markets like Rwanda, Uganda, Cameroon and Nigeria, and kept it up and running in war-torn countries like Côte d'Ivoire and Afghanistan.

Today, much is said about the power of telecoms to transform life for people in countries such as these. International institutions like the International Telecommunications Union (ITU) and the Global Network Initiative (GNI) enthuse about the role of communications technologies in economic development and stimulating democracy. Aid organisations such as USAID and Oxfam all now have extensive mobile initiatives. United Nations Secretary-General Ban Ki-moon praised the 'phenomenal spread of mobile phone technology' which he said has 'touched every corner of the world and empowered billions of people'. But there was little such enthusiasm in MTN's early days. Indeed, there was even some outright hostility to the mobile phone: some African National Congress politicians labelled it 'white elitist technology',[47] arguing it would benefit only a privileged few.

From the outset, MTN was determined that the reverse would be true, as Karel explains. 'We were a country that was very clearly orientated between the haves and the have-nots, and that was always part of our vision,' he tells us. 'Our focus from day one has been, "how do you address the whole market?" That was always our ticket.' His story demonstrates how it's often business that has the vision, the appetite for risk, and the operational capability to make a difference.

In MTN's case, the initial scepticism that there would even be a demand for mobile didn't just come from the non-commercial sectors, but also some parts of the business world – especially as the company began to expand out of South Africa and across the continent. Karel remembers a conversation with an employee from one of MTN's main competitors, in the early days: 'He said, "why the f*ck are you going into Africa? It's just potholes and squalor."'

One of the first markets MTN took on outside of South Africa was Rwanda, which was up and running in 1998. The country was still reeling from the genocide, and many questioned MTN's decision. Themba Khumalo, who ran the operation in Rwanda, describes the scepticism: 'People said, "There's no money in these rural areas, these people don't even have houses!"' But once again, MTN saw things differently, says Themba: 'We knew people had one fundamental need: to communicate across long distances. So we built the coverage and the demand was so strong that we had to add capacity within three months.' Today, the bright yellow of MTN's logo has become an integral part of Rwanda's lush landscape: every village in the so-called land of a thousand hills has independent MTN distributors jostling to sell airtime from yellow-painted huts, or booths, or bicycle-trailers. You get the impression that MTN really means its slogan: 'Everywhere You Go'.

In 2001, as operations elsewhere began to settle, MTN set its sights on the big prize: Nigeria, a market of 160 million people and widely expected to become the largest economy in Africa. Then, as today, Nigeria was a notoriously difficult environment to operate in: poor infrastructure, badly maintained roads, a patchy power grid and a reputation for endemic corruption. Other network operators had tried to enter Nigeria, only to crash and burn: Vodacom, for example, ditched its V-Network Nigeria business after only six months, finding it too tough going. Unsurprisingly, the markets reacted with alarm when news leaked that MTN had paid $285 million for a licence. At the time, it seemed to many an eye-watering amount. 'People thought we were crazy, and our share price dropped,' says Christian de Faria, who was the company's Chief Commercial Officer. 'But we knew we could make it work, and it's turned out to be one of the best decisions we ever took.'

Make it work they did: MTN in Nigeria now has over 45 million subscribers. What made it possible for MTN to succeed where others had failed? Listening to the company's managers tell the story, two themes sing out: the sheer on-the-ground, get-it-done executional ability of the company, coupled with a really clear vision for the potential of mobile in Africa. 'When we encounter a problem, we deal with it,' says Khumo Sheunyane, who is in charge of strategy for the group. 'When we need to build a road, we build a road. If we need 10,000 generators, we buy 10,000 generators. We do what it takes.' This make-it-happen mentality is rooted in a real sense of purpose for MTN. Khumo tells us: 'It all starts with the vision that mobile telephony would revolutionise the continent.' It's a theme we also hear from Karel, MTN's Employee No. 1: 'We always believed in the absolute catalyst that a cellular infrastructure brings to a country,' he says – and he's seen it first-hand. As soon as MTN was awarded the licence, Karel was sent to lead the team in Nigeria setting up the network. It was hands-on work: 'I used to walk the streets looking for places to put switching centres,' he tells us, 'knocking on doors, getting it started. That's how it happens. We get going, we invest with conviction, we go in boots and all, hire the right people, and build the network.'

This risk-on, get-it-done approach has proved hugely rewarding: in the eleven-year period from 2001, shareholders saw their earnings rise by 26 per cent each year on average, and the share price climbed by 16 per cent a year over the whole period.[48] But getting the network up and running is only the start of it: *keeping* it up and running can also be a major operational challenge. Spend time with MTN people, and you soon hear a rich lore around what it takes to keep the network going – especially in war-torn countries. We hear that in Afghanistan, base-stations have been regularly burnt down by the Taliban, who were suspicious that networks were being used against them. We're told of an MTN employee who was kidnapped by jihadists while doing maintenance work in a remote part of the country, only to return to work upon his release to finish the job in hand. In 2011, as civil war broke out in Côte d'Ivoire, MTN employees refused to leave the country – even as hundreds of thousands of people were fleeing for their safety. As chaos spread through the country, MTN staff knew that people needed the network more than ever. There is a deep sense among the company's front-line employees that people depend on them, especially people who are experiencing difficult times.

Few places have proved more challenging than Syria, where MTN has nearly six million customers – almost half of the market. In 2011, the demonstrations against President Assad developed into a national uprising, which soon slid into violent civil conflict claiming tens of thousands of lives. From the start, the war had no clear front lines, with flashpoints erupting in towns and cities across the country. In such a volatile and chaotic situation, people needed their mobile networks more than ever. But aside from keeping people connected in a time of great crisis, the network played another crucial role: it was the eyes of the world. Even as dozens of journalists were being killed, imprisoned and tortured by the government, the country's citizens had a new weapon in their hands: the camera phone. Amateur footage soon began flooding the international media: shaky images of violence and confusion, taken on the streets by a brave new legion of citizen journalists. The government may have done its best to terrorise the press in Syria – it's been ranked as the world's most dangerous country for journalists[49] – but as long as the network was up and running, anybody with a camera phone could broadcast to the world.

A similar story had unfolded across the region during the Arab Spring, with mobile playing a central role as the spirit of revolution cascaded from country to country. Many have called this the 'social media revolution', and while social media was undoubtedly an important tool for protest leaders, the impact of mobile is likely to have been far greater – especially in the form of SMS text messages. For example, as the revolution began in Egypt, there may have been around 15,000 Twitter users, but there were up to 80 million mobile phone subscribers. Without mobile networks, the transformative changes that got under way with the Arab Spring may never have gathered momentum.

The people we spoke to at MTN are clearly proud of their company's determination to keep the network up and running, even in environments of real adversity. However, MTN's role in countries like Syria is not uncontroversial. Bloomberg News, for example, obtained a document with details of the SMS censoring activities imposed on the networks by the Syrian intelligence services: MTN was ordered to block politically sensitive terms such as 'revolution' or 'demonstration', or even 'Syrian men'.[50] The *Financial Times*, in a piece with the headline 'Syria finds means of financial survival', explained how the government was reaping revenues from MTN under its pre-war licensing agreement. Critics of the company have used stories such as these to paint a picture of a morally bankrupt business supporting a murderous regime. Some argue that MTN should pull out of Syria. It's a logic that many in the company find deeply vexing. 'People are looking at the short-term benefits of frustrating a dictator, rather than the consequences for the people of the country,' says Jennifer Roberti, the group's overall head of marketing, explaining that shutting down the network would 'create chaos and reverse development' for the people of Syria. Themba agrees: 'The implications of a closure of an MTN service are dramatic. To take the service out is like winding back the clock.'

MTN's CEO, Sifiso Dabengwa, articulates this as a deeply held philosophy. 'At the heart of human existence is *communication*,' he tells us. 'We see telecommunications as a basic human right no different from water or medicine.' You get the impression this is an outlook that pervades the company, from the very top right through to the front-line workers who risk their personal security to keep the network running. It's not just Syria that has tested this philosophy: MTN's presence in Iran has also been heavily criticised. Mark Wallace, a former US ambassador to the UN, has been one of the more vocal detractors: 'At any hour the regime could be using MTN cellular technology to monitor dissidents,' he is reported as saying.[51] Wallace is the chief executive of United Against a Nuclear Iran, which believes that all businesses should withdraw from the country. 'Any company that does business in Iran is not only financially enabling the regime but also risks having its products misused for nefarious ends,' Wallace says.

For MTN, this view overlooks the benefits they have brought to the country, in terms of access to communications, and the political and social benefits that flow from that. Not long ago, getting hold of a SIM card used to take months and cost hundreds of dollars. When MTN was awarded the licence it got the network up and running in just six weeks, shipping in containers of pre-assembled base-stations. Suddenly, anyone could walk into a shop and walk out again with a SIM card for a few dollars. For Iran, MTN's arrival marked a step change in access to communications, a fact even acknowledged by some of MTN's critics. Access, a digital rights campaign group that has also expressed concerns about the company's involvement in Iran, is anxious precisely because of the importance they ascribe to mobile access:

> At the time that MTN was awarded Iran's second private mobile communication licence, cell phone services were outside the reach of much of the public, plagued by waiting lists, high costs, congested networks, poor service quality, and low network coverage. MTN Irancell presented the first serious challenge to the state telecommunications company's effective monopoly, becoming the most popular service within six years (49 per cent market share) and, in doing so, entered into a moral obligation to defend the free flow of information to the Iranian people. The availability of stable, open and inexpensive internet and communications connectivity must be vigilantly protected and encouraged.[52]

To a large extent MTN seems to share this sentiment, although it's not obvious that walking away from the country would help to 'defend the free flow of information'. MTN's instinct is to stay and keep the network running, in Iran, as elsewhere. There is an interesting parallel with Google's highly publicised withdrawal from China in 2010, following sustained criticism from anti-censorship campaigners. What is less known outside China is that this decision provoked a backlash among Chinese internet users. On a visit to Beijing, we met an executive from one of China's leading web companies who told us: 'People felt that Google had just given up and walked away, instead of staying and working a way through a difficult environment... Chinese web users are very sophisticated, they know what's going on, they understand the pressures that companies face. Google pulled out of China to satisfy Western critics – it had nothing to do with its users in China.'

From the outset, MTN was intent on addressing 'the whole market' – including those on very low incomes, not just the affluent. Any company looking to build an inclusive business like this needs to do more than cut costs and lower prices: real affordability usually requires a complete overhaul of the business model, to make sure the economics work in the long term. For MTN, affordability has been the 'north star' for the company's innovation. In the 1990s, as the company began rolling out the network in South Africa, it became clear that the contract-based model that had been dominant in the developed world wouldn't work for many people in Africa. In a largely informal market, there was usually no way to verify identities or credit histories, and most people would be unlikely to be able to afford a big monthly bill. A new approach was needed, and so MTN became pioneers of the 'pay as you go' model for pre-paid mobile phone use, which is now a global standard for lower-income customers, and has extended into other industries such as electricity.

Another breakthrough in the business model was 'MTN

Zone', a pricing tariff that adapts charges according to how busy the network is, and displays the current rate on the phone's screen. At quieter times, customers can be offered up to 95 per cent off the charge, allowing users to save money by deciding when to make calls. Some users even move around looking for cells where the call traffic is lower and the price is cheaper. It sounds simple, but it took some careful planning to get the technology right, and to make sure the business model worked – get it wrong, and MTN could soon find itself out of pocket. MTN partnered with Ericsson to develop the hardware and software, and ran tests to understand how the dynamic pricing would affect call volumes. Launched in 2007, MTN Zone has been a huge success: it's made mobile services available to many who couldn't afford them before, which in turn has helped to grow MTN's customer base. It's also helped MTN to manage network congestion, resulting in a better service.

In launching this new service, MTN hit upon another idea that would transform the market: the MTN Zoners, an informal distribution network of street vendors and hawkers that sell airtime, as well as signing up new customers. It began when MTN was planning the launch of the new MTN Zone tariff. Simo Dabengwa, who runs the Zoners from MTN's Innovation Centre in Johannesburg, explains how the idea came about: 'MTN decided that the first launch of MTN Zone will be below-the-line, it won't be above-the-line. We won't go with big events, we won't be going to the media. We actually have people go out there and explain it to the customers, help them change the settings on their phones, so they can enjoy the discounted calls.' Instead of a slick advertising campaign, MTN Zone recruited around 250 enterprising street vendors, trained them up, gave them MTN uniforms, and sent them out on a mission to switch existing customers onto the new plan. It really took off: pretty soon they had switched a million customers onto MTN Zone. Simo and his team were taken aback by this swift success. They had plugged into a high-voltage new channel that could do much more than switch customers to a new plan: these energetic young vendors could become a major sales and customer service network.

'After that we put together a board paper to scale it up, and put together a management structure to support the running of this channel,' Simo tells us. 'We need to make sure people report for work, we need to be able to collect the cash, we need to give them airtime, we make sure they're properly trained, properly dressed in uniforms.' The board approved the paper, and soon there were 3,000 vendors on the scheme, supported by 200 'Zone managers'. The Zoners were immediately popular with customers – in fact, it was customers who first started calling them Zoners. Suddenly it was much easier to buy airtime. 'Some of the guys are up at 4am, they're at the train stations, they're at the bus stations, they're on the commuter routes, making sure they capture the customers going to work,' says Simo. Some of the Zoners build up a loyal base of customers, who buy airtime from them every day. 'A customer might send them an SMS asking for airtime, "Load my phone with 50 Rand", and the Zoner knows that when the person gets off the bus they will pay this money. There is that rapport and that trust between them.' The Zoners help resolve service problems customers might have, and they run MTN marketing promotions. 'They become the MTN champion for their area,' says Simo.

It's become an integral part of the street-scape in many African cities: the bright-yellow MTN umbrella stands on the roadside, and the Zoners with their bright-yellow flags and rucksacks selling airtime scratch-cards in the commuter-flow, blending seamlessly into the continent's hawker culture. As many parts of Africa struggle to deal with high levels of youth unemployment, the scheme is a great opportunity to make something of yourself, Simo tells us. 'It's mainly young people in their mid-twenties; some of them are single parents, some of them haven't had the opportunity to get a formal job somewhere, and this is an opportunity to earn a good living,' he says. Being an MTN Zoner is considered a prestigious job: aside from making good commissions, they each get regular training and their own 3G BlackBerry. Some of the more successful Zoners see big changes in their lives. We hear of Dudu Nkosi, a Zoner in Mpumalanga in South Africa, who is the sole bread-winner for her extended family. Dudu is building a seven-bedroom house, and Simo shows us a photograph of her standing proudly in front of the half-complete structure: the walls are up, the roof is on, and she's currently saving for the plastering and the windows. Dudu doesn't own a car, but the house includes a garage – a sign of her optimism for the future.

'Some of our Zoners were about to go destitute, and we help them set up businesses that are now thriving,' says Simo, who clearly finds his job running the Zoners extremely rewarding. 'I have the pleasure of seeing these young people, their stories of how they are making a difference for themselves and supporting their families.' He shares with us an internal paper on the scheme, which describes MTN as 'a people's business'. It goes right to the heart of the central idea behind this book: when businesses are smart about their place in society, they can grow in ways that bring benefits to a broad range of people – not just their shareholders. MTN is a great example of this: by pioneering new ways to get mobile into the hands of more people, the company has had a profound impact in its markets. 'My team says I sound like a politician when I say this,' Simo smiles modestly, proud but not boastful. 'We make changes in the lives of people. We are impacting the lives of people, and we do it whilst we are making money and making profit for MTN.'

MTN's network of umbrella stands and street hawkers has worked especially well in Nigeria, where the informal market is particularly vibrant. At first, MTN had tried to build a formal distribution network modelled on the car dealerships and mobile phone distributors of the UK. According to this plan, independent, registered businesses would set up chains of MTN shops, selling contracts. It soon became clear that this wasn't the best approach for a low-income country with such a fast moving, energetic market culture. Mobile needed to be cheap, instant, and easy to buy – and Zoners provided the perfect model. Instead of an established, formal distribution chain, MTN now has a dynamic network of dealers, subdealers, sub-subdealers and street-retailers. It's the perfect fit for Nigeria – and indeed for many developing world countries, which have thriving informal economies. The American journalist Robert Neuwirth gives a striking description of informal economies in his book *The Stealth of Nations*:[53]

> There is another economy out there. Its edges are diffuse and it disappears the moment you try to catch it. It stands beyond the law, yet is deeply entwined with the legally recognised business world. It is based on small sales and tiny increments of profit, yet it produces, cumulatively, a huge amount of wealth. It is massive yet disparaged, open yet feared, microscopic yet global. It is how much of the world survives, and how many people thrive, yet it is ignored and sometimes disparaged by most economists, business leaders, and politicians. At the same time, many major corporations make their money through [the informal economy].

The MTN Zoners operate on the untidy edges between the corporate world and the informal economy, where big business meets individual improvisation. It's not easy doing business at this unruly interface: corporate structures don't easily lend themselves to ongoing economic relationships with large numbers of individuals. In Chapter 1 we saw how Coca-Cola used the NGO TechnoServe to facilitate its relationship with thousands of smallholder farmers in Uganda. For MTN in Nigeria, a private company stepped in to help MTN run its network of distributors – and it was the kind of institution that was used to handling financial relationships with large numbers of individuals: a bank. When Access Bank first started working with MTN, they were a relatively obscure bank. In 2002, they were number sixty-eight in Nigeria; by 2013 they were number four. A big part of this stellar growth is what they describe as the 'Value-Chain Model': helping big corporate clients to grow by making sure that all of their suppliers, distributors and employees have the financial products and services they need to be successful. For MTN, this solved a major problem: how to manage the many small increments of cash that began flooding in from thousands of street vendors – cumulatively, a significant flow of income. Access Bank went out and made sure that they all had bank accounts, into which they could regularly deposit cash. And so Access Bank became an important part of the cash-cycle for MTN, which positioned them well for managing the company's other requirements, such as advancing credit to distributors, and paying salaries to employees.

When you see Access Bank's work with MTN, it's a reminder of what a bank can be: directly enabling economic activity by understanding its clients' businesses, so it can empower their employees, suppliers and distributors. We visited Access Bank in Lagos, and discovered a company ambitious to be part of taking Nigeria to a new level. In 2002 a new, young management team took over the bank, determined to adopt international standards – especially in the area of business ethics. In a country mired in corruption, they set about building a different type of organisation. 'It started with some restless young men,' says Herbert Wigwe, the bank's incoming CEO – referring to himself and his colleagues. 'We believed that we could create a new type of bank, in an environment where not much is said about ethics: a new type of bank which we could control.' They single-mindedly applied global principles of transparent reporting, which won the trust of investors, as well as partners like the International Finance Corporation. In the context of business in Nigeria, this set them apart. When shockwaves from the 2008 financial crisis hit Nigeria's banking sector, Access Bank were able to raise sufficient capital to weather the storm. It was a massive shake-out for the country's banks. Not only did Access survive, but it was able to grow through a series of acquisitions and mergers. Only a decade ago, the bank was nothing special; now it's one of five so-called SIFIs (Significant Financial Institutions) in Nigeria. 'Access Bank is the perfect example that you can do business in Nigeria, grow, make good profits by applying rigorous ethics,' says Omobolanle Babatunde, the bank's head of corporate affairs.

Access Bank lists as one of its values 'courage to be the change we want to see' – a sentiment that may sound high-minded coming from many organisations, but when you appreciate the scale of ambition, you realise they really mean it. 'The perception of Nigeria from the outside is not always the best,' says Herbert. People assume the banks are fiddling the books: 'External commentators say the reported numbers of many institutions are not representative of the true state of their affairs. We wanted to create an oasis of sanity: an institution you could trust – to show that Nigerians can do the right thing.' Omobolanle agrees: 'We want to show you can do clean business in Africa.' The bank's then CEO, Aigboje Aig-Imoukhuede, was keen to point out this is about business first and foremost: 'It's not about being altruistic – it's because

Access Bank cannot achieve its objectives if things in Nigeria stay as they are.' It may not be about altruism, but there's no doubt that many people see the bank playing a role in taking Nigeria to the next level. Okey Nwuke is one of the bank's Executive Directors, and in his words:

> In ten or twenty years when history is written, we hope that we will be part of the change – of fighting for governments that function well and aren't open to corruption. We hope that this momentum builds, and that we earn respect and that we make money and that we are known for this.

Back in Johannesburg, MTN's management feels a similar sense that their company has a broader role in society. 'We want to be a good news story of a good company coming out of Africa,' says Serame Taukobong, who looks after MTN's marketing in South Africa. Like any large company doing business across Africa, MTN has had its fair share of struggles with corruption, but the people we spoke to are determined to get on top of the issue. 'This is the first example of a company operating on a global scale with a black African leadership,' says Khumo. 'This company has a special responsibility in the way it behaves because it represents a black African success story.' Jennifer picks up this theme: 'MTN has a huge responsibility because we are a role model on the continent and a beacon of what is possible: an African company solving African problems.'

Solving African problems: that's no small scope of ambition. But MTN have a sense of what is possible, having seen first-hand how access to communications has driven progress in Africa and the Middle East. And of course this is a global story: in developing countries around the world, people have seen tangible improvements in their lives thanks to mobile, whether that's through access to health information, educational resources, market information such as crop prices, or financial services. Having a mobile phone in your pocket gives people a new sense of security and freedom – especially for women. Across the developing world, what was once a luxury has become a necessity. Keeping your phone in credit has become a top priority, even for those on very low incomes. One report showed that those living on as little as $2.50 a day (the World Bank's standard definition of poverty) would choose to walk instead of paying for the bus, or even skip a meal, rather than run out of credit.[54] Economist Jeffrey Sachs told a conference at the London Business School:

> The cell phone is the single most transformative technology for development. I've been in the development sphere for thirty years and I've never seen anything as amazing as what mobile has done. It's a unique combination of fantastic technology and business model for the poor as well as the well-to-do. Everybody loves their mobile and everybody has multiple uses for it. The transformation power is phenomenal.

It's not hard to find evidence of the 'phenomenal' impact that mobile businesses are having. Meet people in any part of the developing world, and you soon hear stories of how mobile connectivity has made a practical difference – as the GSM Association's 'Mobile For Development' team found out when they made a series of short films capturing some of these stories. Here are some examples:

Jaipal is a 27-year-old farmer from a remote part of rural India. Like many smallholder farmers, his livelihood depends entirely on his crops doing well. He uses a mobile phone information service to get advice on how to protect his crops, control pests and increase productivity. 'It's really helped me,' he tells the GSMA team. 'Though I trusted my elders before, they weren't right 100 per cent of the time. I can be a lot more certain about which pesticide I should use when insects and other pests affect my crops.'

Florence lives in Kibera, Kenya, the largest slum in Africa and home to approximately one million people. She lives with her husband Nicholas and her one-year-old son Joseph. For her, access to mobile communications has proved a real life-saver – literally: 'The day my kid felt sick, the mobile phone gave me a chance. I just called the doctor direct and asked for the first aid I could perform to the baby.'

Muniba is a seventeen-year-old student in Bangladesh, and she's learning English using a mobile phone service run by BBC Media Action called Janala. 'I want to work for a multinational company,' she says, explaining to a researcher why she wants to learn English. Anyone can call the Janala service for an English lesson, all for the price of a cup of tea. At her college, Muniba's English teacher, Mr Sazzad, says it's really boosting opportunities for his students. 'A lot of our girls are going for jobs,' he says. 'Without learning English they won't get any good jobs, because the job market is getting so squeezed these days.'

John runs a small taxi service on the busy streets of Nairobi. He uses mobile money every day, to make a variety of payments. 'I have a couple of cars on the road,' he says. 'When one of my drivers runs out of fuel or he needs some cash, he will just call me and I will text him the money.' He also uses his mobile to send money back to his parents. 'I come very far from Nairobi and I can't visit my parents weekly or monthly. So I used to look for who is travelling back home, a friend or a relative. You give them the money to drop to your parents, but sometimes you have many problems. Sometimes they use half of the money.' Now John can regularly send money directly to his parents using his mobile phone.

This is a story we heard repeated in many parts of Africa we visited: using mobile to transfer money to relatives, eliminating the need to make long, time-consuming journeys, and reducing the risk of carrying cash around. Of the many mobile applications, mobile money is proving to be particularly powerful. It began in 2007, with a service launched by Safaricom, the Kenyan local operator owned by Vodacom. The system is called M-pesa, and allows customers to charge their phones with credit bought from an agent, which can then be transferred by SMS and cashed in with another agent. The service has become part of life in Kenya: according to Safaricom, M-pesa has 15 million users and up to a third of the Kenyan GDP passes through the system – it handles $21 million a day. Mobile money is reaching such a scale that the African Development Bank is worried that it might actually be driving inflation, because it has increased the speed and efficiency with which money moves through the Kenyan economy.

Assuming central bankers are able to adjust their anti-inflationary policies, mobile money promises to be a great boost to economic activity in the developing world. In many countries, the majority of people don't have bank accounts, and so mobile money provides an alternative way for them to participate in the formal economy. In Indonesia, for example, mobile phone penetration is 106 per cent (in other words, there are more phones than people), while only 20 per cent of the population hold a bank account. There are already more mobile money accounts than bank accounts in Kenya, Madagascar, Tanzania and Uganda, and there are now more mobile money agent outlets than bank branches in at least twenty-eight countries. Across the developing world, people are using their mobile phones to pay electricity bills, water bills, school fees and even taxes.

Across the developing world, mobile phones are changing the way that people work, the way they learn, and the way they do business. Mobile services are improving the productivity of farmers, and improving access to health information. It's not surprising that the number of mobile phone users in Africa is soaring towards 1 billion. But behind the astonishing growth and the stories of transformation lies the hard graft of companies like MTN, who were prepared to take on the risks of building a network in some difficult environments, and were ready to invest heavily to make it happen. Renaissance Capital, an investment bank that operates exclusively in emerging markets, calculated that over a seven-year period to 2012, business invested $80 billion in Africa – and MTN alone accounted for almost 20 per cent of this – some $15 billion of capital investment. This means that MTN has probably invested more in Africa than all other private sector investment, apart from the resources industry.

For MTN, this is all only the beginning. 'What we've done is built the first layer – sheer connectivity. That's the phase we've passed,' says the CEO, Sifiso Dabengwa, talking to us over a healthy lunch in the calm expanses of the Innovation Centre. 'Now the phase is to convert this connectivity into commercial activity.' And so the company that set out to put a mobile into everyone's hands in the 1990s has set itself a new mission, according to Sifiso: 'We want to make the capabilities of the internet available for all,' he says. 'Our vision is to roll out internet for everybody by 2020.' Revenue from data services will be the next wave of growth for operators, and so this is the new frontier of investment for MTN: the company has invested more than $230 million in fibre-optic cables since 2009. That's why MTN is a great example of the theme of *Everybody's Business*: a positive force for change coming from a business acting purposefully, understanding how it can grow by improving the world around it. Karel, MTN's Employee

No. 1, remains as excited as ever by the impact MTN can make. 'I've been expecting it, hoping for it, advocating for it, and now it's here,' he says, brimming with enthusiasm for mobile internet. Like many at MTN, he is full of optimism for the future:

> It's fantastic technology. You only need a certain amount of literacy and you have the world's knowledge at your fingertips. It's a way of equalising the opportunities around the world. Imagine a community that has been totally isolated, and now they can connect to the worldwide web, and access the same information as anyone in the first world. That's what we're doing now.

9

REWRITING THE SOCIAL CONTRACT

It's become a global symbol of over-consumption: images of the overweight and the obese, chomping down on super-sized burgers, or guzzling from buckets of sugary soda. It's a symptom of a deeper discontent: in Michael Kimball's novel *Big Ray,* the eponymous hero is driven by a ceaseless need to consume: he 'never felt like he had enough of anything. He always wanted more of everything – money, food, shoes, clothing, magazines, hair, children, etc.' Obesity, it seems, is the product of a corpulent culture. 'I'm starving' is a fridge-raiding *cri du siècle* – oblivious to the millions of people around the world who live in genuine hunger. But it's not just a developed-world phenomenon: millions of new consumers are swelling the ranks of a new global middle class. They're enjoying new-found spending power, and access to food and drink products that were largely unknown to their parents – and, like Big Ray, it seems they can't get enough. The result is a growing international health problem: as long ago as 1997, the World Health Organization declared obesity a global epidemic.

Today, the Red Cross estimates that obesity kills more people than malnutrition. Obesity rates have doubled over the past thirty years. Globally, 1.4 billion people are overweight and 500 million obese. By 2030, up to 60 per cent of the population in many countries will be obese. Childhood obesity is a particular worry: there are close to 8 million overweight children living in developed countries and 35 million in developing countries. The rising tide of obesity places a great burden on overstretched health systems around the world. The annual cost of obesity-related illness in the USA alone is estimated at $190 billion – which is almost 21 per cent of the country's annual medical spending. The cause of this epidemic is simple enough: we eat more high-calorie foods that are packed with salts, fats and sugars (but typically low in vitamins, minerals and other nutrients) while at the same time we do less physical activity. It's a deadly combination: more calories in, fewer calories out.

The food and drinks industry is firmly in the firing line. Books like *Fast Food Nation* and documentaries like *Super Size Me* have pointed the finger squarely at the big companies in the industry. Governments are starting to act: countries like Denmark, France and Finland have already introduced taxes on sugary drinks or high-fat foods. The UK is considering following suit and many US states already have specific sales taxes on soft drinks and snack foods, although none is explicitly a 'fat tax'. New York City mayor Michael Bloomberg banned the sale of drinks larger than 16 ounces (473ml) in the city's food-service establishments – but a judge, who described the move as 'arbitrary and capricious', blocked the ban. It's a heated debate, and an increasingly litigious one.

As the biggest food and beverage company in the USA and one of the biggest in the world, PepsiCo is in the eye of the storm. PepsiCo has become a global food and drink powerhouse because they have an enormous portfolio of products that people love, including twenty-two products with sales of more than $1 billion a year each. As well as its namesake cola, PepsiCo is famous for Mountain Dew and Gatorade, Lay's, Ruffles, Doritos, Fritos, Cheetos and Walkers. It's a company with a long history, stretching back to the 1880s when a pharmacist called Caleb Bradham launched his own cola made from cola nuts and a digestive enzyme called pepsin – from which the drink gets its name. PepsiCo quickly became a star in the

American corporate universe, and remains one of its long-running success stories. In the 1950s, when arch-rival Coca-Cola was focusing on small-town America, Pepsi championed the 'new' lifestyle of upwardly mobile city living. It became the epitome of 1950s corporate glamour when CEO Alfred Steele married Hollywood diva Joan Crawford. Together they travelled the world attending gala openings of new bottling plants, and they hosted company parties in their opulent Manhattan apartment. Joan Crawford even became the company's first female board member. Pepsi was one of the world's first truly global brands: in 1959 Soviet leader Nikita Khrushchev tried the drink after his famous debate with Richard Nixon in Moscow, and Pepsi-Cola subsequently became the first capitalist product sold behind the Iron Curtain.

We visited PepsiCo at their global headquarters, located in a quiet hamlet called Purchase in New York. It's an understated low-rise building, with no brash corporate branding. A long straight drive rolls through a sculpture garden with water-lily ponds and immaculate lawns, featuring work by Rodin, Henry Moore and Giacometti. A line of carefully tended shrubs leads to the quiet entrance, above which a PepsiCo flag furls next to the stars and stripes. It's one of the most restrained offices you're ever likely to set foot in. Amidst the tranquility, it's hard to believe that a few days earlier Superstorm Sandy had lashed through this area, tearing down all the power lines. PepsiCo, whose backup generators immediately whirred into action, had provided its neighbours with a place to warm up and get a hot meal. On the day of our visit there's little evidence of the storm – other than the sky, which remains a resolute steel grey. Neither does this feel like a company in the middle of an onslaught from the global health lobby: the clamour of concern about obesity seems far off. And yet what we encountered was a company intent on aligning its business strategy with the interests and expectations of society.

It's become a mantra for CEO Indra Nooyi: 'fun for you, better for you, good for you'. It's at the heart of the vision for what she calls 'PepsiCo's transformation journey' – and you can hear her repeat it on any public platform she takes. The essence of this strategy is a shift in the product portfolio: alongside the company's core 'fun for you' brands (the salty snacks and sugary drinks that rile health campaigners) PepsiCo has set out to grow the 'better for you' brands (low fat content, less sugar, fewer calories) and 'good for you' products (nutritious drinks and foods including fruits, vegetables, whole grains, low-fat dairy, nuts and seeds). For some time, the company has been adding healthier brands to its portfolio. Indra explains:

> Going back to 1997 when we bought Tropicana, and then 2001 when we bought Quaker and Gatorade, we expanded the portfolio to include 'good for you' products. Now fast forward. If you look at the ageing of the population, as you look at the focus on health and wellness, this part of the portfolio represents a gigantic growth opportunity.

The company is really throwing its weight behind this opportunity. In 2012, PepsiCo made a big investment in a joint venture with Theo Müller, the European dairy company, to build a facility that will churn out around five billion cups of yoghurt a year. Yoghurt sales have been increasing on the back of the trend for healthier eating – from $4.5 billion dollars a year in 2000 to an anticipated $9 billion in 2016. Put this alongside fast-growing brands like Naked Juice – named for its insistence on no artificial flavours, added sugar or preservatives – and soon the shape of the portfolio will begin to look different. 'It's all about growth,' says Indra. 'We are a growth company, and the growth of "good for you" is about three times the growth of "fun for you".'

Undoubtedly, many will be pleased to see PepsiCo making

strides towards transforming its portfolio, and putting its marketing muscle behind healthier foods – but that does not change concerns about sugary sodas and salty snacks. Indra took the helm as CEO in October 2006, and was quick to push these concerns up the corporate to-do list. Within a year, the company had committed itself to some ambitious targets around cutting the salt, sugar and fat content of its foods. All of these goals are set against a 2006 baseline, and apply to the company's key brands: cut the salt by 25 per cent by 2015; cut the saturated fat by 15 per cent by 2020; cut the added sugar by 25 per cent by 2020. Achieving these targets is a considerable technical challenge: aside from maintaining the taste that consumers expect, these ingredients play an important role in the texture and appearance of the products. Take out too much sodium and your Doritos become bland, soggy and anaemic. Saturated fats have become a public health enemy, but they help to maintain the shelf life of products. PepsiCo's food scientists need to reformulate these products to meet the targets without losing the essential taste, crunch, colour or shelf life – and they need to do this without pumping them full of artificial ingredients and preservatives. Finally, all of this needs to be achieved without disrupting the economics of the product, which needs to remain competitively priced. It's a real challenge: the demand from society may be simple enough, but it requires a complex response from the company.

Momentum behind healthier products is growing. By 2012 almost half the beverages sold by PepsiCo in the US were zero or low-cal, sports nutrition drinks or fruit juices. Someone who's learnt a lot about what it takes to deliver that change is Derek Yach. He has the kind of résumé that would once have been very rare in a major multinational corporation: he is a former Executive Director of the World Health Organization, he was Professor of Global Health at Yale University and he was heading up global health at the Rockefeller Foundation when he was invited to meet Indra Nooyi, when she had just taken the reins as CEO of the company. 'I thought it was just a chat,' he says, 'but it turned out to be a job offer – which, if you know Indra you'll know was in fact a job demand. I was being offered the chance to lever the work I'd done at WHO and see how you could apply it within a private company to bring about change.' In many ways, it would turn out to be a continuation of his work at the WHO, but with a chance to reach the billions of PepsiCo consumers around the world. 'I never thought I'd join a private food company,' he says – indeed, many of his public-sector colleagues were taken aback at his move, as if he were a 'traitor to the cause'. But as he told us, 'When I saw the seriousness of the planning and the investments that were going to come in R&D and innovation, it was impressive.'

Derek had been a global health campaigner and critic of the industry. In fact, he originally penned many of the papers calling for food companies to cut the salt, sugar and fat content of their foods. 'That's very easy to write about what's wrong from the outside, and then you come into a company and you get insights into the realities of what appear often on the outside to be very simple things to do,' he reflected when we asked him about how his experience of being inside one of the biggest companies in the business had changed his perspective. 'You realise there are many roadblocks, even if you want to do it: you may not have the ready supply of healthy oils, you may not get the taste or the price right at the outset – or you may want to lower sugar but your consumers don't accept the product. What sounds so simple and alluring turns out to be much more complex to achieve, and that's the intellectual challenge.'

Derek had an interesting job title: Global Head of Health and Agriculture Policy, not an obvious role to find in a company most famous for its fizzy drinks, but of course PepsiCo has a wide range of products, such as cereals, cookies, nuts, nachos and hummus. 'People don't really think of PepsiCo as being an *agriculture* company,' Derek tells us, 'but everything the company sells has to be grown – and there's going to be rising pressure focused on the health aspects of the core products, so that's the link'. It's a profound link to make: PepsiCo can't respond effectively to the health challenge without seeing it in the context of the global agriculture system. 'The issue goes all the way down the chain,' Derek explains, 'Many of the basic commodities that the industry uses have been subsidised dramatically over the last few decades and so it's not surprising that many food companies tend to still have a high proportion of high fructose, corn syrup or sugar derived products, or palm or soy derived products, as opposed to fruit, vegetable, nuts and grains, which are more expensive and are not really receiving the same level of public subsidy.'

One of the most contentious ingredients is palm oil. It's great for the food companies: it has a longer shelf life and a lower price, making it ideal for food production. As a result, the food industry has developed a big palm oil habit: global consumption of palm oil in food has quadrupled over the past twenty years. The trouble is palm oil isn't so great for human health. In fact, it's one of the least healthy oils, containing 45 per cent saturated fat, compared to only 10 per cent in sunflower oil and 6 per cent in rapeseed oil. To meet PepsiCo's goal of reducing the saturated fat in its key brands by 15 per cent by 2020 means finding practical alternatives to palm oil. It's a big innovation challenge, but the company has had some significant wins to date. From Smith's potato chips in Australia, to Cheetos snacks in Russia, to Lay's Forno in Saudi Arabia, brand by brand, market by market the business is changing the formulation of its products. In Mexico, for example, the business partnered with the Inter-American Development Bank to help farmers revive the farming of sunflower seeds: the farmers get a guaranteed market for their

A whole society, rising up: the traditional grass-thatched hut that Alfred Omoding used to live in (right) and his new brick-built house (left).

Sorghum farming in Uganda: Lucy and Jon look at the crop which is providing stable livelihoods for farmers.

Shaping the future: looking across Silicon Valley towards the San Jose skyline.

Cottonopolis: looking across Kersal Moor towards Manchester, the 'shock city of the age', as shown in a painting by William Wylde in 1852.

In the 1990s, working conditions in factories making products for big Western brands became a cause for global concern.

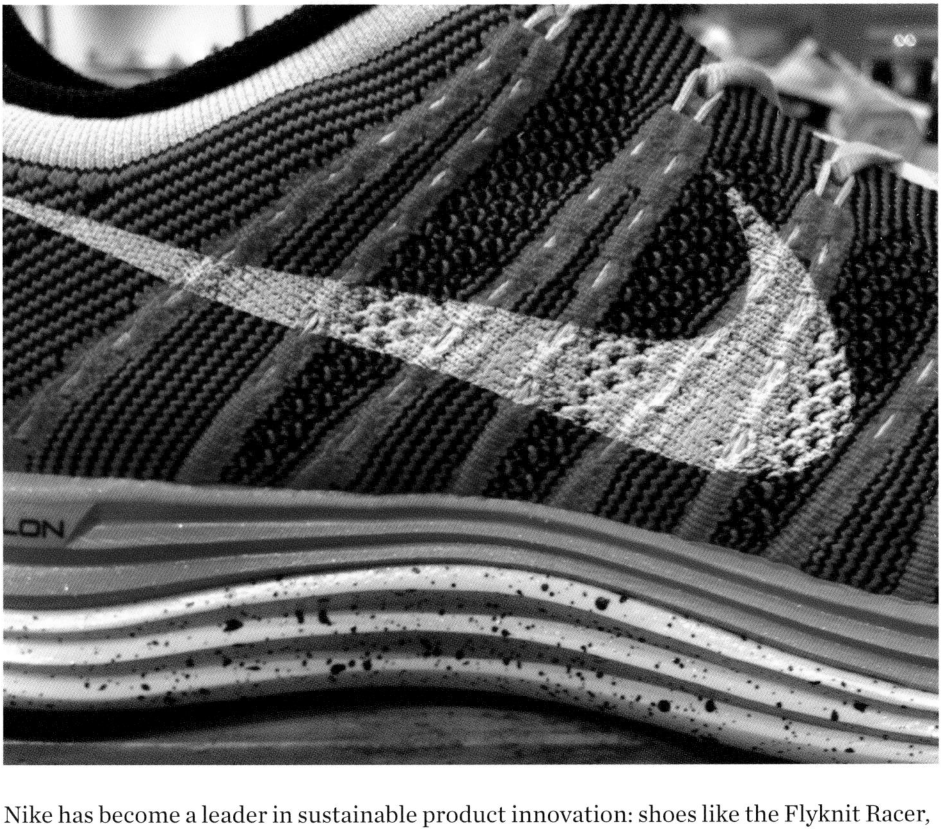

Nike has become a leader in sustainable product innovation: shoes like the Flyknit Racer, which is knitted like a sock, have lower environmental impact.

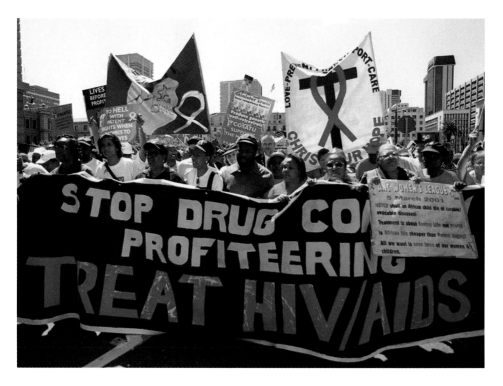

In 2001, as thousands were dying of HIV/AIDs, protestors in South Africa called on Big Pharma to make treatments affordable.

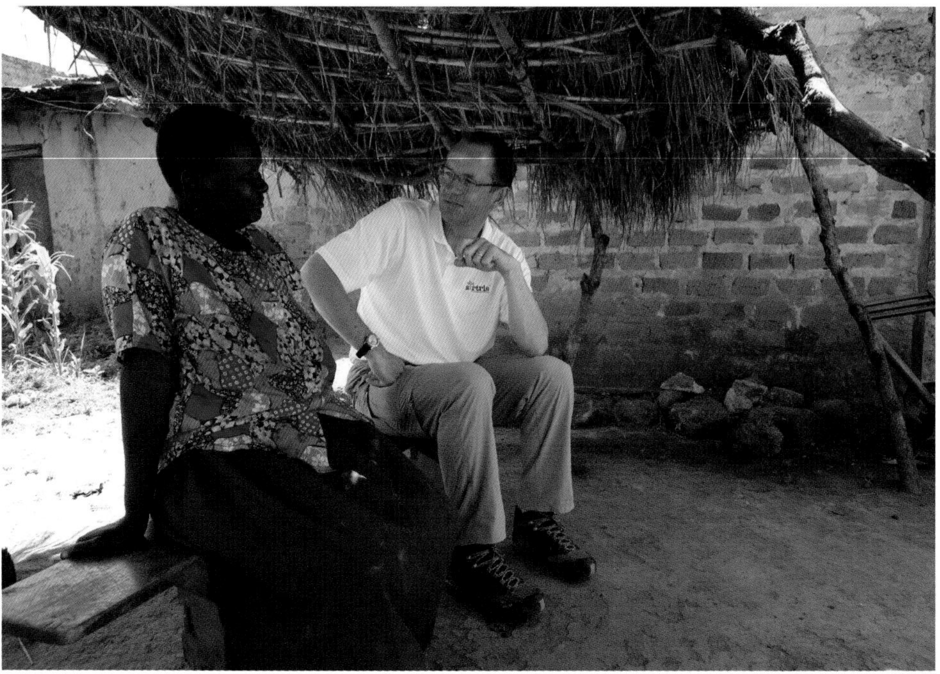

Andrew Witty, CEO of the pharmaceutical company GSK, with Aduwe Nosiante in Uganda. The company introduced new approaches to making life-saving drugs available in the world's poorest countries.

At any one time, 400,000 people are in the air on planes powered by Rolls-Royce engines. Each engine is assembled from thousands of precision parts from hundreds of suppliers.

A Rolls-Royce engineer shows us a single crystal turbine blade – literally grown from one crystal – which has been able to function in surrounding temperatures 200°C above its own melting point.

A familiar sight in rural India: farming is hard, back-breaking work using traditional methods such as ploughing with oxen.

A farmer demonstrating Mahindra's Yuvraj tractor, designed to be compact and affordable even for smallholders with only a few acres.

A 'system of systems': the City Operations Centre in Rio de Janeiro, part of IBM's *Smarter Cities* programme, makes the city work better.

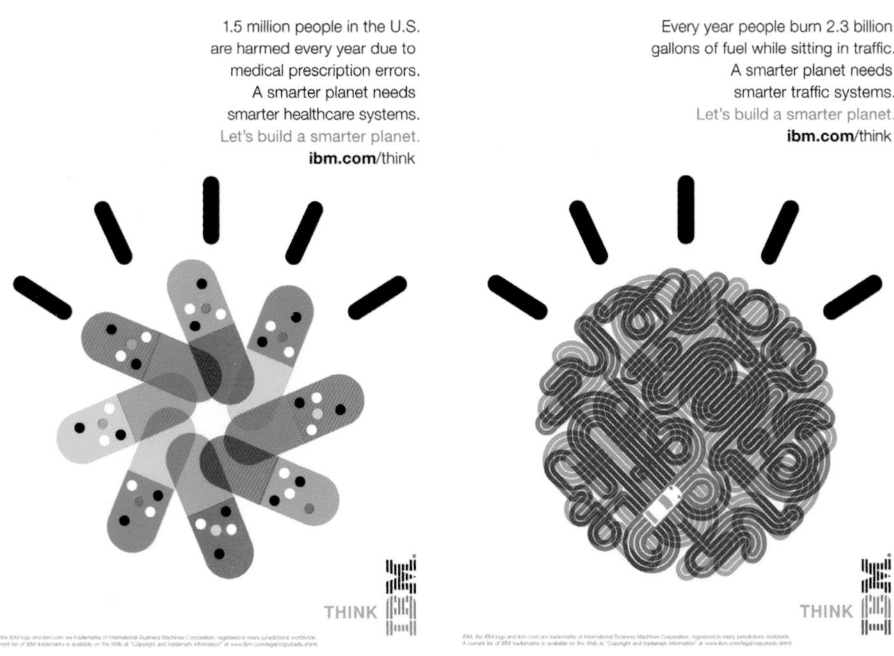

1.5 million people in the U.S.
are harmed every year due to
medical prescription errors.
A smarter planet needs
smarter healthcare systems.
Let's build a smarter planet.
ibm.com/think
THINK
IBM
Every year people burn 2.3 billion
gallons of fuel while sitting in traffic.
A smarter planet needs
smarter traffic systems.
Let's build a smarter planet.
ibm.com/think
THINK
IBM

IBM's *Smarter Planet* strategy has 'reconnected the business to society'. Even the ad campaign focuses on solving world problems.

LEFT In 2003, people across India demonstrated against perceived 'water thievery' by Western soft-drinks companies who, as a result, came close to losing their licence to operate in that country.

BELOW Water has risen up the agenda of many corporates. PepsiCo is recycling up to 75 per cent of its water at this plant in Arizona, part of a global programme to reduce the company's water use.

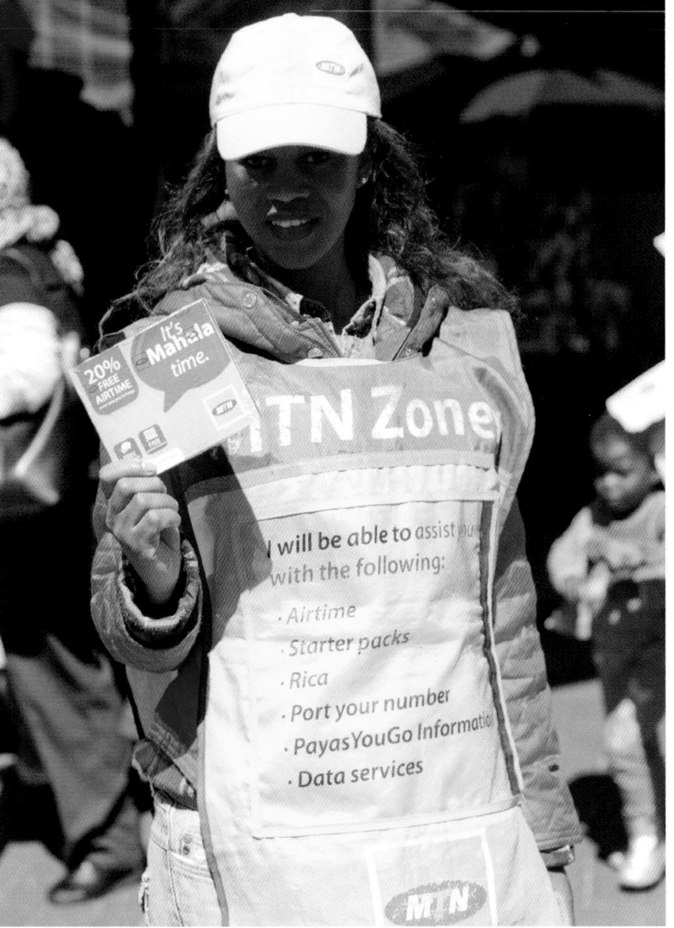

ABOVE A mobile is a lifeline for people in remote areas. MTN is the leading network operator in Africa and the Middle East and keeps the network running even in conflict zones such as Afghanistan.

LEFT An 'MTN Zoner' sells airtime on the roadside in Johannesburg. Through an informal network of street vendors, MTN is supporting livelihoods whilst generating additional revenues.

BHP Billiton operates the Escondida mine in Chile, which produces around 7 per cent of the world's copper. Extractive industries have long raised significant environmental and social concerns.

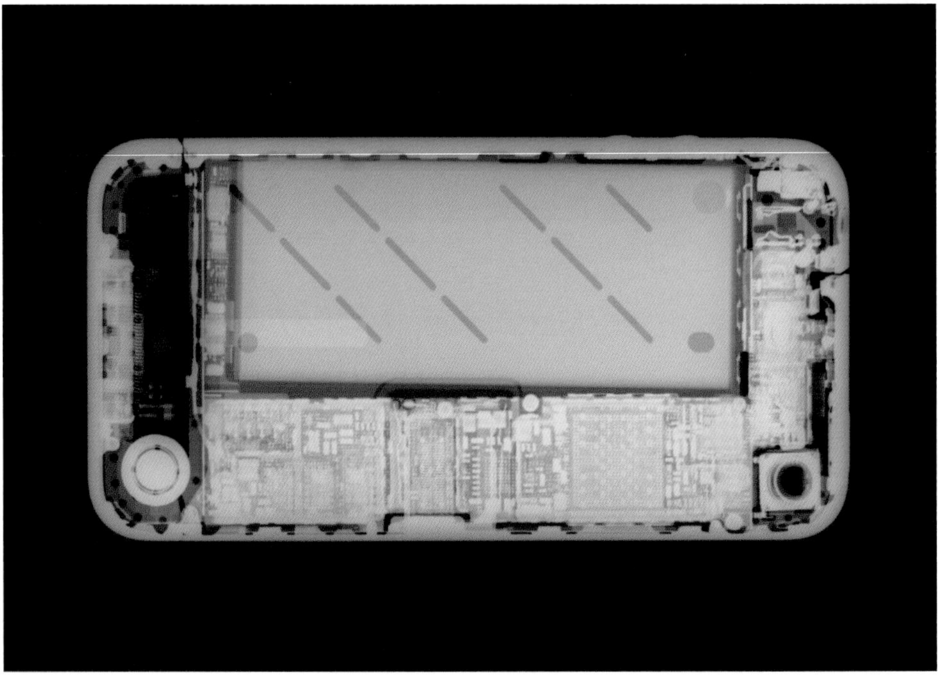

Modern lifestyles depend upon mining companies. Smartphones contain dozens of different metals and minerals, and there are concerns that some of these may come from conflict zones.

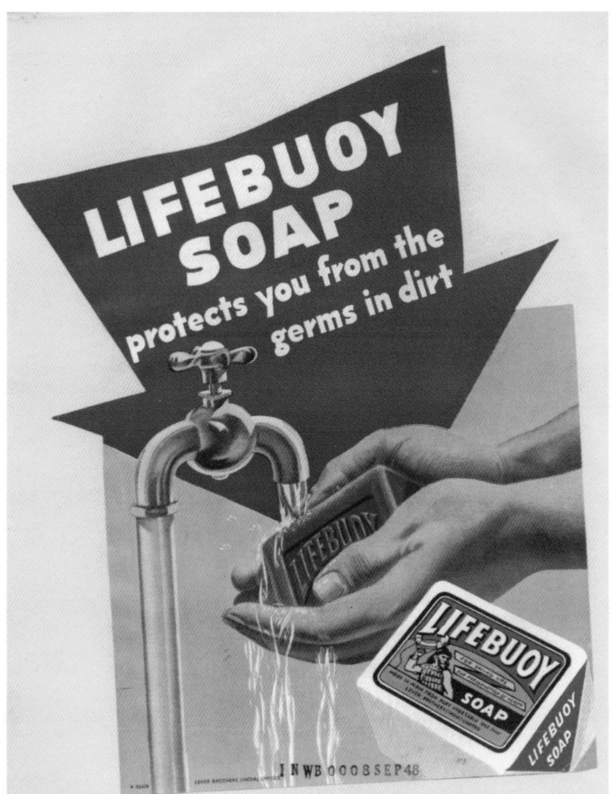

Unilever's Lifebuoy was the world's first branded, packaged soap. In cholera-ridden Victorian cities, it was a lifesaver. It was launched with the ambition 'to make cleanliness commonplace'.

Unilever's Lifebuoy runs hand-washing programmes all over the world. Every day 3,000 children die of diarrhoea: this could be halved by raising standards of hygiene.

On 1 January 2013, APP stopped their bulldozers clearing rainforest in Indonesia. The company had been reviled by environmentalists, and this was a moment many thought would never come.

Working to bring an end to deforestation in Indonesia: an agitator, a mediator and a corporate activist (Bustar Maitar, Scott Poynton and Aida Greenbury).

product and PepsiCo has established the basis of a reliable, scalable supply of sunflower oil to make healthier products. It sounds like a straightforward goal – reducing saturated fat – and so it's remarkable to see how it has unleashed such a wave of fresh thinking and new approaches across the company's operations: new ingredients, reformulated products and unexpected partnerships.

PepsiCo grows or sources four million tonnes of potatoes a year, three million tonnes of oranges and other fruits, and over half a million tonnes of oats for Quaker; the company is deeply involved in farming practices as well as policy. Take rice: growing rice is very water intensive. In India, with traditional growing methods it requires a mind-boggling 3,000 litres of water to produce one kilo of rice. That's a challenge for the company, for the farmers, as well as for the world. So scientists from inside the company worked in collaboration with the International Rice Research Institute and the Punjab Agricultural University to introduce a new technique into the process, called direct seeding. Where it's used, it eliminates the need to flood the fields. They're excited about the results: it's saved over 30 per cent of water consumed, reduced greenhouse gases by 70 per cent and improved the profitability of farmers. So far, their direct seeding technique has been adopted in seven states in India. And if it were to be taken up across the country for even half of the land used for paddy cultivation, they estimate, it just might save more water than is consumed by all industry combined. It's often hands-on, on-the-ground initiatives like these which are moving agriculture and sustainability forward in the developing world.

A few years ago, if someone had told you that a fizzy drinks company would be at the forefront of sustainable farming around the world you would have thought they'd been drinking their own Kool-Aid. Yet that's what's been happening at PepsiCo.

Dan Bena has become one of PepsiCo's leading authorities on water. He's easygoing and articulate – but this wasn't always the case. 'I was a pathologic introvert when I started at PepsiCo, twenty-eight years ago,' he tells us. 'I was a chemist in the lab, afraid of my own shadow. I didn't want to speak to anyone and I was so shy that my colleagues used to actually leave the lab just to get my coffee for me.' It's hard to imagine this now: Dan regularly appears on public platforms, addresses international institutions such as the World Economic Forum and has even testified before the US Senate. So what happened to the shy lab rat? 'It was the proverbial spark being lit, maybe fifteen years ago, when I attended a senior management meeting to talk about water scarcity,' he says. He had laid out the business risks that came from water scarcity, and found he had their undivided attention. Dan knew this was an issue of great importance to the business, and to the communities in which it operated – and the senior management wanted to hear what he had to say. It felt good. 'That was the spark, and once that spark got ignited I just ... there are not enough hours in the day, I mean I don't shut up! I love to talk about what PepsiCo is doing and I love to harness the power of what the private sector can bring.'

Increasingly, the topic has become a major area of concern for the world: global water use doubled between 1951 and 2002, and already three billion people live in areas of severe water scarcity. Within twenty years, demand for water is expected to outstrip foreseen supply by 40 per cent. Water scarcity is now recognised as one of the biggest challenges facing the world in the twenty-first century. And by the nature of what it does, water use has become a major issue for PepsiCo.

We asked Dan to describe for us the journey that PepsiCo has been on around its use of water. 'I think it's important to share the story, warts and all,' he says. 'Sharing all the lessons we have learnt is just as important as sharing all the awards and prizes we have gotten.' In 2003, PepsiCo faced the ire of communities in India who accused them of 'water thievery' – using up the water supply in their bottling plants, so there wasn't enough left for local people in water-stressed areas. PepsiCo commissioned hydro-geologists, who concluded the bottling plant wasn't the cause of the problem – but the local people simply refused to believe the data. 'They would see trucks every day go in and out of these plants filled with bottled water and filled with Pepsi and other beverages,' reflects Dan. 'How could they not draw the conclusion that we were stealing their water as their wells were dry?' Indian activists and politicians took up the cause, and the media fuelled public outrage. Calls grew for PepsiCo to be thrown out of India, together with Coca-Cola. A campaign was launched by Sunita Narain, an Indian activist from a family of freedom fighters who supported Gandhi's struggle for independence. Sunita Narain subsequently won the prestigious Stockholm Water Prize for drawing attention to water issues in India. PepsiCo had found themselves firmly on the wrong side of this story. 'You soon find out what the social licence to operate really means when you almost lose it overnight,' says Dan.

It began as a local problem but soon became a national issue in India; and whatever was happening on the ground, it soon became another global story of corporate malfeasance. It was a turning point for PepsiCo. Dan elaborates: the company became acutely aware that it could not take its licence to operate for granted. At a local level, the solution was surprisingly simple. 'I will never forget it and it cost just $15,000. We went into that community and built a well with the same rigour that we would build our own industrial wells. And we put in taps about every 150 feet in the village. So we were providing easy access to better quality water for the community,' Dan tells us, shaking his head in disbelief that it turned out to be so straightforward. 'It was just remarkable!' he exclaims, as if to say, *why didn't we just do this in the first place?*

Indra Nooyi made the issue a priority for the business when she became CEO in 2006. She grew up in India in a 'middle class' family, but even so she recalls filling up buckets with water before breakfast, before the municipal supply would shut off. Taking a bath still feels like a guilty pleasure. And aside from her personal understanding of what water access can mean for people, Indra sees it as a business issue for PepsiCo. She puts it bluntly: 'If we're going to do business in countries that are water starved, we can't be water hogs: we've got to figure out a way to help conserve water or we all lose.'

In the first phase of their work on water, beginning to understand and scope out the challenge more fully, the company did a project in partnership with The Nature Conservancy, a global NGO with a million members and water conservation programmes around the world. Kicking off their joint report on the work, The Nature Conservancy made a clear statement of their reason for collaborating with a big corporate:

> The Nature Conservancy is drawn to this partnership with PepsiCo because we want to work with companies that can help us bend the trajectory of our common water future toward a more positive outcome by promoting widespread adoption of sustainable water practices.

The Nature Conservancy's expertise in freshwater conservation deployed across PepsiCo's network of sites around the world created a powerful combination for real-world testing of methodologies and solutions. Together, they selected a number of very different geographies where PepsiCo has manufacturing facilities: Boxford in England, Zhanjiang in China, Sangareddy in India, Phoenix in the USA and Mexico

City. The task was to examine the local watershed, assess the sustainability of water use and design restoration activities to improve water availability and quality.

As PepsiCo had learnt the hard way, water scarcity may be a big global issue, but the impacts are very local. Each area has its unique pattern of rainfall, geographic features and water use. They developed a methodology which looked at every local watershed as a kind of 'water bank account' – representing the challenge to balance the deposits and withdrawals from the local water supply. Analysing how those things work together creates a vivid picture of the stresses and strains on water availability. And the pilots confirmed the merits of taking a local approach. As The Nature Conservancy reported: 'In contrast to the bleak appearance of the global water situation, we're finding that when we look closely at local watersheds and communities, many opportunities for better water management become apparent.'

With growing confidence that it would be possible to develop action plans that could make a practical difference, PepsiCo made three public commitments on water. First, to improve the efficiency of how they use water in their operations by 20 per cent by 2015 (against the base line of 2006). Second, to provide access to safe, clean drinking water to three million people in developing countries by the end of 2015. And finally, to aim for a positive balance in the 'water bank account' in all the water stressed areas where they work.

So how's the progress been? On the first goal – improving efficiency in their own operations – lots of relatively small wins across the world added up to hit the target in 2011, ahead of time. In total, PepsiCo conserved nearly 14 billion litres of water in 2012 in their factories, from a 2006 baseline, and saved the business $15 million in the process. Many projects contributed to this, and each has its own spark of ingenuity. In the USA, for instance, Gatorade devised a technique for cleaning bottles which uses purified air instead of water – which is now being adopted in bottling plants around the world saving billions of litres of water a year. In the UK, Walkers Crisps has developed a new technology to capture the natural moisture which comes from the processing of potatoes to make their major manufacturing facilities self-sufficient in water – making it possible to unplug from the water mains. In Colombia they've introduced a new technology, called a membrane bioreactor, which enables the food production facility to reuse three quarters of the water coming into the plant and conserve almost 90 million litres a year. Meanwhile back in the US, in recent years the state of Georgia has faced serious drought with aquifers running dry – and PepsiCo's plant responded by setting up 'leak patrols' with teams of people checking on every bit of their water system several times a day to put a stop to any leaks even as they spring up – and that approach has been picked up and adapted elsewhere across the PepsiCo network.

When it comes to the next of the big three water commitments – to provide clean water for three million people in developing countries by 2015 – the PepsiCo Foundation has been busy putting together a portfolio of partnerships with a cluster of not-for-profit organisations – each of which comes at the challenge from a different angle. The Earth Institute out of Columbia University, led by the economist Jeffrey Sachs, has played a significant role in trialling agricultural techniques, taking sophisticated technologies and making them affordable for the developing world. The Safe Water Network is focused on water purification; the China Women's Development Federation works with women in communities to get drinking water into some of the most water-scarce regions of China. The business has partnered with The Inter-American Development Bank in helping to finance a huge scheme to provide clean water for 500,000 people in Latin America by 2015; while Water.org has pioneered a microcredit scheme to provide tiny loans for access to water at the village level. Through the business and the foundation, PepsiCo has put around $35 million philanthropic dollars into schemes to deliver access to clean water since 2005. The funding matters, of course, but a key part of the value the business can add is the ability to scale a successful model. And it seems to be working: the 2015 goal to reach *three* million people with safe water was achieved in 2013 – and it was promptly doubled: the new goal is to reach another three million, making it a total of *six* million by 2016.

The third and final ambition – to create a positive balance in the water bank account in the water stressed areas where they operate – came alive most vividly in India. The full range of water conservation activities were brought into play, inside and outside their facilities, to add up to a positive balance for the first time in 2009. On the debit side of the account is always the manufacturing process. So all the work done to minimise their own operational water use – as part of the first water commitment – played a major part in achieving the positive balance. In the decade between 2001 and 2010, the water required to produce one litre of Pepsi in India was reduced sharply from 7.1 litres to 2.2 litres. Then on the credit side of the account is an array of schemes to replenish and recharge the local watershed. Action plans were developed on the basis of local water resource assessment studies. Many of the company's philanthropic projects in the country were directed towards access to water. For instance, around their plant in Paithan, Aurangabad, the business worked with the local community and municipal authorities to construct thirteen small dams, dig over 100 wells and establish water harvesting initiatives. It all added up to a billion litres of water recharged into the supply around the Aurangabad facility. And the PepsiCo corporate website for India proudly declared that they were the first business to achieve a positive water balance:

> 2009 was a year of immense pride and joy for PepsiCo India. We were able to give back more water than we consumed through our various initiatives of recharging, replenishing and reusing water.

The positive water balance at a country level was achieved again in 2010. And in 2011 the company restored almost 15 billion litres, against around 6.5 billion litres used by the manufacturing facilities. The reports which track progress on the work are stiff with numbers, audited by Deloitte. But the numbers lead directly to the impact on human experience. The pipe laid in Paithan to take drinking water into the local school had the knock-on effect of making it possible to cook meals for the children, which had the knock-on effect of increasing school attendance. With the improved availability of water, many farmers have found they can now plant twice in the year instead of once, and their incomes are rising.

Working in this way and in this detail over the years, PepsiCo has built up considerable technical expertise on the issues – from eco-efficiency in agriculture to the economics of water provision. Water has become an integral part of the way PepsiCo does business. The approach to achieving a positive water balance has evolved with experience. The trend is towards even more local understanding, with balances being weighed watershed by watershed. The emphasis is on even more sophisticated collaboration. So in Jordan today, for instance, PepsiCo is working in support of the Ministry for Water and Irrigation's national strategy for a positive water balance. As part of that, the company funded the construction of the Wadi Al-Ahmar dam project in Tafileh, which will harvest rain water for local community use and to restore natural ecosystems.

The company's approach weaves together three strands: the technical and process improvements in their own operations; hands-on programmes with a variety of NGOs all coming at the challenge from different directions; and the overall commitment to collaborate with governments, communities and other businesses – even competitors – to work towards a positive water balance.

PepsiCo is held up now as an example of what businesses can achieve when tackling the world's water issues. The story has turned around. In 2012 – seven years after the Stockholm International Water Institute gave their prestigious prize to Sunita Narain, a prominent critic of the company – the Stockholm Water Prize went to PepsiCo 'for its work to reduce water consumption in their operations and to help solve water challenges on a broad scale.'

Sanjeev Chadha went to Stockholm to receive that award on behalf of the company. He was a founding member of the PepsiCo business in India twenty years ago and has seen the whole story unfold from the beginning. Now as President of PepsiCo in the Middle East and Africa, he told the assembled experts of the continued progress in Paithan: transforming an arid landscape to put water in the wells, grow a second crop each year in the fields, and bring more children into the schools. It's only one project in the overall strategy but it captures their approach to the problem of access to water. As he said, it is 'Arguably, a life changing initiative, at a total cost of less than $100,000 – less than $10 per person.' It was evident how much the success meant to him personally:

> I have to tell you – experiencing Paithan first hand changed my life for sure. I was amazed that so little could transform so much so soon. It had also been personally one of the most gratifying experiences I have ever had.

PepsiCo has become an advocate on water issues, even leading the corporate sector in recognising access to water as a fundamental human right. As the United Nations declared in

2002: 'The right to water clearly falls within the category of guarantees essential for securing an adequate standard of living, particularly since it is one of the most fundamental human conditions for survival.' At the time, there was little response from the corporate world – in spite of the huge amounts of water consumed in manufacturing processes in all industries, few realised they had any role to play. PepsiCo set the pace when it formally recognised access to water as a basic human right in 2009 – and acted on that premise. Indra says becoming champions of the cause of the human right to water shifted the perspective in the business: it created a strategic requirement to actively protect and replenish water supplies, rather than simply to take measures to mitigate the demands made by its operations. Indra explains,

> We have a short-term responsibility to many stakeholders, but we also have a long-term responsibility. Companies must lead. We must lead in the marketplace. And we must lead in society. That's not just good for society, that's smart business.

It's smart and defensive. If you're a business that is dependent on plentiful supplies of water to manufacture your products, you need to secure that supply. If you operate in areas where water is scarce and demand is getting greater, you have to ask yourself why that society would continue to grant you access to their precious resource. If what you produce is not essential to life and the farmers around you cannot produce enough food for their communities to eat, you develop a strategy that makes you part of their solution to that problem. Along with many other multinationals today, PepsiCo is aware of the imperative to protect its licence to operate in society. Where businesses consistently fail to respond, they pay the price in ever greater penalties, high taxes and more stringent regulation that stifle their ability to operate commercially. It seems an abstract concept until you see it in action. Dan has found himself describing this to business leaders at meetings such as the World Economic Forum. He describes a complacency when it comes to a company's licence to operate:

> When you mention licence to operate to virtually any business leader, their heads will invariably shake in agreement, because they understand the concept and they understand the danger if that is taken away. What I think some people don't quite understand is the *magnitude*: the removal of the social licence to operate isn't a theoretical thing – it's a real, real possibility.

If the licence to operate is one motivator for business to get engaged, another is the sheer urgency of what needs doing. Sanjeev Chadha conveys that spirit when he urges action on the global water challenge:

> Being a person from the business world, the one thing I have been taught all my working life is that it is *action* that yields *results*. In the case of water and food security too, I believe we need – to borrow a phrase – JUST DO IT. Let's not wait for the perfect solution. Or 100 per cent funding. Or a totally risk-free strategy. These do not exist most of the time in the real world. We have no time to lose. If we have 80:20, or even a 60 per cent solution, it's time for action – at least to pilot the initiative.

Back in the quiet of the headquarters, in Purchase outside New York, we talk to Richard Delaney, PepsiCo's Senior Vice President of Global Operations. People in the company had described him to us as something of an elder statesman figure. Rich joined the company twenty-seven years ago, starting off as a project engineer, working his way up through plant, country and regional management and today running the entire operational machine – that means bringing together the manufacturing, engineering, quality control, logistics, transportation and purchasing activies of the business worldwide. It's not uncommon to hear a sustainability expert wax lyrical on the subject of water, maybe, but it is quite unusual to find a hard-core operations guy who dives into the subject with such enthusiasm and grasp of every detail. So we asked him why he sees it so central to his role:

> It's been amazing to see how the sustainability agenda has energised our organisation. Not just the operations personnel but right across the organisation. Whenever I speak about it with groups of people internally, the response is just overwhelming due to the subject matter. I mean, I've never been involved in a subject which is such an open door for folks in PepsiCo. And it's because every single individual connects with the fact that the work they're doing impacts the community that they live in. That is the way we wanted to set it up: we say it's about making a positive impact in the communities where we do business.

The proof, he tells us, of the energy in the business around water conservation is in how people have got behind the goals. 'When we first set out our goal to reduce our intensity of water use in our operations, looking back, we didn't fully know what we were signing up for,' he admits. 'And I can say that personally because I was right in the middle of that process. But the issue really speaks to people in the organisation, they got energised and they just blew right past the goal. We hit it four years early. That means literally tens of thousands of people put their minds and hands into achieving that result. And I'm very, very, very proud of that. Then when it came to what we could do to help get access to clean water to three million people in the communities we operate in, they blew right past that goal too a couple of years early'. But there are sceptics out there, we say to him; not every operations director sees sustainability as core to the day-to-day business: what would he say to them?

> I talk them through how we came to that conclusion ourselves. There are a number of proof points that got us there. First, we say that conservation and sustainability is a critical component of our licence to operate. Think about the nature of what we do: we produce beverages – which require heavy water use. We sell in over two hundred countries and produce in almost as many, so by definition our operations are extremely diverse and local, and our licence to operate is dependent on how we manage our resources in every one of those communities. Second, it resonates with all the constituencies we want to connect with: customers, consumers, governments, NGOs. It's a topic on which we all agree and a topic on which we can collaborate. Third, and not least, it drives productivity. We're in the business of reducing our cost structure and resource conservation helps us do that.

We were talking to Rich as the PepsiCo delegation was flying out to Stockholm again to World Water Week, one year on from winning the international prize. He sees being awarded the prize last year as an affirmation of their strategy of working internally on the operations and externally with partners, simultaneously, 'But it's far from the end of it, far from the end. Every year we know more than the year before. And therefore every year we're setting our sights higher.'

This year, the team is travelling with a cluster of their major NGO partners to share what they've learnt about the relative merits of the different approaches to making water more accessible to more people. It was a conscious strategy in PepsiCo to have a portfolio of partners and test out a variety of ways of tackling the challenges. Between them all, the business and the NGOs, they've now got considerable practical experience, they've developed methodologies and evaluated progress, and they're keen to present what they've found so far; what works and what doesn't. There's a growing community of experts gathering around the subject of the global water challenge and PepsiCo sees their role as bringing what they know to the table and participating in the dialogue with the broader world to figure out what is possible. 'There are a lot of areas where as a corporation we compete, but this isn't one of them,' says Rich. 'We believe that everything we do should be open and available in the public domain.'

Reminding ourselves that Rich's day job is running the global operations, we return to the subject of why all this matters to the business. 'While my role today is at headquarters, over my time in the company, I've spent many years working outside the US, all over the world,' he says. 'While our reach is global, really wherever we have facilities or distribution chains, our operations are very local. Our employees live in the communities they work in and care about those communities. We have to have a licence to operate in those communities. Access to safe drinking water in those communities, and having enough water for everyone's needs – including ours as a business – is a pressing issue.' Stepping back from the detail of the delivery challenge for a moment, he speaks in his capacity as a senior executive of one of the world's biggest businesses:

> I think we play an important leadership role as a multinational, as well. Maybe I flatter us, but through the

> example of what we're doing, we can draw people in this direction. And I find it's not a hard sell. People see it. People get there. More and more corporations I think are seeing their responsibility and acting on it in their communities.

Indra Nooyi was born and raised in India, but she didn't yield to traditional ideas of how a young Indian woman should behave. She played guitar in a rock band, and was one of the first women cricketers who played for her country. But mostly she studied. 'I had a very strict upbringing which said, "As long as you get good grades you can do anything you want, but if your grades are not good forget it."' It was a useful lesson for a woman who would become Chief Financial Officer and then CEO and chairman of a major multinational: keep delivering the results, and you buy yourself room to manoeuvre. When Indra took the helm of PepsiCo, one of her first big overseas trips was back to India, where she made a speech that would define her leadership. It was a December evening in New Delhi, and the city's business elite assembled to welcome a daughter of India at an event hosted by the American Chamber of Commerce. She told her audience that financial achievement 'can and must' go hand in hand with social and environmental performance. Business can do well for itself, she explained, by contributing to societal problems – citing as examples population growth, urbanisation, poverty, health, access to water and climate change. She summarised this philosophy with a phrase: 'performance with a purpose'.

This point of view was ahead of its time. Indra made her speech shortly after an article appeared in the *McKinsey Quarterly*, entitled 'When Social Issues Become Strategic', that lamented the failure of many business leaders to come to grips with the 'social contract':

> Businesses have never been insulated from social or political expectations. What's different today is the intensifying pressure and the growing complexity of the forces, the speed at which they change, and the ability of activists to mobilise public opinion. Yet even as the social contract evolves, the typical corporate response appears to have become increasingly flat-footed.[55]

Nobody could accuse Indra of being flat-footed in this area. She can often be heard reminding people inside and outside the company about the social contract – 'Business does not operate in a vacuum – it operates under a licence from society,' she says. As she told the *Financial Times*, 'We're constantly watching the changing societal trends and looking at the interplay between corporations and societies.' She made these remarks in an interview at the World Economic Forum in 2010, as the global economy was still freshly rocked by the financial crisis. It was a rude awakening for many business leaders, who sensed a sudden loss of legitimacy. The social contract was more fragile than they had realised. 'Everybody is talking about the new rules of capitalism,' Indra had told the *FT*. 'Don't just think about the company within the four walls of the company, think about your obligations to society.'

Against this backdrop, PepsiCo crystallised this approach into a business strategy which they called *Performance With Purpose*. Indra describes the thinking:

> Increasingly the focus was shifting from corporate capability to corporate character. A new understanding was taking shape that responsibility and growth are not just linked, but inseparable. We encapsulated that thought into a simple phrase: *Performance With Purpose*. In short, it is our belief that our long-term profitable growth (our Performance) is linked intrinsically to our ability

> to deliver on our social and environmental objectives (our Purpose).

Talking to people at PepsiCo, you're struck by the seriousness of the intent behind *Performance With Purpose* – whether it's shifting the portfolio towards healthier foods, reformulating products to cut down on the salt, sugar and fat content, or taking on wider issues such as water use. *Performance With Purpose* seems to be more than a corporate brand position – although it does have a positive effect on the company's reputation. Within the last few years, PepsiCo has been named one of the World's Most Admired Companies by *Fortune*, one of the most innovative by *Fast Company*, one of the most respected by *Barron's* and one of the most ethical by *Ethisphere*. Indra Nooyi, meanwhile, spent five consecutive years in the number one spot on *Fortune* magazine's '50 Most Powerful Women' list. Having a clearly articulated, purpose-driven stance on the relationship between the business and society has generated significant goodwill towards the company.

One of the major business benefits, everyone recognises, is recruitment. It has proven itself to be a differentiator, especially in the younger age range – employees between twenty-five and thirty years old. Indra talks about it as a 'signal to our employees that we recognise that they are first wives, husbands, mothers, fathers, daughters, sons and citizens of every country in which they live and work.'

But key to it all is that it is core to the company's business strategy. It aims to secure the long-term supply of vital raw materials, including water. At the same time, it focuses attention on the long-term revenue growth to be gained by reorienting the company towards healthier products. So it creates the impetus to shift resources, R&D spend and marketing efforts to support that new direction. 'To do that you've still got to use the powerful engine of the profit that comes from the classic core. Without that you can't make the changes needed to achieve long-term growth: that's what *Performance With Purpose* is trying to do.' Even so, it all takes time, so this commitment has not been without its critics. Some investors have called for a greater focus on the original core business: selling potato chips and soda. And the pressure is always on to deliver the next quarter's results. It's a tension facing many businesses that are attempting to align their strategies with big societal trends, in order to achieve long-term growth.

Reflecting on the issue, Derek Yach described how he sees these dual demands:

> I think we're living in this interesting era where, on the one hand, businesses are being hit for going too fast and, on the other hand, they're being hit for going too slow. That's why Indra's consistently said it's not a question of either/or, it's a question of both/and. The tricky thing, of course, is that the stream of benefits to investors flow at different times for different parts of sustainability programmes. For example, many environmental initiatives – lowering water use, lower energy use – hit the bottom line relatively quickly. So the returns are more immediately obvious to many people inside a company and to shareholders: you use less stuff, you pay for less stuff. Whereas shifting a core portfolio takes longer and is more complex for many reasons.'

Indra is acutely aware of managing this balance, summing it up as having 'to think in terms of both quarters and generations'. When asked how she responds to those people who say PepsiCo should focus more on its traditional 'fun for you' products, she explains patiently, 'We're investing in both parts of the portfolio. As many critics as we have who say "forget the good for you" and focus on the "fun for you", we have an equal number of critics who say "why aren't you focusing more on 'good for you'?".' Finding the right path through these competing demands is central to her job. 'I think the role of the CEO is to be able to thread this needle,' she says. 'You have to balance it. You can't say to Wall Street, "Oh give me a few years whilst I develop this portfolio and then I'll give you a return".' Instead, the company needs to continue delivering the results, while reshaping the business for the future. It's a journey PepsiCo seems wholeheartedly to have embraced – and many across the world of business are watching to see if they pull it off.

Over a billion PepsiCo products are consumed somewhere in the world, every day, and that gives the business huge reach, influence and operating capability. Indra recognises that companies the scale of PepsiCo have become significant actors on the world stage. 'Companies should not forget that we are big, we are engines of efficiency and effectiveness,' she says. 'Many times we are bigger than small countries. Today's problems of the world cannot be solved by governments alone, or by people alone, but only by partnership between companies and governments.' Still, Indra is clear that *Performance With Purpose* isn't just about solving problems in the world, but about keeping the business on track: 'We have to disrupt our businesses before they disrupt us. We have to transform our strategies and our business models to cater for these new world realities'.

10

THE WEALTH IN THE EARTH

The business of mining incites anger and concern. Whatever you're digging up, extraction is a brutal process. Resources are finite. The money involved is huge. The power of the companies equipped to do it is enormous. So there's a lot to be concerned about.

Many of the cultural archetypes of bad business are drawn from the mining sector. The highest grossing film of all time when it was released in 2010, *Avatar* tells the story of a native tribe of the planet Pandora whose existence is threatened by the ruthless and cynical expansion of mining for a precious metal, called Unobtanium. The film *Blood Diamond* puts the spotlight on the grim reality of diamonds mined and sold to finance conflict in fragile states in Africa. They're dramatic storylines, drawing on real-world contrasts: some of the world's biggest most powerful and technologically advanced companies landing from an alien culture to work the land inhabited by some of the world's least powerful and least technologically advanced communities. Desperate boy soldiers toting guns to traffic gemstones that will glitter around the necks of beautiful, rich women. Pristine landscapes and delicate ecosystems transformed into craters and mountains of discarded waste.

For all those reasons, there are some who'll find it impossible to countenance that the mining sector could appear in a book on the potential for business to play a positive role in society. For us, that's all the more reason to include it. If so many people feel the potential for harm is so great, why do we even do it? What is it doing for us? How is it being done? Where will progress come from?

Mining is a vast industry. The world's appetite for minerals is voracious: aluminium, copper, lead, zinc, gold, silver, uranium oxide, diamonds, iron ore, coal. These companies generate enormous sums of cash, and they invest at a colossal rate. Just one of these mining giants, BHP Billiton, is expected to invest around $18 billion in 2014. To put that in perspective, that's twice Unilever's entire operating profit for 2012. It would take Twitter eighteen years to earn that much money, at current revenues. So the major mining companies are giants of business. We wanted to take a closer look and so we started with one of the biggest. BHP Billiton is headquartered in Australia, with operations in 100 countries. We went to meet Chip Goodyear, who was CEO of BHP Billiton for several years in the 2000s – a period of immense change for the industry. We met him in the elegant lounge of a hotel in London's Mayfair – but make no mistake, Chip has heavy industry in his blood. Charles Waterhouse Goodyear IV – known across the industry as Chip – grew up in the USA with a family history rooted in traditional American industries, such as lumber and rail and, of course, tyres. By the time Chip Goodyear became CEO, BHP Billiton was one of the largest publicly listed companies in the world – though many people don't even know its name.

'I remember when I arrived at BHP in 1999, mining was definitely something that nobody in the developed world cared about. Nobody appreciated that the way we live today wouldn't be possible without resources,' he told us. It was the time of the dot.com boom and the virtual world seemed more exciting than the physical world, and the heavy-lifting industries seemed somehow old-hat. 'I remember one reporter saying to me, 'Why would you want to come here? I mean this is yesterday's business.' And I said to him, 'Without the stuff we do, what you do wouldn't be possible.'

The products of the mining industry are all around us, an ever-present but often unnoticed part of our daily lives. Take the mobile phone, for example: it is the icon of our time, ubiquitous and democratising. There are now more of them than people on the planet. And recently there's been growing awareness that for them to work their magic, they require tin, tungsten and tantalite – the '3Ts' of mining. Similarly, our laptops and tablets wouldn't work without a cocktail of minerals and so-called 'rare earths' that many of us had hardly heard of until a few years ago. The mining industry underpins our new digital technologies, as much as it underpinned the arrival of railroads, cars and planes when they first revolutionised everyone's lives.

It's not always obvious, but many of the high priority items on the global agenda rely on mining – even the search for renewable energy sources. Politicians proudly announce new investments in green tech, companies win applause for shifting their operations away from oil dependency to renewables. Wind power is the fastest growing renewable in many countries – yet none of it could happen without the aluminium and steel for the great blades and towers, and the cobalt and rare earths in the batteries – and the copper cable that takes the electricity to the grid. Copper is the great conductor.

Reducing poverty in developing countries is another priority globally – and mining plays an unseen role even here. 'Lack of access to electricity results in health, environmental, and livelihood challenges,' according to Worldwatch, an independent research institute. Although two billion more people on the planet got electricity between 1990 and 2008, more than 1.3 billion still don't have it. 'Eradicating energy poverty is a moral imperative,' declares Maria van der Hoeven, Director of the International Energy Agency. The single naked bulb lighting up the night in a remote village is an evocative image of progress – but it too relies on the copper cable to conduct the power. A new device which can get electricity to millions of people who live beyond the reach of a grid is a solar-powered lantern that stores energy from the day's sunlight: this needs copper as well, along with around fifteen other minerals and metals required to produce solar panels. If access to electricity is an imperative for rural development, then copper is a basic building block of development.

The value of what mining companies like BHP Billiton bring to society is evident. In many different ways, the materials that are dug out of the ground underpin today's world, and tackling tomorrow's challenges would be impossible without access to these resources. So the issue isn't *what* they do, but *how* they do it. During the 1990s, the spotlight turned on the big miners for their role in environmental disasters and human rights scandals. BHP Billiton invested in the Ok Tedi mine in Papua New Guinea where the waste dam burst, and Rio Tinto, another of the mining majors, has also faced long-running criticism for environmental damage caused in Papua New Guinea by its Grasberg mine. In both cases, environmental activists say that tens of millions of tonnes of waste from the mines were disgorged into the rivers, destroying life in the river, polluting the surrounding land and ruining livelihoods for people around the sites.[56] For many, these terrible cases epitomised the behaviour of the mining industry.

Public pressure was mounting. Chip agrees that the way the industry used to act would be unacceptable today: it paid less regard to the concerns of society and often viewed critics as 'getting in the way'. It had grown inured to criticism. But, slowly, mining was embarking on its own journey, and Chip credits Bob Wilson, the chairman of Rio Tinto at the time, with making the first move: 'Bob took a leadership role. He was concerned that we would lose our licence to operate in society. And it was as a result of those incidents, no doubt about it. The industry leadership began to say, "We've got to change the way we do things."'

In 1999 Bob Wilson assembled nine of the top chairmen and CEOs in mining and kick-started the Global Mining Initiative. It became clear the industry was changing its stance. Speaking at an international conference two years later, Bob Wilson explained how the initiative began: 'Crucial to the programme was a willingness by the company leaders concerned to acknowledge that the industry has a case to answer in terms of both its environmental and social performance. The way forward should not be by hopeless efforts to sway public opinion but rather to accept that we have made mistakes and to actively engage with and listen to our critics, to help us to define priority areas to try to improve performance.'[57] He talked about the original impetus behind the need for reform:

> Increasing public antipathy has been evident for at least two decades. The industry had made a number of attempts to balance these perceptions with public relations campaigns, advertising and education programmes. Our products, after all, are fundamental to modern economic life and our fiercest critics are dependent on mined materials for their transport, cooking, power transmission, communications, indeed just about every aspect of their lives. The industry campaigns of rebuttal therefore tended to focus on either the ignorance or the sheer hypocrisy of its critics. It is clear though that this sort of industry response has achieved absolutely nothing. It was time for a rethink.

Their starting point was to take stock of the issues. They recognised the need for that to be done independently and worked with the International Institute for Environment and Development (IIED), the well-respected NGO led by Richard Sandbrook, who carried out an analysis of the main challenges facing the industry and put forward a plan of action. It was the beginning of a new journey for the major mining companies. The informal group first gathered by Bob Wilson had set a new agenda and – as important – a more responsive attitude. They took a shared set of principles into the global arena at the World Summit of Sustainable Development in South Africa in 2002:

> Instead of being seen as part of the problem [as we were] ten years ago, we intend to show that we are part of the solution by defining what our contribution to sustainable development will be. The Global Mining Initiative itself is a change agent; it has no institutional structure and it is not intended to be permanent. But its processes are designed to serve the future. We realise this is not a quick fix. Sustainable development is a journey rather than a destination.

The Atacama Desert in Chile is the driest place on the planet. In the vast open landscape of dusty red earth, you could be on the surface of Mars. It's the site of Escondida, the world's biggest copper mine, operated by BHP Billiton. It's an extraordinary man-made spectacle: two huge craters, 600 metres deep, have been carved out in sharply cut terraces. Enormous trucks, with wheels twice the height of a man, carry rough rock for crushing or transport the copper for export to BHP Billiton's own port at Coloso. Escondida produces around 7 per cent of the world's copper.

'Copper is the biggest earner for the Chilean economy,' says Chip – in fact, this one mine represents 2 per cent of the Chilean economy. But, as he explains, the value isn't just at a national level: 'What you see there is how the operation is integrated into the community at a local level as well.' The mine is a vivid demonstration of the journey that mining companies have been on: an example of a systematic approach to delivering social and economic value to the host countries they work in.

One of the more surprising impressions of the place is the massive scale of the operations juxtaposed with the detail of life in the local community. Under the tall cranes in Coloso harbour, beside the great cargo ships, tiny colourful fishing boats bob around festooned with flags. One fisherman remembers back to the time before Escondida came: 'If Minera Escondida hadn't come to Coloso we would have been in a bad way here. Fishing was going badly and we were having a really hard time.' What they lacked was basic infrastructure, so Escondida built the dock with loading areas around it, which has made it much easier for the fishermen to get their catch to market. But beyond that, what the local people value most is the mine's social investment into the area, according to the President of Coloso Fishing Group, Henry Rodrigues: 'The most remarkable work we're doing with Minera Escondida has been in health and education for the development of our community, especially training for our women and our young adults,' he says.

There's no local community around the mine itself in the desert but its closest neighbour, 100 kilometres away, is San Pedro de Atacama, a small town which earns much of its living from tourism. Intrepid travellers come for the hot springs and the pre-Colombian history. Escondida has put money into the local museum and built a library. As part of its community programme, the mine set up English language courses for the people who work with the town's foreign visitors. 'English is an international language and everyone speaks it except us, so we were at a loss,' explains Sandra Berna, San Pedro's Mayor. 'We hope our children learn English so they can use it as a tool for the future.' The company built two language labs, one at the primary school and one at the high school.

At the higher education level, Escondida works with the University Catolica del Norte to help develop centres of scientific expertise in this 'second region' of Chile, as it's called. As well as funding, the mine brings professional engineers into the university setting. Cecilia Demergasso, Director of the Biotechnology Institute, says it's this link with the mine that helps to elevate the status of the university: 'It means that there are labs all around the world who are interested to come to our labs to learn new techniques,' she says. It's a pattern that's repeated in the company's involvement in other universities around Chile, including Antofagasta and Santiago.

Each of these makes its own contribution and helps to weave the mining operation into the fabric of the local communities it works in. Yet the real story on education is building technical skills for the country. In Antofagasta, for example, the Centro de Entrenamiento Industrial Minero is where people come to learn the skills they need to prepare them for jobs in the industry. Set up with an initial investment of $10 million from Escondida to train people for its own operations, it's been opened up to other students. And with thousands coming every year – including some from as far afield as Peru, Bolivia and Argentina – the centre has become a leading technical training college for mining in the region.

Chile has been one of South America's most stable economies and in the World Economic Forum's Global Competitive Report it ranks higher than any other Latin American country. Mining accounts for more than 20 per cent of GDP, provides more than 100,000 jobs directly and supports 500,000 more through the supply chain. Escondida may be the biggest single operation but it's only one of thousands of mining companies of many different kinds in the country. 'Mining is Chile's engine,' according to Hernan de Solminihac, the Minister for Mining.

The country has an enormous wealth of natural resources, but without the skills in the population, it quite simply cannot get it out of the ground. Yet Chile has a significant skills gap looming: it's estimated that there's a need for an additional

25,000 skilled people by 2020 to work at all levels of the industry: engineers, operators, technical and maintenance. Unsurprisingly, BHP Billiton is very involved in tackling this, working with the government on an ambitious national programme. Osvaldo Urzua spearheads that effort for Escondida. Though he's an industrial engineer by training, Osvaldo tells us that what's dominated his thinking for twenty years is getting to the core of what drives successful development in an emerging economy, like his native Chile. So he's worked in government, in consultancy and in academia before arriving at BHP Billiton. He travelled to the UK to the internationally renowned centre of Science and Technology Policy Research to do his PhD on what it takes to create world-class supply chains. BHP Billiton hired him to put his thesis to practical use.

Osvaldo sees this huge skills programme as one way in which he can do that: he sees it as equipping Chile for the future: 'It's building the core strength of the country,' he says. Extensive research has gone into modelling and adapting the competencies, training systems and qualifications frameworks of advanced mining economies, such as Australia. 'We have to develop new capabilities that will enable us to grab the opportunity we have here.' Fundacion Chile, set up by Escondida, will be the first place to trial the new system. 'This programme requires a collaborative approach, a high degree of coordination,' he stresses. 'We can't be doing this instead of government, we have to work together. And with the other major mining companies and the education institutes. This is about agreeing the development agenda and working on it together.'

Osvaldo speaks passionately about the scheme funded by Escondida which offers fifty postgraduate scholarships a year to young Chileans. 'Social mobility is very important to Chile. This is a fragmented society – so giving people the skills to progress in their lives is essential to our continued development. It's how we will close the gap between rich and poor,' he says emphatically. It's a philanthropic programme but it plays its part in the overall strategic objective of Escondida to contribute to the socio-economic development of the country. 'The scholarship helps to support social mobility because it makes it possible for people to participate in a Master's programme who would never have been able to afford it otherwise,' he continues. 'It's for studies which have a focus on globalisation: people who want to be entrepreneurs, or, who want to work in multinational organisations as managers. They don't have to work for us afterwards. But it lifts them to another level in their lives and then that will have an impact in the next generation too.'

Nurturing the growth of local businesses is perhaps the most direct way that BHP Billiton can strengthen the skills base of the community it operates in. Escondida buys from many local companies, spending billions of dollars with them every year. Its goal is to build the capabilities of the local supply base and enable 250 of them to become world-class operators in their own right. This programme is at the heart of Osvaldo's work: he's designed it, it's his baby, and he's very proud of it. 'It's a challenge-based programme which really stretches them,' he tells us. 'We set each of them a challenge: for example, to reduce water use, to automate certain processes, to monitor dust levels more effectively. They have to innovate to come up with new solutions – ideas they have never tried out before.' The suppliers participating in the programme get to test out their solutions in the real working environment of the mine – and, as he explains, that's a rare and valuable opportunity for any small entrepreneurial tech company. The challenge is designed to prompt them to expand their networks across the industry and make links with universities to develop their research. When it began in 2009 there were just five suppliers involved and now there are more than sixty. It's already won awards and recognition from the

Chilean President, and Escondida is now sharing the methodology to get other big mining businesses on board. 'Because of the programme, these businesses are beginning to develop cutting-edge technologies of their own. At the same time, we get stronger suppliers and, for Chile, the programme helps to identify potential knowledge-based exports. It's designed to work for everyone.'

Conymet is one of Escondida's success stories. Manuel Medel is Managing Director of Conymet, the firm his father founded in the 1970s. He tells us how the company went from a small family firm to a global business. 'In the early days, all we were capable of doing was repairs,' he says ruefully. Then in the 1990s, as foreign investment came rushing into Chile's mining sector, the company began to grow very fast. Manuel took his cue from Escondida. As he puts it, 'One of the main signatures of Escondida's style in our region is to encourage the development of new technologies to increase production for the mine.'

The big win for Conymet came in 2001 when they came up with a new design for the large trucks which transport the rock. The tray, as the immense container on the trucks is called, takes a battering with every shovel load of 80 tonnes that gets tipped into it. 'We introduced a suspended rubber base under the tray to cushion the impact on the truck. It protects the whole of the chassis and the tyres, which means the truck needs less maintenance, less hours off the road, and offers increased productivity.' Simple but very effective. It worked on Escondida's trucks and turned Manuel into an urbane international businessman. There's a real sense of achievement in his smile as he lists the countries he exports to today: Australia, Canada, USA ... France, England, Finland ... New Guinea, Indonesia, Vietnam, Cambodia... 'The opening for that was the fact of working with Escondida locally,' he grins.

It's become part of how the big mining companies work: building social infrastructure around their operations. It's part of the deal. Roads, ports, water treatment plants, energy grids, community centres, clinics, schools, training centres and university labs. It's almost taken for granted by the people we speak to. Today, when people are talking about the positive impact the mining companies can have, it's often about enabling people to raise their game for the future, and that takes many forms: it may be literacy levels at a community level, or skilled jobs for local people, global links for universities, access to new markets for suppliers, exports for the country. The commitment of Escondida to create social and economic value in Chile represents progress for the mining sector – and seems a far cry from the days when the mining industry paid scant regard to the concerns of society.

Relationships between the big mining companies and the local communities are not always harmonious, however. Examples like Escondida are not easy to achieve, and conflicts continue to flare up. Recent times have seen significant protests and disturbances all over the world, including Australia, Canada, South Africa, USA and Peru. A study in 2012 by the Harvard Kennedy School of Government explored the factors involved by bringing together employees from a number of mining companies in Peru, where demonstrations and violence have brought mining operations to a halt in the past few years.[58] The study found that sometimes the challenges come down to the simple matter of human interaction. It was summed up by one of the participants in the study: 'It's a culture loaded up with a bunch of engineers and project types ... how do you give many of those people, especially the business types who've never worked in a context like this ... [an understanding of what's involved?].'

Engineers – often more comfortable with equipment than

people – with large projects to deliver, big budgets and tight timelines don't always communicate well with local people about what worries them. One of the conclusions of the study is that success relies on the ability of the community relations team to 'translate' the communities' priorities to the technical staff, as well as to the senior management. These days all the major mining companies have teams focused on community relationships and in BHP Billiton, we were told, in some places where the issues are complex and sensitive there may be as many as fifty people whose job it is to get this right.

Meanwhile, communities have become a force to be reckoned with. Social media tools mean that an egregious local incident can become a global crisis instantly. People have the means to learn about the experiences of other communities like themselves, even if they live on opposite sides of the world. They know how to contact activists who can take up their cause. And they have greater expectations than before about how they should benefit from the profits that a big business generates by extracting resources from the land they live on.

Getting it wrong with local communities has proved very costly for the corporates. A study by Goldman Sachs showed that the time it takes for a project to come on line had almost doubled in the previous ten years, leading, of course, to significant cost increases[59]. An analysis of delays associated with a sample of 190 of the world's largest oil and gas projects showed that only 21 per cent were due to technical risk, while 73 per cent of project delays were for non-technical reasons – such as objections from local communities. Small wonder then that competent handling of community relationships has become an integral part of risk management. And investors have learnt to ask about it. When BHP Billiton took investors out into the Atacama Desert to see Escondida for themselves, for example, the introductory presentation for the visit outlined the mine's approach to health, safety, environment and community as reassurance of the basics of a well-run operation before turning to the main business of the day: the production capacity and growth potential of the asset.

Risk management is a core competency of mining; in fact, delivering any large project is all about managing risks. So once building strong relationships with the host community becomes recognised as an integral part of project delivery, it tends to get incorporated into plans, and monitored and acted on effectively. Nowhere illustrates that more vividly than Mozal.

On the other side of the world from Escondida, Mozal is the aluminium smelter operated by BHP Billiton in Mozambique. Entering Mozambique in the late 1990s was risky and the company's commitment to build Mozal was the first foreign investment in the country after the long civil war. A million people had died from fighting and starvation and the economy was devastated. To get the aluminium smelter up and running required not just building the plant but the road and bridge to reach to the port, expanding the port facilities and strengthening the electricity grid to cope with the demands of large-scale production.

Aluminium production requires a continuous electricity supply – which was a tall order in the country at that time. Chip Goodyear remembers securing the go-ahead from the board. 'If you lose a pylon that brings power into the plant, you're in trouble. The aluminium pots freeze up and it's a huge task to get that sorted,' he explains. 'So to get approval for the investment we had to demonstrate that we could replace a pylon in four hours – and we were able to prove we could do it!'

The country needed the employment and the infrastructure, certainly, but maybe more important was the vote of confidence it represented in the future. 'Mozal was very important because it was a kind of flag which signalled to the world that Mozambique is an attractive country for investment,' said Antonio Fernando, former Minister of Trade and Industry in Mozambique. The whole operation came together where nothing like it had been there before, which is why it's a good place to see the BHP Billiton model at work.

Producing over 560 thousand tonnes of aluminium a year, Mozal is a state-of-the-art facility and one of most efficient operations of its kind in the world. Around a hundred huge trucks a day make their way directly from the smelter to Maputo port, and the length of the waterfront is stacked with gleaming ingots of aluminium.

It's a source of pride in BHP Billiton that Mozal is run almost entirely by Mozambicans. It took intensive training to build a local workforce at the beginning. There's a real appetite among employees to grasp the opportunity the plant provides to make a better life for themselves. 'Everybody feels the need to just do better and get better and get more accreditation ... and just seek what's out there in the world. The sky's the limit and I think that's what Mozal's offered to a lot of people,' says Etelvina Mausse, a young supervisor at the plant. She wears her orange uniform as a badge of honour because it signifies her status as part of a highly valued and skilled workforce.

The knock-on effect into the local economy is cultivated in parallel. The smelter's spend with small and medium-sized enterprises has risen to around $8 million a month and the number of companies on the roster has gone from around 50 to 200 over the years. The destruction left by the war meant that the supplier base had to be built from scratch. So it looked very different from the more technology-led engineering companies of Chile. In Mozambique, small and medium-sized businesses supplied everything from protective equipment to welding, from transport to uniforms to brooms. Initially, the suppliers were assessed by BHP Billiton for safety, quality and maintenance practices, as well as HR and financial management.

Each of them was given their own development programme, six months to implement it and another assessment to monitor the improvement. The objective was to ensure these businesses could become self-sustaining. They may have started with 100 per cent of their revenues coming from the smelter but over time they've grown and expanded to take on other customers, and become less dependent on Mozal.

Mozambique's lush subtropical climate makes it a happy home for mosquitoes, and malaria is endemic in the region. In the early days of the smelter, it was taking a heavy toll on people and on business. Absenteeism at 20 per cent or more was a real problem, making it impossible to run an efficient operation. Mozal introduced a programme aimed at controlling the disease, which has gone on to win international acclaim in the global health community. 'I think the success of this programme was that, since the beginning, we decided to put Mozambicans in charge of the project. Very qualified people – but most important, Mozambicans,' explains Carlos Mesquita, who was Mozal's General Manager at the time. 'Because controlling malaria is also about education. Simple things like convincing people to use bed nets. If you don't speak the language of the community, if the people don't understand the benefit of what you're doing, they won't let you spray their house.'

Incidence of malaria in the area fell from over 80 per cent to less than 15 per cent. Absenteeism at the smelter fell dramatically and the killer disease was brought under control in the region. True to the spirit of the operation, a programme that began with Mozal issuing bed nets to the local community evolved to establishing a small enterprise run by local women to manufacture bed nets for the surrounding area. Delivered through a tripartite collaboration with the governments of Mozambique, South Africa and Swaziland, the Mozal programme proved such a success it was rolled out across the region.

BHP Billiton's operations in Mozal have played a significant role in establishing stability in the country after the long civil war – and, alongside the impact of the operation itself, there is a range of philanthropic initiatives delivered through a foundation set up by the company. The principle that's applied to the local supply chain – that the system around Mozal needs to become self-sustaining – is also applied in its approach to social investment. Mozambique is still largely an agricultural economy and most people in the area earn their living by working their own smallholding. So Mozal's community programme includes support for local farmers; better quality seeds and equipment, and training in new techniques. Production per family, which used to be around 350 kilos per year, has risen five-fold. As yields improved, Mozal built a market site to help farmers sell their produce on into local towns.

'Everything we're doing here is about being self-sustainable. That's why when we build a school it's in partnership with the local government,' says Alcido Mausse, who was manager of the Mozal Community Development Trust for the first ten years. 'The school we found here when we first arrived had no roof, no windows and was accommodating only 130 kids. Since then, we've built eleven primary schools, each for an average of 700 kids.' And now there's a secondary school and a technical college as well. One of the common criticisms of funding educational or health schemes in developing markets is that the building goes up but there's no attention given to ensuring the community can support sustained activity in the shiny new structures. So that issue is high on the risk register for community investment in BHP Billiton. Therefore, at the outset, Mozal's involvement in these schools included setting up effective administration systems and even teacher training. But, once a school or college is built, equipped and peopled, it's taken forward by the government and Mozal takes no further role.

Against a backdrop of stories around the world of conflict and disharmony around the mining sector, BHP Billiton's Mozal operation offers a sense of how mining can work to create social value – from the economic contribution to investment in health to education. Issufo Caba, speaking for the World Bank's International Finance Corporation, saw it as a platform for growth:

> What we'd like to see in the country is more Mozals coming. Not only for aluminium, but you could imagine Mozals in the different areas. This will impact the development of a country like Mozambique that's in huge need of investments like this.

BHP Billiton is not alone in developing a methodical, comprehensive approach to how it works with its host communities. Anglo American, another of the world's mining majors, has its own award-winning Socio-Economic Assessment Toolbox (SEAT), which every operation around the world is expected to use. 'We have to be able to answer the question from host governments and communities, "What's in it for us?"' says Jon Samuel, Head of Social Performance for Anglo American. Even the existence of the role, Head of Social Performance, shows how far the industry has travelled and puts him at the forefront of the debate about what it takes for a mining company to be recognised as a good neighbour and a good citizen. He thinks the NGOs have made a very effective contribution by raising the issues which needed to be tackled by the industry, 'And these days they are becoming more sophisticated,' he says. 'When you meet them across the table, they often know as much about the detail of regulation or the technical issues as our guys.'

Jon's seen the industry evolve and recognises what a long journey it's taken: 'You could say that fifty years ago, as a mining business, you didn't have to worry about your impact. Twenty years ago, you had to minimise impact. Ten years ago, you were expected to have no impact. And now we are working towards having a positive impact,' he tells us. As the architect of SEAT, which he's developed over the past ten years, he's gained a wealth of experience in the most effective ways that mining companies can act to the benefit of the community around them. In an interview with the International Business Leaders Forum he explained how he sees it:

> The best way for mining companies to contribute to the development of their host countries is to focus on the core business – things like procurement and things like who they hire and how they train them. Social investment will remain important but it's a small part of the overall picture. Anglo American procured $14 billion worth of goods and services last year and three quarters of that was from developing countries – that compares to a social investment budget of around $130 million. So you can see the relative size of the two budgets.

His point goes to the heart of the argument that it's through how it operates *as a business* that a business can contribute to society most effectively. And that shows up in the nature of the choices it makes.

One area where Anglo American is recognised globally for its positive impact is HIV/AIDS. The company has the biggest workforce treatment programme in the world, with 11,000 HIV-positive employees on treatment. In South Africa, home to its largest operation, it estimates that around 16 per cent (12,000 of its 70,000 full-time employees) are affected.

As with malaria for Mozal, the problem first showed itself

when its own employees were suddenly sick and dying. The speed at which the disease took hold shocked everyone. Dr Brian Brink, Anglo American's Chief Medical Officer, remembers that, 'There was a time when investors were getting on the phone and asking whether the disease was going to bring down the organisation. We were training two people for the same role in case one died on the job. It was that bad.'[60] Dr Brink has been on the front line of the battle against HIV/AIDS ever since.

In 2002 Anglo American was the first major employer to provide free anti-retroviral treatments for their workforce. But they found they were grappling not only with the disease but with the tangle of inhibitions and perceptions that surround it. At first it was hard to persuade people to come forward and get tested. In the first year, take-up was only around 10 or 15 per cent. By 2006, it was up to about 60 per cent. Today in South Africa around 90 per cent of employees volunteer for testing annually.

Over more than ten years, they've been learning as they go. Each new stage of the programme represents another hurdle overcome. At the start, it was clear that employees were worried that testing might cost them their jobs, so the business had to send an unambiguous message that people wouldn't be fired for being found HIV-positive. As the problem of transmission to women and children became evident, they decided to expand the programme to include treatment for employees' dependents. Another big step was achieved with the introduction of home testing: families proved to be much more willing to participate in the programme if they were in familiar surroundings. And recently the scheme has been extended again to include local contractors and suppliers.

It might seem logical that near universal testing would get the problem under control. But the next hurdle turns out to be that, even when people test positive, they're often reluctant to take up treatment because it could amount to a confession of infidelity which leads on to painful repercussions at home. And, as many health and welfare schemes have found, the contribution of 'peer educators' is invaluable. So the business has trained up more than 2,000 volunteers around the world to take on the role of mentors to help their colleagues to come to terms with what living with HIV involves and to break through the social stigma that still surrounds the disease.

The new frontier for HIV/AIDS in the global health community is stemming the continued rise in mother-to-baby transmission. Brink points to what he calls the 'array of conditions that systematically work against girls and young women'. A UNAIDS study highlighted that in South Africa a third of women between twenty and twenty-nine years old are HIV-positive – and the big risk is that they pass it on to their children. Anglo American joined the global campaign of WEF's Business Leadership Council, with UNAIDS and others, investing $3 million into the effort to end mother–child transmission by 2015. 'We have to reach a point of zero new infections in adults; that's a huge thing, changing a society, changing attitudes, changing the way people behave,' says Brink.

Anglo American has done the sums. The programme costs the business around $18 million a year globally, yet it pays for itself in reduced absenteeism and by keeping skilled people at work and healthy. And it proves its worth in the loyalty and motivation of employees. 'I can't claim perfection on any of the goals we have achieved. I would rather just look for progress and determination. And we are determined, we will make progress and we will make a difference,' says Brink.

Social impact and environmental impact are intertwined at a local level. Water availability is an increasingly important priority in many communities, for example, and yet mining is a water-intensive industry. Emalahleni is a coal mining town in Witbank, South Africa and we went to see the water treatment plant which Anglo American set up in collaboration with BHP Billiton. It started as a solution to a perennial technical challenge: water from underground sources fills up the cavities left by extraction – it becomes toxic and can contaminate the local water supply and, for the miners, it makes the coal harder to access. Meanwhile water is a scarce resource in the area – and expected to become scarcer with growing demand in the coming years. The mines compete with farms and towns for limited rainfall.

At the plant, we climb the iron mesh stairs to get a vantage point over the large tanks of slurry. The liquid in the vats is murky and evil looking. It's drawn from the mines full of toxins, salts and heavy metals, but by the time it's been through a series of sophisticated filtration processes at the plant, it's purer than the water in the local municipal supply. For some years now, the plant has been able to meet all of the mine's demands for water and the surplus provides 20 per cent of the water supply for the local town. 200 million dollars has been invested over the years to establish what is now a world-leading reclamation plant, with visitors coming from around the world to see how it's done. And recently it's expanded, doubling capacity to produce 50 million litres of clean, drinkable water a day. As we're walked through each step in the process by the plant manager and his team, we hear how they've begun working with the local authorities to improve the standards of the municipality's operations to cope with growing demand from the community. 'Ten years ago our mine water was considered a liability and now it's integrated into the national water strategy,' he tells us with a real sense of achievement. 'It's about going that extra mile – so the mining operation becomes a resource for the community, not a drain on it.'

At the end of the tour, we come across tall piles of dusty,

grey gypsum: a waste product resulting from the water filtration process. In the spirit of making the detritus of the operation useful, they had been sending the gypsum off to become raw material for a local cement producer. Then they hit upon a new possibility. Since the gypsum could be used for building materials, maybe it could help solve a completely different problem: housing for their employees. Finally sloughing off the long legacy of hostel accommodation for mine workers and creating an adequate stock of modern affordable local housing is a priority for the mining industry and the South African government alike. The team shows us round the prototype homes constructed using gypsum-based materials from the plant. Pleased with the ingenuity of the whole scheme, they explain that the pilot project to build sixty-two three-bedroom family homes was a great success: employees who'd been sceptical about the very idea of homes from waste at the start were delighted when they saw the end result. The company is now committed to another 400 units and the plant manager sums it up, 'We've shifted our mindset. I keep reminding myself to use the word *by-product,* not *waste* – because there's probably a use for everything.' In fact, the project has now become a local employment opportunity: a small enterprise has been set up to manufacture bricks using the gypsum from the plant and another is busy building affordable houses for the community. It's as if the business today is remembering the ethos of Anglo's founder, Ernest Oppenheimer:

> ... the purpose of the company is to make profits for its shareholders, but to do so in a way that makes a real and lasting contribution to the countries and communities in which it operates.

Thanks to rising demand for finite resources, the mining sector is likely to remain at the centre of live debate for some time to come. With rapid development around the world and the prospect of billions more consumers, people are worried. So, though it's evident that leading companies in the sector have changed how they operate to improve their social and environmental impact, an underlying concern remains: scarcity.

BHP Billiton's new CEO, Andrew Mackenzie, aims to reframe the debate. Speaking to the Geological Society, he argued that the crux of the issue is not so much the *quantity* of resources available to us but the *management* of those resources. Counter to the general tenor of the debate on this issue, his message is one of abundance, optimism – and caution.

Like his predecessor Andrew is a scientist, with a PhD in Chemistry. And his history tracks back through Rio Tinto, the world's second biggest mining company, where he ended up running the diamond and minerals business, to BP where he joined the research unit in the 1980s; back to his school in a small town in Scotland where he won science prizes sponsored by a local miners' welfare group. With five languages to his name and a period as chairman of the trustees at the think-tank Demos in his background, he seems in some ways a surprisingly reflective figure in this very practical action-oriented industry. Now at the top of the world's largest mining business, his view can significantly influence how the industry relates to society in the coming years. So we went to see him to learn about how he sees the future of resources.

What he means by the abundance of resources available, he tells us, is that 'the amount of resources we're taking out is small relative to what's available in the earth's crust.' While he recognises, of course, that the resource is finite, for him, the key misunderstanding is that debate is often focused on price alone:

> People see big surprises in a commodity price and worry

> that it's a signal of resource scarcity. It's actually more a signal of technological difficulty and, in practice, that is continually being overcome in many ways. Those price signals trigger the ingenuity that triggers more supply but it's not because the stuff is about to dry up.

He cites examples of that technological ingenuity: seismic detection used to gather geological data in exploration, floating platforms to drill directional holes under the sea floor for testing, or heap leaching and solvent extraction techniques which make it a viable proposition to mine lower grades of copper. Exploration technology is making it possible to be ever more precise in locating mineral deposits. Extraction technology is reducing the price of accessing those reserves and reaching them more accurately, while minimising environmental damage in the process. Processing technologies are finding new ways to extract the useful materials while reducing the waste.

His optimism about the potential of innovation to deliver new solutions is not based on the prospect of a single breakthrough that solves everything – one bound and we're free. He's counting on the multiple, incremental, continual advances in technologies being taken to the next level. 'Ingenuity comes at a price. You do something once, it's expensive. Do it twice and it's a bit cheaper and so on. You have to go through an activation barrier but then the price goes down.' He wants the debate to distinguish between absolute availability of resources and supply of resources.

What happens beyond the mining industry itself is part of the overall picture of resource management as well, Andrew argues. Manufacturers are using metals and minerals differently and more efficiently, which can have a knock-on impact on intensity of resource use: high bandwidth telecoms switching to glass fibre-optic cables in place of copper cables, for example, or cars designed to use less steel than they used to.

And Andrew opens the conversation out towards recycling and reuse: 'If we really want to reduce our footprint as a society, we have to think more about how we substitute things that have less of an impact, recycle more, reuse more. And think of energy and resource efficiency as the best and most profitable mine in the world.' Increasingly that's become part of the public agenda. To illustrate the point, he turns to the example of aluminium reuse. In 2010, recycled aluminium accounted for 29 per cent of global demand. Meanwhile, China's twelfth five-year plan sets out the intention to build industries dedicated to recycling and 'remanufacturing' resources.

Pressure is mounting on consumer-facing industries to rethink the way they use materials, as well. Greenpeace has turned its attention to the 'e-waste crisis'. The aim of its campaign is to shift the 'current out-of-sight out-of-mind approach' towards the use and disposal of metals and minerals. As ever, its strategy is to focus on high-profile brand names which have the potential to change practices across an industry. In India, for example, the electronics company Wipro comes out top in the Greenpeace 'Guide to Greener Electronics', scoring well for the effectiveness of its 'take-back' policy with systems and logistics in place to provide over 300 authorised collection points around the country.[61] In time, the imperative to recycle will increasingly spawn whole industries in its own right.

None of this changes the reality that the resources of our planet are finite – and society's appetite for those resources seems almost infinite. Yet considering both availability and supply, along with the scope for materials substitution, waste reduction and recycling has the potential to open up a more informed and rounded debate about how, as a society, we want to manage the resources available to us. To be effective, Andrew argues, we have to attend to the pressing issues around how those resources are governed. That's the caution that accompanied his message of abundance in a speech to the Geological Society:

> The governance of mineral and petroleum resources and the policies put in place by national and intra-national governments is the single most dominant factor controlling the accessibility, availability and economics for their supply to the world's population. This factor overhangs those of geological abundance and quality.

Many would agree that how to achieve strong governance in and around the mining sector is the most pressing issue on the agenda today. It's at the core of dispelling what came to be called the 'Resource Curse' in the 1990s and has been debated ever since. Coined by Richard Auty, the phrase captured the apparent paradox that resource-rich countries have so often ended up worse off, with more corruption and greater conflict. Unaccountable governments, weak institutions or plainly corrupt elites mean that the wealth coming into a country fails to reach its citizens. Grappling with this today means focusing on transparency.

The global NGO, Transparency International, campaigns on the cause of anti-corruption and publishes an annual index of corporate transparency. It's counter-intuitive to think that the extraction sector could do well in such a survey, yet in 2012 six out of the top ten slots went to extraction businesses, with Statoil, Rio Tinto and BHP Billiton taking first, second and third places.[62] But the reasons quickly become clear. On one hand, these companies have worked hard over recent years to make their contribution to wider society more visible, through more transparent measurement and reporting. On the other hand, most of today's intractable problems continue to fester in the areas where they can't be seen – where there's little or no transparency. Given that, committing to transparency about their own operations is one vital step the big mining companies can take towards establishing new global standards for the industry as a whole.

The Extractive Industries Transparency Initiative (EITI) was launched in 2002 to forge new rules for global governance. We asked EITI's Eddie Rich for his view on the subject. 'The most important thing for the major companies is to create a level playing field,' he tells us. To explain his point, Eddie tells the story of how EITI began. Back in 1999, a report called 'A Crude Awakening' by Global Witness focused attention on the dire social consequences of what they identified as the corrupt mismanagement of oil proceeds in Angola. The report urged the industry to engage with the problem directly and called on businesses to break the cycle by 'adopting a policy of full transparency'. It grew into a campaign – still active today – under the banner 'Publish What You Pay'. In 2001 John Browne, then CEO of BP, committed to publish the company's payments to Angola – only to encounter the sharp displeasure of the Angolan government. In his recent memoir, Browne concluded that, 'Clearly a unilateral approach, where one company or one country was under pressure to "publish what you pay", was not workable.'[63] Supported by the British government, Browne's efforts to establish a collaborative forum led to the creation of EITI, which today has a membership of seventy leading companies and thirty-seven of the resource-rich governments of the world – with others lining up to join.

What began as an initiative to create a voluntary standard for companies has evolved into a minimum standard of disclosure for member countries. In EITI's reports 'companies publish what they pay' and – the other half of the equation – 'countries publish what they receive'.

As Eddie reminds us, transparency is only a tool, not an end in itself: 'It's not the same as doing what needs to be done.' He's been involved with the campaign for transparency from the start and, in his view, the debate has moved on from publishing revenues. 'Today it's about cost of production, project by project visibility, tax arrangements, ownership of licences,' he explains. And according to Eddie, although it was BP in the person of John Browne whose actions led to the creation of EITI as a forum for governance, today the oil and gas sector lags the mining sector.

'The major mining companies have got hold of this agenda – they have a strong interest in being open,' he explains. Often the 'majors' face competitive challenges from smaller, local and less accountable companies – the 'juniors', as they're called. So in situations where there's weak governance, they may operate with an unfair but undisclosed advantage, in commercial terms. And in social and environmental terms, the juniors can cause great harm. This is where so many of today's investigative activities are focused: Blacksmith Institute's report on the toxic pollution from mercury caused by small-scale gold mining;[64] Global Witness's report on the need for traceable supply chains to prevent conflict in the Congo;[65] Shefa Siegel's article on 'The Missing Ethics of Mining'[66] conjuring up the vulnerability of people who literally scratch their living out of the dirt to feed their families, to select only a few examples.

This is not to say that the mining majors are not open to challenge, but they are now under immense scrutiny – and know it. As Eddie acknowledges, 'There's been a transformation over the past decade,' and there's increasing belief among the businesses themselves that growth is compatible with creating a positive social impact. However, while they may be powerful, they are only few in number. The question on the horizon is what they can do – separately and together – to use their influence to establish new ground rules right across the industry, for companies big and small, private and state owned.

We met Andrew Mackenzie at the headquarters of BHP Billiton, looking east over the sprawl of London, towards the Palace of Westminster, with the Shard looming in the distance. It was just before he took the helm as CEO at BHP Billiton, and he was reflecting on the role of mining in the world. 'You know, this city is a massive disturbance in the natural order,' he says, directing us to the view. 'People find it beautiful, they find the architecture beautiful. But ultimately if you're going to build great cities like this, if you're going to develop mankind, then obviously you are going to have some negative impact on nature.' In a sense, it's an invitation for everyone to share some responsibility for an industry we all rely on, that underpins the lifestyles many of us enjoy. It's a controversial industry, but one that seems to be reaching a new understanding of its responsibilities in the world.

Ten years on from the first meeting of the Global Mining Initiative, another independent study by the International Institute for Environment and Development reviewed progress. They credit the major companies with implementing many of the initial recommendations, with having established a set of global rules for the industry and a credible base for collective action. And no one disputes that there are standout examples of success among the leaders in the industry. But the review throws the focus forward to where the progress of the next ten years will come from. The theme which runs through it all is that the priority now is to move towards consistent and universal implementation across the sector. They conclude: 'While the mining CEOs at the time ... could afford to be visionaries, the CEOs of today have to focus on action that reaches beyond industry leaders.'

They finish by raising a question:

> ... it is no longer about seeing what mining companies can do for communities, but communities and wider society deciding what they want to see from mining.

Andrew is also aiming to open up the question of what society wants from the companies that manage the earth's resources. But he's well aware of the compelling archetypes which shape the perception of the industry in the public imagination: 'We're in a world where many see us as something of an *Avatar*,' he tells us, 'And many people even think we'd be better off without mining companies.' Yet seeing how metals and minerals extracted from the earth underpin our lifestyles in the developed world, the aspirations of the new rapidly growing economies and the desire for progress among people in developing countries, mining companies are here to stay. So we ask Andrew what his best hopes are for the business he's running: 'I want us to be seen as one of the great companies of the world. Not because we control the world's resources but because we manage them with transparency and integrity and concern for global harmony.'

11

TURNING AN INDUSTRY INSIDE OUT

The start of the twenty-first century was the lowest point in the relationship between Big Pharma and society. The world's attention was gripped by the epidemic of HIV/AIDS. With millions more people becoming infected each year, there was a sense of horror and helplessness. Resources were mobilised globally. Money poured in from governments and foundations. The pharma industry got busy looking for solutions and, by the end of the 1990s, the early drugs were seen, at least, to slow the disease. In the USA the number of deaths began to fall, though the cost of treatments was running at $10,000–15,000 per patient per year.

Meanwhile Africa had been hit hard. In South Africa, more than four million people were infected and dying – and with the cost of medicines so high, they had no hope of treatment. The number of orphans was growing. The South African government, desperate for solutions, hit upon the strategy of manufacturing its own generic versions of the anti-retrovirals, which would make them much more affordable.

The Big Pharma companies of the rich world reared their heads. The idea struck at the central tenet of their business model: the protection of intellectual property. They ganged up, and together, thirty-nine companies sued the South African government, naming the President as first respondent. In effect, Big Pharma sued Nelson Mandela. Leaving aside the reality of patients in urgent need, Mandela – maybe more than any other living soul at the time – had become a symbol of hope for the world and the corporates had set out to squash him.

The action awoke protests in the developed world. Activists in New York were on the streets with banners: 'Patients before patents'. Students in the UK added their voice with 'People before profits'. The European Parliament passed a resolution urging the companies to drop their lawsuit. The companies were powerful and rich – their revenues had grown seven-fold over the previous few years – and they owned life-saving drugs. People in Africa were powerless and poor – many living on a dollar a day – and they were dying because they couldn't afford to pay. The picture was made of such sharp contrasts it crystallised public sentiment about what was wrong with the industry.

On 19 April 2001, after three years of legal battles, during which time hundreds of thousands of people died of the disease, the industry backed down. South Africa won the right to manufacture HIV/AIDS drugs and people danced in the streets. And the watching world celebrated with them.

GSK, one of the giants of the pharma industry and the maker of medicines which are recognised around the world such as Ventolin, Malarone and Zantac, was one of the group taking legal action. Looking back, Duncan Learmouth, a director in the company during those years, recognises the industry was too slow to react. He talked to us about the significance of those events:

> It was the point at which the business got disconnected from its human impact. And with HIV/AIDS, the fact that the disease evolved so rapidly created a unique set of circumstances. People weren't thinking quickly enough about it: how do we deal with this problem?

The barrier to action was the intransigence of the business model they were working with. Big Pharma companies spend billions and years developing new drugs, on the expectation that they will use the intellectual property which comes from their discoveries to generate earnings – and to invest in the next generation of research. It was impossible for the industry to imagine how the whole system could work if it couldn't protect the revenues flowing from the medicines it brings to market. 'Of course, without intellectual property the industry can't survive, because you can't invest in something if you know that, as soon as you launch it, someone is going to copy it,' Duncan explained. 'It's never going to be worth the investment and the failures in R&D to do that. So IP is essential to the survival and the success of the industry. But I think that, as an industry, we had lost sight of the impact of taking that to its extreme conclusion. It's as simple as that.' Inflexible enforcement of patents had led the industry down the road that ended up in the South African courts, but Duncan believes that it was also the turning point:

> The message got through to people in the industry. Because we couldn't pretend it never happened and keep going. So the experience was a catalyst. It was a scary thing, but I think everybody realised then that we couldn't stay entrenched in that position.

For GSK, it was the beginning of an extraordinary journey away from that entrenched position. Today Duncan heads up a unit in GSK with a mandate which would have been inconceivable in the context of the industry ten years ago. The unit is dedicated to finding health solutions for the world's fifty least developed countries, as identified by the World Health Organization. So he spends around half his time out on the road and when we met him in the company's Head Office, sitting in his glass walled, open-plan office in an open-necked shirt, he was full of stories from the front-line of the health systems in the poorest countries. At a desk right by him sits Allan Pamba. Allan is a doctor who grew up and trained in Kenya, and he remembers that time too. He told us what life was like as he experienced it. 'I was one of nine children raised in an African village in the western end of Kenya where it was all bush. I wasn't meant to be here at all, it was a pure accident of history,' he begins.

Allan was the 'middle one', the fifth of the nine children. A local priest got him into school and from there he got himself scholarships into secondary school and then to medical college in Nairobi. He tries to distil the experiences that still drive him today:

> The most important thing about that part of my life is that when I grew up in the village I saw the challenges that we're dealing with today. I saw malnutrition, I saw children die from malaria, from pneumonia. I saw that lots of the kids I was growing up with didn't make it. There was always someone crying in the village because a child had died.

Later, as a practising physician in a government hospital, he had to turn away severely ill patients because there were no medicines.

> We had women who came in and couldn't get a caesarean section because we didn't have oxygen to go into theatre or there was no anaesthetist. I had many colleagues who had to do caesareans with a local anaesthesia, one of the cruellest things that you can ever do to a woman. And many, many women laboured to death, and lost their lives and their children's lives because there was nothing you could do.

It was at the time when HIV/AIDS was sweeping across Africa. Allan's professors at medical school would say there was little they could teach the students because nothing could be done in the face of this new disease: 'There were ten beds in the ward, and beds one to eight were occupied by people with AIDS. The professor told us, it's going to be a short ward round because these people are here until they die.' So they walked past those people to visit just the few beds at the end of the ward. 'It was a horrible experience training as a physician,' Allan says levelly. He ran an HIV/AIDS clinic for a while where, in the absence of medicines, much of his job was listening to and talking with the patients. 'I finally broke,' he says.

> Those stories break your heart. I felt so angry with the pharmaceutical industry because I knew that there were patients in the USA, in the UK and other places who were getting a decent shot at life because of available treatments. And I knew that the drug companies were fighting Mandela in court. I was really angry when I left Africa. I wanted to be a voice for those patients with institutions that could make a difference.

With the ambition to join the United Nations as a platform to argue from, he studied Public Health at the famous London School of Hygiene and Tropical Medicine. At the end of it and many application letters later, he had no joy and still no job. 'But there was this one advert hung up on the student notice board that never moved,' he told us. 'It was a job with GlaxoSmithKline. We all looked at it and dismissed it because Big Pharma was evil so you don't even consider it. The notice just stayed there.' It was to work in the HIV/AIDS team in GSK and eventually a friend pushed Allan to get in touch. Resistant at first, he met the team and they gave him the job. He didn't tell his friends, and those who found out felt he'd sold out. It was going to be a one-year stint, he said, while he worked out where he should go on to.

Of course, we had to ask what changed his mind. 'I thought they were going to be this group of money-hungry, suit-wearing, white men sitting in a room working out how to suck more money off poor patients all the time. I was surprised to find they were just human beings,' he laughs. But what really hit home to him was seeing the significance of the decisions made about what disease areas to back and how. 'I think for the first time it occurred to me that actually it's not a bad idea to be *in*. If you think there's a need for change, this is a way to create change. I thought, I might be here longer than I planned.' He's been there for eight years now, first overseeing drug trials for Phase 4 studies for HIV/AIDS in Africa and then as lead physician of the assessment of a new anti-malarial.

When you see Duncan Learmouth and Allan Pamba sitting within arm's reach of each other you realise what an extraordinary transformation the industry has been through. And it's been a long journey for both of them.

In the first few years after the infamous court case in 2001, GSK – like all the pharma companies – explored a raft of different ways to make a meaningful contribution to health care in the developing world. Heavy discounts for medicines going to the poorest countries was the first and most obvious solution. From 2002, GSK provided its anti-retrovirals to Africa, and low income countries elsewhere, at cost. Other companies took similar action. Licences were granted for generic versions of critical medicines still in patent, allowing local companies to produce them more cheaply for Africa. As Duncan explains, this was an important period because the industry was gradually getting more confident that it was possible to flex the IP model without breaking it: 'The licences were given to companies which could demonstrate they were serious about supplying Africa specifically because, while getting the medicines into the poorest markets, we also needed to manage the risk of parallel imports back into the developed markets.' In other words, the industry needed to be sure that if large quantities of drugs flowed into the poorest countries at cost or thereabouts, they would not be imported back into the developed world at prices that undercut the market and unravelled the industry's business model entirely.

Over the next few years, GSK, along with the whole industry, was casting around for ways to respond. A wide variety of community health projects sprang up in collaboration with NGOs on the ground. Drug donation programmes were scaled up significantly. Each company focused their efforts where their drug portfolio meant they had a special role to play: in leprosy, for example, Novartis donated enough to treat all patients worldwide; Merck provided hundreds of millions of free treatments for river blindness; GSK committed to provide medicine for as long as it took to eliminate lymphatic filariasis. These initiatives, and many similar ones, moved up the corporate agenda. But no amount of dropping prices or giving away medicines could actually solve the problem – and, anyway, taken to its logical but absurd conclusion it would put the companies out of business. To create change it would be necessary to look at the problem the other way up.

'There are still two billion people on the planet without access to medicines, across the range from painkillers to antibiotics for life-threatening diseases,' says Wim Leereveld, a Dutch entrepreneur who made his money in a publishing business providing information for the pharmaceutical industry. He sold his business to set up 'The Access to Medicine Index', which ranks the efforts of the twenty biggest pharma companies on how well they are doing on getting their treatments into the hands of the poorest patients in the world. His great insight was that the competitive instinct of the big industry players could be used to good advantage:

> The thinking at the time was to place public pressure on the pharmaceutical industry in such a way as to force them to act. There was an element of shame in this tactic that I knew would not work. What people didn't realise is that the pharma industry was willing to improve their access to medicines programme but they simply didn't know how... Having worked in the pharmaceutical industry for fifteen years and knowing the industry as I did, I understood that a driving force within that sector was a sense of competitiveness. Rather than working against this instinct, I thought why not use that characteristic to help redirect efforts towards social issues.

The result of his brainwave was 'The Access to Medicine Index'. It took a hard slog of four years to get it up and running but Leereveld stuck with it. Through a wide consultation process with industry participants coming from many different perspectives, he succeeded in codifying the essential elements of what it takes to provide access to medicine. The sophisticated ranking system won general acceptance and the index was first published in 2008. GSK's Duncan Learmouth agrees it's helped to move things on: 'It's clever, it worked,' he says. 'Because people don't like to be at the bottom and they have strategic discussions about how they're going to improve their position, which is a really good thing.'

The premise is straightforward, Leereveld explains: the companies at the top of the index, at minimum, have to be given credit for what they do well – meanwhile, they have something practical to share, which shows what's possible and that gives others courage. Leereveld tracks everything back to his original inspiration for the index: 'Two billion people don't have access to medicine and that is a problem for us all.' His philosophy is clear: 'The pharmaceutical industry is not part of the problem, they are part of the solution. They have the know-how to make life-saving drugs and that's why we need to help them to perform better.'

GSK has topped the rankings on the Access to Medicine Index each time since it started and the business is recognised as leading the way in the industry. A defining moment came for the company in 2009 when, a year into the job of CEO, Andrew Witty set out his strategy. One of his strategic priorities was building trust: a common theme for CEOs, especially in industries with battered reputations. What's less common is laying out a comprehensive plan to change the game. He chose Harvard Medical School as the setting for what he wanted to say on the subject of 'Big Pharma as a Catalyst for Change'[67]. In his address, he pledged that, for the fifty least developed countries in the world, GSK would cap the price of *all* its patented medicines at 25 per cent of developed world prices.

Even by critics, the move was recognised as a step change in the business model of the industry. Oxfam has long been one of the fiercest critics of Big Pharma and in its landmark report 'Beyond Philanthropy', published in 2002, it had been scathing about the stance of all the big players.[68] But following GSK's strategic announcement in 2009, the headline on the press release issued by Oxfam read, 'GSK breaks industry ranks to improve access to medicine'. Rohit Malpani, an Oxfam policy adviser, wrote, 'This is the first time a company has acknowledged that access to medicines is relevant to its entire portfolio of medicines, not just for HIV/AIDS, TB and malaria.'

So pricing was the first big hurdle for access to medicine in the developing world. But once you break the back of the pricing challenge – even in such a dramatic way – the scale of the next challenge becomes clearer. Health infrastructure in the poorest countries is heartbreakingly fragile. That's why the second plank of Andrew Witty's strategy was a pledge to re-invest 20 per cent of the profit made from selling medicines in the least developed countries back into improving the health care infrastructure in those countries. As he put it:

> We have to move from being a supplier of drugs to a partner in delivering solutions. We need to stop saying, 'it's not our fault there is no infrastructure to deliver health care' and start saying, 'who can we work with to ensure that the infrastructure does exist?'

So the focus shifted: the goal was no longer just getting the medicines into the countries, but into the hands of the people who need them. And that's no small logistical challenge. Speaking in Kenya about the problem on the ground, Andrew points to the large warehouses in the ports, full of medicines, and then to the shelves in the rural health clinics, empty of medicines. It sums up the problem. So GSK is working in partnership with the African Medical Research Foundation on a project which uses mobile phones to connect rural clinics to a central organising hub which helps to manage the distribution of medicines to the front line. It's just one of many such projects around the business. 'We have to be never complacent,' he says. 'Because we can never stop. We can't sit still in a comfortable environment and say we've done enough.'

Before becoming CEO, Andrew Witty lived for ten years in Africa and Asia running different parts of the GSK operations. Duncan Learmouth worked closely alongside him on the launch of his strategy and, in Duncan's view, it's his consciousness of the realities of life in the developing world that created the context and the impetus for change. 'There's personal feeling in this for Andrew. He believes that the things ex-CEOs regret they didn't do is stuff like this. He said he didn't want to be looking back and thinking he should have done more on this but he was too busy elsewhere. He says: "When I'm sixty-five, I want to look back and think I did what I could on access, not that I regret not doing it.'"

Intellectual property is the lifeblood of the pharmaceutical industry and its big players are in a permanent race to register the next blockbuster patent. So when GSK set out its strategy, the clearest evidence that it was serious about finding a new way of operating came with the announcement of a Patent Pool which made all the GSK intellectual property which could be relevant to neglected diseases available for others to use: academic researchers, charitable foundations or even other businesses – anyone else trying to develop solutions to the health-care challenges of the poorest countries of the world. The Ethical Corporation, another of the industry's long time challengers, called it 'by far the boldest' of the company's strategic moves:

> Sharing intellectual property has to date been a taboo for drug companies. Patents enable the industry to spend huge amounts on drug development, all leading to high prices. Now GSK and Witty have challenged the commercial logic of the industry.[69]

As incoming CEO, that's certainly what he intended: 'Collaboration is something that the pharmaceutical industry doesn't do – and doesn't want to do. There's been a fear around collaboration that it would destroy the fundamental business model.' But a big part of the global health challenge is that for decades there has been little research and development into drugs for diseases which can offer no prospect of financial return because the customers for them simply can't pay. In the global health-care community they've become called the NTDs, neglected tropical diseases, and there are seventeen of them, according to the World Health Authority, including fearsome infections such as dengue fever and leprosy.

The purpose of creating the Patent Pool was to accelerate progress towards new drug development. Duncan talks about it as a Knowledge Pool rather than a Patent Pool because, he says, 'It's not just that we're sharing IP, it's about all the information behind that as well. It can be just as valuable to know about a product in development or a line of enquiry that fails, as it is to have a patent made available. So we feel we've really been able to step up to enable greater innovation.' The logic sounds so obvious that it's easy to miss how much it represents a break from convention in an industry which had become notorious for its closed culture.

Three years on and with more to show for his efforts, Andrew Witty spoke to the Wellcome Trust about GSK's approach to what they call 'open innovation'. He spoke with pride about the creation of the Patent Pool:

> We were the first company to put all of our IP in the field of neglected tropical diseases into the public domain. That was really a seminal moment in the history of the company and I would argue the history of the industry in terms of acknowledging that you can have a different approach to intellectual property to solve different problems.

In the Wellcome Trust, he had the perfect audience to talk to about the need for progress in R&D in tropical diseases. The huge company that GSK is today has been built out of a series of massive transactions. SmithKline with Beecham in 1989 and Glaxo with Wellcome in 1995. And eventually, in 2000, the merger of GlaxoWellcome with SmithKline Beecham, requiring the complex layers of corporate history to be simplified

– and hence the initials the company is known by today, GSK. But that means that hidden deep in the heritage of the company is the origin of the Wellcome Trust – and also the story of Henry Wellcome.

As a child in the mid-West of America in the 1840s, Henry Wellcome travelled across the prairies in covered wagons with his family to settle in a home in Minnesota. He left school at thirteen and worked for his uncle in the local drug store, which gave him the chance to do his own earliest experiments in creating compounds. A few years later, as the railroad opened up the USA, he found himself working as a travelling salesman taking medicines out into new territories for a New York-based drug company. For his next employers he explored Ecuador and Peru looking for new sources of quinine, one of the most treasured medicines in America at the time because of the protection it offers against malaria.

Tablets had just appeared on the scene, transforming the possibility of distributing effective medicines. Curiously, the opportunity had been opened up by William Brockedon, an artist on a quest for better quality pencils for his sketches, who patented a mechanised method of grinding and compressing graphite to produce leads for pencils. The potential of that innovation was quickly spotted by the pharmaceutical industry in the USA and the technique was applied to medicines to create tablets. Wellcome was invited by an old college friend, Silas Burroughs, to join him in setting up a business to take the innovation into the UK: 'I think we would make a pretty lively team in the pharmaceutical line,' he said. He was right: starting in 1880 and built on vigorous marketing of their own trademarked 'Tabloid', Burroughs Wellcome & Co. grew fast to become the leading pharmaceutical company in Britain and eventually one of the biggest in the world.

When the company was founded, scientific research was on the verge of discoveries that would lead to a vaccine for the killer disease diphtheria. In the 1890s researchers had proved that it was possible to immunise humans against diphtheria, but producing large quantities of a pure enough serum remained an impossibility. Henry Wellcome established the first ever research lab to be set up inside a business and charged it with coming up with a way of manufacturing the vaccine to scale – which it achieved. Twenty years later, as he travelled up the Nile with Lord Kitchener, he was appalled by what he saw in Egypt of people and communities devastated by a vicious cycle of poverty and disease they had no means of combatting. Believing the company had a role in changing that, he wrote, 'One thing that impressed me greatly when I was at Khartoum was the possibility of making that city as healthy as New York, London or any other place.'

Within two years, Wellcome had set up the Tropical Research Laboratories in the Sudan, concentrated especially on malaria. And later, back in the UK, he established the Bureau of Scientific Research, which became the R&D arm of Wellcome plc when the business was listed on the Stock Exchange in the 1980s. Looking back through time, the story carries the romanticism of the academic adventures and entrepreneurial scientists of the nineteenth century. Yet many of the elements of the early business are still evident today: the search for new compounds, the commitment to research, developing manufacturing processes to make breakthrough drugs widely available, entering new markets through the exploitation of new technologies, drug magnates coming face to face with the urgent need of the world's poorest communities – and that crystallising a sense of the purpose of the business.

In Spain, on the outskirts of Madrid is Tres Cantos, a small town which is home to a cluster of high-tech innovative businesses and to GSK's specialist research institute dedicated to diseases of the developing world. Outside, the institute is surrounded by beautifully planted gardens. Inside, in a protected biosecurity lab, a team of five scientists have been working with some of the deadliest malaria strains on the planet. In a marathon project, lasting over a year, the team screened all two million chemical compounds in GSK's portfolio and came up with 13,500 'hits' – each hit representing a possible lead for developing new malaria medicines. Even though these are GSK proprietary compounds, the company took the radical step of publishing the data in the public domain. It was an invitation for other scientists in other research institutes to pursue those leads, thereby accelerating the chance of somebody somewhere finding a route to developing the next generation of malaria drugs. Already fourteen institutes and universities have grasped the opportunity and a number of new research projects are under way. Encouraged by their first step towards a more open approach to R&D, the team repeated the process, this time to find new leads for TB. The results proved more modest: just under 200 hits. But as Andrew Witty said when the data was published in 2012, it goes to show how difficult breakthroughs in TB will be and 'two hundred hits in the public domain tomorrow are 200 more than we had yesterday.'

Dr Mike Strange is director of operations at the institute, so it's his job to make the spirit of GSK's new commitment to open innovation real in practice. 'This lab is where drug discovery happens,' he tells us. 'So we asked ourselves the question: in the absence of a commercial market to incentivise innovation, how can we use what we've got here to get more done? How can we open up this resource to stimulate more activity outside GSK?' They decided that the Tres Cantos Institute should literally open its doors to external researchers from universities, not-for-profit partnerships and other research organisations. GSK has put up $10 million to fund the work of visiting scientists and assembled a high-ranking external board to take the programme forward. 'The idea is that they can tap into our expertise and resources to progress their projects. We have the industrial tools to perform tests quickly and the kind of high-throughput screening facilities that you just don't get in an academic or other setting,' he continues. 'So we can offer them rapid acceleration of their work – and there's no strings attached. If you go back two or three years, we just wouldn't have imagined we could ever do this.'

As evidence of how their open innovation approach has acted as a catalyst to significant change in the world of pharma, what pleases Mike most is that the Patent Pool pioneered by GSK has evolved into an independent industry-wide project. Under the wing of the World Intellectual Property Organisation (WIPO), most of the big players are now signed up to sharing their IP in order to kick-start fresh research into the world's neglected tropical diseases. Drug discovery today means working across many different highly specialised areas, so collaboration is the only way forward, according to Dr Liotta, Professor of Chemistry at Emory University, Atlanta. Dr Liotta's work has won him multiple patents and he's behind the invention of two front-line HIV/AIDS drugs: 'These days in science, no one person or research group has sufficient expertise to do it all. If you want to do big things that are going to positively affect the health of the public you'd better find some good partners.'

In his view, this more open approach to innovation which has made the WIPO project possible is 'a win-win for everybody'. It's a win for global health because it's reigniting interest in neglected diseases which continue to cause millions of deaths. It's a win for the researchers who get to take their own work to the next level. And it's a win for the companies because they develop expertise in areas which may one day become commercially significant. 'There is some great science to be done here,' says Dr Liotta. 'While academic institutions are fabulous places for doing discovery research, pharmaceutical companies really bring something special to the table when it comes to drug development.'

On a conference platform at the end of 2012, Andrew Witty was asked whether GSK's strategy on access to medicines in low-income countries had a clear commercial incentive or whether it's about corporate social responsibility, CSR. The question got at what everybody wants to know. His answer was unequivocal, 'Neither.' He went on to explain how he sees it:

> CSR is the add-on pieces to everything else you do. To us, this is a pivotal part of the structure of the company. GSK has 104,000 people. And they're not going, 'How can we protect this knowledge and make money from it – only in the West?' They're asking: 'How can we leverage this technology to improve health around the world?' That's what really drives us – and that's different from CSR in the traditional sense.

Improving health around the world is a sizeable challenge. The fifty poorest countries in the world have a population of 800 million people, more than half of whom live on less than $1 a day. The structural inequalities with the rest of the world are stark. For example, according the WHO, Africa shoulders 24 per cent of the global disease burden yet has only 1 per cent of the global health budget. Responding to that challenge led to the next major milestone in GSK's journey on access to medicines.

In 2010 the company announced the formation of a new business unit dedicated to the least developed countries – and Duncan Learmouth was appointed to head it up. Duncan laughs as he tells us of the day Andrew called him into his office and pointed across the table at him to say, 'One of the advantages of this unit is that now I've got *you* – and you're accountable for it actually happening.' So Duncan is no longer just playing his part in the team behind the scenes, he's in the driving seat himself, delivering strategy for the least developed countries. But, given how much GSK was already doing in this area, we asked him why it was necessary to establish a separate unit. The point, he told us, was making it a reality. 'We wanted to be sure we could operationalise these principles and integrate them into the business agenda.' The shared concern was that it should not become only an attractive vision, stranded at corporate Head Office but not alive in the day-to-day priorities of the operating companies.

The idea is to develop a profoundly different and sustainable business model for the poorest countries in the world: to build a low price and high volume business that benefits patients, payers and GSK. That's involved setting some new rules. For these markets, there are new measurements of success and new incentives, which reward volumes not price – something of a quiet revolution in itself. There's a new rule about establishing long-term investment horizons for marketing spend in order to build the business for the future – which is reminiscent of the view Henry Wellcome took more than a hundred years ago on pricing the first ever diphtheria vaccine low enough to get it out to where it was needed most and, later, growing the volumes to a point where the business could get what he called a 'fair profit'.

Allan Pamba says that working in the unit gives him the opportunity he has always been looking for: 'A business unit that moves us away from a model of pure philanthropy to one where we're saying, "We want to trade with you, and we'll try as best as we can to meet you halfway – or even closer to your half than our half, recognising what your circumstances are."'

He sees it as sound business strategy because these markets will be the next frontier of growth, but he also believes it's the right approach for the people in those countries:

> I think the world is just now waking up to the fact that people who are considered poor don't necessarily want hand-outs. If you go to the slums in the poorest parts of Nairobi, you'll find micro-economic activity there. People are trading. There's nothing evil about making money in that environment. I have no problems with that. I actually think it's great because you keep people's dignity intact. They value the product and they can challenge you on the quality of it.

'Our instinct is that not all the least developed countries will be least developed for ever,' explains Learmouth:

> By focusing on volume you're obviously supporting the access agenda but you're also supporting the business agenda through growing market share – volume is where the pieces overlap. Growing our market share is part of our bet on economic growth in the developing world. As some of these markets move from *least* to *low*, or from *low* to *middle income* countries, we want GSK to be in a great position to benefit from that economic wave.

The company's commitment to cap the price for all its patented medicines sold in these countries at 25 per cent of the developed world price is a good start. It assumes that the business can cover its costs and make a 5 per cent margin. But given that price is such a critical factor and resources so meagre in these markets, we asked Duncan, why insist on the 5 per cent margin? Why not provide the medicines at cost? 'Because we want to keep being able to do more – and that means developing some kind of business rationale,' he explains. The intention was to not to embark on an enormous philanthropic effort, but to fund the growth of the unit from its own P&L. Since the unit began in 2010, the model has begun to prove itself with volumes growing by almost 50 per cent in the first two years.

Frustratingly, very often, the low price provided by the pharma companies doesn't reach the patients. GSK's Ventolin inhaler, to take one example, is a life-saving medicine which could be bought for $2–3 in New York, but might cost $5–6 in Kinshasa, twice the developed world price. Many structural issues lead to that outcome: mark-ups by other players along the value chain, in-country taxes, lack of scale efficiencies among small local businesses. In the Democratic Republic of Congo, the government charges high import duties on medicines. In Namibia, pharmacists control the distribution and value in the market. In Zimbabwe, rampant inflation has driven mark-ups as high as 200 per cent. Each circumstance needs its own solution. And the challenge of the day for Duncan, when we met him, was working out how to provide evidence to all the different parties who put a mark-up on the product along the way that bringing their prices down will drive volumes up sufficiently to compensate – the lesson his own unit has been learning.

He introduces us to another member of his team, Katrina Tyson, whose responsibility is to wrestle with exactly these kinds of distribution and supply chain problems. Katrina had been working in Head Office for a while when, a few years ago, she began to think she wanted to get closer to the front line of the challenge in health care. She was wondering whether to take time out and get involved with some charity work when she got the chance to be in the first wave of the company's new volunteering programme, which arranges for people to take a six-month placement with an NGO, matching the individual to an organisation that can make good use of their skills. She jumped at the opportunity. 'The experience was eye-opening, amazing,' she tells us. Katrina's placement was in Johannesburg with Direct Relief International, an NGO which specialises in getting donated products out across the world, and her assignment was to look at the supply chain in Africa. 'Previously, I think my understanding of the challenges people have in terms of getting hold of medicines was far different from actually being out there and seeing the reality,' she says.

Most important, she spotted a gap she didn't even know was there: 'One of the key things I learnt was that the supply chain was almost completely forgotten in Africa.' She found a lot of work going on to train health-care professionals, but people running pharmacies, clinics and hospitals weren't receiving any support to get the supply chain working effectively. 'So they have no business capabilities. Yet everyone's expecting them to make sure medicines are on the shelf, and to do the ordering and procurement. Then, you see, they have no understanding of what's needed to manage distribution systems either,' she says. 'Giving people even some basic capability to manage the supplies for their pharmacies or their health centres better seemed a really big way of making medicines more accessible – because it had been completely forgotten. And it seemed like a big gap.'

At the end of her project, Katrina wrote a paper on what she'd learnt and now she's leading the effort to find solutions. A great result for her from her volunteer assignment and a valuable addition to the unit's work on strengthening health-care infrastructure. When we met, she'd recently returned from a trip to Bangladesh. 'Dhaka is the busiest place I have ever been to in my entire life. The traffic and the distances are measured in minutes rather than miles because it is so hard to move through the traffic,' she tells us. The objective of the trip was to understand the journey a patient has to make to reach the treatment they need. 'It's really important that you go out there and see a patient's route to medicine, you actually see it with your own eyes. Otherwise you just focus on the route the medicine takes and then you can make a lot of false assumptions,' she continues. 'Every single country has a slightly different route and we need to have an understanding of how things happen: what is the price that is paid and what influences that price, what influences a patient's choice, do they have a choice, does the medicine have to have a prescription? All that helps us to understand what more we could be doing to help here.'

What she brought back with her from that trip is a heightened awareness of the role of pharmacies. Because patients in Bangladesh have to pay to see a doctor, they often bypass clinics and turn instead to the pharmacies for medical advice, she explains. So now she's working out how to partner with pharmacy networks to see how they can contribute more effectively within the whole system. It's very evident how fired up Katrina is about making a practical difference to health care on the ground. And she's a vibrant example of what the volunteering programme was set up to achieve: to bring inspiration back into finding better ways to do things for the most challenged communities in the world. As Andrew Witty said when he set up the scheme, the over-arching aim was 'to change the organisation from the inside out'.

Duncan's entire unit can be seen as an indication of how the business is working to change from the inside out. He sees their commitment to reinvest a fifth of any profits made in the least developed countries back into strengthening the health-care infrastructure in those countries as one of the most powerful signals of GSK aligning its interests with the wider community. Currently that amounts to around $5 million a year, which is small in the context of the company's entire community spend of over $300 million. But Duncan says that it is providing for the training of 10,000 health-care workers. For him, the crucial factor is 'the reinvestment is going on in the country where we make the profit and that plays well with the governments.' Against a history of African countries distrusting the pricing of pharmaceutical companies, these specific, close-to-home projects funded by the revenues earned in that country are helping the company to establish much more positive relationships for the future. Strategic philanthropy has become integral to the success of the unit.

Gunther Faber is a striking, almost military looking man, white haired, tall and elegant in his dark blazer with shining buttons. A veteran of the pharma industry, he's retired already and might have been expected to sit back and take it easy. Instead he decided to become CEO of a small NGO working on the front line of health-care delivery in Rwanda. One Family Health, as it's called, sets up nurses to own and operate their own small clinics in the remotest rural areas where people have to walk miles to get any medical help. And Gunther brings the energy of an activist to the cause:

> I will go to one of our clinics, right out in the rural areas, and see these women walk with their children into a facility that is clean. The nurse is wearing a coat with an emblem on it: it's clean. Everything is clean and tidy – and they've never had that before. You can just see the hope in their eyes that maybe they can get something to help their children. And they go out looking relieved because they got an answer to something.

Gunther explains to us that, for millions of people, front-line health workers are the first and only link to health care. They offer a very direct, hands-on and cost-effective way of saving lives. Yet in 2006 the UN identified a shortfall of 4.3 million trained health-care workers globally. GSK, along with the other major pharma companies, has answered the call to action. Most of the philanthropic investment from Duncan's unit goes to supporting that effort. Gunther's One Family Health is one of the most innovative programmes they fund, with almost $1 million committed so far to set up sixty clinics in Rwanda. Duncan is enthusiastic: 'We like the model. It's scaleable, it's sustainable and we're looking to take it into other countries.'

The model operates on a franchise system and Gunther explains to us how it works: experienced nurses are set up as owner-managers of their own small clinics with a portfolio of medicines which can tackle around 70 per cent of the biggest health threats to communities: diarrhoea, malaria and asthma, for example – though there's no obligation for them to carry GSK drugs. To expand what they can offer patients, the nurses are equipped to do basic stitching, blood tests and maternal care. And Gunther puts its success down to the huge appetite among Africans today to run their own businesses. On the day the scheme launched, it was covered on Rwandan television and immediately 189 nurses called up wanting to join.

To get started, each franchisee has to put up $500 of their own money. That commitment is important, he tells us, because they're signing up to run their own operation: 'So they liquidate assets, such as a car loan, or they might go and sell chickens or borrow from their family.'

As well as the portfolio of medicines, the nurses get financing and training to show them how to manage their books, their cash flows and their own P&L. It's all carefully worked out so if the nurses see just fourteen patients a day, they'll break even. And within a year, they're covering their costs and managing their own sustainable business. As he tells us, the franchising model answers health-care objectives and contributes to local economic development as well:

> Within the first week of opening, the nurse needs a cleaner, so a local woman who may never have worked before suddenly has money in her pocket. As the clinic gets busier, it needs a receptionist and many of the nurses employ their husbands or daughters. As the clinic becomes established they hire additional nurses. And the women become important figures in their local community.

It's a picture of development we've seen elsewhere. The Shakti Ammas in India are a female network trained, equipped and supported by Unilever to run their own micro-enterprises. The women get money in their pockets and the opportunity to expand the scope of what they manage. And with it comes a sense of mastery over their own destiny, and a trusted and respected role in the village.

There's a business-like mindset at work in One Family Health. Gunther calls it 'a commercial enterprise with a social benefit.' A central IT system manages the flows of medicines and money transparently throughout the network. Training and processes ensure quality standards are maintained across the franchise. And the expansion strategy has been mapped out: the first round of clinics are located where people have had to walk three and a half hours or more to reach a health centre. The next phase is clinics where the walk is two and a half hours, then one and a half. Just how far people have to come to get treatment is a sharp reminder of just how desperately the clinics are needed. Gunther is yet another example of the people we've met who demonstrate the blurring of the line between business and wider society. While some, like Allan Pamba, move from NGOs into business, his journey has been in the other direction. An experienced businessman now leading an NGO, he's on a mission to get more of these clinics established as fast as possible.

Meanwhile, Duncan talks about trained front-line health

workers as the back bone of the health system in Africa. Strategic philanthropic investment in this area works for GSK on all fronts: it offers a practical solution to an urgent problem on the ground, a visible demonstration of how the company can contribute to the systemic challenges facing governments, and a more robust infrastructure on which to build a long term business.

Partnerships with not-for-profit organisations have become integrated into how the business works. One Family Health is only one of those dedicated to the workforce in front-line health care, there are more than thirty others: for example, 2,000 community workers in Nigeria working with Save the Children; 1,000 nurses getting new skills in Tanzania with AMREF, 1,700 female community workers for birthing centres in Nepal with CARE International. We asked Duncan how he sees the different contributions made by the NGOs and corporates:

> What NGOs bring is an insight into the base of the pyramid, the marginalised populations; what their needs are and how to get to them. That's an understanding we just don't have in the business because, by definition, these are marginalised communities. And that's why we're very keen to further these partnerships. The thing big business brings to the party is a kind of rigour; the power of incentives and the capability to operationalise in a disciplined way.

So we were curious to understand whether there's still a role for straightforward drug donations. The answer is yes, and they've been increasing. GSK's major drug donation programme is for lymphatic filariasis – which most people know as elephantiasis, a graphic description of the enormous and debilitating swellings it causes. Spread by mosquitoes, it destroys the lives and livelihoods of people infected. Over 100 million have it and there's no cure. But GSK's drug, Albendazole, offers the possibility of relief and the potential to break the cycle of infection in whole communities. Back in 1999, GSK made the bold commitment to donate Albendazole treatments for as long as it takes to eliminate the disease. They've manufactured and shipped three billion doses so far, for repeated mass treatments administered by government and charity organisations around the world. When the UN turned its attention recently to the challenge of parasitical intestinal worms, which are the cause of malnutrition and stunted growth in 600 million school-age children worldwide, GSK expanded the Albendazole programme to contribute to the UN's global campaign, taking its donation to the equivalent of one billion doses a year through to 2020.

These days there's a tendency to look at drug donations as old-fashioned because, based on philanthropy alone, they're ultimately not sustainable as long-term business models. So we asked Duncan where they fit in. 'They matter where we've got a product in our existing portfolio that's really only relevant in the very low-income countries,' he explains. 'There is simply no commercial market but we can see it has an urgent use. So we feel we have a moral obligation to produce and supply it where it's needed.' So for existing drugs with special application to diseases which hit the world's poorest communities, the donation programmes continue. All the Big Pharma companies have them and, recently, in support of the WHO ambition to control or eradicate ten of the seventeen neglected tropical diseases by the end of the decade, they have been scaled up. But it leads straight back to the question which looms over the global healthcare community: how to generate more R&D to generate newer, more effective drugs for the diseases of the developing world.

Malaria remains one of the biggest killer diseases. Western globetrotters these days pick up their tablets as they set off on a journey and consider themselves protected. But still over 600,000 people die from it a year, half of them under five years old. 'It's easy to forget just how prevalent malaria is,' says Andrew. 'Almost every hospital bed has a woman or a child febrile or dying with malaria – just think of what that's doing to that society.' GSK has what promises to be the first ever malaria vaccine in late-stage trials. And the hope is that vaccination will not only protect people from disease but, as a consequence, make a big contribution to reducing the burden on the health system overall.

It's been a thirty-year journey so far to develop the vaccine, so there was a mounting sense of anticipation when it got through to third-stage trials and was proven to reduce the risk for babies over five months old by around 50 per cent. Excitement was tempered by disappointment though when it turned out to be less effective in babies only six to twelve weeks old – meaning it couldn't be introduced neatly into the infant vaccine schedule, which is becoming a more routine feature of the health system in developing countries. The requirement for a separate delivery process would present a huge logistical challenge. So everyone involved is reconciled to the exploration continuing to the next stage.

Vaccines offer a massive opportunity to change the game in global health care and GSK's strong portfolio of thirty vaccines puts them in the centre of the debate about how to achieve that. Of the 1.1 billion doses of vaccines they produce every year, 800 million go to the developing world. The vaccine programme is also the largest initiative for the Bill & Melinda Gates Foundation, and Bill Gates has become one of the world's most vocal campaigners on the subject. His aim, he says, is to achieve equity: 'We have to take the very latest vaccines that the rich countries take for granted and get them to the poor kids. That will save millions of lives – and vaccines are the miracle intervention that allows that to happen.'

Through the Global Alliance for Vaccine and Immunisation (GAVI), the Gates Foundation has put more than $200 million into the development of the malaria vaccine and GSK has invested upwards of $300 million. However, some voices in the NGO sector are concerned that, by working through these partnerships, the Foundation is in effect paying the industry for these drugs. Gates is unapologetic in the face of that challenge. In his view, where the governments of the poorest countries can't afford to pay – even at a fraction of the rates which apply in the developed world – it's the Foundation's readiness to buy in bulk, and to commit to large-scale, long-term contracts which gives the companies the confidence they need to invest in scaling up their manufacturing capacity to respond to that requirement. He believes it's the NGOs working on the ground who should most welcome the Foundation's collaboration with Big Pharma because it's what will produce the new drugs they so urgently need to fulfil their own healthcare mission. 'This is medicine at work,' he says.

GSK has taken a position on access to medicines: they state that they're working to make their products available 'to as many people who need them as possible, regardless of where they live or their ability to pay.'[70] *Regardless of where they live or their ability to pay* is the critical phrase which speaks of the mindset shift that's happened in the business in the last ten years. Talking about the unit he heads up, Duncan told the *Telegraph* newspaper in 2011 that 'We would rather make £1 million of profit supplying a million patients, than £1 million of profit supplying 100,000 patients.'[71]

This galvanising effort to respond to those most in need

means that GSK now operates explicitly on a tiered pricing model. Duncan explained to us what that means: 'We have a clear feeling about tiered pricing: the least developed countries should pay nothing towards R&D, high income countries should pay the most towards R&D and middle income countries should pay something in the middle. Not nothing, but not the highest amount.' He acknowledges that it leads to some tough choices about places which are developing fast but still struggling to support large poor populations. 'Of course, we recognise there are poor people – in India, for example. But when a government is starting to generate a significant amount of income, where does our responsibility end and where does the government's take over?'

Meanwhile the challenge can come from the other direction: does this amount to the rich world subsidising the health of people in the poorer countries? Andrew Witty has a robust response: 'I make no apology for that. It's unreasonable to expect someone in the poorest countries to contribute to shareholder profits and the R&D of the future – because the challenge here is to make sure that access is achieved.' The argument is that the business model is not simply a sliding scale of revenues, but a mechanism which works overall to sustain the resources needed for a long-term commitment to R&D. Dr Richard Sezibera, Secretary General of the East African Community, is quick to defend that proposition: 'What industry is doing with tier pricing is exactly what governments across the world do. Through social health insurance schemes, you make sure that the more well off pay relatively more for their health than the poorest – and so what the industry is doing is absolutely the right way to go.'

Reflecting back on the journey the business has been on over the past ten years, Duncan says, 'Once we got some way down the road on this, we've increasingly seen it as a competitive advantage. We've seen the impact that it has on employees and we've seen the impact it has on new people; talented people wanting to join the company because they see what work we're doing.' Participating in a panel discussion recently, Andrew was asked how to get more companies involved in working to solve some of the biggest challenges in the world. In answering, perhaps surprisingly, he turned attention on the shareholders:

> I think you need to talk to shareholders. I'm amazed how often people say to me: how on earth does your shareholder base allow you to do what you're doing on this agenda? I have never been asked – once – by a single shareholder why we do what we do, in a negative sense. And this is a company that spent $500 million or so on the malaria vaccine project, so I'm not talking about a million bucks here or there: it's a big deal for GSK. And no shareholder has ever criticised us. I think there are a lot of corporate managements who have not properly embraced this yet. If I was you, I would go to the shareholders and ask them: why don't you ask your corporate managements what they're doing on this agenda? That's the way to encourage more companies to get involved.

It's true too that investors know that the future for the pharmaceutical industry in the developed world looks tough. Headed for a 'patent cliff' as established medicines are due to come off patent protection, combined with pricing pressures from cash-strapped payers in the health-care system, companies are going to find growth increasingly hard to come by. At this point, it looks like it's the emerging and developing countries that will offer the real potential for the long-term. But to build sustainable businesses that can work for everyone in these markets, the pharma companies and their investors have recognised that a completely new model is called for.

Duncan's unit in GSK, focused on the least developed countries, is still small in the scheme of the overall business, too small to register strongly on the radar screen of the investors – but it's at the forefront of the next chapter of the story for the pharmaceutical industry. The challenge is to build a successful business while, at the same time, expanding access to health care to even the poorest people in the world.

Radically rethinking pricing came first, then a commitment to invest in health-care infrastructure, breaking open the traditional approach to intellectual property, and a huge push on R&D to deliver new medicines for the developing world. Each represents a step in the journey so far. Partnerships between industry players, governments and not-for-profit organisations, big and small, have established new ground rules for engagement. And new ways of operating are turning the industry inside out.

Reflecting on his early impressions of GSK – coming fresh from the front line of health care in Africa with the desire to be a voice for the world's poorest patients – Allan Pamba retains his belief in the power of the business to make an impact:

> This institution is a huge platform. From here, you can influence the movement of millions of dollars for R&D and the shape of global health-care strategy in a way that will make a big difference, you know. Much more than I could where I was sitting ten years ago in my little clinic.

12

THE AGITATOR, THE MEDIATOR AND THE CORPORATE ACTIVIST

On 5 February 2013 at a press conference in Jakarta, journalists gathered for a press conference that would stun the world of environmental campaigners. For many years, Asia Pulp and Paper had been reviled as the main culprit of deforestation. They had remained obstinate – belligerent, even – in the face of years of campaigning, pleading and petitioning. Deforestation was their business model: APP made money by cutting down forest to make pulp and paper. For rainforest activists, the company was Public Enemy No. 1. But that morning, APP announced they were halting deforestation – 'in their own operations and their suppliers'. It was a moment corporate watchers thought would never happen.

Everyone knows that pristine natural rainforest is being destroyed around the world at a breathtaking rate. When it goes, it's gone for ever and, with it, the habitat of a huge variety of species, including iconic creatures such as orang-utans and tigers whose very existence seems to express something of the magic of life on our planet. The loss of the forests is a problem for the world: the carbon dioxide that's released when the trees are felled accounts for a fifth of global carbon emissions and accelerates climate change – creating a vicious cycle of forest collapse.

The destruction of Indonesia's vast forests is so extensive that the country is now the world's third largest emitter of greenhouse gases – behind only China and the USA. As one of the leading perpetrators of deforestation, APP has been the target of mounting criticism for over a decade. Pulp and paper are used in a wide variety of products, and a long list of famous brand name customers walked away, including Disney, Danone, Adidas and a string of others. More than once in the past few years the business had made promises on forest protection that didn't materialise and scepticism had grown. There's no question about it: in the drama of saving the planet, APP has famously been playing the role of villain.

But this announcement was different. Teguh Ganda Wijaya, chairman of the APP Group, was there in person in front of an audience of the world's press, government and civil society organisations. Indonesia's Minister for Forestry was there to congratulate the company. And, almost unbelievably, their fiercest NGO critics were in the room to support the plan. Greenpeace, The Forest Trust and APP had forged an unlikely collaboration that resulted in APP's decision to halt deforestation. Aida Greenbury, one of APP's directors, delivered the announcement to the expectant audience:

> This is one of the most significant days in the history of APP, and I'm very proud to be representing the company on such an occasion. Our sustainability journey has been, and continues to be, challenging ... We have been extensively criticised in the past – sometimes fairly, sometimes unfairly ... We would like to share that effective January 1st 2013 we have suspended all natural forest clearance ... This means there will be no more natural forest cut by our company, or anyone that supplies us...

The press conference broke into applause – surely a novel experience for any APP director. For all concerned, it was a scarcely hoped-for victory – and a startling example of how collaboration is proving to be the key to change in the corporate arena.

We've seen collaboration at work in earlier chapters. We heard Nike's CEO Mark Parker reflect that 'we learned that the path to change ... is paved by collaboration with multiple stakeholders'. At GSK, we saw how drug companies that once fought tooth-and-nail are now collaborating to fight diseases in the poorest countries. We saw how IBM's *Smarter Planet* brings together a broad range of collaborators to make cities work better. On the road with Unilever, we saw how some imaginative NGO partnerships are enabling the drive to reach consumers at the 'bottom of the pyramid'. PepsiCo's work on water scarcity depends upon a portfolio of partnerships. Time after time, the same theme emerges: collaboration – even with your critics or your competitors.

For APP, it had been a long journey to their momentous announcement, and the announcement was only the start of a long journey ahead. To understand how it began, we need to trace the story back to the announcement made by APP's sister company, Golden Agri Resources, which had been on its own transformational journey two years earlier. Golden Agri, like APP, is part of the Sinar Mas business empire. They are Indonesia's largest producer of palm oil, and the world's second largest. Like APP, Golden Agri was built on the model of clearing forest and turning the land into plantations; and like APP they had been heavily targeted by activists. They even found themselves out of step with the government, which had committed to a 26 per cent reduction in greenhouse gas emissions by 2020. Significant customers, such as Unilever and Nestlé, intent on improving their own environmental performance, delisted them as suppliers. The situation looked hopeless. As positions became ever more entrenched, it seemed impossible to see how any progress could be made.

The story of Golden Agri is a story of collaboration – and so let's begin by introducing the *dramatis personæ* of the action: the *agitator*, Bustar Maitar from Greenpeace; the *mediator*, Scott Poynton from The Forest Trust; and the *corporate activist*, Peter Heng from Golden Agri.

First, the corporate activist: Peter Heng of Golden Agri. Peter heads up Golden Agri's sustainability efforts, and was a key figure in breaking the deadlock. He is a managing director of one of Indonesia's most powerful companies today, yet he grew up with no such expectations. His father died when he was eight years old, leaving his mother extremely poor, and alone with him and six siblings. The older ones went out to work and he got the chance of an education. 'My father, even though he was just a street hawker, always emphasised education. So I come from a background where I know that if I hadn't had that education, I wouldn't be here having this conversation with you today,' he tells us. In Peter, you meet a huge energy in a small, delicate frame, and an earnest commitment to telling this story.

As challenges from environmentalists intensified, the company had struggled to know how to respond – but Peter knew it couldn't just be ignored, he tells us: 'If you have a determination to be the best, you have to recognise these challenges: NGO attacks, customers leaving. So we asked: "What do we need to do?"' To begin with, Peter simply wanted to understand the situation, and so commissioned reports from two independent bodies – their job was 'to get the facts on the table'. His next priority was to get from conflict to collaboration. 'You need to move to a place beyond conflict. How to do that was obviously something we were thinking about. To do that you will need a *mediator*,' says Peter.

The mediator was Scott Poynton. Scott is Executive

Director of The Forest Trust, the organisation he helped to found in 1999 to prevent deforestation by working collaboratively with businesses and changing the way they operate. Scott grew up in a remote area of Australia, and had planned to be a vet. He loved nature and was rarely indoors. One day he was stuck inside on a rainy afternoon, and he happened to hear a radio programme featuring the grand old man of forestry, Sir Richard Baker. He was talking about his vision of replanting the Sahara. For Scott, it was like hearing a voice from another world, full of reverence for nature. One detail locked into his imagination: Sir Richard explained how a stone propped carefully against the root of a tiny sapling in the desert can begin the process of making the soil that makes reforestation possible. 'It captured me and straight away I knew I wanted to work with trees,' he told us when we first met. So Scott grew up to be a forester.

With Scott playing the role of mediator, the unlikely alliance with Greenpeace was established. And so we meet our third cast member, the agitator. Bustar Maitar has led the Greenpeace campaign against deforestation in South East Asia since 2007. He's lived most of his life in Papua New Guinea, for eight years with the indigenous communities in the remote areas of the forest. And he says that it was seeing their struggle to protect the forest, their livelihoods – and even their lives – that motivated him to work not just at the local level but also at the national and international level. And in the crusading culture which defines Greenpeace, Bustar's something of a legend for his dedication to the cause.

Early on, Scott told Peter the tale, apocryphal of course, of two fighting armies and one side holed up in a church under siege. The likely end is destruction and desolation. But the wise leader of one army decided to negotiate for peace, and was looking for a way to prove his good faith. He hacked a hole in the door of the church and stuck his arm through, hoping to shake hands with the people on the other side – but risking that it would be chopped off. The people on the other side saw the significance of what he had done and shook his hand, and the two sides began to resolve their dispute. He remembers telling Peter early on, 'Look Peter, you've got to chance your arm, mate?'

'So what's that in our context?' says Peter, picking up the story. 'We chanced our arm.' They understood from the start that the NGOs are concerned only about deforestation, he tells us. There are large areas of forest that may have already been marked out as 'degraded', and Peter explains that by Indonesian regulations companies are encouraged to convert this degraded forest into plantations. But the NGOs were raising a big question: what exactly constitutes degraded land? There might be significant areas of forest that are worth saving in land that's classified as degraded – but there was no way of quantifying that. Peter could see the point. 'We agreed that the parties should come together and map out where we thought these areas might be. And we paused our bulldozers while the work was happening,' he says. It was a significant step in building trust between the different parties, Peter recalls. 'So that's where we chanced our arm.'

Meanwhile Bustar makes the Greenpeace position clear: 'What Greenpeace is doing challenging a company like Golden Agri is not about stopping their business. We're not against palm oil – palm oil is important for Indonesia and the local people. We're looking to find the best solution for the environment, for the local people but also how business can grow to fulfil global demand. The thing is how to make it happen on the ground so that there's a business still growing and the forest is still there.'

The basis of the collaboration was agreeing on the common ground. They agreed on three objectives: conserving forest, creating much needed employment in Indonesia, and ensuring long-term sustainable growth for the business – and, as Peter told us, 'We're a business, we mustn't shy away from that.' Bustar is very clear too on the spirit of the collaboration, 'There is no piece of paper we signed with Golden Agri. So this is more a matter of a gentleman's agreement. So they trust us and we trust them. This is very important, for me this is very unique.'

It's astonishing to think that a gentleman's agreement could be possible against the backdrop of antagonism that made it hard for them even to get into the same room only months before. Bustar is explicit too about the fact that Greenpeace takes no money from the company. They are absolute in their insistence on their independence, on retaining their right to be critical and their ability to walk away if they feel they must; it's vital to their own effectiveness and also to their value as partners in the exercise. 'When we work on the ground together it shows their people that Greenpeace is really involved in helping them to build the credibility of their operation. So I think the trust grows from there.'

With the common ground established, as Scott tells us, the fieldwork could begin:

> The Greenpeace guys were out in the field with our guys and the Golden Agri guys to measure the trees. They're out in the swamps, measuring trees in Indonesia so it's not a pretty sight, having to cut lines through the forest, up hills. And they did it, they were in it. So this is collaboration and there were three equal parties – we need to protect the forest, and we're going to get rid of some trees and we're going to do it together. It's not a cosy partnership, it's about collaborating to reach a common goal.

But in Scott's experience, the fieldwork has to go hand in hand with the strategic choices at the top of the company:

> We have to get out in the forest, but we can't do it from there either. We've got to be in the boardrooms as well. That's where we've been able to bring change where maybe others hadn't expected us to be able to, because we've been able to bring the story of the field into the boardroom. So when they say to us, 'We can't do that', we can say, 'You can. We're out there with your people and if you change the way you worked it, you can do that.'

The technical issues of land management are intertwined with complex social issues. Bustar has had a lot of experience in defending the rights of indigenous communities in the face of the onward march of the forestry industry, 'Sometimes people are just looking for quick cash, and that's why they give up their piece of the forest for compensation – and it's a very small amount of money. Afterwards they don't have access to the forest to fulfil their needs any more, and in the end they realise it's not sustainable for them.' So there's a job to do to persuade local people to value and protect the forest for the long-term. That will require companies to take a much more active role in ensuring the economic viability of the fragile communities whose livelihoods depend on the land which they turn into plantations. On this journey, Golden Agri made new commitments to working directly with local communities, which Bustar sees as 'bringing a hope that local people will get the chance to sit down together with the company to find ways of making a better future for themselves.'

'We call ourselves the Team – Greenpeace, The Forest Trust and Golden Agri, looking together to find solutions,' says Peter. In June 2012 they jointly published a report on their fieldwork.[72] A crucial outcome is the first mutually agreed and scientifically robust methodology for categorising areas of forest that are worthy of conservation. It is 'pioneering work', as Scott says, because it provides a new way of tackling the problem on the ground that land is being marked down for clearance even though it's only slightly degraded.

Their shared excitement is that the methodology offers a practical cost-effective tool that can be used by any other company. Peter explains that its potential to influence others comes as a result of the collaborative nature of the venture. Its value, he says, is that 'for any business which is serious about stopping deforestation, this is a methodology they can look at to help them make their own decisions.' The project has turned Peter into an activist exhorting the corporate world to get serious about stopping deforestation.

Bustar also believes that the work can lift standards across the industry. He wants the methodology to inform regulation in the emerging palm oil industry in Africa before it's too late for their forests. And it creates the opportunity to push for tougher certification levels from the Roundtable on Sustainable Palm Oil (RSPO), which provides accreditation for the sustainable production of palm oil:

> Golden Agri policy is really challenging the Roundtable on Sustainable Palm Oil to strengthen its principles and criteria. For example, in the RSPO they don't have greenhouse gas emission criteria and Golden Agri has now already set that. RSPO still allows peat lands to be developed, Golden Agri is saying no to peat land. So what Golden Agri has done is to set the bar higher.

Peter is more mellow in tone. He sees the Round Table as 'part of the journey of palm oil' and a potential partner in working with the Indonesian government. To get to the next level, collaborating with government will be vital: it means bringing in new measures to protect forests and revising existing regulations on land use and tax regimes based on converting forest to plantation. That's why building what he calls 'a multi-stakeholder platform' is essential. Although Golden Agri is the country's largest palm oil producer, it represents only 6 per cent of production. If the ambition is to halt deforestation in Indonesia others must join the effort, other businesses, communities and government.

So Golden Agri found itself out in front, taking the lead in the effort to halt deforestation. And that inevitably intensified criticism of Asia Pulp and Paper. As sister companies in the Sinar Mas group, it was easy to highlight the contrast. And, as with palm oil, consumers may not know the companies but they're well acquainted with the products – newspaper, wrapping paper, toilet paper, copy paper and packaging are in everyone's lives. When it emerged that Mattel, the makers of Barbie, used APP product in their packaging, Greenpeace ran a spoof video in which Ken, Barbie's toy boyfriend, dumps her, appalled by her association with rainforest destruction. Meanwhile, APP had been watching Golden Agri's success in changing direction and slowly resolving to attempt the same journey themselves.

Ever the mediator, Scott put APP's predicament in context: 'They were business people running a business model that up until a few years ago was considered just fine in our countries too. It's not an unusual business model.' Scott reminds us that most of northern Europe was once covered in dense forest, and deforestation is still occurring in parts of North America. 'But times have changed and it's just not appropriate any more,' he says. APP's growth had been completely dependent on cutting down natural forest and The Forest Trust set out to explore alternatives with them. Nevertheless, when Scott agreed to support APP on that journey, he felt the heat of real antagonism from some in the NGO universe:

> People hear you're working with APP and there's a sharp intake of breath. I got attacked by one NGO who said,

> 'We knew you were dodgy – working with the most evil of the evil.' Others said to me, 'But what if you fail, what would that do to your reputation?' I'm not worried about my reputation; I'm worried about the forest. We haven't got that much time – the window for the world's forests is closing, we're losing them all. If I don't get in there and try, I can guarantee the forest is going to be gone. And if I fail, at least I can look at myself in the mirror.

Indeed, during 2011 The Forest Trust had been talking with APP, on and off – as much off, as on – but they had not found common ground. Characteristically, Scott introduced the company to a parable:

> I used a story. In Chapter One: I'm walking down the street and I fall into a hole. It's really annoying I'm in this hole – and I can't figure out how to get out of it. It takes me a long time, but I finally do it and off I go. Chapter Two: I'm walking down the street and I fall into the hole again – and I think, it's not my fault. And it's really annoying and it takes me ages to get out. And then Chapter Three: I walk down the street and I fall into the same hole – and I'm really annoyed with myself because I should know better. Chapter Four: I walk down the street – and I avoid the hole. But I'm still walking down the same street. And Chapter Five: I'm walking down a different street.
>
> In August 2011 I said to APP, you're at Chapter Two because you're still falling in the same hole and blaming someone else. The hole you're in is that you're chopping down natural forest with all the consequences that has, and you're blaming someone else for the criticism and the campaigns against you. As the year unfolded, the company was attacked again in a report identifying the use of ramin, a protected tree species, in their

> products. In the past they might have denied it and gone on the attack. But this time they said, 'There's ramin in our factories, why have we even got that there – that was our fault. We need to tighten our systems to be sure that doesn't happen again.' I didn't see it at the time, but then I realised: that was their Chapter Three moment – they were annoyed at themselves for falling into the same hole.
>
> In June 2012 the company published a report committing to cutting down no more high conservation rainforest. That was when they went from Chapter Three to Chapter Four. They were trying to avoid the holes. Then in October I thought, they're on the threshold of Chapter Five: delinking themselves from deforestation – walking down a different path before there's no forest left to save. I wrote and told them that.

Scott tells us that when he met with the company in the autumn of 2011, 'They were saying, "We can't stop talking about Chapter Five and how we are going to do it." They were talking about how to change their business model to delink it from natural forest fibre.' That was the start of APP's collaboration with The Forest Trust and Greenpeace. And, once again, it involved a period of intense fieldwork by a team drawn from all three of the organisations, combined with strategic conversations in the boardroom.

An important operational challenge for the company was ensuring there would be alternative sources of fibre to keep up production levels in the mills, in the absence of using natural forest fibre. The answer came from the fieldwork which identified that the improved yields which APP had been able to deliver in its plantations in recent years could provide the additional fibre needed. Spotting the link between the two was the result of looking for an answer to the new question: how do we stop deforestation in our operations?

Over the years, APP had invested in tiger protection projects – and their response early on was to want to point towards them as evidence of their good intentions. As someone used to acting as an interpreter of the outside world, Scott explained, 'Those projects are terrific but every time you talk about them you will get hit again. They get written off as greenwash – because, over there, you're also killing the forest. But suddenly, those projects – which you're quite proud of – take on a whole new meaning if you're not cutting down that forest. Suddenly, as a company you have a holistic platform, rather than all the grief and destruction here in your core operations – and some silly little greenwashing things over there.'

When it came to the announcement, in the press conference on 5 February 2013, APP committed to ending the use of natural forest fibre – in their own business and throughout their supply chain. And to demonstrate their determination to implement the new policy, they opened up the process to public scrutiny, inviting civil society organisations to help them monitor and alert them to failures. When we ask Scott what gives him confidence that this time is for real, his answer is emphatic: 'They stopped the bulldozers.'

Fresh from the event, Bustar's blog expressed his sense of elation:

> Today was a day I have at times feared might never come, but I've just emerged from a packed press conference in Jakarta for the launch of Asia Pulp & Paper's new 'Forest Conservation Policy' aimed to end its involvement in deforestation. I've personally invested, along with many of my colleagues, endless hours into our campaign to persuade APP to make this step. After a great deal of blood, toil, sweat and tears, today the company did just that – announcing an immediate moratorium on further

> forest clearance and a range of measures to stop its role in deforestation.

On the morning after the press conference, we were fortunate to find ourselves with some Greenpeace campaigners on the other side of the world in San Francisco. They were the team behind the work which had targeted a number of high-profile consumer brands, linking them to deforestation by exposing them as APP customers. And they still had sore heads from celebrating the night before: to have both Golden Agri and APP as committed leaders in the cause is a big boost. Bustar told us, 'Mostly our campaigns challenge the market-facing companies. But this is changing the practice of producer companies. For this kind of company, it's really hard to change. When we started this six years ago, even for us – even for people in Greenpeace – it was really hard to believe we could manage it. It's been such a long journey to this announcement – but it really shows that the business sector in the developing countries can do something to end deforestation.'

Meanwhile, Aida Greenbury, APP's Managing Director of Sustainability, was on the platform that day alongside the chairman and the minister, voicing the details of the company's commitment which, as she said, 'represent a major milestone for our company'. And she also has much invested personally in the announcement. In an interview with BusinessGreen Plus, she spoke in a heartfelt way about how it had been a journey of several years for the business:

> We did not know what it meant to stop deforestation. We were not sure we could do that. Our business is about conversion: converting land into plantation, and then making pulp and paper out of it. We couldn't understand how to do what the NGOs wanted us to do. We didn't

> understand what the impact to our operations would be if we did what they wanted us to do.

Scott gives the company great credit for persevering on this journey. APP has indeed made a transformational shift, but what inspires them all is the opportunity this sets up for creating change across the industry. In Scott's words:

> The really significant thing to me is that if APP can do this, anyone can do it. So what it tells me is that there is no excuse for any company, anywhere in the world, to be chopping down forests as part of their business. That's the joy of this announcement.

In these portraits of collaboration, agreeing on the common ground – right from the start – is what allowed each of them to take their own victory out of it in the end. And in this world where new partnerships, alliances, coalitions and collaborations seem to spring up almost every day, what sings out in these examples is that their success came from people being actively engaged in a difficult and shared project. They had literally cut a path through the forest together, they all had skin in the game – and yet no one knew for sure how it would work out. In both instances, this was a practical, problem-solving collaboration, not a diplomatic, face-saving exercise.

Yet even with the unity provided by a common purpose, the boundaries never blurred. The collaborators stayed in character. It's a symbiotic relationship; each needs the other to play their role to get where they're headed. Greenpeace remains the implacable agitator, on the outside, carrying the banner for the cause. And mediating between the different players, The Forest Trust reframes the issues so they can be looked at afresh – and sticks around on the inside to help the business deliver on the commitments they've made. But in any drama, the protagonist is the one who undergoes the great change; in this case, it was those on the inside of these companies, the corporate activists, who had to wrestle with the operational challenges and make the change happen. As Scott says, 'They swallowed their pride and recognised they had to sort the problem out: that's courageous. I think it was humbling in some ways and energising and liberating in others. They feel they've regained control of their destiny.'

TRANSFORMING INDUSTRIES

The story behind turning off the bulldozers in Indonesia reflects a broader movement: corporates and NGOs are finding new ways of working together, to find a way through difficult issues. Without exception, the companies we have met are collaborating in ways they would have found unimaginable a decade ago. Today, this seems like a common sense, practical approach, and so *collaboration* and *partnership* have become watchwords of the age – sounding platitudinous, even. But it hasn't always been like this. *Suspicion* and *conflict*, rather than *collaboration* and *partnership*, may be better words to describe the relationship between NGOs and corporates over the years.

Jonathon Porritt is co-founder of Forum for the Future, and former Director of Friends of the Earth. As a long-time environmental activist, he has witnessed attitudes towards business shift from instinctive hostility to constructive engagement. 'The business world was demonised as the principal source of environmental destruction and social exploitation. People wanted to point the finger of blame, it made them feel good about something, and business was right there', he tells us, remembering a Green Party conference he chaired in the 1970s, when a speaker was roundly booed simply for introducing himself as a businessman. This was still the prevalent attitude when he took the helm at Friends of the Earth in 1984. He recalls:

> There were the goodies and the baddies and it was very clear who was on which side of the moral divide. It really was a *Star Wars* model of moral involvement: we at Friends of the Earth were all kind of Luke Skywalker look-a-likes and had our wonderful lightsabers to put the world to rights. And I'm not joking – we honestly did think like that: we were doing battle with umpteen legions of storm-troopers and Darth Vaders in business who were all on the side of the wicked, the Dark Side. It was so crystal clear, and it was so convenient because we honestly didn't have to nuance it very much. There wasn't any requirement to get into complex discussions.

For its part, the business world played right into this 'Dark Side' casting, dominated by large secretive corporates, intent on spreading like malevolent empires. 'In those days business was mostly in denial around any notion of environmental impact, even responsibility,' says Jonathon. 'It was down to governments. It's amazing to think that not one country had a Department of the Environment until 1973: they all came during the mid- to late seventies.' During this period, governments around the world generated an avalanche of environmental law. Most of today's regulations date back to then, in areas such as air pollution, water treatment, waste management, soil protection, species and biodiversity protection. Jonathon describes it as a 'fantastically effective period of time' for regulation. It was as if lawmakers had experienced a sudden awakening, prompted perhaps by the disturbing predictions made by the Club of Rome, a think-tank, in their 1972 publication 'The Limits To Growth', or by the bleak world described by Rachel Carson in her book *Silent Spring*, which had prompted

President John F. Kennedy to order an investigation. The authors of *Only One Earth*, a recent history of the environmental movement, offer another interesting perspective:

> It is perhaps difficult to remember the powerful – and complex – impact that the Apollo 11 landing had on people all over the world ... it provided, almost without anyone realising it, a transcendent but almost-subversive image of Earth – breathtakingly beautiful, but also extraordinarily fragile – an image that steadily seeped into the collective consciousness of people everywhere. It fundamentally reshaped the common understanding of how interdependent life on Earth was, and of how tenuous was our existence on this our only planet.[73]

Whatever had prompted the environmental legislation of the seventies, one thing is clear: the landscape had changed for businesses. Gone were the days when corporates could easily disavow their role in environmental and social issues. 'So business had to move out of denial,' Jonathon tells us. 'The evidence was incontrovertible that there was a growing problem, and then the regulations kicked in, and business moved into compliance-based mindsets. And so that was the dominant behaviour of business: compliance with legislation.'

This culture of compliance characterised business during the eighties and nineties: doing the bare minimum, fulfilling their legal obligations, adhering to the regulations. For most companies, to declare '*we comply with the law wherever we operate*' was to discharge their responsibility to society. Any talk of 'doing the right thing' was deemed fanciful: the 'right thing' was encoded in the letter of the law. However, even then a small raft of companies began exploring a new approach: beyond mere compliance, they saw the possibility that 'the right thing' might be a driver of profitability. Among them was

3M, who back in 1975 developed a programme that went far beyond the regulations in order to reduce their negative environmental impacts. They called it the 3Ps – pollution prevention pays. Joe Ling, the 3M executive who introduced the programme, would describe the business case with a simple maxim: 'Pollution is waste, and waste today leads to shortages tomorrow.' Nearly four decades later it's still running, and the figures are impressive: according to 3M, the programme has prevented more than 1.36 billion kilograms of pollutants being tipped into the environment, and has saved 3M over $1.2 billion. This doesn't count significant repeat savings from lower operating costs, decreased raw material requirements, and reduced fuel consumption.

Examples like this encouraged companies to move beyond a compliance-based mentality, and to start thinking about the business case. As it became mainstream, some of the world's biggest companies became leading advocates for this way of thinking. Walmart, for example, expects to add $150 million to the bottom line in 2013 from renewable energy projects and its zero waste programme. This would be in addition to the $231 million the company says it saved last year from waste reduction and recycling. In the UK, Marks & Spencer's Plan A sustainability programme has made a net profit of $286 million from achievements such as reducing food waste (by 40 per cent) and improving energy efficiency per sq. feet (by 28 per cent). P&G, meanwhile, claims to have delivered over $1 billion from sustainability efforts in their operations, over a ten-year period. Gradually, cutting waste and reducing environmental impact became hallmarks of an efficiently run operation. Over time, it became clear that there were a broader range of potential business benefits, as Jonathon Porritt explains:

> To begin with it was all about tangible, monetisable, bottom-line benefits. If you look at the evolution of the

> concept of the business case [for sustainability] it is now much more sophisticated. Now it's all about things like recruiting and retaining talent, competitive advantage, and good relationships with regulators.

And so businesses began to pay serious attention to their role in society – and not just as a driver of business efficiency, but as an area of potential business opportunity. In 1990, the World Business Council for Sustainable Development (WBCSD) was formed to strengthen these arguments, asserting that: 'The business case is also an entrepreneurial position: it looks to the next point on the business curve – the point at which business can be more competitive by being more sustainability driven.'

At the same time, the scope of '*sustainability*' was beginning to span the full extent of a business's role in the world – including its social and economic impacts. After all, when you think about it the business case for fighting poverty is quite straightforward: business cannot succeed in societies that fail. Poverty is a waste of human resources: it results in an uneducated, low-skill workforce and a consumer base with limited potential. The WBCSD goes on to say:

> Smart companies, applying sound business thinking, are already beginning to see the benefits of pursuing poverty reduction. The potential for market expansion, discernible to merchants who see the advantages of dealing with the world's four billion poor, indicates that the best is yet to come.

Today, an astonishing breadth of concern has found its way onto the corporate to-do lists – environmental issues, health issues, social issues, the list has become a long one. If you had told a CEO from the 1960s that his company might one day be working at the forefront of global efforts to eliminate poverty, or conserve water, or save energy, he would most likely have thought you mad. Yet now that is exactly the situation for many big corporates. These are monumental global challenges, and all are inextricably linked. For example, it's impossible to tackle poverty without tackling health, and vice versa; and issues such as global food security cannot be tackled separately from issues like water conservation or energy management. It's a complex picture. There has been a growing realisation that no single actor, government, NGO or business, can define meaningful solutions by working in isolation. Everybody needs to work together. That's why collaboration and partnership have become watchwords of the age for business.

Collaboration is more than a zeitgeisty buzzword; it's not just the smart way of getting things done – sometimes it's the *only* way. Most tough problems require a systemic change. For example, when Starbucks made a commitment to promote recycling of its coffee cups, it quickly realised the issue required both a change in consumer behaviour and an improvement in the recycling infrastructure. This clearly wasn't something Starbucks was able to do alone, so it began by convening all players in the system: local government representatives, manufacturers, suppliers, recycling companies, conservation groups, academics, as well as competing retail and beverage businesses. Together, these partners were able to start work on an effective solution that would benefit the industry as a whole. This is an example of companies collaborating in a pre-competitive space. Another example is the Plant PET Technology Collaborative, in which competing businesses like Heinz, P&G and Coca-Cola are working on plastics made of plant-based materials, with the aim of developing fully commercial solutions and common methodologies and standards.

It seems as though every conceivable dimension of collaboration is now covered: single industry, multi-industry, local and national governments, international organisations, NGOs and activist groups, academic institutions. Some of the most interesting of these partnerships have been formed between corporates and their erstwhile critics, as we saw with APP and Golden Agri. Facebook and Greenpeace are working together to switch the social network's data centres to renewable energy, following a typically vociferous campaign by Greenpeace, urging Facebook to 'unfriend coal'. Greenpeace had galvanised 700,000 Facebook users to poke and pressurise Facebook into changing its ways. This brought the company to the table, where a partnership was forged. It's becoming a classic NGO play: mobilise, agitate, negotiate, collaborate. Greenpeace hopes that Facebook's decision will show the way for others in the industry. Under the headline 'Victory! Facebook 'friends' renewable energy', the Greenpeace website declared, 'Facebook founder and CEO Mark Zuckerberg has shown today what other IT leaders should be doing.'

It's a clear strategy: focus on the big businesses that can change *at scale,* and they will pull entire industries behind them. At The World Wildlife Fund they call this 'market transformation', and we spoke to Jason Clay, the WWF vice-president who leads their work with business. 'We have a theory of change for how we get the most influence with the least work, the fewest touches.' He tells us:

> We have a clear goal: we need to figure out how to produce more with less land, less water and less pollution. So how do we do that? Changing consumer behaviour is important, but we have seven-plus billion consumers on the planet, in different cultures, speaking different languages – so that's a daunting task. Changing producer behaviour is essential – but there are 1.5 billion producers on the planet – farmers, fishermen, etc. But there are just one hundred companies who control 25 per cent of

> all commodities. Just one hundred. We can get our arms around that. And what's more, we think that getting these companies to change will pull 40–50 per cent of the industry behind them. And we're seeing this happen.

He calls it the 'champagne glass' theory of change: seven billion consumers fizzing away at the top, with a base of 1.5 billion producers, connected by a fine stem of just one hundred big companies. Working with these companies, Jason believes, is the fastest way to change the system. One of WWF's long-standing partnerships is with Coca-Cola on water conservation. The partnership was established in 2007 to achieve Coke's goals of improving water efficiency in its own operations, as well as conserving some of the world's most important freshwater basins – including the Yangtze, Mekong and Danube. Numerous projects and initiatives are under way on the latter goal, and the company is on track to hit its five-year target to reduce its water use by 20 per cent. Coke's own journey towards sustainable water use began in controversy: in 2002, local women began protesting about the degradation of the water supply around a new Coca-Cola bottling plant – and these local protests quickly became a global news story. To add to the company's woes, a study found that Coke's drinks contained twenty-four times the maximum level of pesticides allowed – which prompted embarrassing news footage of Indian farmers using cola to debug their fields. MPs in the Indian parliament called for the company to be thrown out of the country, and the Indian Supreme Court ordered that it publish the ingredients of Coke – one of the most closely guarded secrets in corporate history. It was a rude awakening: an issue in a local bottling plant had threatened its national licence to operate, and damaged its global reputation. To understand these risks better, and to plan a response, Coca-Cola turned to WWF. Today, Coke has a Vice

President for Environment & Water Resources, Jeff Seabright, who states:

> Watersheds are nature's water factories, and the first line of our supply chain. But they are also a vital resource that underpins the health and well-being of communities and ecosystems. Our work with WWF has shown that by protecting this 'natural capital', we can help sustain business while benefiting people and nature.

And it's not just Coca-Cola. Having identified the 100 biggest food and fibre companies, WWF has now signed agreements with fifty-five of them – some 'transformational' scale partnerships with companies like SABMiller, M&S and United Biscuits, as well as a number of 'toe in the water' partnerships. WWF is also heavily involved in working with round-table bodies such as the Marine Stewardship Council, the Forest & Trade Network and the Finance Lab. It's new territory for both the corporates and the NGOs, forcing both to work in new ways. For NGOs, it requires working with a broader and deeper set of skills – and this can be challenging. 'It's very hard for the culture of NGOs to change,' Jason tells us. 'It's hard to expect very good conservationists, like foresters with decades of experience, to design strategies that bring in vastly different skill sets.' For example, you might need to work with financiers or international bankers, he explains – 'people who have very different ways of working, very different pay scales, it's a huge shift'. Even so, WWF is developing a very distinct way of working with these big corporates. 'In 75 per cent of meetings we just sit and listen,' says Jason. 'We're not there to tell them what to do, but to solve problems. Some NGOs will go in there and lay down the law. We go in and listen. If we're going to help solve their problems, we need to really understand them.' Many other NGOs, of course, take a far more confrontational approach to big business. Jason views this as an important part of the bigger picture:

> It's important to have NGOs that are very critical of businesses. It gets companies to take it seriously, it puts the issue on the agenda. It shows them that people really do care, that people are watching. To have a Greenpeace campaign, on deforestation for example, is very helpful. It becomes an open, public discussion. It pushes them in our direction, and we can help them understand what's important, why these issues matter and what they can do about them.

Jason grew up on a farm in Missouri, and was driving a tractor by the time he was four years old. Like many kids of his day in rural America, he grew up helping to raise the animals and tend the crops. His father died when he was still young, and he ended up running the family farm before he went to college. It was a daily struggle to make ends meet, and it gave Jason a lifelong appreciation for the realities of life for many farmers around the world. After college, he spent some time working for the United States Department of Agriculture, and lecturing at Yale and Harvard. 'I tried to work in government, I tried teaching – it just wasn't stimulating,' he says, explaining to us how he came to be working at WWF. He had become increasingly interested in figuring out how humanity can continue to thrive without destroying the natural world that supports us: 'This is the problem that has to be solved,' he says emphatically. 'I don't know if we will solve it, but this is where the change has to happen. This is the work that has to be done.'

We asked Jason how he came to the conclusion that this work could be done by partnering with business:

> In September 1988 I went to a Grateful Dead benefit concert for the rainforest. At the time I was working on human rights issues for indigenous peoples in the rainforests. I met this guy called Ben, and he asked me what he could do to help save the rainforest. He sold ice cream [with his business partner, Jerry]. I said he should make an ice cream with nuts from the rainforest, to show how the rainforest has value, to provide livelihoods for the peoples that live there. And so within a year, Ben & Jerry's *Rainforest Crunch* was on the shelves. I set up a trading company to buy and sell products from the rainforest. We had over 20 per cent of the global Brazil nut market, and we paid three times the market rate, which pushed up prices across the board. It generated $100 million in sales. It was the first time I saw that it is often through business that you have the power to change things.

Scott Poynton's passion is trees and he's made it his life's work to save the forests. And he shares Jason's Clay's conviction that it's through working with business that things change.

Of The Forest Trust he says:

> From day one, we've said we've got to work with the companies. It's no good going to the UN because it's not the UN that's chopping down the forests. It's no good going to the governments to create the policy context because what they need is examples of what it could be changed to; don't expect them to lead. It is the private sector that is chopping down the forest, so go to work with the private sector. Yes, they're the problem but they're also the solution. So let's work with them to show a model: Golden Agri is doing it, APP is doing it – show how it can be changed.

Yet while the public debate continues to discuss the role of business versus government versus the NGOs, Scott believes the key to collaboration is to focus on the people as agents of change. 'At the end of it all, we're all people. Let's talk about coming into the middle ground and work out solutions together; that's the creative space.'

While the world watches the continuing corporate journey for Golden Agri, the whole experience has been a personal journey for Peter Heng as well:

> When this began I visited almost every one of the reporters who were writing about us. And I can recall an incident where I was talking to one journalist – from a magazine which, coming from my background, I couldn't even afford to buy when I was young, and now here I am now being interviewed by their reporter – and at the end of the conversation he leaned forward to me and said, 'Before you came here today, Peter, I thought you had horns.' That right there talks about the need there is to reach out. And to do it one-to-one because that is where the trust is, it's not on a piece of paper. People need to look at you and decide whether you have integrity.

Peter sees it as vital to communicate the journey he has been on. The story he tells is one of the examples that shows real change can happen, even where once it seemed impossible:

> What excites me is that when you start to share your story, you begin to persuade people that they can begin their own journey. They start to think that this can also be their story.

13

EVERY STORY IS A JOURNEY

Whether it's been about the hard graft of agriculture or the mental sweat of technology, the old journalistic truth has proved itself: every story is a journey. From the quarries and pits of mining to the fast-moving hustle of consumer goods, each one of the stories in this book has been a journey of its own – and for many of these companies, their journey has been transformative. As David Mitchell's Zachry declares – sounding every bit like Huck Finn – 'there ain't no journey what don't change you some.'

Nike, for example, had a dark night of the soul in the 1990s, as public anger grew over its use of sweatshops in Asia. The company began with a disavowal of responsibility towards the people working in factories making their products: *not our factories,* they shrugged. It was a matter for their suppliers. The company trod an uphill path from this nadir, and is now setting new standards for both social and environmental behaviour. Nike had the world's first corporate responsibility department, and they published the world's first CSR report. Nike was the first major corporate to have a fully transparent supply chain – complete disclosure of every factory used to make a Nike product. Most businesses are still struggling to catch up. Today, Nike's decision to make a positive impact on the world is embedded in its product design process, through a merged Sustainable Business & Innovation unit. As we saw in Chapter 3, it's been a challenging journey – and a long one: Nike has been tackling these issues intensely for two decades.

Many of the stories we have seen follow a similar pattern. As one of the world's biggest pharmaceutical companies, GSK was widely loathed for enforcing patents on HIV/AIDS medication while millions were dying of the disease across Africa. The low point came when the industry decided to sue the South African government for patent violation – in effect, Big Pharma sued Nelson Mandela, bringing protestors out onto the streets in capitals across the world. As the AIDS epidemic grew and the suffering mounted, people in GSK started to question how they had become so disconnected from the human impact of their business decisions. In the years that followed, the company has been turning the business model inside out, introducing new pricing structures to improve access to treatment. Today, GSK is collaborating across the industry to improve treatment for the killer diseases of the world's poorest countries. The journey has been long and hard, but their determination to set new ground rules for how pharma relates to society seems to be working – both for the company, and for those who might use its medicines. In a sense, it's a return to the original spirit of the pharmaceutical industry: to make money by making people well.

With IBM, we saw the journey of a company that was struggling to define its relevance to the modern world – a lumbering giant in a new internet age. It had become a dull, sprawling megacorp, cut off from people's lives. As we heard from one of its executives, 'the company practically lived in its data centres'. The 2008 financial crisis forced IBM to dig deep and ask some difficult questions about its strategy and purpose. This led to *Smarter Planet*, a strategy to grow by making the world work better, which insiders say has reconnected the company to society. PepsiCo, a company that was widely criticised as a 'water hog' in water-scarce areas, became an advocate for making access to drinkable water a human right. In a very different industry – mining – BHP Billiton, once characterised as a predator in the countries that hosted it, has become a partner to governments wanting to generate viable economic growth for their citizens. The list goes on. All of these companies are now recognised role models for doing business purposefully, acting in ways that benefit a broader scope of stakeholders – but all of them have made a long journey to get there.

In the archetypes of storytelling, a scholar of literature might tell us, these are all tales of *rebirth*: the protagonist falls under the compulsion of some dark desire, or into the doldrums of a deep malaise, and the action is always a journey of some kind. In *Peer Gynt*, for example, the hero is a callous and incorrigible liar who is no longer welcome in his hometown: he finds redemption on his journey through the subterranean kingdom of the trolls, emerging with a new sense of purpose. Literature is full of such stories: some kind of awakening takes place, and the cold grip of winter is replaced by the summer's warmth. Some of our stories are redolent of this plotline: businesses that have struggled to win back society's approbation, and in so doing become leaders in their fields. Others follow a more straightforward archetype: the *rags to riches* story, where the protagonist has a great sense of conviction – often incurring scorn and mockery – and is driven to some great achievement, bringing benefit to those around it. We saw this with MTN, for example: a start-up from South Africa, who believed in the potential for mobile in Africa when others dismissed the continent as too poverty-stricken; today they are one of Africa's biggest companies, and millions have benefited from mobile access as a result.

Of course, these archetypes come from the world of fiction, where stories have a beginning, middle, and an end; in the real world, journeys continue. All of the companies we have met are now recognised as role models for doing business purposefully, acting in ways that benefit their customers and shareholders for the long-term, and also contribute to wider society. They have a broader view about what matters, and a stronger sense of identity. Still, in public perception, these companies remain the exceptions that prove the rule. Big business is often seen as narrowly focused on the pursuit of profit, to the exclusion of all else. In the public imagination, they fit into an archetype of antihero: these big beasts are miserable creatures, much like the Selfish Giant in Oscar Wilde's story:

> *'My own garden is my own garden,' said the Giant; 'any one can understand that, and I will allow nobody to play in it but myself.' So he built a high wall all round it, and put up a notice-board.*
>
> TRESPASSERS
> WILL BE
> PROSECUTED
>
> *He was a very selfish Giant.*
>
> *The poor children had now nowhere to play. They tried to play on the road, but the road was very dusty and full of hard stones, and they did not like it.*

WHY EVERYBODY HATES THE BANKS

Ever since the news broke on 15 September 2008 that Lehman Brothers had collapsed, the world has been dealing with the consequences. Countless words have been written and uttered on the subject: hearings have been held, investigations conducted, reports written and regulations rewritten. Years later, there's still continuous media commentary on the question of what happened and what's to be done. A raft of genuinely enlightening books have explored how things came to such a pass and how to ensure that it can never happen again. The whole financial system has been called into question.

The financial sector has not been our subject here. Our focus has been on businesses and their place in society. In the lead-up to the crash, the balance between the two was out of kilter: one of the symptoms of the over-heated system was that businesses were in thrall to the financial sector, rather than the financial sector being in the service of business. And these days, in popular debate, *the banks* often engulf any conversation about *business*, and bankers' bonuses seem to make any consideration of the positive contribution of business laughable. So it's been our intention to disentangle the role of business from the heat that continues to surround the banking sector.

Nevertheless, banks are everybody's business. If the crash showed us anything it was the degree to which the banks are systemically important in all our lives, and that holds true for individuals, for businesses, for countries and for the global economy. So we need to pause to ask where they are in this story. Recognising that banking has a core purpose and a social value is not hard. And getting banking to people who don't have access to it is commonly understood to be a social good. Like electricity, the product is invisible and how it actually works is a mystery to most of us, but we understand that it is of great practical significance to our quality of life.

How essential banks are to everyone is directly proportionate to how deeply betrayed people felt when it all went wrong. Suzanne McGee's gripping telling of the horror story of the financial crisis, *Chasing Goldman Sachs,* includes a scene from a public debate hosted in New York by the not-for-profit organisation Intelligence Squared, where 'a twenty-something laid-off banker who gave his name only as Peter' took the floor with the declaration, 'We're the most hated guys out there.'[74]

That hatred was given expression in the Occupy movement.

When thousands turned up in Zuccotti Park in New York's financial district to *Occupy Wall Street,* the idea was quickly taken up in more than 100 cities across America and spread to 1,000 sites across the world. 'But what do they want?' was a question often asked in the boardrooms which looked down on the site of mass protest. Paradoxically, incoherence was part of the power of the phenomenon at the time. Occupy was not an activist group with specific demands or a political uprising aiming to wrest power for itself. It was a broad social movement – everyone, young and old, radical and establishment, working and workless came to stand under the banner of Occupy to convey quite simply that what had happened was not right and not fair. As they said, 'We are the 99 per cent', they are – almost – everybody. So Occupy is literally a demonstration that the banks and the powerful system they were part of had lost their connection to society. The movement succeeded in putting inequality and fairness centre stage in the political debate, and it's still there. But over the months, the encampments settled in and the placards became just part of the scenery in the world's financial centres. Then they moved on. The impetus seemed to fizzle out.

In parallel, the process of formal reviews came to a similar conclusion: it wasn't right and it wasn't fair, and it was caused by the people in charge right across the system. The language of the Financial Crisis Inquiry Report, published in January 2011 in the USA, jumps from the page:

> The crisis was a result of human action and inaction ... a crisis of this magnitude need not have occurred ... The captains of finance and the public stewards of our finance systems ignored warnings and failed to question ... Theirs was a big miss, not a stumble ... We conclude there was a systemic breakdown in accountability and ethics.

Lord Turner, heading up the Financial Services Authority in the UK, damned as 'socially useless' the activities that had led to the spectacular rise – and fall – of the financial services sector.

It's obvious that some important changes have been made since the crash. Heads have rolled and new heads are running the show. Capital ratios have increased. Business units have been sold, products have been wound up in the worst offending areas. Some practical and structural problems have been sorted. The overall feeling is that normal service has been resumed. And that's what drives everyone else wild.

People don't want the banks as they were; they want banks of a different character. The reason people express the same visceral fury – hatred even – is because they don't believe the banks have changed fundamentally. Bonus time keeps on coming round, providing a fresh reminder to the outside world that the underlying assumptions don't seem to have changed much. New scandals get exposed, reinforcing the sense that the real problem is not a series of isolated incidents but rather the underlying attitude of the industry to doing business. It's the attitude that 'symbolised what was wrong with the system', according to Susan McGee. She cites the on-air remarks of the chairman of Citigroup on Brian Lehrer's radio chat-show that following its billion-dollar bailout, the priority of the bank was to recover as quickly as possible so it could 'do the right thing by its two most important constituencies', meaning its employees and its shareholders – with no reference to the government, the tax payers, its clients or the wider financial system. She is describing an industry with no recognition of the true price paid by society for its actions – and little desire to reconnect to the wider world. In our view, that's why anger stays so close to the surface: people lack that flicker of recognition.

In the preceding chapters, we've told stories of companies

that were vilified once and set out on a journey that transformed their relationship with society. We saw them come hard up against the reality that their actions had broken faith with a social contract, or that their operating model could not withstand the glare of public scrutiny. What mattered is what happened next. We saw them recognise that their success as a business was costing others dear. The leaders of those businesses talked in a forthright way about what needed to be fixed and began to adapt their businesses accordingly. Crucially, they showed that they grasped what people were so concerned about. Those businesses created a pivot point and changed their direction of travel. Quite clearly, they set off on a new journey.

A striking characteristic that all these leading businesses share is that they make the cause their own. Whether it's sustainable sourcing, human rights in their supply chain, access to drugs or halting deforestation, they step out in front of what regulation is demanding of them and what common practice has set as the standard. They start to grapple directly with the problem as the outside world sees it. Because of that, they earn the right to be champions for change in the public arena. They set the pace on the journey for others.

Granted, heroes are few in this life. Transformation takes time and the stories we've told have been years in the making. At the moment the space is wide open for any of the big banks to step out into a leadership role for the sector. So the question of the moment is whether there are any signs of that. Maybe. Bank of America has embarked on its Transformation programme. Barclays has articulated a new strategy with the aim of becoming the 'Go-To' bank, with the promise from the CEO that 'there will be no going back to the old way of doing things'. HSBC's chairman has spoken eloquently on industry platforms, acknowledging that the responsibility for transformation lies squarely with the banks themselves:

> Our greatest risks are from within our own industry and the needed rehabilitation of our industry in terms of public trust. And confidence can only be earned by demonstrating both that lessons have been learned and that social contribution trumps self-interest.[75]

Social contribution in place of self-interest is certainly what the world is looking for from the banks. Matthew Bishop, New York Bureau Chief of *The Economist* and co-author of *The Road from Ruin,* is not alone in arguing that the financial system overall needs a decisive shift to a longer term orientation – but he strikes a more unusual optimistic note in his belief that this could provide a new context for innovation when he says, 'My hope would be that ... the ingenuity of financial innovators would be directed more towards socially useful ends.'[76] But as yet there's not that story to tell. If some years down the road, there is such a story, we look forward to telling it.

BREAKING THE MIRROR

Many of the companies we have met in this book are much further along in their own stories than the banks. We've seen in detail how their journeys progress, and the themes that emerge – and what comes out is that it takes great leadership. We wanted to hear directly the voices of people who have led that change. In Chapter 11, we saw how GSK helped to transform the pharmaceutical industry's approach to doing business, and begin the process of reconnecting with society. We spoke to the CEO, Andrew Witty, to hear his perspective on this journey.

'Big organisations can be remarkably stubborn,' he tells us – and he should know about big organisations: GSK is one of the world's Big Pharma giants, employing 100,000 people. GSK spends $600,000 an hour on research and development. Andrew joined GSK when the company was really struggling with demands for better access to medicine for the world's poorest, and its research and development efforts needed resuscitating. 'I felt it was a moment when we had to break the mirror, to move on,' Andrew recalls. 'I came to the conclusion that small incremental change wouldn't be enough. We needed to do a few things that were quite surprising to people.' It's a striking image – 'to break the mirror' – and so we asked him what he meant by it:

> Because it's impossible to put it back together, isn't it? I mean I wanted something where it was impossible to go backwards; you just have to go forward, it's not an experiment that you're able to lose faith in; you just have to make it happen.

Andrew was appointed in 2008, when he was forty-three, and brought with him a fresh sense of dynamism. 'I felt that we needed to re-energise the people. There wasn't sufficient energy or direction; there was something missing with the engagement of the organisation. I wanted to inject a sense of change, to create some momentum.' A key part of this, for Andrew, was finding a way to reconnect the business – and pharma as a whole – to the outside world. 'I had a sense that the whole industry was behind where society wanted it to be,' he says.

In Chapter 6 we met another company that has set out on an ambitious journey: Unilever, whose CEO Paul Polman crystallised the mission for the company. Polman became CEO of Unilever in 2009 – at the height of the financial crisis, he points out. As with GSK when Andrew Witty took the reins, the company was not performing well. 'There was a high level of insecurity,' Paul tells us:

> The company had become very internally focused and was actually shrinking. We had lost quite a lot of business over the preceding decade. Just to tell the company to run faster and run harder and to squeeze the costs would not be a very successful long-term strategy. We needed a vision: we needed to bring the outside in.

The vision, when they framed it up, was dramatic: to double the size of the business while at the same time reducing environmental impact by half. Called the Sustainable Living Plan, it also contained the ambitious targets of improving the health of a billion people, and including 500,000 smallholder farmers in the supply chain. It was a bold move, aimed at shifting the internal focus that had developed in the organisation, and forcing it to look at the world outside. It put Unilever ahead of the pack on building environmental and social impact into the core business strategy – but not everyone in the organisation, or outside, warmed to the approach at first. Paul shrugs them off: 'Cynicism, I say, is the easiest form of abdicating responsibility.'

For Unilever, the Sustainable Living Plan placed the agenda for change at the heart of the organisation. There is no separate Corporate Social Responsibility department: meeting the ambitious targets is the job of the business itself. This is a common theme in many of the stories we've encountered: don't simply tinker with activities at the periphery of the business – take it into the core business model. In some cases, this might involve shifting the basic product offering, as PepsiCo is doing by transforming its portfolio towards healthier foods and drink. In the spirit of Andrew's 'breaking the mirror' analogy, we heard PepsiCo's CEO Indra Nooyi reflecting that 'We have to disrupt our businesses before they disrupt us. We have to transform our strategies and our business models to cater for these new world realities.'

In other cases, it requires a change in processes, such as Nike's fusing of innovation with sustainable development, or the decision by APP to cease deforestation of the rainforest and rely instead on plantation-grown wood. For GSK, as we saw in Chapter 11, it involved a new, open approach to research and a more flexible approach to pricing. As Andrew explains to us, 'so many of the things we've changed involve the business model rather than simply adding an activity without really changing the core business model.'

For Paul Polman, the journey starts by looking for the issues that are relevant to your business, and embracing them. 'I have grown up in the way that you take full responsibility for the issues you are part of,' he tells us. It's about having a point of view about what matters, a perspective on the contentious issues in which the company may play a role:

> Many businesses operate under the principle that as long as they are on the right side of the law, they are fine. So many businesses think 'how can I use society and the environment to be successful?' We think about it slightly differently: how can we improve society and the environment to be successful?

At GSK, Andrew tells us that change requires you to become highly attuned to the signals coming from the outside world. 'When an issue hits you, you have to recognise it very quickly and begin to respond. If you don't, you are almost never forgiven.' GSK has recently found itself having to mobilise fast to do battle on the front line of corrupt selling practices in China. Of course, the frontier of public debate about the role of business in society is always changing, new areas of friction emerge, and an issue can flare up so intensely that it eclipses the broader discourse. Corporate taxation is an example: a succession of businesses have found themselves in the spotlight over their tax affairs, mainly companies with complex global operations. Often, their response has been to point out that no laws have been broken – which, to their detractors, is entirely unsatisfying. We discussed corporate tax when we met Paul. 'Oh, it's a hot topic,' he agreed:

> Tax is a morality issue ... Some companies have set out to misrepresent economic activity ... It is unacceptable to have business in a country, and make money in a country, but pay zero tax. That is a morality issue. They might claim it's the law that allows me to do that, but to hide behind the law is a cheap escape. And society will hold them accountable, which is exactly what is happening.

A morality issue: interesting to hear him stress this point, and so we ask about it. 'We need to not shy away from the discussion about morality in business, and in how business acts in society.'

'Really it's about the mindset,' Andrew says. 'As with all challenging issues, the companies in the limelight on tax need to really understand what the question is, or they'll find it hard to justify themselves to the public.'

Understanding what the question is coming from the wider world means developing a new capability within the business, a sort of *active listening*: 'I've found that you need to get good at really understanding society's concerns, so you can get there at more or less the same time as your critics, rather than a year or two later.' For Andrew, what's needed is a new attitude to the outside world:

> The mindset actually is humility – which, five or ten years ago, is not a word that many people would have used in the same sentence as GSK. But everything we're trying to achieve is underpinned by humility. It means

> understanding that we have a small role to play in a very big world, and that we ought to be really thoughtful about how we do it. We need to be out there listening and connecting and being open to evolve in our business model, to help society do better. And if we can learn to do that well, we will do well.

Many of the businesses we have met have a sense that there is a vacuum of leadership on the global stage, and feel that big companies have to step up and play a role. 'The world has become very interdependent, there's no doubt about that, but the political system hasn't adjusted,' Polman tells us:

'There's a lack of leadership, for sure, but also a system that has come to a grinding halt. And politicians have become shorter and shorter term. So the role of business – where you are global, where you are a bit more long-term – is to anticipate the issues and lead the initiatives.'

Big businesses are on the front line of some of the world's most pressing challenges, such as water scarcity or food security. The leaders of business have themselves become players on world issues: Paul Polman was invited by the UN Secretary-General Ban Ki-moon to join the high-level panel that will decide upon the next round of Millennium Development Goals. Global health is a perpetual challenge, and Andrew Witty has become a prominent voice on issues such as improving health infrastructures in poorer countries. It's an important part of the journey for many companies: the awareness that they have the potential to play a broader role in the world. Alongside this comes the recognition that companies should serve the interests of a broader set of constituents than just shareholders. Andrew is emphatic on this point:

> I'm very resistant to the argument that a corporate exists to service its shareholders. These are very large economic institutions. They have a broad stakeholder interest and it's entirely reasonable to me to argue that you can in fact achieve substantial social engagement and be a highly successful economic entity, and therefore think of a broad pallet of stakeholders rather than creating this 1980s self-constrained dimension of one stakeholder. So yes, I think the shareholder is crucially important. I simply don't believe they are the only important stakeholder.

Polman agrees. For him, all shareholders are not created equal, and he has set out to attract those who buy into the company's long-term vision. 'Just because someone has the money to buy 1 per cent of this company, which many can do, doesn't give them the right to change the strategy,' he tells us. For Unilever, a landmark moment in the journey came when the company announced it would stop providing quarterly updates on earnings – a brave step in a market intensely focused on short-term returns. 'I can now have much more intelligent discussions about strategy with my shareholder base,' he says, pointing out that the share price has doubled in the past four years. It's an important shift in perspective for any company setting out on its own journey: from a narrow focus on shareholders, to a broader view of society; from a short-term financial mindset, to a longer strategic horizon. As Paul puts it:

'It's very easy to get this company to produce 10 per cent profit more in one year. I stop training; I stop investing in IT; I don't do any market research; I get rid of all my agencies – and frankly all that is what this company *was* doing, because it was shrinking and it had to make its profit. So to give into these people, because they want a short-term move on the share price, would be very dangerous I think.'

Most people would agree that the companies we have featured in *Everybody's Business* are a group of leaders, not the typical run of business – and occasionally we have heard concerns that they're so far ahead in their own journeys, that they may simply leave the bulk of the business world behind. Polman dismisses this. 'There is always a normal process: some adapt and some don't adapt,' he explains. 'Are we concerned that some newspapers don't get the digital world? No, because the ones that don't get it will go.' It's a case of creating a critical mass on a specific issue to change the market itself, he suggests:

> Companies like ours need to be market transformers, and need to want to go on a journey. You have to ask, what is the force you need to create to make the change you want to achieve? I am convinced you need about thirty of the right companies or coalitions behind an issue to make things happen. And you just need to get to that tipping point.

Both Andrew Witty and Paul Polman find it inadequate to talk about companies as somehow 'good' or 'bad', although the debate around business has become very polarised in recent years. 'In my experience, much better than calling people "good" or "bad" is to recognise this as a journey,' Andrew tells us:

> You can't really see a company in a snapshot – but 'good' or 'bad' tend to be very static assessments. All organisations are typically on a migration from somewhere to somewhere. It'll never be finished. And once you get engaged in a conversation I think it's amazing how much a company can move, in very large agreement with very

> wide numbers of stakeholders. But the company needs to have a sense of dynamism or willingness to move, which is what I've tried to create.

When you consider the scale and complexity of these huge corporates, operating in fast-moving environments, and dealing with many competing internal and external agendas, it seems highly reductive to think of them as 'good' or 'bad'. It's a theme Paul picks up on:

> It's frustrating when people think in end points; there is no end point anywhere, there is no end point in life, there is no right or wrong. It is in the eye of the beholder. So what you need to do is get people on the journey. And the journey needs to be one of *measured, continuous improvement.*

He gives a special emphasis on the last three words: *measured, continuous improvement*. For both of these CEOs, leadership is about constantly raising the game, stretching the business. As Andrew tells us: 'you need to be constantly asking yourself what more you could be doing, constantly anxious about missing things: are we missing challenges or opportunities, being restless for improvement. And for me that's really the sensation I'm trying to create in the company.'

These two individuals, running two of the world's largest companies, each have the feel of two men who find they have caught a tiger by the tail. As Andrew puts it:

> I just think when you're in a job like this you have a temporary period when you have command of a remarkable portfolio of skills and resources. What a shame to get to the end of it all and only to be able to measure it in money. I mean that would be ... quite sad actually.

PART III

HOW BUSINESS CAN FIX THE WORLD

14

THE 11 CONVERSATIONS

Early on, in the first part of this book, we visited places where you can see what businesses mean to the societies they operate in. Whether they are the technology giants of Silicon Valley or the farming collectives of rural Uganda, they create livelihoods in those communities – and whole ecosystems are established around them. Their activities create the fabric of the culture and economy in those places.

In the second part of the book, we took a journey through the world of business to understand the ways in which a big corporate can have a positive impact on the world. We saw how they are themselves on a journey, discovering and working out how to connect constructively with wider society.

And because this is a book about the role of business in society, in this final section, we step back to look at what society is concerned about. What are the big debates in the world today and the big challenges we face? And we look at how business fits into that and how it can make a meaningful contribution.

THE AGE OF CONVERSATION

A single edition of the *New York Times,* we are told, contains more information about the world than the average person from the seventeenth century was likely to encounter during their entire lifetime. We now have instant access to knowledge that would have been unimaginable a few generations ago. We're even bombarded with statistics about how information-rich our environment is: every day nearly 300 billion emails are sent. In 2012 YouTube hit 4 billion views per day. This explosion has been made possible by the exponential increase in communications power: we now have the prefixes kilo-, mega-, giga-, tera-, peta-, exa-, with zetta- and yotta- waiting to take the stage.

Take an average day in our times. More than 2 million blog posts are written – that's enough to fill *Time* magazine for 770 years. Meanwhile, 526 million people check Facebook every day and upload 300 million photos. On top of this, each day there are 3.2 billion comments and 'likes' on Facebook. That's a whole lot of liking going on. And each day on YouTube, 86,400 hours of video are uploaded, and 14 million people like, share, and comment on these videos. It's a continuous cycle: post, comment, upload, view, like, respond, share. It's often said we live in the Age of Information – although it might more properly be called the Age of Conversation.

This sprawling, continuous conversation is changing our culture. Ordinary people have a voice in big events, and powerful people participate in the mainstream debates. Nothing is more emblematic of this than Twitter – which, at the time of writing, is heading towards half a billion accounts and approaching 200 million tweets a day. Founded in 2006, Twitter already lays claim to some historic moments. In May 2011, the raid on Osama bin Laden's compound was live-tweeted by Sohaib Athar, a concerned neighbour. Later that summer, after riots shook the city of London, thousands took to the streets to help clean up – mobilised by the hashtag

#riotcleanup, which was started by three local residents, Dan Thompson, Sophie Collard and Sam Duckworth.

President Paul Kagame of Rwanda surprised many when he joined a Twitter conversation about human rights in his country. Journalist Ian Birrell had tweeted that Rwanda's leader was 'despotic' and 'deluded' – and was taken aback when Kagame fired back with fourteen tweets defending himself. A global conversation ensued across news channels and Twitter, as the journalist and the President traded tweets.

Twitter has even found its way into space. On 12 May 2009, astronaut Mike Massimino made history with an extra-terrestrial tweet:

> From orbit: Launch was awesome!! I am feeling great, working hard & enjoying the magnificent views, the adventure of a lifetime has begun!

His words may not quite carry the sense of history that Neil Armstrong managed with his timeless 'That's one small step for a man, one giant leap for mankind', but Twitter is not without its literary advocates. Salman Rushdie (@SalmanRushdie) – winner of two Whitbread Awards, the Booker, and the Booker of Bookers – is an avid user, with 235,000 followers. Margaret Atwood (@MargaretAtwood), who at the time of writing has over 300,000 followers, told *The Guardian* newspaper that she fell into Twitter 'like Alice down a rabbit hole'. She says, 'let's just say it's communication, and communication is something human beings like to do.'

Twitter is one of the many Silicon Valley businesses to have made a significant impact on the global conversation – but it hasn't yet found a way around the Great Firewall of China. However, a Chinese alternative is now well established: Weibo, which means simply 'microblog'. The service is approaching

400 million users. Quietly, without the clamour surrounding social media in the West, Weibo is changing the public debate in China. The Propaganda Department has urged government officials to 'embrace Weibo with more openness and confidence'. This was followed by a directive from the Ministry of Public Security instructing bureaux and police officers across China to set up Weibo accounts to 'use correct, authoritative, transparent news to answer people's concerns in a timely way, clarify facts and clear up misunderstandings.' In other words, China's state is exploring new ways to engage with China's public.

According to the Ministry, some government officials' Weibo accounts have already attracted millions of followers. The long-term implications of this are uncertain – but one thing is clear: Weibo has created a momentum towards public conversation that may be difficult to reverse, even for Communist Party hardliners. Over the past decade, a number of statutes and regulations have been issued to keep the internet firmly within the influence of the state, but shutting down Weibo would be an impossible task. Zhan Jiang, a journalism professor at Beijing Foreign Studies University, takes the view that it would generate tremendous unrest in the Chinese public, especially among a well-informed generation that has come to cherish open dialogue.

Visiting Beijing, we connected with Kaiser Kuo, Director of International Communication at Baidu, China's leading web search engine. Kaiser is a large and larger-than-life character, who is better known in China as a guitarist with the heavy metal band Tang Dynasty in the 1990s than in his role as roving ambassador for Baidu over the past couple of years. He brings with him the easy extrovert manner, leather jacket and ponytail that cast him as a veteran of the music scene. He's a long-time commentator on China for Silicon Valley and on Silicon Valley for China, which puts him in exactly the right spot to interpret the cultural shift being brought about by online media. He describes the rise of Baidu as part of the 'larger mission of the internet in China'. Whether it's for search, social networks, video channels or microblogs, he's talking for the band of tech entrepreneurs leading internet businesses in the country when he says:

> We definitely feel we are changing lives. Expanding people's information horizon. Information builds choice and choice builds freedom. Even the lowliest person in the fields has access to information. And that's a noble mission.

Not all internet use in China is high minded: as in the West, millions of people simply want to share videos of cute kittens and embarrassing photos of drunken nights out. But beyond the layer of entertaining trivia, Kaiser credits the internet with establishing a brand-new public sphere, which never existed in China before: 'Until the internet, there was no major outlet for the voice of the people.'

Everyone knows, of course, that the internet can be used to bully, as well as to liberate; to incite discord and violence as well as to engage; to spy and pry as well as to open up and include – and is used in those ways, in China as elsewhere in the world. Kaiser is sanguine about the challenge that as a search engine in China, the business compromises to operate within the context of internet censorship. 'We don't labour under any illusions that users prefer bowdlerised text – but we work within the boundaries of the law in China,' he explains. While the West tends to focus on the efforts to restrict the flow of information in China, Kaiser thinks the Chinese public's imagination has been captured by the momentum that is forcefully pushing in the direction of opening channels that had been firmly closed before:

> We're making it easier to understand public sentiment. We're a force for public participation in the decision-making process. We've seen the online conversation become the national agenda.

In the West, access to information and freedom of expression are felt to be intrinsic to our cultural inheritance, but in modern China they've been given a completely new lease of life through the online conversation.

If we are in the Age of Conversation, it was the world of consumer marketing that first woke up to this fact. Gone is the *Mad Men* age of broadcast marketing; corporates are adapting to the new paradigm, and it was in the marketing department that this first happened. In 1999 a book was published which gained a cult following in the world of branding. It was called *The Cluetrain Manifesto*, and in many ways it presaged social media. *Cluetrain* became famous for its central thought: 'Markets Are Conversations':

> The first markets were filled with people, not abstractions or statistical aggregates; they were the places where supply met demand with a firm handshake. Buyers and sellers looked each other in the eye, met and connected ... For thousands of years, we knew exactly what markets were: conversations between people who sought out others who shared the same interests. Buyers had as much to say as sellers. They spoke directly to each other without the filter of media, the artifice of positioning statements, the arrogance of advertising, or the shading of public relations.[77]

The sheer scale of modern business drove a wedge between buyers and sellers, creating a world of mass production, mass distribution, mass media and mass consumption. The modern consumer came into being – in the words of industry analyst, Jerry Michalski, 'a gullet whose only purpose in life is to gulp products and crap cash.' The word 'market' became a verb, something done to somebody, rather than an exchange between people.

As the growth of the internet made itself felt, marketers took this critique to heart. In the age of social media, the idea that markets are conversations seems very intuitive. Back in 2007, David Armano wrote a *Business Week* article called 'It's the Conversation Economy, Stupid', arguing that brands should start to think in terms of conversations. 'Conversations lead to relationships lead to affinity,' he wrote, going on to ask:

> Can you see the old-world residue in the word 'communicate?' It lacks the dimensions of experiencing something and having an ongoing two-way dialogue. 'What are we trying to communicate?' implies a one-way conversation. Maybe we should ask ourselves: 'How can we facilitate?'

This now seems obvious in the world of consumer marketing – and slowly corporates are beginning to adopt this same attitude to their relationships across society as a whole. Recent years have seen a shift of power away from established structures and small elites, towards broader ground-up networks. In business and in politics, leaders can no longer control the conversation in the way they used to, and long-standing power relationships have been upended overnight. Many corporates are adapting to this new environment; those that don't risk being swept away or simply rendered irrelevant.

Corporates have long suffered from what psychologists call 'conversational narcissism' – an inability to talk about anything other than yourself. But many of the companies we have met in this book have moved from this constant 'transmit' mode, and are beginning a dialogue with those around them – including their critics. They are moving beyond 'messaging' and 'audience targeting'. Instead of asking, 'What are we trying to communicate?' they are asking 'What's the conversation?' They understand that they have the skills, expertise, resources and influence to make a real contribution to the big conversations. In the Age of Conversation, business leaders are growing their businesses by joining the effort to tackle the global challenges we all face. They're joining the big conversations, and asking a powerful question: *how can we help?* It's a big shift and it requires a new way of looking at the world.

THE SIGNAL IN THE NOISE

In our modern world there are ever-widening circles of conversations: TEDTalks, Do Lectures, RSA Animate, SXSW, PopTech, the Skoll World Forum, Google Zeitgeist, the World Economic Forum, the Clinton Global Initiative, the Mobile World Congress, One Young World. Traditional print media have created their own forums; the *Wall Street Journal* has its CEO Council, *The Times* has its CEO Summit, *Fortune* has set up the Most Powerful Women Summit. The online network Avaaz connects 15 million activists worldwide in their shared commitment to social action. Hardly a week goes by without a high-level global summit, platform, conference or forum. It just keeps growing and sometimes it feels as though the noise is deafening.

The question is, what on earth is everyone talking about? We set out to explore the places where some of the most influential conversations are happening. What's on the radar screen of the major global institutions? What's on the agenda at the major global forums? What issues concern the global NGOs? What are the policy priorities of national governments, in the developed and developing world?

In total we looked at around thirty institutions, each with a global perspective: intergovernmental institutions, big governments, multinational companies, and major players in the not-for-profit world. We analysed reports and publications, conference agendas, policy positions and strategic priorities. We found a wide range of tone and style – some analytical and academic, others eclectic; some corporate and strategic, others by 'big thinkers'. What we found is, everywhere you look, you see different versions of the same agenda.

- We began by looking at the global institutions. The United Nations (UN), for example, lists its top thirty 'Global Issues', racing through the alphabet from Africa and Ageing through to Climate Change, Democracy, Food, Human Rights, Peace and Security, Refugees and on to Water and Women. The World Economic Forum (WEF) has a different tone, flowing from its origins in the business world, but the topics are similar, covering areas such as environmental protection, food supplies, governance, and global health-care challenges.

- McKinsey is a renowned management consultancy that has many of the world's top corporates as clients, and is familiar to many people through the publication of the *McKinsey Quarterly*. McKinsey identifies five global forces shaping the future of business and society, which inform the content it publishes. They are *the great rebalancing* – which discusses the significance of the growth of the fast rising economies; *the productivity imperative* – which talks about the need for the developed economies to drive new growth through innovation; *pricing the planet* – which discusses the issues around resource scarcity; *the market state* – looking at the balance required between economic growth and social safety nets, and between national governments and international strategies; and *the global grid* – explaining the ever greater connectivity of the global economy. These are all different perspectives on the issues we saw identified by the global institutions.

- As we continued to explore public platforms, we saw similar themes recurring. TEDTalks – billing itself as 'Ideas Worth Spreading' – is another global platform which brings a range of voices into the conversation. They cover a bewildering range of subjects: *Cheese, dogs and pills to end malaria* – on eradicating one of the world's great killer diseases; *A reality check on renewables* – on new energy technologies; *The other inconvenient truth* – on the world's 'skyrocketing demand for food'; *Unlock the intelligence, passion and greatness of girls* – on the untapped potential of young women. So, again, some big topics recur: health, energy, resources, environment, and the role of women.

- We found the same pattern of overlapping and intersecting priorities in the work of some of the world's most respected NGOs. The World Wildlife Fund, Oxfam and Amnesty International may have different ultimate goals – environmental protection, poverty alleviation and human rights – but reaching these goals inevitably leads them to turn their attention to a similar set of big challenges, such as water, population growth, and employment. The world of politics, meanwhile, is dominated by the same big debates: wherever you look, governments are grappling with areas like health care, security, and energy.

- We explored a whole host of other platforms and organisations, including the Commonwealth Secretariat, the IMF, the OECD, the World Bank, the G20, USAID, the UK's Department for International Development, and the Clinton Global Initiative. Ranging across this territory, it's possible to trace how the various agendas weave in and out of one another. They often converge. The topics appear to multiply continuously – jostling and ceaselessly subdividing, like cells in a bacterial culture. It's an unending churn, constantly drawing in new voices, fresh data, the latest momentous events.

Yet within this burgeoning, ever-evolving swirl of conversations, we reached the conclusion that you can find the signal in the noise; that there are only a finite number of themes being discussed. According to Christopher Booker, in the great creative proliferation of plays, novels and films produced in human history, there are only seven basic plots.[78] The way the stories are told seems to have infinite variety, but they unfold from a few underlying dramatic structures. In a similar way, we think there are only eleven big conversations about the challenges facing the world today – The 11 Conversations.

THE 11 CONVERSATIONS

So what are the eleven big conversations? This is what they look like: *Population, Health, Environment & Resources, Security, Consumer Culture, Communication, Human Rights, Communities, Global Economy, Education & Skills, Energy & Climate Change.*

Underlying each of the 11 Conversations are three enduring drivers of change: technology, globalisation and sustainability. Together, these three drivers are creating new realities for all of us – and have done throughout human history. Countless books have been written on these three, and here we only define these terms in relation to the 11 Conversations:

- Technology is essentially the creation of new tools, and has long been a major driver of social change – from the agrarian revolution and the industrial revolution, to today's information revolution. Each of the 11 Conversations today is heavily influenced by advances in technology – from digital media raising new concerns about privacy which may infringe *Human Rights,* to the ethics of genome research in *Health.*

- Globalisation is the intermingling of human activity across the world: ideas, views, products, resources, languages, systems, infrastructure... This has long shaped human culture – today's world would look very different without the Phoenician sailors, the Greco-Roman traders, and the medieval explorers. Globalisation continues to impact each of the 11 Conversations – from debates about migration flows in *Population,* to the quest for globally competitive workforces in *Education & Skills.*

- Sustainability is defined by the Bruntland Commission as the ability to satisfy the needs of the present without compromising the ability of future generations to do the same.[79] From the earliest human settlements and agrarian communities, this has been a major factor in how society is organised. Today, sustainability drives intense debates in each of the 11 Conversations, such as arguments over the use of finite resources in *Environment & Resources,* or concerns about potential conflict over water in *Security.*

These three forces are driving the big conversations, and so the next question is: what are these conversations *about*, today? What are people actually talking about when they discuss Health, or Security, or Human Rights? Where are the points of contention in the big debates about, say, Population or Communities? In other words, where's the heat in these conversations today? At any one time, there are areas of real friction. While the big conversations endure, where the heat is will shift.

In *Health*, to take one example, we found that a great deal of the current debate is focused on non-communicable diseases – so-called, NCDs – which are expected to account for some 60 per cent of the global health-care burden by 2020 and include diabetes, heart disease, obesity and cancer. The heat around this topic is relatively new: not many years ago the spotlight was on the devastating impact of HIV/AIDS – which is still a priority but much progress has been made, and the heat on this topic is less intense than it was. In each of the 11 Conversations, we see that the heat rises and falls to reflect new priorities.

Many people today share a sense that we live in an extraordinary time. Other generations have experienced extraordinary times, of course – and they have adapted to new realities. We're not the first to have been enthralled and disoriented by massively disruptive technologies, threatened by alarming pressures on the natural resources we depend on and jolted by tectonic shifts in the global balance of power. But this one is our one; we're in the thick of it and it's down to us to grapple with the challenges it throws up. Big business has a role to play in this. Some companies are already stepping into these big conversations, and asking how they can play a positive role in the world. The 11 Conversations is a way of laying out the landscape that can help corporates to locate themselves in the big debates in the world, and understand where their contribution may be most relevant.

The following pages present a snapshot of each of the 11 Conversations, to give a sense of the big themes and where the heat is in today's debates. After that, we pick up the story of how the business world relates to these big conversations.

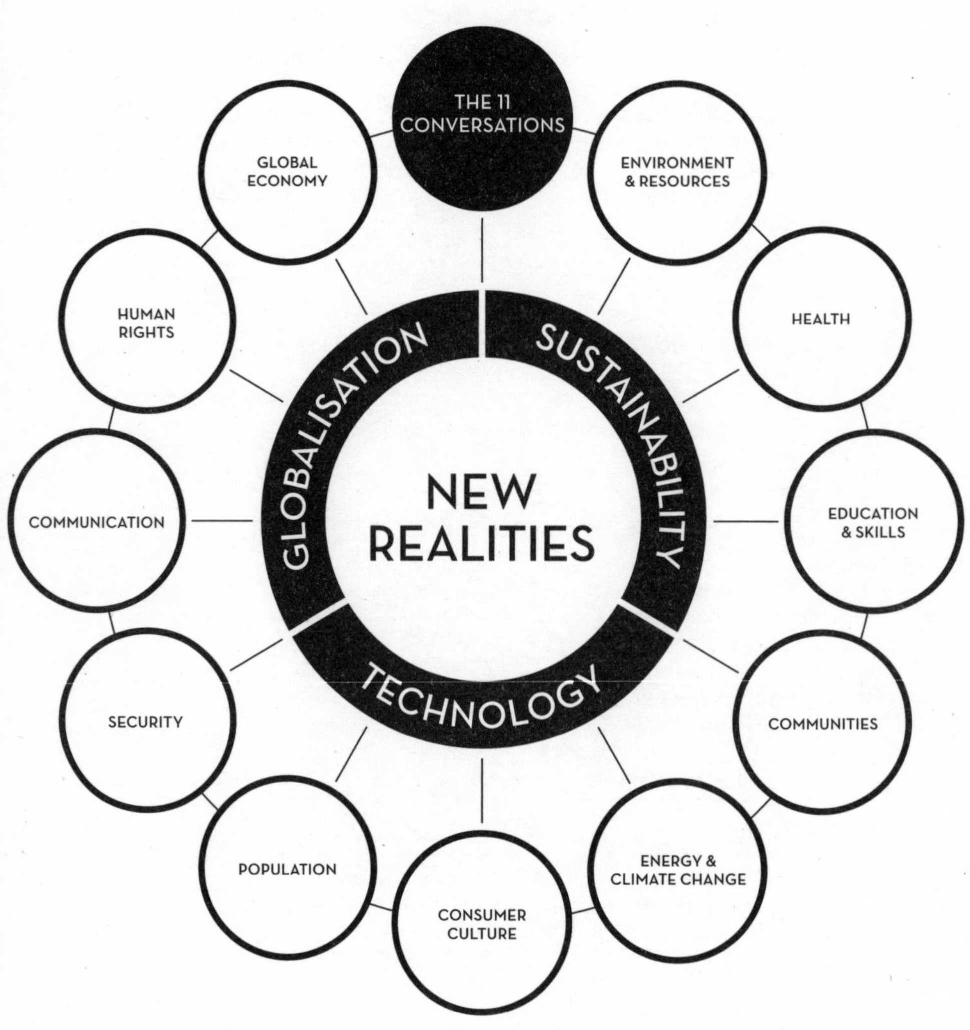
THE 11
CONVERSATIONS
GLOBAL
ECONOMY
ENVIRONMENT
& RESOURCES
HUMAN
RIGHTS
HEALTH
GLOBALISATION
SUSTAINABILITY
NEW
REALITIES
COMMUNICATION
EDUCATION
& SKILLS
TECHNOLOGY
SECURITY
COMMUNITIES
POPULATION
CONSUMER
CULTURE
ENERGY &
CLIMATE CHANGE

1. ENVIRONMENT & RESOURCES

/ Resource scarcity
/ Extraction
/ Pollution
/ Waste
/ Biodiversity
/ Food security

2. HEALTH

/ Communicable diseases
/ Non-communicable diseases
/ Medicine
/ Health-care systems
/ Nutrition
/ Workplace health

3. EDUCATION & SKILLS

/ Basic skills
/ Participation
/ Funding
/ Education systems
/ Curriculum
/ Competitive skills

4. COMMUNITIES

/ Multiculturalism
/ Unemployment
/ Public/private structures
/ Social enterprise
/ Community financing
/ Volunteering

5. ENERGY & CLIMATE CHANGE

/ Fossil fuels
/ Alternative energy
/ Carbon emissions
/ Nuclear power
/ Energy security
/ Smart grids
/ Transport

6. CONSUMER CULTURE

/ Resource use
/ Consumer empowerment
/ Brands
/ Emerging middle class
/ Crowd power

7. POPULATION

/ Population growth
/ Youth bulge
/ Ageing
/ Refugees
/ Women
/ Urbanisation
/ Migration

8. SECURITY

/ Peace and reconciliation
/ Terrorism
/ Changing nature of warfare
/ Defence industry
/ Arms proliferation
/ Crime
/ Cybersecurity

9. COMMUNICATION

/ Mobile technology
/ Access to information
/ Social networks
/ Citizen empowerment
/ Transparency
/ Power of the media

10. HUMAN RIGHTS

/ Labour rights
/ Child labour
/ Supply chains
/ Diversity
/ Democracy
/ Freedom of expression

11. GLOBAL ECONOMY

/ Economic growth
/ Development
/ Trade
/ Financial systems
/ Income inequality
/ Jobs
/ Corporate tax

1. ENVIRONMENT & RESOURCES

/ Resource scarcity
/ Extraction
/ Pollution
/ Waste
/ Biodiversity
/ Food security

'After a century of cheap resources, few institutions, in either the private or the public sector, have made resource productivity a priority.'
— Mobilising for a Resource Revolution, McKinsey

'Perhaps our greatest distinction as a species is our capacity, unique among animals, to make counter evolutionary choices.'
— Jared Diamond

1.1 BILLION

people lack access to clean drinking water and more than 2.6 billion people do not have access to basic sanitation.

4

If we all lived the average US lifestyle, we would need the resources of four Earths to regenerate humanity's annual demand on nature.

2,500

It takes up to 2,500 litres of water to make a cotton T-shirt.

The word 'sustainability' was listed as one of the world's 'jargoniest jargon' words by *Advertising Age* – alongside 'monetise,' '360', and 'the new normal'. The magazine says, 'It has come to be a squishy, feel-good catch-all for doing the right thing.' For most people, 'sustainability' means *environmental sustainability* – and whether you love or loathe the word, it has become one of the biggest conversations in the world today: how can business be more sustainable?

It's a question that is gaining urgency, as pressure on the planet's resources continues to grow. According to WWF, our demands on the natural world have doubled since the 1960s. There is a wide disparity in the needs of countries. WWF estimates that if every human being enjoyed the average US lifestyle, we would need the resources of four Earths to regenerate humanity's annual demand on nature. Furthermore, within the next two decades, an additional 3 billion people are forecast to be added to the global middle class, ready to spend, acquire more goods, and increase our need for resources.

Advances in technology can produce more outputs for given inputs, but this requires investment. It's one of the biggest challenges we face: we need to think long-term, and balance a narrow, localised view of the world against a recognition that we all share the same planet.

WHERE'S THE HEAT?

/ **RESOURCE SCARCITY** There are more of us making greater demands. We do not just need more core commodities, such as steel or copper, but more scarce resources too, such as the rare earth metal cerium, used in flat-screen TVs. Prices are already climbing steeply.

/ **EXTRACTION** Our search for resources takes us to increasingly remote and inaccessible places – which pushes up the social, environmental and financial cost. There's a lively debate about how to minimise the impact, or whether we should extract at all.

/ **POLLUTION** More industry, more manufacturing, more transport – all this means more pollution. Mining and industrial production, for example, generate hundreds of millions of tonnes of toxic waste each year – often polluting rivers and ground water. Air pollution causes more than 3 million deaths a year worldwide.

/ **WASTE** Throwing away 'stuff' does not make sense as resource scarcity bites. Waste can become a source of value and a spur to innovation. China is the world's largest importer of waste, taking material from the USA, processing it and shipping it back.

/ **BIODIVERSITY** Ecosystems can be destroyed when land is used for building, agriculture and accessing resources. Most alarming is the continued destruction of rainforests around the world: where there were once 16 million square kilometres, today there are fewer than 9 million square kilometres.

/ **FOOD SECURITY** Almost a third of food along the global value chain is wasted. In developing markets food security is still very much a pressing issue; production is often small-scale, lacking investment and infrastructure. Meanwhile, global trade in food means that while for many food is plentiful, in a crisis no country is self-sufficient.

2. HEALTH

- / Communicable diseases
- / Non-communicable diseases
- / Medicine
- / Health-care systems
- / Nutrition
- / Workplace health

'Health is a state of complete physical, mental, and social well-being and not merely the absence of disease or infirmity'
– World Health Organization definition of health

'Every minister is a health minister'
– Professor Sir Michael Marmot

121 MILLION

Depression affects 121 million people worldwide, almost ten times as many as those living with HIV/AIDS.

X3

Spending on cancer care in the USA has increased from $27 billion to $90 billion per year over the past two decades.

20%-40%

The WHO estimates that between 20 per cent and 40 per cent of global health spending is wasted.

Health is one of the great arenas of human progress, from the eradication of smallpox to the development of prosthetic hands that are nimble enough to type. But this all comes at a cost. Treatments are more sophisticated, diagnostic techniques are getting better and populations are growing – all of which puts a huge burden on health-care systems.

In many countries patients have become better informed and more demanding, while access to health care and medicines has become a challenge around the world. Life expectancy varies wildly: if you're born in Japan you can reasonably expect to see your ninth decade; in Angola, about two in ten people don't make it past the age of five. An Angolan woman is nearly 100 times more likely to die in childbirth than her Japanese counterpart. But health is more than just the absence of disease; the World Health Organization defines it as 'complete physical, mental, and social well-being'. Changing lifestyles mean people don't exercise enough, they eat too much junk food and they get stressed. These issues are starting to appear in rapidly-growing countries as they get wealthier, leading to an 'epidemic' of diseases such as diabetes and heart disease.

The global conversation around health is drawing in players from all sectors – not just health departments and pharmaceutical companies. 'Every minister is a health minister,' said Sir Michael Marmot, President of the British Medical Association. To some extent, every business is a health business.

WHERE'S THE HEAT?

/ **COMMUNICABLE DISEASES** Our track record at dealing with infectious diseases is good: from cholera to HIV/AIDS, progress is being made. However, growing urbanisation creates the conditions for disease to spread and drug resistance is increasing for malaria and tuberculosis.

/ **NON-COMMUNICABLE DISEASES** 'Lifestyle' diseases are now the biggest global killers – diabetes, heart problems, and some cancers. These diseases are skyrocketing in rapidly-growing economies: China now has the most diabetics, and Mexico has the world's highest level of obesity. Tobacco use claims more than 1 million lives a year in China alone.

/ **MEDICINE** As the medical industry conquers more illnesses, some ask whether we are going too far in pathologising complaints. For example, Attention Deficit Hyperactivity Disorder (ADHD) is not a disease, but 3 million US children are medicated for it. At the same time, millions of people are still excluded from the medicines or treatments they need.

/ **HEALTH-CARE SYSTEMS** With rising costs, how best to organise health care is a subject of intense debate in every country. World Health Organization reports estimate that between 20 per cent and 40 per cent of global health spending is wasted.

/ **NUTRITION** As millions of people in low-income countries suffer from under-nourishment, millions of others elsewhere consume excessive amounts of food, often of an over-processed variety. The role that business can play in redressing this imbalance is a live conversation.

/ **WORKPLACE HEALTH** In developing countries, basic safety is a priority in the workplace. In the developed world, stress-related illnesses are the top concern. Across the world, employers are increasingly aware that it can be cheaper to address employee well-being than to ignore it.

3. EDUCATION & SKILLS

- / Basic skills
- / Participation
- / Funding
- / Education systems
- / Curriculum
- / Competitive skills

'Learning happens in the minds and souls, not in the databases of multiple-choice tests.'
— Sir Ken Robinson, educator

'If you go to one of these tough schools, your chance of going to a four-year college is even less than your chance of going to jail.'
— Bill Gates

59%

of young adults in developed countries are in university, up 25 percentage points from 1995.

6 MILLION

China is producing 6 million graduates a year, six times more than a decade ago.

55%

A study found that differences in average skill levels among OECD countries corresponded with a 55 per cent difference in economic growth over a 34-year period.

A few years ago, a viral video called 'Shift Happens' clocked up a few million hits on YouTube. Among the many startling factoids was the following: 'The Top 10 most in-demand jobs in 2010 didn't exist in 2004. We are currently preparing students for jobs that don't exist yet, using technologies that haven't been invented, in order to solve problems we don't even know are problems yet.'

It's something that many businesses are grappling with: as the pace of innovation continues to grow, the skills base that companies need continues to shift. Many businesses are partnering with universities to close the skills gap. At the other end of the spectrum, Douglas Coupland famously popularised the term McJob to describe 'a low-pay, low-prestige, low-dignity, low-benefit, no-future job'. McDonald's responded to this by supporting its staff in getting basic qualifications, even going so far as to get several hundred McDonald's outlets accredited as exam centres. Skills development is relevant for every business.

Education has a transforming effect – on individuals, businesses and economies. A skilled workforce does wonders for increasing national competitiveness: UNESCO reports that differences in average skill levels among OECD countries corresponded with a 55 per cent difference in economic growth over a 34-year period. For an individual, getting a degree can double earning power. Getting people into and through the system, and making sure they acquire the skills they need to succeed in life, remains a challenge across the world.

WHERE'S THE HEAT?

/ **BASIC SKILLS** Certain core skills are necessary to function in modern society, such as how to manage money, use a computer, work with others, have good ideas, and turn up to work on time. How to equip people with these skills is an ongoing debate.

/ **PARTICIPATION** In developing countries, it is a struggle to keep children in secondary education. In developed countries, the proportion of young adults in university has increased 25 percentage points since 1995 to 59 per cent today.

/ **FUNDING** Educating a nation does not come cheap. In most countries, it represents a sizeable proportion of public spending. For example, Norway spent an average of about $15,000 per student, per year in 2007, whereas Mexico spent $2,000 per student in the same year.

/ **EDUCATION SYSTEMS** Schools have been around for thousands of years but it's still not clear how best to organise education. Simply pouring in money is not the answer and is no longer an option; the debate is intensifying.

/ **CURRICULUM** Some argue that school should make us fully rounded individuals and citizens. Others complain that traditional education is too academic and want more vocational training. Finding the middle ground is one of the big conversations in education. Should the curriculum be imparting knowledge or building capabilities?

/ **COMPETITIVE SKILLS** In today's globalised economy jobs can go anywhere. China is producing 6 million graduates a year – six times more than a decade ago. Being highly educated is not enough – it is the application of cutting-edge skills that drives innovation and creates jobs.

4. COMMUNITIES

- / Multiculturalism
- / Unemployment
- / Public/private structures
- / Social enterprise
- / Community financing
- / Volunteering

'We cannot seek achievement for ourselves and forget about the progress and prosperity of our community ... Our ambitions must be broad enough to include the aspirations and needs of others, for their sakes and for our own.'
— Cesar Chavez

'We cannot solve complex horizontal problems with vertical command-and-control solutions.'
— Stephen Goldsmith

100

languages spoken in London, one of the world's most multicultural cities.

190 MILLION

people in some of the world's poorest countries are being helped by microfinance.

28%

The average daily saving in US prisons operating as private partnerships.

Many companies have felt the sting of community activism at a grassroots level. In parts of the developed world, local communities have organised opposition to the opening of chain retailers' stores such as Walmart or Starbucks. Across the world, communities have pushed themselves up the agenda of the extractive industries – mining, oil and gas. Getting it wrong can be very costly: an analysis of the world's largest oil and gas projects found that only 21 per cent of delays were due to technical risk, while 73 per cent were for non-technical reasons, such as community resistance.

Increasingly, large companies deal with communities across the world – and this raises the stakes. Sometimes, mismanaging issues with the local community can damage relations with a host government, putting at risk a company's licence to operate. In extreme cases, there have been violent incidents. Social media tools mean that an egregious local story can very quickly become a damaging global issue – with negative effects on a company's reputation.

Many factors are at play. Multiculturalism has become a big issue around the world, redefining local communities. The shape of the family and the structure of households are changing, as are patterns of economic activity and jobs. Governments are experimenting with new community-based solutions and financing models. Meanwhile, for many people, online networks are dramatically reframing the idea of community, empowering people to join together wherever they live in the world on the basis of shared interest.

WHERE'S THE HEAT?

/ **MULTICULTURALISM** Across the world, different cultures rub shoulders in our big cities. The big debate is the age-old one of assimilation versus amalgamation: whether it is better to absorb new arrivals into the existing culture, or to allow various cultures to live in their own way side by side. At the moment, fears of extremism lend weight to the former view.

/ **UNEMPLOYMENT** This can be deeply toxic and corrosive, causing communities to collapse. It is not just about money, but the lack of opportunities and the erosion of a community's aspiration. Tackling the issue requires innovative approaches involving both government and business.

/ **PUBLIC/PRIVATE STRUCTURES** Asking private companies to deliver public services can be controversial. They need to overcome the suspicion that profit will come before fully delivering the service. In the UK, around a third of public services are already provided by private and other non-government sectors.

/ **SOCIAL ENTERPRISE** At the heart of social enterprise is making a positive impact on communities. It is an area of great creativity and innovation and includes looking for positive ways businesses can address social problems.

/ **COMMUNITY FINANCING** Innovative funding approaches, such as micro-credit, help the less empowered to get their ideas off the ground – though some argue that this can become just another way for vulnerable individuals to fall into a poverty trap.

/ **VOLUNTEERING** In the USA, 26.8 per cent of people say they volunteer; in the UK, 49 per cent. Many organisations report they have lots of unused volunteer hours, suggesting that red tape and limited resources can get in the way.

5. ENERGY & CLIMATE CHANGE

/ Fossil fuels
/ Alternative energy
/ Carbon emissions
/ Nuclear power
/ Energy security
/ Smart grids
/ Transport

'The race is now on between the technoscientific and scientific forces that are destroying the living environment and those that can be harnessed to save it. ... If the race is won, humanity can emerge in far better condition than when it entered, and with most of the diversity of life still intact.'
– Edward O. Wilson[80]

'I have a feeling that climate change may be an issue as severe as a war. It may be necessary to put democracy on hold for a while.'
– James Lovelock

X5

China accounts for most of the world's new nuclear capacity, forecast to grow five-fold by 2020.

X100

Since the industrial revolution, total global commercial energy use has increased a hundredfold.

X25

A 40-watt LED bulb can last 25 times longer and provide a 77 per cent energy saving.

Rising living standards have resulted in a dramatic increase in demand for energy. Since the industrial revolution, total global commercial energy use has increased a hundredfold. Today's demand growth comes from different parts of the world. China overtook the USA as the world's biggest energy consumer in 2010: only a decade earlier, its total energy consumption was just half that of the USA. Most energy still comes from fossil fuels: oil, gas and coal. Meanwhile, rising global temperatures threaten to alter the planet's climate, with potentially damaging consequences for fragile ecosystems in many regions of the world.

There is often seen to be a trade-off between the environment and the economy. A similar logic is applied to business: 'green' choices are seen as dragging down profitability. The debates are heavily balanced towards this zero-sum argument, casting big business as the bad guy who sacrifices the planet for the sake of short-term growth.

But for a number of companies, energy efficiency has become a 'north star' for their innovation. 'Smart grids', for example, are a central part of IBM's *Smarter Planet* strategy. GE has 'Ecomagination' – an R&D initiative with a substantial focus on developing more energy-efficient products. As usual, there is a flip side – the Jevons Paradox: as efficiency increases, prices fall and demand rises. In other words, the argument goes, new efficient technologies may actually push up energy use. There are no easy solutions, but many companies are taking up the challenge.

WHERE'S THE HEAT?

/ **FOSSIL FUELS** Four-fifths of our energy comes from fossil fuels – a finite resource. Estimates of how long existing resources may last range from forty to 120 years, depending on how quickly we can change the rate and composition of our energy consumption.

/ **ALTERNATIVE ENERGY** Non-hydro renewable energy delivers around 5 per cent of the global electricity supply. Last year, China led the world in terms of wind turbine installation and solar panel manufacturing. Developing economically workable alternative energy is one of the world's big challenges.

/ **CARBON EMISSIONS** Reducing emissions is widely considered to be critical. Levels of CO2 in the atmosphere have reached 400 parts per million – the highest level for five million years. And yet a global agreement to reduce emissions has proved extremely difficult to achieve.

/ **NUCLEAR POWER** Nuclear power generates about 12 per cent of the world's electricity. Since Japan's Fukushima disaster, the debate about the industry's safety has reignited and some countries – Germany, for example – have turned away from nuclear power. The industry's future is uncertain.

/ **ENERGY SECURITY** Natural disasters, political instability, conflict, terrorism, and restrictions over access can all threaten energy security. Many countries are heavily dependent on others for their energy supplies, as illustrated by Europe's plight when Russian gas supplies were halted.

/ **SMART GRIDS** Electricity infrastructure with embedded intelligence can ensure a more reliable, safe and efficient supply. One estimate sees smart grid spending growing by about 17 per cent a year to $46 billion in 2015.

/ **TRANSPORT** Energy and climate change concerns have focused interest on low-carbon transport: vehicles powered by electricity, biofuels or hydrogen. Greater energy efficiency increases the value of public transport and has intensified the road-versus-rail debate.

6. CONSUMER CULTURE

- / Resource use
- / Consumer empowerment
- / Brands
- / Emerging middle class
- / Crowd power

'I'd rather cry in a BMW car than laugh on the backseat of a bicycle.'
— Ma Nuo, 22-year-old Chinese model and TV celebrity

'As the number of choices grows further, the negatives escalate until we become overloaded. At this point, choice no longer liberates, but debilitates.'
— Barry Schwartz

40%

By 2030, Asian consumers could account for over 40 per cent of global middle class consumption, and 64 per cent of the world's middle class could be in Asia.

$410 BILLION

The size of the global waste market, from collection to recycling – and not including the large informal segment in developing countries.

70%

Consumer spending represents around 70 per cent of the US economy.

Consumer culture is defined by the brands that surround us: the food we eat, the shoes we wear, the phones we use, and even the water we drink – much of our everyday lives is packaged and positioned by brands. Around the world, hundreds of millions of people have new-found disposable income, and they're showing a healthy appetite for brands of all kinds.

As a result, consumer culture is spreading like wildfire across the globe. But not everybody approves. It's a 'pandemic', according to Latin American writer Jorge Majfud. He calls it a collective delusion: 'Development is confused with consumerism, wastefulness with success, and growth with fattening. The pandemic is considered a sign of good health ... There is no ideology or political system in the world that is not bent upon reproducing and multiplying it.'

Consumerism stands accused of turning the world into a bland mono-culture, destroying local interest and diversity. Many argue that consumerism undermines spiritual values and leads to dissatisfaction and unhappiness. Most of all, critics point to the problem of over-consumption, where use of resources is growing faster than the available supply. It's a very live conversation. Millions of people from rapidly growing economies around the world are becoming fully paid-up consumers. They share the same aspirations as consumers anywhere in the world – and in particular, they have a love of luxury brands that shows no sign of flagging.

WHERE'S THE HEAT?

/ **RESOURCE USE** Our modern consumer lifestyles require abundant natural resources. Growing numbers of new consumers around the world want to join the party – but this places a significant strain on the world's limited natural resources and is a source of concern. The business world stands accused of both fuelling and fulfilling unsustainable levels of consumption.

/ **CONSUMER EMPOWERMENT** Consumer attitudes, values and behaviours are dominating global culture. As access to information proliferates, power is shifting from producers to consumers. Many businesses are playing catch-up with consumers, who have a growing number of options from which to choose.

/ **BRANDS** The global megabrands of today can't take their dominance for granted. A new generation of brands is gaining power in countries such as China and India and it is only a matter of time before they set their sights on global consumers.

/ **EMERGING MIDDLE CLASS** By 2020, more than half the world's middle class could be in Asia. One of the big debates at the start of the twenty-first century is whether these new emerging middle classes will shift towards Western consumer culture and democratic values, or conform to their own particular interpretation of consumerism.

/ **CROWD POWER** Consumers are getting used to exercising their collective muscle. A succession of big brands has been forced by consumer activism to reverse a position – whether that's a change of fee structure or a corporate tax policy.

7. POPULATION

/ Population growth
/ Youth bulge
/ Ageing
/ Refugees
/ Women
/ Urbanisation
/ Migration

'Every one of [our] global problems, environmental as well as social, becomes more difficult – and ultimately impossible – to solve with ever more people'
— Sir David Attenborough

'The fastest way to change society is to mobilise the women of the world.'
— Charles Malik

6/10

By 2030, six out of ten people on the planet will live in a city.

9/10

By 2050, nine out of ten youths will live in the developing world.

45.2 MILLION

People forcibly displaced worldwide in 2012 – the highest number in eighteen years.

By 2050, there may be as many as 9 billion of us – a seemingly unstoppable human juggernaut rolling over the global environment: over-fishing, deforestation, water shortages and loss of species are placing considerable strain on the resources required for survival. Still, there are those in the world of business who are asking what would happen if we saw population growth as an opportunity, rather than a risk.

Certainly there are plenty of new areas for innovation. Vast new urban sprawls have emerged – many are overcrowded, putting pressure on housing and infrastructure while a 'youth bulge' places the focus on providing education and finding jobs. For global policymakers, the youth bulge presents a risk and an opportunity: it can fuel an economic boom, or it can lead to a social bust.

A burgeoning youth population isn't something that Western countries have to worry about: their ageing populations present a very different set of challenges – from an increased health burden to reduced numbers in the workforce. Whether these countries can act in time to manage pension deficits is critical to their future prosperity.

It's a very different global picture. Most business leaders are familiar with an average consumer who is about forty years old. In the developing world, a forty-year-old is a member of an ageing niche; the average consumer might be around twenty years old – and that is where today's economic power lies.

WHERE'S THE HEAT?

/ **POPULATION GROWTH** The most populous nations are China (1.3 billion), India (1.2 billion), the USA (313 million), and Indonesia (242 million), whereas most growth in the future will be in Africa. Other nations will shrink: Japan's population will decline by a third in the next fifty years.

/ **YOUTH BULGE** In many parts of the world there is a 'youth bulge' where the size of the younger generation is disproportionately large – close to a third of the total population. This could be a source of creative energy or social unrest – or both.

/ **AGEING** Even with the youth bulge, the collective age for mankind is gradually increasing as, across the globe, people are living longer and having fewer children. The big challenge is to ensure that older generations remain an asset for society, and not an expensive burden.

/ **REFUGEES** Globally, there are almost 45 million displaced people – fleeing conflict, climate change or natural disasters. This can place a strain on the countries they move to, and cause tensions between nations.

/ **WOMEN** There only around twenty female CEOs of Fortune 500 companies; barely one in eight women in Afghanistan is literate. However, change is happening: more than 500 million females have joined the global workforce in the last thirty years.

/ **URBANISATION** In 1900, some 13 per cent of the global population was urban; now more than half of us live in cities. Some benefit from increased opportunities and options for work and leisure, while others may remain poor and live in crowded, unhealthy conditions.

/ **MIGRATION** The global population is on the move, presenting opportunities to expand and improve the workforce. However, this shift can present challenges for social cohesion. Today, one in every thirty-three individuals in the world is a migrant.

8. SECURITY

- Peace and reconciliation
- Terrorism
- Changing nature of warfare
- Defence industry
- Arms proliferation
- Crime
- Cybersecurity

'The same global advances in communication, transportation and commerce that lead to economic growth, social exchange and political integration can also be conduits for transnational security threats.'
— The Brookings Institute

'Violence has been in decline for thousands of years, and today we may be living in the most peaceable era in the existence of our species.'
— Stephen Pinker

$50 MILLION

The US army is investing $50 million over five years in gaming systems designed to prepare soldiers for combat.

$388 BILLION

Cybercrime is bigger than the global black market in marijuana, cocaine and heroin combined ($288 billion).

4.7%

US defence spending as a percentage of US GDP in 2011. For many countries defence is a major part of the economy.

Security is high on the risk register of any business or government. The array of possible threats is rapidly evolving, as the world becomes more interconnected and tech-enabled. Clashes between different ideologies remain a concern, while securing access to vital resources is re-emerging as a potential source of conflict. The nature of conflict itself has changed, too, with new technologies, such as unmanned drones, and increasing use of new urban guerrilla tactics. Cyberspace is now thought of as the 'fifth domain' of warfare – alongside land, sea, air and space. Of course, cybersecurity has become indivisible from *hacking*.

Hacking comes from a subculture most of us know little about. For most people, it's the digital equivalent of breaking and entering: finding weaknesses in a security system and exploiting them. But hackers have their own ethics and language. They have a natural suspicion of authority and secrecy, and place a high value on information sharing and openness. Hackers love the challenge of stretching a system to its limits and pushing its capabilities.

Many 'hactivists' are motivated by political or ideological reasons, and include groups such as Anonymous in the USA or the Red Hacker Alliance, a network of Chinese nationalist hackers. It's the 'black hats' who are most problematic. They are motivated by personal gain, or just pure maliciousness. They're often after financial data such as personal banking information, and they're a big threat to individuals, businesses and governments.

WHERE'S THE HEAT?

/ **PEACE AND RECONCILIATION** Economic development is seen as key to creating lasting peace in troubled regions. It used to be said that no two countries with a McDonald's ever went to war – until the Russia-Georgia conflict of 2008.

/ **TERRORISM** The USA spends more on counter-terrorism than all other anti-crime activities. Governments are struggling to find the right mix of hard power combined with diplomacy and strategic aid.

/ **CHANGING NATURE OF WARFARE** At the start of the last century, land warfare using infantry dominated. Now, guerrilla tactics and terrorism demand increasingly sophisticated, precise and technologically advanced responses.

/ **DEFENCE INDUSTRY** Defence spending can be a major part of a country's economy – 4.7 per cent of GDP in the USA in 2011. Some argue the industry creates employment and fosters innovation, though others raise concerns about the ethics and political swag of the 'military-industrial complex'.

/ **ARMS PROLIFERATION** Controlling the spread of arms requires an ongoing series of multilateral talks and agreements. The illegal trade in small arms is estimated to be worth between $2 billion and $10 billion a year.

/ **CRIME** Global organised crime is worth $1 trillion a year. Aside from the human cost, it damages economies: drug-related violence costs Latin American countries the equivalent of nearly 15 per cent of their GDP. At the other end of the spectrum, low-level antisocial behaviour undermines local communities.

/ **CYBERSECURITY** Two in three internet users have been affected by cybercrime. Cybersecurity has become a matter of national security as hackers from hostile governments could wreak havoc on critical infrastructure. In 2010, the Pentagon set up a new US Cyber Command.

9. COMMUNICATION

/ Mobile technology
/ Access to information
/ Social networks
/ Citizen empowerment
/ Transparency
/ Power of the media

'It (transparency) is the new operating standard.'
– Debbie Weil

'Can we go back to using Facebook for what it was originally for – looking up exes to see how fat they got?'
– Bill Maher

90

Today, there are freedom of information laws in more than ninety countries. In 1990, just thirteen countries had such laws.

91%

According to Morgan Stanley, 91 per cent of US cell phone users keep their phone within arm's reach at all times.

60%

The compound annual growth rate of the amount of data being generated – truly a deluge.

The communications revolution goes far beyond Facebook updates or satellite navigation systems: it means rural farmers in India can have up-to-the-minute data on crop prices and plan their harvests accordingly. It means it is possible to get a diagnosis from a doctor without a visit. A shopkeeper in remote Kenya can become a bank with just a basic handset. Information flows fluidly in this new world. Governments and companies find it harder to control the story, and transparency is the new norm.

The free flow of information is essential to the health of society – this is a deeply held democratic value. The growth of the internet has put this at centre stage in recent years – but it's just the latest chapter in a long struggle for freedom of expression. In 1792, speaking in a debate about the circulation of American newspapers, Senator Elbridge Gerry said, 'However firmly liberty may be established in any country, it cannot long subsist if the channels of information be stopped.'

Today, social media has created a 'reputation economy' – your digital profile becomes your real currency. As digital technology journalist Clive Thomson writes,

> The reputation economy creates an incentive to be more open, not less. Since internet commentary is inescapable, the only way to influence it is to be part of it. Being transparent, opening up, posting interesting material frequently and often, is the only way to amass positive links to yourself and thus to directly influence your Googleable reputation.

WHERE'S THE HEAT?

/ **MOBILE TECHNOLOGY** It's thought that there are now more mobile devices than there are humans on the planet. In developing countries, mobile phones can bring real transformation; in developed countries, they're a part of everyday lives.

/ **ACCESS TO INFORMATION** We are generating data at a faster rate than ever – it is growing at a compound annual rate of 60 per cent. Some can feel overwhelmed, while others feel as though the world is at their fingertips and they can shape the future.

/ **SOCIAL NETWORKS** The way that we communicate with each other is changing profoundly, whether it is groups of friends, consumers, investors, activists, employees, journalists – social networking is changing forever the way we organise our lives.

/ **CITIZEN EMPOWERMENT** New ways of communicating are shifting power from the ruling elites towards networks of organised citizens. The role of social media, mobile and Al Jazeera during the Arab Spring shows the power of media in the hands of those hungry for change.

/ **TRANSPARENCY** Being open and transparent is now a cultural – and often legal – standard. More than ninety countries now have freedom of information laws. A succession of companies has been forced into the open by whistleblower websites such as WikiLeaks.

/ **POWER OF THE MEDIA** Control of the news media has consolidated into fewer companies. Today, just six big companies dominate the vast majority of US media output. Around the world, accountability and control of the media are issues of public debate.

10. HUMAN RIGHTS

/ Labour rights
/ Child labour
/ Supply chains
/ Diversity
/ Democracy
/ Freedom of expression

'No substantial famine has ever occurred in a country with a democratic form of government and a relatively free press.'
– Amartya Sen

'The next two decades are going to be [about] privacy. I'm talking about the internet. I'm talking about cell phones. I'm talking about health records and who's gay and who's not. And moreover, in a country born on the will to be free, what could be more fundamental than this?'
— Sam Seaborn (*The West Wing)*

700,000

Walmart has 700,000 workers outside of the USA.

23/25

Every economy in the top twenty-five of the Global Innovation Index is a democracy, except semi-democratic Singapore and Hong Kong.

211 MILLION

An estimated 211 million children between the ages of five and fourteen have to work.

The power to protect (or abuse) human rights used to reside almost exclusively with nation states, but multinational corporations have an growing role to play, as they increasingly wield substantial direct power and practical influence. They employ thousands across the globe – Walmart has 700,000 workers outside of the USA – and extend their reach further via partnerships and supply chains. Respecting the rights of workers can be challenging and has been a major area of contention for many businesses.

The international recognition of human rights grew in the wake of the horrors of the Second World War. Dignity, liberty, equality and brotherhood – these principles underpin the Universal Declaration of Human Rights, which has become central to the basic laws and constitutions of many different countries throughout the world. There has also been much debate in recent years about the extent of human rights: in 2009, for example, broadband access became a legal right in Finland.

It is no surprise that controlling the media is high on the agenda of any would-be autocrat. An unfettered quality press is essential to any healthy democracy, holding governments accountable and promoting informed debate. Similarly, human rights depend upon the rule of law – a system of transparent legal principles that exist for everyone's benefit. Around the world, the rule of law is variable and sometimes non-existent. This was what prompted Peter Benenson, an English lawyer, to found Amnesty International in 1961 to stand up for human rights.

WHERE'S THE HEAT?

/ **LABOUR RIGHTS** In the developed world, the big debate has been whether labour rights have gone too far, cramping business competitiveness. In the developing world, many argue that a bad job is better than no job, and that strict conditions put people out of work.

/ **CHILD LABOUR** There are areas in the world where child labour is considered normal. An estimated 211 million children between the ages of five and fourteen have to work. In many cases, they may be the only breadwinner in the family.

/ **SUPPLY CHAINS** The global supply chains of big companies have become sprawling and complex – crossing national boundaries and cultural norms – increasing the risk of human rights abuses. The role of multinationals in preventing such abuses has been a hot issue in recent years.

/ **DIVERSITY** Equality of opportunity is a basic human right – but how to achieve this is a point of contention. Many governments have imposed quotas for women and ethnic minorities, with some success. France, for example, has a law requiring gender diversity on company boards.

/ **DEMOCRACY** A new wave of 'people power' has swept the globe. A strong case can be made for democracy as a force for progress: the Global Innovation Index's top 25 economies are all democracies (discounting semi-democratic Singapore and Hong Kong).

/ **FREEDOM OF EXPRESSION** Never has this been more debated. Global interconnected media make it inevitable that cultures will clash: from cartoons of the Prophet Muhammad and banning the burqa to censoring Google search results, freedom of speech is a big global issue.

11. GLOBAL ECONOMY

/ Economic growth
/ Development
/ Trade
/ Financial systems
/ Income inequality
/ Jobs
/ Corporate Tax

'Obscene rewards for success are as socially corrosive as obscene rewards for failure.'
– George Monbiot

'To Westerners, the glass is half empty; to the rest of the world, it's half full.'
– Simon Silvester

36%

Developing countries now account for 36 per cent of world exports, about double their share in the early 1960s.

$639 TRILLION

In June 2012, the global derivatives market was worth $639 trillion, close to ten times the value of global GDP.

40%

Unemployment is hitting young people hard: 40 per cent of the world's youth is unemployed.

It's impossible to have a conversation about the global economy without running into some pretty astronomical numbers. It is estimated that the size of the world economy was around $65 trillion in 2010 – up from about $3 trillion four decades before. It is easy to become blasé about the scale of these very large numbers. The mathematics professor John Allen Paulos helps us get to grips with them in his book *Innumeracy*. 'It takes about eleven-and-a-half days for a million seconds to tick away, whereas almost thirty-two years are required for a billion seconds to pass,' he writes. And a trillion? Our own species of *homo sapiens* is thought to be less than 10 trillion seconds old. These large numbers define the global economy.

The global financial system is a complex network of global institutions and regulations, national agencies and private organisations. Many have argued this system is in need of reform. Critics have ranged from economist Joseph Stiglitz and journalist and economist Paul Krugman, to financier George Soros and former Pope Benedict XVI. Banks are a crucial part of the global financial system. They provide credit to businesses, which is essential for growth and job creation. They facilitate flows of payment across borders, thus making international trade possible. However, trust in banks has been badly damaged by the financial crisis and ensuing banking scandals.

WHERE'S THE HEAT?

/ **ECONOMIC GROWTH** The overriding goal of most governments is creating or maintaining economic growth – the assumption being that this is the way to increase quality of life and lift people out of poverty. More and more, people are starting to question whether growth is a good thing.

/ **DEVELOPMENT** Many argue for a strong role for businesses in helping poorer countries develop – creating jobs, training workers, investing in infrastructure. Others are worried by companies that exploit natural resources without helping local communities.

/ **TRADE** It's the lifeblood of the global economy. In 1950 it accounted for 5.5 per cent of world GDP; today, it represents more than 20 per cent. While some countries struggle to protect industries and jobs, others are trying to reduce their reliance on exports.

/ **FINANCIAL SYSTEMS** Even after the crisis, financial institutions work with complex and interlinked financial products at a global level, and national regulators struggle to keep up. A string of scandals around rate fixing and money laundering has deepened public anger at financial institutions.

/ **INCOME INEQUALITY** In many countries, inequality is rising. According to economist Joseph Stiglitz, incomes for the top 1 per cent in the USA are up 18 per cent over the past decade, while those in the middle have seen their incomes fall.

/ **JOBS** According to the International Labour Organization, one in three workers worldwide is either unemployed or living in poverty. In developed and developing countries, policymakers are looking to businesses to create meaningful and productive jobs.

/ **CORPORATE TAX** Reports of apparently successful companies paying very low rates of tax have led to rising public anger. Multinationals operate across a patchwork of different jurisdictions and competing national interests, so there is inevitable tension between the global interests of corporates and politicians who fly the flag for their own country.

STEPPING OUT OF THE CITADEL

Imagine the traditional corporate as a citadel: a huge fortress, built for defence and designed to keep the world out. From inside, if issues that concern the world appear on the horizon they are seen as a threat, and dealt with. When the corporate wants to communicate with the world outside, it develops a 'messaging strategy', and messages are shot out like arrows through the slits in the castle walls.

But the world has changed. The very structure of a corporate has changed: a modern company runs through a series of complex networks, with multifaceted connections to the outside world: systems of supply and distribution, global workforces, mobile employees, commercial alliances, NGO partnerships, empowered communities, connected consumers – running a successful big business today means managing a vast system of relationships. It's the Age of Conversation, and a quiet revolution is taking place in the way that corporates engage with the world. As we've seen in many of the businesses we encounter in this book, companies are beginning to see that communications is not about bombarding people with messages but about stepping out and joining the conversation.

All the 11 Conversations are conversations about the big problems in the world today: the challenges that need to be tackled for the future. People gather around them, worry at them, argue over them because they are about our fears – and hopes – for the world. In other words, they are the things that need fixing. By the very nature of what they do, every corporate can contribute to these conversations: they have the skills, scale, resources, and influence. They have experience to bring to bear, and they are already active in these areas. To see this in practice, we look at the conversation around three big topics: water, transparency, and women.

(I) TALKING ABOUT WATER

In the *Environment & Resources* conversation, one of the areas of real contention today is water. In 2009 the world was alarmed by a McKinsey study showing that within two decades the global demand for water would exceed the current level of supply by 40 per cent.[81] In preceding chapters, we've seen a number of companies getting heavily involved in the global conversation around water. We saw how Coca-Cola found itself embroiled in a global controversy over its voracious use of water in India. Now Coke is working with WWF to reduce its water use, and help to conserve some of the world's most important freshwater basins – 'nature's water factories', as the company calls them. SABMiller has also formed a partnership with WWF, working together on a 'water footprinting' methodology to understand the impact of the company's operations on local water resources. Andy Wales, the company's head of sustainability, tells us 'we clearly have to get our own house in order.' Still, in Andy's view it's the corporates who have been driving the global agenda on water:

> Big businesses saw that water scarcity was an issue long before governments did, because we have operations all over the world. That's what led, five years ago or more, to big conversations with governments about how we can get a better grip on how water underpins economic growth and quality of life around the world. And we pushed to manage water resources better, not just as a niche issue for the environment department in a country, but as a core resource underpinning your economic growth and success.

This thinking led to the 2030 Water Resources Group – a major cross-sector initiative, hosted by the International

Finance Corporation (a part of the World Bank), including governments such as India, Mexico and South Africa, NGOs such as the World Wildlife Fund, and big companies including Nestlé, PepsiCo, SABMiller, and the Coca-Cola Company. Coca-Cola's chairman Muhtar Kent describes this as a 'Golden Triangle' of collaboration. As he told a conference in 2012:

> We must rely on partnerships that connect across what I call the 'Golden Triangle' of business, government and civil society. Indeed, more and more companies are finding that we have something more valuable than our dollars or yen or euros to contribute. And that's our expertise, our know-how, our unique and specific strengths.

Not everyone has welcomed this 'Golden Triangle' approach with open arms, and the role of corporates has itself become part of the conversation on water. Some are cynical about corporate involvement with organisations such as the 2030 Water Resources Group. Kristin Urquiza, a campaigner with the NGO Corporate Accountability International, wrote an open letter to Coca-Cola about their participation in a number of water-related initiatives:

> These examples along with your description of the 'golden triangle' make the case that Coca-Cola wants to be treated as if it is equal to governments when it comes to the governance of what is a public resource – water. However, corporations are fundamentally different from governments and in cases of the interest of the commons often collide with the public interest. With governments in charge, they are accountable to the people they serve and must prioritise the human right to water and

> equitable access to water. Whereas corporations – 'golden triangle' or not – are only accountable to profit.

Many people may feel circumspect about corporates getting involved in the global conversation about water, but it's hard to imagine having a productive debate without them. Businesses build and maintain the water infrastructure, they run the water-intensive food chains and energy systems that we all rely on, and they are the main sources of innovations to make fresh drinking water more accessible.

Because they have acquired much experience and expertise on water, many companies have become activists on the subject. PepsiCo has also been very voluble in the global conversation about water security – and has led calls for access to water to be recognised as a human right, as we saw in Chapter 9. PepsiCo has become a prominent voice in this space, underpinned by three serious public commitments. First, to improve their own use of water; second, to provide access to safe, clean drinking water to six million people by 2016; and third, to aim for a positive balance in the 'water bank account' wherever they operate. The company is working towards these commitments through a range of partnerships at global, national and local levels.

Of course, each of the 11 Conversations links to others. The topics form multiple, ever-shifting connections between each other – and this is especially true of water. As the renowned American naturalist John Muir observed, 'when we try to pick out anything by itself in nature, we find it hitched to everything else in the universe.' Try to have a conversation about the global water challenge without talking about agriculture and food, or energy, or security – it's impossible. Even financial services companies have become an important part of the conversation. Standard Chartered made a commitment at the Clinton Global Initiative to provide $1 billion in financial services – a mix of debt, equity and advice – to water related projects. HSBC published a study showing the critical role of the major river basins in economies around the world. Against these findings they launched a $100 million, five-year partnership with WWF, WaterAid and Earthwatch to tackle water risk. A big conversation like water can draw in major players from all sectors.

(II) TALKING ABOUT TRANSPARENCY

In the *Communications* conversation, transparency has been an increasingly hot topic. Don Tapscott is a leading commentator on how business has responded to the challenge of transparency, since the publication in 2003 of *The Naked Corporation,* written with David Ticoll. We asked him a very basic question: what exactly *is* transparency? 'Well, it took us about two months to come up with this definition,' he tells us:

> Transparency is the opportunity and obligation for institutions (not individuals) to communicate pertinent information to stakeholders – pertinent, meaning it can help them if they receive the information, or hurt them if they don't.

Many of the companies we met would recognise that there is an 'opportunity and obligation' in transparency. Nike, for example, is now widely recognised as a corporate leader on transparency. Today you can go onto the website of the Fair Labor Association and read hundreds of independent reports of factory inspections. On Nike's own website, you can see a complete list of Nike suppliers – the first major corporate to move to full supply chain transparency. All of this would have been hard to imagine twenty years ago, when the company was in the depths of its sweatshop misery. With Nike, it's possible to see both the positive and the negative aspect of transparency: negative, in the sense that Nike wants to be seen to have nothing to hide; positive, where Nike is proactively putting information into the public domain where it may help others – such as the Materials Sustainability Index, used by product designers, inside or outside of Nike, to evaluate the environmental impact of their designs.

Of course, when it comes to transparency, not all companies are created equal. Each year Transparency International publishes an index of corporate transparency, and the top of the list is dominated by a sector most people wouldn't immediately associate with openness: the extractive industry. In 2012 six of the top ten spots went to extraction businesses. Statoil, Rio Tinto and BHP Billiton took first, second and third places. For them, it's about creating a level playing field: these big companies face competition from smaller, local players who often create an unfair advantage through cutting corners on their environmental and social behaviour, or through corrupt practices. The big players want to raise the level of transparency within the industry, to flush out these unaccountable players – and, in the process, prevent the harm they cause.

There's a clear logic here: bringing business out into the light leads inevitably to improved standards of behaviour. As Don Tapscott explains to us:

> There was the traditional notion of Corporate Social Responsibility – that you can do well by doing good. I don't think it was true. Lots of companies did well by being really bad – by having terrible labour practices or exploiting the developing world, or by externalising their costs on to society. But increasingly I think, because of transparency, that idea of social responsibility is becoming true. We know for sure that you can do badly by being bad – look at the banks on Wall Street. Increasingly, I

think, companies are going to have to build integrity into their business models.

(III) TALKING ABOUT WOMEN

When Sheryl Sandberg, COO of Facebook, saw the 11 Conversations, she leaned back on her chair and furrowed her brow. Often when we talk about the 11 Conversations, people play with the concepts: *I think you should merge those two topics,* or *I think there are Fifteen Conversations,* or *I think there's a new priority emerging.* Of course, these are all valid challenges – and there's really no right answer. In fact, that's the whole point: to prompt a conversation. But Sheryl asked us an important question: 'Where's women?'

She wanted to know why *Women* wasn't one of the 11 Conversations in its own right – and she wasn't completely convinced by our answer: we think that women are a central part of *every* conversation: how can you talk about *Health* or *Human Rights* without talking about women? What kind of conversation can you have about *Communities* or *Education & Skills,* if you don't talk about women? But Sheryl wasn't buying it. 'I see your logic,' she said. 'But I think it's too important. And I guess it's my job to make sure *Women* is one of these big conversations,' she declares.

What women are to the future of the world is a hot topic, undoubtedly. 'The fastest way to change society is to mobilise the women of the world,' says Charles Malik, former President of the UN General Assembly. 'Send a girl to school even just for one year and her income dramatically increases for life, and her children are more likely to survive and her family more likely to be healthier for years to come,' says Hillary Clinton, talking on the platform of TEDWomen. The UN tells us that 'women's poverty is directly linked to the absence of economic opportunity.'

Among the corporates we've featured in this book, all of

them who are active in developing countries direct their energies towards lifting the role of women in the communities they work in, one way or another. Setting out to provide economic opportunities is, naturally, one area where they can play a major role. We saw how Unilever, for example, employs a network of tens of thousands of Shakti Ammas – women who sell their products in remote rural villages. For the first time, they earn income for their families and, maybe even more important, they get a voice and central role in village life. Coca-Cola's *5by20* programme follows a similar logic, aiming at 'economic empowerment' for 5 million women by 2020 through business training, access to credit and peer mentoring. Coca-Cola now even has a Global Director of Women's Economic Empowerment, Charlotte Oades, who explained why backing women is also smart business:

> We know that women, as future consumers, account for $20 trillion of consumer expenditure. People talk about the emerging economies of China or India. Women, as a market opportunity, represent more [opportunity] than China, India, and the United States combined.

'Girls are the most powerful force for change on the planet,' declares Girl Effect – which is a Nike Foundation initiative launched in 2009, based on research that demonstrated how investing in adolescent girls could reduce global poverty. The foundation now runs programmes across the developing world, aimed at ending early marriage, delaying first birth, and increasing secondary-school completion. Their conviction is that if you give girls the same access to opportunities as boys have, you unleash a powerful force for economic development.

But, for some people, the connection to Nike may not be immediately apparent. Why is this Nike's concern? 'The question I get asked more than any other is "why doesn't the

Nike Foundation just focus on sport?"', says Caroline Whaley, who runs creative development for the foundation. 'I tell them, Nike is about innovation, it's about world-class brand communications – and we're focusing these core capabilities on where they can really make a difference in the world.' Caroline, who spent fourteen years working at Nike, responsible for marketing across Latin America and Canada, before becoming General Manager for their Running business, knows a thing or two about the Nike brand. When you look at the work of the foundation, there isn't a swoosh in sight – and yet somehow it really resonates with the spirit of Nike. Caroline explains: 'Nike Corporation is about a belief in human potential. And so Nike Foundation is about the potential of adolescent girls – girls living in poverty. What could be more true to the brand than that?'

In our journey through business, we've come across a great variety of imaginative work focused on supporting women. The mining company Anglo American, which runs the world's largest workforce programme for HIV/AIDS, has invested millions into the global effort to end the cycle of mother-to-baby transmission. The pharmaceutical company GSK is training thousands of female health workers and nurses in the world's poorest countries. In India, Mahindra's education trust funds 75,000 girls to go through school, 'out of the conviction that empowering women through education would have a tremendous positive impact on the nation in the long run'.

These big businesses seem to be right with Charles Malik's message that the fastest way to change society is to mobilise the women of the world – and, from all different angles, they're actively involved. Meanwhile in the developed world, the equality of women in the workplace remains an issue: there are significant gaps in the level of pay between women and men, and women are still under-represented on the boards of big companies. Sheryl Sandberg takes up the cause in her book, *Lean In*, which sets out to inspire women that they can make both their career and their family work. In it, she outlines her vision: 'In the future, there will be no female leaders. There will just be leaders.'

THE CONVERSATION ABOUT BIG BUSINESS

This book itself is part of a bigger conversation – about business, and its role in the world. Big business is seen by many as part of the problem, not part of the solution. Survey after survey shows levels of trust in business on a steady decline over the years. Exorbitant pay-packets symbolise the growing inequality between the super-rich – who have the money, the status, the power – and everybody else. The economist Joseph Stiglitz claims that the top 1 per cent saw their incomes rise 18 per cent over the past decade, while those in the middle have actually seen their incomes fall. He argues that this inequality distorts society: the corporate elites have a firm grip on power, and we live in a system 'of the 1 per cent, by the 1 per cent, for the 1 per cent'.

The companies themselves are often vilified: Big Oil, Big Ag, Big Pharma – the major players in each of these industries are seen as faceless corporates. To their detractors they seem insatiable profit-machines, inhuman and impenetrable, making money at the expense of the world around them. Any conversation about big business has to accommodate a strong cultural archetype: corporate as anti-hero – from *Avatar* and *Superman*, to *Erin Brockovich* and *The Constant Gardener*. Big companies make good villains. It can be a fraught conversation, so to get a perspective on this we went to an organisation with an unrivalled vantage point on the world of business. As the world's leading consultancy firm, McKinsey advises big businesses in all sectors, all over the world – and so we met Dominic Barton, the firm's managing director.

'I think the problem has been building up over the last forty years,' Dominic tells us. 'In my view it began in the early 1970s, with the focus on shareholder value. Especially in the West – it became an obsession that *the business of business is business,*' he says, referring to the maxim of free-market economist Milton Friedman, who thought that companies have only one responsibility: to increase their profits. Dominic thinks this narrow focus is self-defeating:

> If you don't, as a business leader, think about stakeholders, not just shareholders, think about the stakeholders – and that's not just employees and customers, but also the communities in which you are operating – if you don't think of those stakeholders as core to what you do, you will not maximise your value. The two go well together: shareholder value and stakeholder value are synergistic, they are not trade-offs.

This is at the heart of the problem, according to Dominic: a narrow focus on shareholder value, which has led to a short-termism in corporate decision making, especially among big companies based in the West. During his time at McKinsey, Dominic has spent time living in Toronto, Sydney, Seoul, Shanghai and now London. The most marked difference between East and West, he tells us, is the time frame managers consider when making big decisions. 'I do think we have become way too short-term orientated in the West,' he says. 'Some of the challenges that we have to deal with, like education, cannot be fixed on a quarterly basis.' Dominic feels strongly about this, and wrote an article calling for a shift from *quarterly capitalism* to *long-term capitalism*. 'You can't deny the power of thinking long-term,' he explains;

'you can't develop a new drug in a quarter – there is a cycle, sometimes of nine years, or nineteen years. Some of the vital business problems are not four-year problems, they are ten-year problems.'

The debate over long- or short-termism has become a central part of the conversation about big business. Some corporates have stopped issuing quarterly earnings guidance: Unilever, Coca-Cola and Ford now only publish their financial results annually, and Google only ever did. Many of the major mining companies now only report results twice a year, including BHP Billiton, Rio Tinto and Anglo American. Unilever's CEO Paul Polman reflected on this when we spoke to him in Chapter 13; he famously told his investors that if they didn't like the company's approach, they weren't the right investors for Unilever:

> Unilever has been around for 100-plus years. We want to be around for several hundred more years. So if you buy into this long-term value-creation model, which is equitable, which is shared, which is sustainable, then come and invest with us. If you don't buy into this, I respect you as a human being, but don't put your money in our company.

Much of the conversation about business is about measurement and reporting, as Dominic explains. 'You know that adage that goes *what gets measured, gets done* – well, the challenge is that a lot of the metrics that we have available right now for performance are short-term orientated, not the long-term orientated ones.' The shifts in reporting we are seeing from companies like Unilever are an attempt to redress this balance, he says – broadening the focus to look at other stakeholders, as well as shareholders. There's no shortage of frameworks and standards intended to facilitate this: ecological footprint reporting, environmental and social governance reporting (ESG), the Global Reporting Initiative (GRI) – the problem, according to Dominic, is being more precise about how shareholder value and stakeholder value are connected. 'Shareholder value is really around the cash flows as opposed to the drivers of those cash flows, if you see what I mean. So there is a consistency between stakeholder and shareholder, but we have to be more articulate about that connection, and how to measure it.' One of the biggest contributions to this conversation was made by John Elkington when he coined the term 'the triple bottom line' (TBL) in 1994. His idea was that companies should report three separate bottom lines: the first is the company's traditional profit and loss account; the second is a 'people account' – some measure of social impact; and the third bottom line is the 'planet account' – its impact on the environment. Reporting on these three bottom lines would ensure that companies are accounting for the full cost of doing business, Elkington argued. It's an idea that significantly moved on the debate about how businesses can account for their role in society, and forms the basis for many corporate responsibility reports. Of course, the conversation continues: many ask how the three accounts can be 'added up', given that it's difficult to place a financial value on the 'people' and 'planet' accounts. As Dominic tells us, 'I think these are good indicators, they are good ideas, but the analysts are not sitting there measuring these elements to the level we would like.'

Ever since the introduction of the 'triple bottom line' concept, John Elkington has been one of the leading voices in the conversation about business in society. He is described by *Business Week* as 'a dean of the corporate responsibility movement for three decades'. John has spent years working on these issues with some of the world's biggest companies, and so we asked him for his take on the current debate. He has the sagacity of a seasoned activist, but this clearly hasn't softened his ardour. When we met him, he was frustrated with the pace of change in the corporate world. 'You look at McDonald's or Coca-Cola or Pepsi, these sorts of companies, they are so hemmed in by competition, by regulators, by their consumers or customers,' he tells us. 'So you can't completely blame companies for doing things that are in the long-term perspective unsound, if that's what they've been asked to do by key people like investors or consumers.' What's needed, John tells us, isn't just a change at the corporate level, but in the system as a whole:

> Somebody once said that culture trumps strategy. And I think a lot of what this movement is trying to do is influence the strategy in companies – but in the end it's culture that counts, and not only corporate culture, there's a cultural context within which companies operate. Which I think is crucial.

Many people are trying to bring about this shift in culture. John Mackay, the CEO of Whole Foods Inc, started a movement he calls 'Conscious Capitalism'; Richard Branson, after publishing a book called *Screw Business As Usual,* founded The B-team – a group of business leaders 'with a single purpose: to make business work better'. The idea of 'Inclusive Business' is often discussed as a way to ensure that a broader range of stakeholders is considered in decision making. Some companies have developed their own philosophies in this area: the UK retail group Kingfisher Plc, for example, talks about 'Net Positive', which it describes as 'a new approach to doing business'. To succeed, business must do more than minimise its negative impact – it must be designed to have a more positive one. Nestlé has adopted the concept of 'Creative Shared Value' (CSV) that was introduced by Michael Porter and Mark Kramer in an article in the *Harvard Business Review.*[82]

The company has formed a Creative Shared Value Advisory Board to help guide its decision making, and John Elkington is a member. When we asked him about it, he was optimistic: 'they have a sense of their own self-interest, which goes back 140, 150 years,' he tells us. 'And they are absolutely determined to be in business 140, 150 years from now, and will do what it takes.' It's possible to see how a company's interests and society's interests can operate hand in hand.

One of the most provocative voices in the conversation about business today is the economist Dambisa Moyo. She has worked at Goldman Sachs and the World Bank, and is the author of a number of forthright books on business and the global economy. She told us that increasingly the world is looking to business to provide the answers to future challenges.

> There are going to be 9 billion people on the planet in 2050. Economic growth means that in 2030 there are going to be 3 billion new people in the middle class. There is simply not enough water, not enough arable land, not enough energy and minerals to support living standards the way that Westerners live today. Yet that is what everybody is aspiring to.

In her view, while governments have a role in providing a clear regulatory structure and appropriate incentives, everybody is looking to business to develop solutions.

We heard a similar view from Bob Zoellick, whom we met just before he stepped down as president of the World Bank. We asked him simply, how is the world doing? 'I think the world is stumbling, but it is stumbling forward,' he said, and told us that 'private-sector dynamism' is an essential part of the answer. His role in the World Bank gave him a deep insight into the role of business in the developing world, where the conversation has a different dynamic, he explains. 'In emerging markets there is not a debate about the role of the private sector; there is a desire to harness it, to recognise that it is a source of increased productivity, a source of innovation and a source of jobs.'

Of course, another contribution that business makes is tax, and this has become a topic of considerable controversy over recent years. In the global conversation about business and society, it's where the heat is today. A telling moment came with the concluding statement of the 2013 G8 conference. The declaration didn't address one of the pressing geopolitical issues of the day, such as nuclear North Korea or war-torn Syria. Neither was it about ending global hunger, or stopping the rise in obesity; it wasn't even about tackling climate change. Instead, announced with much fanfare, the world leaders delivered a grand statement about *corporate tax reporting*. Clearly the issue has risen up the political agenda. It presents a dilemma for governments: on the one hand, they are forced to look ever harder for tax revenues, and they need to respond to public calls to be 'tough' on tax. On the other hand, low tax rates are one of the main tools governments have to compete for the economic activity that big companies can bring; job creation and investment. Politicians find themselves in a lose-lose position on tax.

The picture for business is even more complex. Big businesses have become as adept at minimising their tax burden as managing their costs. As you would expect, they are very efficient about the process, applying the sharpest financial brainpower to the task. Shifting their cash flows across borders, transferring costs across geographies, investing according to global priorities, they have the wherewithal to keep one step ahead of local treasury departments. And here's the problem: the result, to many, looks distorted. It can seem like a multidimensional, multi-player game of chess which the corporates are winning. So a steady stream of stories make their way into the media about businesses that are clearly doing well but are paying next-to-no tax – and inevitably this has fuelled public anger. Yet it's surprisingly challenging to distinguish all points along the spectrum from impressive efficiency to sharp practice to blatant knavery. It's further confused by the fact that governments are seldom consistent and clear about the rules of the game. And as the outcome of the G8 discussions on the topic highlighted, this is a global conundrum. Governments may be as reluctant as corporates to bare all. And global consensus is likely to prove as elusive as it does on trade or carbon emissions.

These companies have workforces and supply chains that stretch across national boundaries, operations that are deeply embedded in many countries and a global customer base. Corporations are, of course, taxed on their profits – but deciding how much profit should be attributed to any one specific country is a genuine puzzle. Meanwhile, the world is a patchwork of different jurisdictions and competing national interests. So there's an inevitable tension between the corporates who are intent on the best outcome for their business at a global level, the politicians who fly the flag for their own country, and the global institutions which are working to stitch together a coherent system of international rules which everyone can sign up to.

There's no simple answer: tax is one of today's real areas of friction for big business, and the debate will run for some time. But it's already clear that some leading companies have been prompted to re-examine what has hitherto been accepted as common practice – and over the next few years this is going to be one of the defining issues of what it means to be a good corporate citizen in the public imagination.

To an extent, we get the big businesses we deserve. No conversation about the role of business in society is complete without considering the role of the public. Ultimately it is the public – as consumers, as citizens – who create the environment in which business operates. Jared Diamond, in his opus *Collapse: How Societies Choose to Fail or Succeed,* offers a thoughtful point of view on this:

> To me, the conclusion that the public has the ultimate responsibility for the behaviour of even the biggest businesses is empowering and hopeful, rather than disappointing. My conclusion is not a moralistic one about who is right or wrong, admirable or selfish, a good guy or a bad guy. My conclusion is instead a prediction, based on what I have seen happening in the past. Businesses have changed when the public came to expect and require different behaviour, to reward businesses for behaviour that the public wanted, and to make things difficult for businesses practicing behaviours that the public didn't want. I predict that in the future, just as in the past, changes in public attitudes will be essential for changes in businesses' environmental practices.[83]

15

THE PRISM

In our journey through the world of business we met people in company boardrooms and on the front line of operations – in mines, factories and farms, in data centres and distribution hubs. We travelled to the furthest end of the supply chain. We spoke to people in mature economies and developing countries, in North America and South Africa, in Indonesia and India. We listened to admirers and critics of business, insiders and outsiders, and we heard from policymakers and campaigners, partners and suppliers. And we learnt what it takes to get a product to market, whether it's software or soap, a jet turbine or a crate of mangoes. All the time our question has been: what does it look like when business has a positive impact on society?

Give that question to a politician or an economist and you'll get an answer that focuses on investment and productivity, exports and GDP – and employment, of course. More often than not, that's what people have in mind when they think about the role of business in society. And we agree about the importance of that, yet we think there's more to it as well. So in this chapter we present the Prism as a way of making the different aspects of social value more visible. But first, we'll look more closely at what is perhaps the most fundamental contribution of business to society: jobs.

ECONOMIC FOOTPRINT

One of the most vivid ways to demonstrate what business means to us is to look at what happens when it's absent. When a big company collapses, jobs are lost. But it's not long before people notice it's not just employment and money that go when jobs disappear.

Unemployment leads to a deep sense of disorientation, disenfranchisement and pain for individuals. And it can devastate entire communities: desolate images of Detroit's once-grand old neighbourhoods falling into disrepair are a reminder of how the decline of big business can rip the heart out of local economies. And in many countries around the world today, the despair of large and growing populations of jobless young people who feel they have little to lose is the fuse that ignites social unrest.

During the great depression of the 1930s, the social psychologist Marie Jahoda documented how the loss of work affected the people of Marienthal, a village not far from Vienna, when the main factory closed down. In what has become a classic study, she described how formerly energetic men became somehow incapable of what previously had been simple tasks for them, social life declined drastically, family life fragmented and the little money that was available was often spent on trinkets rather than necessities. She concluded that work provided people with a fundamental 'sense of reality' which could not be obtained through any other activity or institution. First and foremost, individuals work to earn a living – the manifest function of a job – but it carries greater meaning than that. People, she said, 'have deep seated needs for structuring their time use and perspective, for enlarging their social horizon, for participating in collective enterprises, where they can feel useful, for knowing they have a recognized place in society, and for being active'.[84] She articulated the profound significance of jobs for personal effectiveness and social identity, as well as for the vibrancy of a community more broadly. Not only is unemployment problematic because of the loss of income and the burden of dependency, but it is in itself a cause of personal and social malaise.

It's hardly surprising then that unemployment is a spectre for politicians around the world. Job creation dominates the agenda for economists and policymakers everywhere – and business plays a central role in this. When we spoke to Dambisa Moyo, she described how this works, using her native Zambia as an example. Zambia, she tells us, is one of the largest copper producers in the world:

> ... but to benefit from these minerals, you need skills and capital. You need money and you need people with the expertise. We have a great mineral endowment, but we do not have enough Zambian engineers to figure out how to extract the copper. Even if we did have those Zambian engineers, we need money. We need to buy the machinery to convert the raw mineral into copper wire to be able to export it. This is a very practical expertise that the mining business can bring to Zambia, but the same principle applies across the board, whether it is in financial services, consumer goods, or telecommunications. Companies should, and do, invest and provide capital and skills in order to create jobs in this country and around the world, and that really is super-essential.

On a visit to Ethiopia we met Bethlehem Tilahun Alemu, a young entrepreneur who appears on Forbes' list of 'Africa's most successful women'. She grew up in an impoverished rural area on the outskirts of Addis-Ababa, and saw the terrible impact that unemployment had in her local community. She made it a personal mission to tackle this. She noticed that although most of her neighbours had no jobs, many of them possessed traditional artisan skills, and so she founded SoleRebels – a small business crafting shoes from local natural fibres. Today, SoleRebels sells in more than thirty countries, courtesy of Amazon's global distribution. When we met her, revenues had just broken through the $1 million mark, and the business was employing more than 100 locals. We meet some of them, leaning over their work with an air of calm concentration: we're shown how the soles are made from old weather-beaten tyres, how the fabrics are hand-loomed, and then the shoes are hand stitched. It's a time-consuming process, and productivity needs to increase as the demand grows. Inevitably, journalists like to refer to SoleRebels as 'Africa's answer to Nike', and at one point our conversation turns to the Nike Foundation – the company's philanthropic effort in the developing world. Bethlehem's point of view was striking: 'Tell Nike that if they want to help in Africa they should build factories here,' she says. 'That's what we need: not charity, but investment, and jobs.'

Jobs are fundamental to what economists talk about as the 'socio-economic impact' of business. Typically, mapping that out begins with understanding the direct employment generated and the indirect employment supported in the supply chain or in the distribution network. It also encompasses investment in skills, in research and infrastructure. It recognises the role of business in paying not only the wages of people in work today, but the pensions of those who are retired. It identifies how the activities of business flow through to productivity, exports and GDP. All of this can be modelled and measured, analysed and evaluated. A company's socio-economic impact is an important articulation of the contribution a business makes. And as companies increasingly feel the need to account for their value to society, some commission independent studies to track their economic footprint in specific countries – and their desire to do so is surely positive. But we don't think that the role of business in society can be reduced to that. It doesn't feel satisfying, and it's not the human experience of business.

In this book we set out to see what it looks like when people choose to work through business to create a positive impact in wider society. We discovered that, wherever we encountered it, we were repeatedly seeing one of five things. Coincidentally, they all begin with the letter 'P': Purpose, Products, Practices, Philanthropy, and Point of View. Together, they offer a new way of looking at how business can deliver social value, and we call it 'the Prism'.

BUSINESS IN SOCIETY

The Prism is a way of seeing more clearly the intentions and behaviour of businesses in society. The companies we met on this journey tend to be driven by a strong sense of *Purpose* – a clear idea of what they are *for* and an ambition that what they do overall will have a positive impact on the world around them. How a company interprets its purpose is the prime mover and it informs the three ways in which any business touches society: through the goods and services that it sells; through how it operates; and beyond the core activities of the business, through the social causes it chooses to support. *Products, Practices* and *Philanthropy.* These are the practical ways that businesses connect with the wider world. Indeed, there aren't any other ways: it's in these areas that businesses act and how intentions become manifest. Finally, the companies we've seen in these stories have a sophisticated awareness of the influence they have in the world, and a *Point of View* about how to use their influence to further the contribution they can make on the issues which are relevant to them.

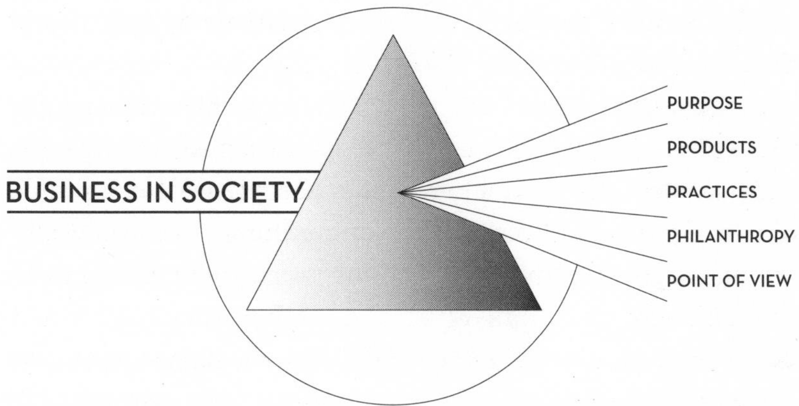

The role of business in society is played out in each of these distinct strands. We see it as a prism: one white light refracted into separate streams of colour. Taken as a whole, they describe how businesses can create social value.

Our proposition in this book is that if you want to fix the world, you're better off harnessing the power of business than fighting it. We've visited many companies in the preceding chapters which make it possible to believe in the potential of businesses to have a positive impact in society. In this chapter, we look at their activities through this prism, to make the elements of what they're doing and how they do it easier to identify and interrogate. So, if you're someone who's concerned to push business to do more or better, look in these areas to understand what could be different and what the potential is for change. Or, if you're someone who's concerned about the state of the world and the need for new solutions to some of the intractable challenges of our time, look in these places to see what business has to contribute.

PURPOSE

All of the companies we have met are motivated by more than the blind pursuit of profit – even though all of them have a track record of delivering handsome returns to their shareholders. Profit, for these companies, flows as a consequence of doing what they do well. How purpose sets the context for profit was described neatly by the economist Will Hutton: 'purpose declares what a business is about and what its capabilities need to be. It creates an animating framework for the pursuit of profit, rather than making profit the sole purpose of the company.'

We've seen how MTN became Africa's largest telecoms company by setting out to make the power of mobile available for everyone. Other telecoms companies thought doing business in rural Africa was too difficult and too risky, but MTN had a conviction that mobile would change people's lives – and are now reaping the rewards. We saw how IBM, a company which has lost its impetus more than once in its long history, has re-energised its business through a fresh articulation of its purpose: to create a *Smarter Planet* by applying the company's formidable intellectual firepower to solving some of the world's complex challenges. We saw how, for six decades, Mahindra has aligned its growth to the development of an entire economy – a clear purpose now expressed in its brand platform: *Rise*. The chairman, Anand Mahindra, articulates it as a simple logic: 'Mahindra helps you rise, because when you rise your community rises, and we rise with all of you.'

All of these companies talk thoughtfully about the purpose of their businesses – but suggest to any of them that profit doesn't matter and you'll get an abrupt response: profit is essential to any well-run business. It's a bit like breathing: essential to life, but nobody thinks that breathing is the *purpose* of life. Without profit, companies wouldn't be able to invest in innovation, or secure capital from the markets. If a company is providing a product or service that has social value, it's in everybody's interest that it stays financially viable. We've met some of the world's biggest companies in industries which underpin our lives, in areas as different as food, aerospace, mining and telecoms. And for the management of these companies, the financial health of the organisation they run is a top priority; but still, none of them would describe it as the *purpose* of the company.

Public sector organisations, charities and NGOs all hold a specific social mandate: social benefit is their only purpose. So it's sometimes assumed that a positive social impact can only be achieved if you put business purpose on hold for a while. We've all grown used to dividing *profit* and *not-for-profit* activities, with the implicit assumption that the not-for-profit sector does *good* things and, by implication, profit-making organisations do ... well, *bad,* or certainly *less good,* things. But on this journey we've met many for-profit organisations increasingly putting a social purpose at the centre of their strategy. And not-for-profits are increasingly behaving with a businesslike attitude in order to achieve their goals. The boundaries are blurring and making an absolute division is an outdated way of looking at the world. The businesses we've encountered show us that the greatest guarantee that the organisation will have a sustained positive impact in the wider world is that the ambition to do so is given expression in the company's purpose, not treated as an offset to its commercial activities.

As more companies start to talk about 'purpose', there's a risk that the idea reduces to a mere rehash of the Mission Statements that were ubiquitous in the 1990s. Today, the Mission Statement has become a Dilbert-style corporate cliché. There is even a Mission Statement Generator app that produces plausibly anodyne offerings, such as: 'Excellence means productising proven systems to benefit our stakeholders through constant innovation.' Still, the original instinct behind the Mission Statement was a good one and tapped into the natural energy of business. Professor Chris Bart was an early advocate and wrote a paper called 'Sex, Lies and Mission Statements' in which he likened them to 'the sex drive of the organisation' – although it's hard to imagine that many of the vanilla mission statements of today's corporate world generate much passion.

Very often, what we've encountered in the companies we've met is a strong *sense* of purpose. There's no doubt that the denizens of the Googleplex or the Facebook campus are very conscious that their work is having a considerable impact in society at large. Both companies have managed to capture this in clear statements: 'to organise the world's information and make it universally accessible', and 'to make the world more open and connected' respectively. These words work because they articulate a deeply held feeling in the people in those companies about the significance of the work that they are doing. Talking about purpose can on occasion elicit a world-weary cynicism, such as we encountered from one seasoned Silicon Valley insider who told us, 'come on, these guys didn't set up their companies because they wanted to change the world – they just wanted to get laid and have a good time.' Which prompts the question, in which sad world are these two things mutually exclusive? Of course, it's unlikely that a fully-fledged social mission was baked into the business from day one; as these companies grew and their potential to make an impact on the world became clearer, the sense of purpose has become stronger. As Mark Zuckerberg puts it, 'Building a mission and building a business goes hand in hand.'

So *purposefulness* is a useful idea: setting out to have an overall positive impact on the lives of employees, customers and suppliers, and on their communities. Today's leading companies are clearly purposeful businesses, intent on making money by creating value for everyone involved. Some have embedded this purposefulness in an overall corporate philosophy, such as PepsiCo's *Performance With Purpose*. For others, it extends to transforming business itself: Unilever's Keith Weed told us of the company's ambition 'to make sustainability commonplace', and Hannah Jones described how Nike aims 'to reposition sustainability as a design concept, as an innovation concept, as a business concept'. These companies are purposeful about a big job they believe needs doing – something which is of the moment, and something that's meaningful for both the business and the wider world. And, as it is for a person, so it is for a company: having a sense of purpose is invigorating and motivating.

Purpose is the starting point for any company considering its role in society: what are we *for*? What is our ambition for the impact we want to make? The answers to these questions inform how the business acts: the products and services it takes to market, the decisions it makes about the practices and processes required to deliver that, and any philanthropic activity it chooses to undertake.

PRODUCTS

The most obvious way that companies can play a positive role in the world is through the goods and services they take to market – and we've seen plenty of examples of this in action.

Mahindra's Yuvraj tractor has revolutionised life for many smallholder farmers in India, bringing compact, affordable mechanisation for the first time. In a country with hundreds of millions of smallholder farmers, this is a sizeable market opportunity. Unilever's Pureit allows people to scoop water straight out of a river and purify it – without requiring pressurised water or electricity. Hundreds of millions of people fall prey to waterborne diseases every year, and so Pureit could be a transformative product on a massive scale – and a big business bet. These are products designed specifically to respond to a social need.

And it's not just a developing world phenomenon: for all of us, the goods and services of big business are woven into the fabric of our daily lives. We've seen the reality of that in day-to-day products we take for granted from shampoo to email, and in high-spec products from life-saving drugs to solar-powered cars. As we saw in Silicon Valley, the big beasts of the technology sector arguably do more to shape our everyday experience than any government or NGO could ever do. Asked why Apple didn't invest more time or money in philanthropy, Steve Jobs would insist that the company's products were its greatest possible contribution to the world.

Of course, for many products there is intense debate about whether the contribution they make is positive, or not. Is the world really a better place for the existence of high-sugar fizzy drinks or gas-guzzling SUVs? Each of us will draw the line differently: for some, colas are a harmless treat; for others, they're an assault on the health of humanity. Our own consciences are our best guides. Most of us may feel some small pang of guilt as we book a flight, knowing that we're adding to the problem of climate change. We're aware that aviation is the fastest growing source of carbon emissions, and it looks highly unlikely that the world's lust for travel will subside any time soon. But, in fact, the answer may lie in the design of the product itself: Rolls-Royce is one of the world's leading aircraft engine makers, and we saw how they've been steadily increasing the energy efficiency of their engines over many years. It's incremental work: the company have been able to improve fuel use by about 1 per cent a year, but that means that the latest Trent XWB engine is 16 per cent more efficient than 1995's Trent 700 model. If society means to slow the rise of carbon emissions associated with aviation, it's continuous product improvement like this that will play a crucial role.

And, as we have seen, energy efficiency is a top priority for product designers in all industries, not just aviation. Consumer electronics especially is an area where global demand continues to soar, and that's where we find one of the world's unsung business heroes: ARM. Everybody has heard of Intel, thanks to a decade of Intel Inside advertising – but few people know of ARM, despite the fact that they design the chips inside more than 90 per cent of the world's smartphones, including for Apple, Samsung, HTC and BlackBerry.

We met ARM's CEO Warren East before he announced he would be stepping down after twelve years at the helm, and he was clear about what had been the driving force behind the company's phenomenal trajectory: energy efficiency. 'When we make our microprocessor twice as efficient, we're doubling the battery life of your mobile,' he tells us. 'If you look at data consumed on these devices, we would say that over the next decade there's likely to be an increase of between thirty and 100 times in the amount of data people want to use, but crucially there's only likely to be a twofold improvement in the energy capacity of a battery. That means the microprocessor has to become fifteen to fifty times more efficient in the work it does. That's what we focus on in the business.'

Without ARM technology, we would still be walking around with mobile devices attached to batteries the size of briefcases. The smartphone revolution simply wouldn't have happened without ARM's chips – but for the CEO of such a pivotal company, Warren is a low-key character. Based in Cambridge, England, both Warren and the company are embodiments of British understatement. As many of his peers gathered in Davos to rub shoulders with world leaders, a *Telegraph* journalist found Warren practising the organ in his local church. But in terms of his faith in the future of ARM, Warren is unwavering: he tells us that the company's greatest contribution to the energy challenge is yet to come. 'In terms of overall energy use, mobile phones and computers don't use that much energy. We could make all the mobile phones in the world ten times more efficient and it wouldn't make a whole lot of difference to mankind's contribution to climate change.' So where, then, is the real opportunity? 'Electric motors,' he says, now with a glint in his eye. Clearly this is where ARM sees the real opportunity for product development:

> Electric motors are huge consumers of energy in the world we live in, and therefore the benefit of changing the current generation of electric motors to smarter ones using microprocessor technology is obvious. I'm talking about motors like those used in your washing machine or winding up the window in your car, through to those powering elevators in skyscrapers. Motors account for around 50 per cent of our overall electrical energy use in the world. Of course, it doesn't have to be ARM technology specifically, but if we can double the efficiency of the electric motor, then we will be making a very big, positive environmental impact.

It's a great vision for tackling the energy challenge, and a vast new market waiting to be created. Warren enthusiastically deconstructs the global energy challenge for us, like any other problem waiting to be fixed. He talks in detail about the efficiency of energy generation, removing waste from transmission, and improving efficiency of energy use. He is an engineer to his bones, no doubt – but even so, he clearly loves the world of business. When we raise with him the debate about whether business is a negative or positive force in the world, he doesn't hesitate: 'I think it's irrelevant,' he says bluntly. Then, on reflection:

> Normally, when people ask that question, they mean business is bad because some businesses exploit people to make others better off. We are talking about businesses making products that make life better and do some good for society. Remember that whenever anybody creates a product that makes life better for society, there is usually a business behind it.

PRACTICES

When a company gets caught in the glare of negative publicity for its impact in the world, it's very often because of how it operates – its practices and processes: an apparel company with suppliers that force people to work in hazardous conditions; a consumer electronics firm whose goods are made in factories where employees are driven to suicide; a beverage company whose bottling plant consumes water so inefficiently there's none left for the local community; a mining company that forces people off their land and then dumps deadly toxins in their river... The list of corporate misdemeanours is a long one, and it usually involves the company's operational practices. Yet while business practices are where so many of the problems are to be found, it's a fruitful place to look for how business can improve its impact on the world.

Much of the effort around *Corporate Social Responsibility* is focused on minimising negative impacts which have become very clear to the world, and which economists call *externalities*: a cost that is borne by third parties who are uninvolved in the business. Every one of the companies we've featured has extensive programmes to reduce waste, carbon emissions and water use. It's the norm now in big business. Sometimes it's continuously improving processes, as we saw with SABMiller, year after year, reducing the water it needs to produce beer, or PepsiCo continuously reducing the sugar, salt and fat in its food and drinks. Other times, it may be a large-scale project such as BHP Billiton's aluminium smelter in Mozambique reducing its carbon footprint by switching from coal to hydro power. These are essential components of a system designed to reduce harm and big businesses now routinely report their progress on a number of such measures.

Yet the leaders in the field today are reaching beyond the confines of their own operations and using their influence to create a positive impact throughout their supply chains. As big businesses, they have a big opportunity to lift standards in the practices of tens of thousands of smaller businesses around the world. The bold commitment from Unilever to source all its raw materials sustainably by 2020 means they have to be active participants in improving the agricultural practices of an enormous number of smallholder farmers worldwide. And, as we saw, it's detailed work: sourcing tomatoes sustainably in southern India is saving water and improving soil quality – while at the same time increasing incomes for local farmers. We followed Nike's progress in improving employment standards throughout its global network of suppliers – while at the same time raising the game on their use of sustainable materials. Managing environmental and social impacts increasingly go hand in hand.

And we've seen companies make dramatic step changes in how they do business. APP is the biggest paper and pulp business in Indonesia and Golden Agri the biggest palm oil producer, and between them they've hacked down a lot of forest in the past. They have fundamentally redesigned the way they operate: devising entirely new approaches to clearing forest and seeking out new sources of fibre to keep the mills running. By consciously setting new industry benchmarks, they are acting as change agents for forest-based business globally. GSK too broke with industry assumptions about what's possible when they moved to a new approach to open innovation. Their patent pool acted as a catalyst for industry-wide initiatives to share data and research costs in order to accelerate the development of new medicines. They challenged deeply entrenched practices in the pharmaceutical sector to establish a new tiered pricing structure and new volume-based incentives for employees as mechanisms to help make medicines more available in the world's poorest countries.

Some decisions on corporate practice are less visible in operational terms but highly significant in their social consequence. For example, the move by BHP Billiton and other major mining companies to transparent reporting on what they pay to host countries is playing a role in international efforts to flush out unaccountable or corrupt practices across the industry. Deciding to guarantee a market price for crops for smallholder farmers, choosing to employ locals in highly skilled jobs and aiming to set global standards for health and safety are all building blocks for development. So it's not all about mitigating the negative in their own operations, there's an opportunity here. A company can choose to design its own systems in ways that aim to create positive external impacts.

We saw similar principles apply in how companies take their products to market: Unilever reaching new consumers at the 'bottom of the pyramid' through its network of *Shakti Ammas* – giving village women an independent income and an important role in village life. Or MTN's powerful new distribution channel for mobile phone airtime with its *Zoners* – providing a good living for urban entrepreneurs who are at home in the hustle of African street life. These 'micro-distribution' initiatives are a big departure from the traditional developed world practices, and a significant rethink of internal processes is needed to make them work.

There are many other such initiatives in the corporate world of companies shaping their commercial practices to provide opportunities for the micro-enterprises which come into their orbit. One of the most ambitious comes from Coca-Cola. It's called *5by20,* referring to the project's aim of empowering five million women by the year 2020. For many years, some of Coke's bottling partners had relied on an informal network to get their products out to the smaller stores: anyone with a bicycle and a trailer could take a couple of crates and earn some money. Coca-Cola became curious about these micro-distribution networks, and commissioned research with the Kennedy School of Government at Harvard. Afzaal Malik was the company's VP of International Public Affairs at the time. He tells us they were astonished with what they found: 'We realised that in certain countries at certain times up to three-quarters of the product was actually being distributed by women.' This was having a positive impact on those local communities, he explains. 'In Tanzania, for example, we found that an outlet was typically being run by a mother with a few children, and this economic activity allowed her to be close enough to home to be playing a role as mother but also allowing her to bring money into the family.'

The team at Coca-Cola hadn't set out to create such a positive external impact – it was a happy side effect of their operations. But once they realised what was happening, they decided to scale it up. After all, why wouldn't you? It seemed a real win-win: the micro-distribution network was great for the women, and really efficient for the business.

And so in 2010 the company launched *5by20*: a plan to bring five million women into the distribution network within ten years. 'We think that's very achievable, very doable,' says Afzaal. 'Obviously finance is key, education is key, and mentorship is key.' *5by20* encompasses a broad range of activities – from teaching basic bookkeeping skills, to financing solar panels that provide energy to chill the Cokes. The programme initially focused on Brazil, South Africa, the Philippines and India, and is now rolling out into many other countries. Afzaal is optimistic about the positive impact that the company can have when its operations are mindful of the world around them. 'We're seeing that we can achieve great things as Coca-Cola if we stay focused and we use our scale,' he says.

PHILANTHROPY

The main focus of this book is, of course, on how business can make a contribution to society *by doing business* – through its products and services, through its practices and processes. However, there is another important way in which business can make a direct impact in the world: philanthropy. And, as we've seen through the preceding chapters, there's a new generation of corporate philanthropy emerging. Once, people would joke that if there were fewer poor people in the world, the chairman's wife would have little to keep her occupied. Now, many companies approach philanthropy with the same imagination and rigour they apply to their core business.

We looked at IBM's Smarter Cities Challenge, where cities compete for IBM teams to spend time understanding their problems and framing solutions. The initiative builds on the *Smarter Planet* programme, and has proved a powerful way to engage employees in IBM's core purpose and a valuable source of insights about the on-the-ground issues facing city leaders. We saw how the marketing flair of Hindustan Unilever is being applied to Lifebuoy's hand-washing campaign to reduce the incidence of diarrhoea, which kills a thousand children each day in India. These are both a 'leverage' model of philanthropy, drawing on the skills and capabilities of the corporate to have a more meaningful impact.

Increasingly, we've seen philanthropy brought into harness to support strategic business objectives. For example, PepsiCo with water. When they realised the business risk of operating in many water-stressed areas of the world, they made some public commitments: aside from cutting water use in their operations by billions of litres, PepsiCo undertook to provide access to safe, clean drinking water for three million people by the end of 2015. Of course, water efficiency in bottling plants is a core operational issue for PepsiCo, but public access to drinking water isn't – and here's where the PepsiCo Foundation comes in. Working together with Columbia University's Earth Institute, the foundation identified dozens of projects in the areas of water conservation, purification, and distribution. And PepsiCo has been working in drought-hit regions of Ethiopia to develop a reliable source of chickpeas. The initiative is a blend of investment from the PepsiCo business and philanthropy from the PepsiCo Foundation: PepsiCo's agricultural experts work with local farmers to improve yields, while the foundation funds efforts to formulate chickpea-based nutritional products. Examples such as this show how corporate philanthropy and business strategy can go hand in hand.

We saw this pattern at work in other sectors. For BHP Billiton, it's of strategic importance to build up the socio-economic resilience of the host countries where it operates mines. They achieve that mostly through strengthening the local companies in their supply chain. But they also establish foundations as a mechanism for community investment into schools and teacher training, clinics and health-care workers, student scholarships and start-up funding for micro-enterprises – all of which are about boosting the vibrancy of the local economy. For GSK, it's of strategic importance to invent a viable business model for operating in the least developed countries and, as part of that, they promised to reinvest 20 per cent of the profits earned in those countries back into those countries. And we saw how that translates into funding for thousands of health-care workers. A common theme runs through each of these examples: they are rooted in the core activities of the company.

Such initiatives are a big departure from the days when companies would simply set up an arm's-length grant-making foundation, detached from the business. Of course, many corporate foundations continue to do great work. Many companies also run extensive volunteer programmes and matched-giving initiatives, and report how popular these are with employees. And in times like these when public budgets are extremely stretched, more conventional areas of philanthropic funding, from the school orchestra to the national opera house, from local sports clubs to international championship teams, keep arts and sports organisations going. If these activities ceased to be, they would leave a hole.

Yet the philanthropic efforts which most effectively connect a business to society are those which come from the heart of the company. We have seen in India how *Rise,* Mahindra's brand platform, beautifully captured the spirit of the entrepreneurial energy of the country and the company in one breath. So – of course – their leading philanthropic initiative is called *Spark the Rise* and is all about getting tiny social entrepreneurial projects off the ground which can help their communities rise. When we met some of the *Sparks,* we found they intuitively made the connection between the philanthropic scheme and the character of the business behind it. Initiatives like these become emblematic of the business, living exemplars of the brand.

The Thomson Reuters Foundation is another business that draws on the essence of its parent corporate, and so becomes emblematic of the business. It was established in 2008 when Thomson – the world's biggest legal services firm – merged with Reuters – the world's biggest news agency. The foundation's CEO, Monique Villa, told us that from the outset she had wanted to 'leverage all the assets of the company, to focus on what we know how to do best'. Monique herself is an ex-journalist, and was managing director of Reuters Media before the merger. 'Thomson Reuters is all about fast and accurate reporting around the world – and we've been doing that for 150 years, so we are quite good at it,' she explains. So one of the foundation's main activities is TrustMedia, which works to promote quality journalism in some of the world's more vulnerable areas, such as conflict zones. 'We train journalists around the world so that their readers benefit from better informed and balanced reporting,' Monique explains. More than 10,000 people from 170 countries have taken the courses, which cover a wide range of topics, such as 'Reporting On Terrorism' and 'Tracking Down Corruption'. 'It is really spreading the highest standards in journalism around the world,' she tells us.

Thomson Reuters is also the biggest provider of legal services to law firms around the world. Monique was keen to make the most of the scale and capability in that area of the business, and in 2010 launched *TrustLaw Connect* – a global marketplace for free legal assistance. The service matches top law firms with NGOs and social enterprises around the world. 'You need a lawyer for everything you do as an NGO or as a social entrepreneur,' Monique explains. 'Contracts, HR, IP problems, tax problems, etc. So we decided to create a marketplace for pro bono.' The idea is that NGOs don't have to spend their valuable resources on legal fees. For the lawyers, the pro-bono work offers a form of personal development: they have access to challenging cases that take them way beyond the experience of their typical caseload and give them exposure to other legal systems. And, Monique tells us, they enjoy being able to put their expertise to use helping people involved in front-line charity work.

The foundation's third major initiative is *AlertNet*, which swings into action after a disaster. 'We thought, at Thomson Reuters, what do we know?' Monique remembers: 'we know how to find information, check it, and then disseminate it. So that's what we set out to do.' In the confusion that follows a major disaster, accurate information can be lifesaving, she explains: 'It's about treating information as a form of aid, and getting it out to the local population.' When a disaster happens, the world's media come to cover the story, and the whole humanitarian machine mobilises. But because they're so busy doing what they do, nobody is thinking about informing the local population, in their language, about vital information. Not news, but vital information. Tim Large, the foundation's editor, saw this first hand in Haiti. 'Port au Prince after the earthquake was like nothing I've ever seen – it was completely devastated,' he says. 'People were desperate for information: they wanted to know how to contact search and rescue teams, where they could go for medical help, where they could get food or water.' The AlertNet team set up a free SMS service, promoted over the local radio. 'Before long we were sending practical, actionable information to tens of thousands of survivors – straight to their mobile phones,' says Tim.

Unsurprisingly, the foundation is popular with Thomson Reuters' employees. 'You cannot imagine the number of emails I receive every time we have a good story,' Monique says. 'Lots of people want to help, to volunteer. It's very good for the culture of the company, for people to feel that pride.'

There was a time, of course, when corporate philanthropy meant simply writing cheques for good causes. There used to be a lot of talk about 'giving back' – which is an interesting phrase, when you think about it, as though philanthropy was some sort of compensation to society for making money. Surely you can only 'give back' something that wasn't properly yours in the first place? But a new attitude is afoot, and many of the companies we have met are approaching philanthropy as a more strategic and creative enterprise.

POINT OF VIEW

If you want to understand what kind of impact a business might have in society, Point of View is a critical factor. It means taking a stance on what matters to the world, taking a position on significant issues that are relevant to the business. On our journey, we found it to be a defining characteristic of the companies which set themselves the ambition of having a positive impact in society. It turns out to be the secret ingredient that distinguishes the leaders from the rest.

So revisiting where we've seen Point of View at work: we heard, for example, how long ago when the world first began to see the shocking conditions that people working in Nike's supply chain were subjected to, the company's first response was that they 'do not need to know'; it was 'not within our scope' of responsibility to do anything about it. In due course, the business did a 180-degree turn on the issue and Phil Knight, their CEO at the time, took a position on workers' rights:

> I truly believe that the American consumer does not want to buy products made in abusive conditions.

He specified what he was talking about: 'slave wages, forced overtime, arbitrary abuse' and the negative impact of all of these on human rights standards. That led Nike into a programme which established the Global Alliance for Workers and Communities, the precursor to the Fair Labor Association that still today champions employment rights. It brings policy-makers, academics and NGOs to the table with businesses in a range of industries and, within that broader movement, Nike still stands out ahead of the pack.

GSK's Andrew Witty expressed a similarly dramatic shift in stance for his business when, launching their new strategy for the least developed countries, he announced: 'We need to stop saying "it's not our fault that there's no infrastructure to deliver health care" and start saying "who can we work with to ensure that the infrastructure does exist?"'

It's a straight line of sight from there to creating a business unit charged with finding a model that enables pharma companies to work effectively in the poorest countries of the world. And that set the business on a path to collaborate with governments on training health-care professionals, to redesign routes to market with pharmacy chains and to support innovative approaches to establishing rural clinics.

In both cases, the company focused on the challenge itself, and decided – because of that – they had to change the way they operated. Once they had a point of view about what mattered *out there* in the world, they had the conviction to follow through with action. And became the leaders of change in their industries.

Typically, businesses are driving for higher standards and incrementally better performance all the time, so their desire to be the best within their peer group is visible for all to see. They aim to hit targets, get accredited, win awards. That's true in social performance as well as financial performance – and an enormous amount of positive social impact comes out of that. However, there's a danger: it can mean that companies are looking backwards, over their shoulders, to check if they're outpacing their competitors; rather than facing forwards to understand the realities of the challenge in the external world.

What we discovered is that the businesses who lead have

stepped outside the echo chamber of industry conventions. They defy received wisdom about how it's possible to respond. That's why Golden Agri's announcement that they were calling a halt to deforestation caused by their business stunned everyone: it was a paradigm shift. They're no longer saying, 'let's be incrementally better than last year' – but 'let's do it differently.' They're no longer saying, 'let's be better than our peers' – but 'let's change the industry.'

These companies are not *self-referencing*: they use the challenge itself as their reference point. They take a position on the problem in the external world and use that to guide their actions. Naturally then, they're more profoundly connected to society by virtue of the fact that it's society's problem they're trying to fix, as well as their own.

As with the other Ps, the companies whose stories we've told here illustrate what's possible, but they're by no means the only businesses today who are speaking out on controversial social issues. In 2013, as the arguments over same-sex marriage continued to rumble around the United States, events took an unprecedented turn when a group of major corporates pitched into the debate. Apple, Amazon, Cisco, Facebook, Google, Microsoft and Twitter were among the companies who filed a brief to the US Supreme Court,[85] arguing that the ban on same-sex marriage was a betrayal of their principles, and ran counter to 'a workplace ethos of transparent fairness'. It was an unusual move: rarely has such an influential group of businesses weighed in on a contentious social issue. Some dismissed it as a cynical marketing ploy, aimed at appealing to a younger tech-savvy demographic – but all of these companies have broad consumer-bases, and taking a position on such a controversial topic was not without risk. Many of these companies have reinforced their position in various ways: an advert for Microsoft featured a same-sex marriage in a TV advert, and Google convened a global

'Legalise Love' conference for campaigners across the world. This might be bold, but not entirely surprising given the *think different* ethos of the tech sector.

A bigger shock awaited YouTube viewers who clicked on a Human Rights Campaign video to hear a bald middle-aged man with a strong Brooklyn accent declare: 'I'm Lloyd Blankfein, chairman and CEO of Goldman Sachs, and I support marriage equality.' So it wasn't just the Silicon Valley companies that had come to the party: Citigroup, CBS Corp, Disney, Ernst & Young, Johnson & Johnson, Morgan Stanley, McKinsey, Nike and Starbucks also signed the brief to the US Supreme Court. It was a remarkable moment in the history of corporate involvement in society, and a striking example of our 'fifth P' – Point of View. These heavyweights of the business arena were not voicing an opinion on a controversial issue simply because it piqued their interest. They were acting as mainstream employers who have painstakingly developed diversity policies within their own organisations and chose to speak up on how the equal rights they defend in the workplace are as relevant in wider society.

Other global businesses we've met have a position on female equality – in MTN, for example, there's a consciousness that as the biggest telecoms player in Africa and the Middle East their policy to allow women and men to work side by side in the same office challenges the social convention of some of the countries they work in. And in SABMiller, as a major employer in Uganda, we heard how their open recruitment policy helps to break down tribal boundaries and create opportunities for previously excluded communities. Of course, it's not about taking a position on any or every issue for the sake of it. But today's sophisticated companies have an expanded awareness of where and how they can make a difference.

Edgar Friedenberg, a radical professor of education writing in the 1970s, said that 'what we all must decide is how we are valuable rather than how valuable we are.' The same applies to business. A time of obsessive and exclusive focus on financial value is ending; successful businesses will be those who look at the world around them and ask, 'how are we valuable?' In this chapter, we offered the Prism as a way of exploring this question. Looking at the activities of business through the Prism, it's possible to distinguish the different strands that blend to form a company's overall contribution to the world. We found that this simple framework helps to open up the discussion to consider more fully how a business can create lasting social value and, through this, also generate rewards for its shareholders. It's a bold ambition for business: to become not just a successful company, but a business of value.

For people inside business – those who are actively working out what it means to play a positive role in society and what to do about it – the Prism spells out the ways in which businesses do have an impact, for good or ill. Together, they spell out the ways that businesses can work on delivering social value with the same energy and imagination that's dedicated to delivering financial value.

For people outside the world of business – especially corporate watchers concerned that the impact of big business is largely negative – often the main signal or commentary they receive is news of another failure, another fine or another disaster. And, of course, the next financial headlines. So our hope is that the Prism makes other facets of the role of business in the world more visible, and the potential for them to make a positive contribution more evident.

Whether you're inside or out, this is not about whether a particular business is good or bad, it's not about who's to blame, or how we got here. It is about recognising where we are, right now, and what's to be done. We've learnt that what matters is the direction of travel. Everyone can see what the challenges are, the question is: what's your point of view on the problem? Are you trying to be part of the solution – and why should we believe in this business?

And the discussion throws light on a fundamental question: what exactly *is* business? These days more people are moving away from the narrow answer given by the management gurus and business-school traditionalists who argued that a business is a structure for maximising profits – and nothing else. We find this an impoverished view of business. It conjures a Scrooge-like existence of fingerless mittens, huddling around a candle for warmth. But a life of business is so much more than this – something that Charles Dickens's character Jacob Marley realised too late, as he came back from the dead, dragging his chains behind him:

> 'Business!' cried the Ghost, wringing its hands again. '*Mankind* was my business... The deals of my trade were but a drop of water in the comprehensive ocean of my business!'

We've met plenty of people in this book who would recognise that sense of business – and it's from them we draw confidence in our view that a business is an assembly of human effort, directed at a common purpose. Most of the stories we've told are of large companies – each one an extraordinary concentration of skills, resources, ideas and influence, and each one trying to figure out how to make itself valuable in the world. Business is about profit, yes – and it is about more than profit: at its best, it is about expanding the possibilities of humanity.

EPILOGUE

'The reasonable man adapts himself to the world: the unreasonable one persists in trying to adapt the world to himself. Therefore all progress depends on the unreasonable man.'
— George Bernard Shaw

This book has taken us to some special places. We've spent time in numerous corporate headquarters – some like bustling college campuses, others in gleaming lofty towers. We've visited vast mining operations and tiny smallholder farms, water treatment plants and smart-grid operation centres, breweries and bottlers. We've watched tractor engines rolling off humming assembly lines, and precision parts for jet turbines being laser-etched in futuristic manufacturing labs. We talked to the vendors selling airtime on busy African city streets, and the women who deliver soaps and detergents door to door in remote Indian villages. We've followed the pulse of business from the corridors of corporate power to the tiniest capillaries of commerce – a few dollars of phone credit, a couple of crates of mangoes.

All of the companies we feature are mobilising to tackle some of the challenges we all face – and not in an incremental way, but by questioning the status quo and challenging their own business models. This is a book about transformation, not about tinkering at the edges. The companies we've spent time with have become big global players: some are long established organisations that have put down roots in many different markets; others are young companies which have grown up to energise the new economy. Some of them are in industries as old as civilisation itself, such as agriculture or mining; others, like the big beasts of Silicon Valley, are busy shaping the future. Many have had dark times when public censure has forced them to ask deep questions about who they are and how they operate; others have grown into an awareness that their power makes them players on the world stage.

We've sought out stories that show the potential of big business to play a positive role in society. Hearing how others have gone about it may offer insight and encouragement to companies beginning their own journeys. At the outset, it can seem a steep hill to climb. The risk is that they withdraw, and find themselves stereotyped as *bad* companies, cornered by a lazy *good-versus-evil* narrative. Each of the companies we feature is a leader in its own way, but we don't mean to suggest that those we've met are fault-free, entirely *good* companies, or that there could ever be such a thing. For sure, the companies themselves would not claim that. The case we make is that the future belongs to companies who can create a positive relationship with society – one that generates value for everybody involved. The companies in this book are leading the way: in transforming themselves they are bringing about a change for their industries and ultimately for the world of business. Our hope is to help make that happen.

Of course, many in business feel they have to live up to a machismo archetype of the big-swinging-dick business leader. They find this whole subject too *soft*. Real business is not for the faint-hearted; it's for the hard-headed. It's red in tooth-and-claw, and focused on the numbers: anything else is a distraction. The business of business, they like to say, is business.

But not according to Dominic Barton, the man who heads up McKinsey. McKinsey is the world's foremost management consultancy, and a flag-carrier for tough-minded business strategy. The firm has an extraordinary record of incubating future leaders, with consultants going on to become CEOs at companies such as Vodafone, HSBC, BHP Billiton, IBM, Boeing and BMW. 'I am all for making as much money as possible,' Dominic told us. 'We are a hard core business, you know, people call us the Jesuits of capitalism. We want people to make money, but I don't think you are going to have a sustainable business if you are not thinking about the stakeholders with which you operate because they can destroy your business very quickly.' Dominic sees a shift from pure business strategy towards companies driven by *purpose*. 'If your only purpose is to make as much money as possible then I don't believe you'll be as successful in the long-term. I'm not saying you won't make money, but you won't sustainably do that unless you make a contribution to the broader good.'

If McKinsey are the Jesuits of capitalism, then this is a striking thing to hear from its high priest. It's a radical alternative to the old paradigm of business as a ruthless zero-sum game. In this book we've explored this emerging picture of business – and the people we've met along the way are far from the bleeding-heart liberals many might expect. They are people grappling with some of the toughest issues facing business today – some remarkable individuals, working at all levels within big companies. We've learnt from them that really getting to grips with a corporate's role in society isn't *soft*: it requires guts, determination and stamina. It's worth quoting at length from an address given in 1953 at Harvard Business School, the seminary of no-nonsense capitalism. Professor Malcolm McNair, who was a pioneer of the school's famous method of teaching by looking at real-world case studies, gave the talk – entitled 'Tough-Mindedness and the Case Method':

> William James, a great teacher of philosophy at Harvard during the early years of this century, made the useful distinction between people who are 'tough-minded' and people who are 'tender-minded'. These terms have nothing to do with levels of ethical conduct; the 'toughness' referred to is toughness of the intellectual apparatus, toughness of the spirit, not toughness of the heart... The tough-minded have a zest for tackling hard problems. They dare to grapple with the unfamiliar and wrest useful truth from stubborn new facts. They are not dismayed by change, for they know that change at an accelerated tempo is the pattern of living, the only pattern on which successful action can be based. Above all, the tough-minded do not wall themselves in with comfortable illusions. They do not rely on the easy precepts of tradition or on mere conformity to regulations. They know that the answers are not in the book.[86]

By this definition, the people we've met during the course of writing this book are surely some of the most tough-minded people in business – defying long-held assumptions, upending business models, turning industries inside out. They're not content to administer the status quo; they want to change the system. They are the *unreasonable people* identified in the George Bernard Shaw quote at the beginning of this chapter. In some ways they're more like tireless activists than business executives. Often they've signed up to the world of business because they recognise that's where the action is. A big corporate, they understand, offers the opportunity to create better products, and to transform industry practices.

Some of the people we met almost surprised themselves by joining business. In Chapter 3, Hannah Jones at Nike told us that as a teenager she had imagined herself scaling the walls as a Greenpeace campaigner. In Chapter 9 we met Derek

Yach, who was a working on world health issues as a former Executive Director of the World Health Organization and the Rockefeller Foundation, and had been a critic of the food and beverage industry before spending some years as Global Head of Health and Agriculture Policy at PepsiCo. He had never thought he would join a private company, but it seemed an irresistible opportunity to make change happen from the inside – even though some of his public sector colleagues thought he was a 'traitor to the cause'. As we heard, being inside a big business gave him a different perspective on the demands that are made of the industry:

> It's very easy to write about it from the outside, and then you come into the company and you get insights into the realities of what appear often on the outside to be very simple things to do. You realise there are many roadblocks... What sounds so simple and alluring turns out to be much more complex to achieve, and that's the intellectual challenge.

Before he joined the drugs giant GSK, Allan Pamba was incensed by the pharmaceutical industry. He told us he was a practising doctor in South Africa, running a clinic in a community torn apart by HIV/AIDS. Without access to treatments he could do nothing for his patients except help them to die, because the industry was rigorously enforcing its patents and prices. Allan told us that his patients' stories were breaking his heart, and finally he could take no more. He left Africa and studied public health, with the ambition of becoming a voice for his patients in the United Nations. In Chapter 11, we heard that as he was graduating, a friend persuaded him to enquire about a job advertised with GSK, working with their HIV/AIDS team:

> I thought they were going to be this group of money-hungry,

> suit-wearing white men sitting in a room working out how to suck more money off poor patients all the time. I was surprised to find they were just human beings... I think for the first time it occurred to me that actually it's not a bad idea to be *in*. If you think there's a need for change, this is a way to create change.

Allan Pamba is not alone in this, as GSK's CEO Andrew Witty described: 'GSK has 104,000 people, and they're not going, "How can we protect this knowledge and make money from it?" They're asking, "How can we leverage this technology and improve health around the world?" That's what drives us.'

There's no doubt that there are many people in these big companies who are on a mission – but we don't mean to suggest that all companies are chock-full of people born with a burning desire to change the world. Often, a sense of purpose grows in people as they become aware of what can be achieved through their businesses. Marilia Bezerra saw this first hand during her time at the Clinton Global Initiative – an organisation set up by Bill Clinton to bring together leaders from corporates, NGOs and governments. Marilia was responsible for working with the corporates, and witnessed the effect that it had on individuals:

> People in business get exposed to what's out there in the world, the big challenges, and the impact that their business can have. Somehow they get moved to make a change. They've found something they can own and run with, and other people join in. They're creating change, and it's good for the business, and it feels good.

In this book, we've told the stories of many businesses – and it would have been impossible to do so without telling the stories of the people working in them and working with them.

Their journeys are intertwined and inseparable. It's an obvious truth, often overlooked: a company is its people. They are melting pots of different skills and experiences, nationalities, and personalities. A listed company may have one share price, but all companies are plural entities. In her time working at the Clinton Global Initiative, this is something that particularly struck Marilia:

> A corporation is not a unit, it's not good or bad – it's a massive amalgam of people and interests. It's not just about business plans, it's about the individual people that can make magic happen. It's about the people that become viruses and infect a whole company.

In each of the companies we've encountered, we've come across these infectious individuals, energised by their work. In South Africa we spent time with Simo Debengwa, who runs an informal network of street vendors for the mobile phone company MTN, called MTN Zoners. 'Some of our Zoners were about to go destitute, and we helped them set up businesses that are now thriving,' he told us in Chapter 8, and then with a note of self-depreciation: 'My team says I sound like a politician when I say this, but we are impacting the lives of people, and we do it whilst we are making money for MTN.' Like many people we spoke to, Simo has a sense of someone who is rewriting the rules. They talk like people who know they are at the forefront of a new way: making money by having a positive impact on the world.

In India, we met many people like this: for example, in Chapter 6, Sudir Sitapati told us, 'It's not a small thing this, it's such a powerful thing to communicate about washing your hands,' as he described how the Unilever team discovered the impact of what they could do: 'We were making a big impact on health and as a by-product of that soap consumption was going up. A lot of us got very motivated about the power of the brand.' In Mahindra, in Chapter 4, we met Abhijit Page, who works with small farmers in Mahindra's growing agriculture business. 'The most important thing is the thought of inclusive growth,' he told us. 'I grow, the farmer grows, my channel grows, my company grows – and India grows. It's a satisfying journey for me.' For many, the motivation comes from feeling that they are a part of shaping the world we live in. The air around Silicon Valley is thick with this sense of significance. Autodesk, for example, are the leading developer of software for architects, engineers and designers – essentially, they are a toolmaker. In Chapter 2 we heard Jeff Kowalski, their Chief Technology Officer, explaining that tools have changed the way we think, throughout the history of mankind. 'It's the arrival of a new tool that opens our minds to new possibilities that we would never have imagined before,' he told us, when we asked him what he loves about his job. 'That's why I come to work.'

We've seen how the boundaries between business and the wider world are beginning to become more porous. Dominic Barton talks about what he calls the emergence of 'tri-sector athletes' – people who can work across business, across government, and in the social sector of NGOs and other non-profit institutions. He should know; as the managing director of McKinsey, Dominic has an unrivalled view of how businesses are responding to today's challenges. There is hardly an industry sector or major business that McKinsey hasn't worked with, and few people can claim access to the inner workings of such a wide range of companies. 'I need to talk to two CEOs a day, to keep my fingers in the external world,' he tells us matter-of-factly, as though this were a perfectly modest requirement. 'I think the lines are blurring across every sector. So if you want to be a very good business leader, I think you have to understand how the public sector works, and the social sector works, and ideally have experience in those.' This is essential for tackling the world's big challenges – and Dominic thinks these challenges will 'accelerate and amplify' in the immediate future. He leaves us with this thought:

> The one quote I always keep in the back of my mind is what a Chinese client said to me: all these major forces at work; many are exciting and transform how the world operates, and the view of the future is going to be wonderful for humanity ... *if* we get through the next thirty years.

John Elkington shares this sense that we are in critical times. John has long been an agitator for new business models, and he agrees that it takes a special kind of person to tackle these challenges from the inside. 'You have to have immense resilience and stamina to drive through these changes,' he tells us. 'I think big companies badly need people who can work in this sort of space – to channel a different reality into the boardroom; to bring the future into a company.' John is, of course, something of a living legend in the world of corporate responsibility. We met him fresh from filming an interview for his induction into a Hall of Fame for the International Society of Sustainability Professionals. Far from seeming pleased with himself, he seemed frustrated. 'We need to do more, do better, do faster, to actually disrupt,' he implored, seeming almost to chide himself. 'It doesn't matter how many halls of fame or whatever you have – it's almost encouraging people to sit on their laurels, rather than to shake the pillars of the temple.' If there's one thing it seems John wants to communicate to us, it's a sense of *urgency*:

> Ten years from now we'll look back at a transformed landscape. The scale of the challenges I think is so great

> that quite a few of the big brand companies that we've got used to – that we buy from, or invest in, or work for – just simply won't be there. We're heading for a period of disruption, as our economies and markets adjust – like when you have an earthquake, and suddenly the landscape goes thixotropic, where the soil, the earth goes fluid. I think we're heading for one of those moments, for better or worse.

We've seen businesses looking at the future, and anticipating disruption. They are responding in ways untypical of the image of large corporations, which are often seen as lumbering hulks, unimaginative and bureaucratic. Changing a big business is like turning an oil tanker, people say. And yet in this book there are big companies adapting fast and changing how they operate to connect with the realities of the world outside them. In Chapter 15 we looked at the role of business in society through a prism to see more clearly the different ways in which businesses can create social value. Described as the five Ps, they are innovating new products and practices that solve real challenges in the world. They're taking their philanthropy spend and applying it strategically, amplifying the core strengths of their business. They're taking a point of view on the contentious issues that are relevant to them, and they're discovering a fresh sense of purpose about what they are *for* in the world.

At the heart of this change are people like those we have met in this book. They are the tough-minded problem solvers, using their vision and political savvy to create change for their businesses and the wider world. They're the ones mobilising big business, unlocking the talent and resources of these vast organisations and directing them at the challenges we all face. They're the unreasonable people, defying the conventional wisdom, trying to create a new reality. They're people working deep in big businesses like Dan Bena at PepsiCo, Andy Wales at SABMiller, Hannah Jones at Nike, Deepak Saxena at Unilever, Katrina Tyson at GSK and Colin Harrison at IBM. But there's a problem. Currently they are the exception, not the rule. Marilia worked with many of these people during her time with the Clinton Global Initiative – and she insists that it's important to keep a perspective:

> Looking at all of these guys, and all of the things they are doing, you would think that the business world is awakened, and they're all really on it – but that's not really true. There are a whole lot of unengaged people out there still and we're not going to get anywhere until we bring everybody on board. It can't just be a few leaders, it has to be a great majority.

When we talked about these people with John Elkington, he described them as 'sparkles of good intention'. Our hope is that they may become beacons of change. They are the people that are taking responsibility for our future, working with their colleagues, their collaborators, and their critics. They see the challenge, and they own it: *this is ours to do – as people, and as businesses. It's not somebody else's to do, some other time. It's ours to do, now.*

NOTES

1 Niall Ferguson, *Civilization: The Six Killer Apps of Western Power* (Penguin, 2012)
2 Professor Ethan B. Kapstein, René Kim and Willem Ruster, 'The Socio-Economic Impact Of Nile Breweries In Uganda And Cervecería Hondureña In Honduras' (May 2009)
3 Oxfam, Coca-Cola & SABMiller Joint Report, 'Exploring the Links Between International Business and Poverty Reduction' (March 2011)
4 Andrew Ross Sorkin, 'The Mystery Of Steve Jobs's Public Giving', *New York Times* (29 August 2011)
5 Joel Mokyr, 'Technological change, 1700–1830', in Roderick Floud and Deirdre McCloskey (eds), *The economic history of Britain since 1700, Volume 1: 1700–1860* (Cambridge University Press, 1994)
6 Thomas Crump, *How the Industrial Revolution Changed the World* (Constable & Robinson, 2010)
7 Steve Wozniak, speech to 'Silicon Valley Comes To Oxford', Saïd Business School, Oxford University (July 2008)
8 Sergey Brin & Larry Page, '2004 Founders' IPO Letter, from the S-1 Registration Statement: "An Owner's Manual" for Google's Shareholders' (Google, 2004)
9 Kartsten Lemm, 'Google's First Steps', *Ubergizmo* (July 2008)
10 H. Maurer (ed.), 'Report on dangers and opportunities posed by large search engines, particularly Google', Institute for Information Systems and Computer Media, Graz University of Technology, Austria (September 2007)
11 Andrew Garcia Philips & Sarah Slobin, 'Google's Widening Reach' (Infographic), *Wall Street Journal* (10 August 2010)
12 Nick Wingfield, 'Microsoft Attacks Google on Gmail Privacy', *New York Times* (6 February 2013)
13 Chris Jay Hoofnagle, 'Beyond Google and evil: how policymakers, journalists and consumers should talk differently about Google and privacy', *First Monday* (14 March 2009), http://firstmonday.org/htbin/cgiwrap/bin/ojs/index.php/fm/article/view/2326/2156
14 Charles Arthur, 'Apple chief insists on commitment to improve Chinese labour conditions', *The Guardian* (15 February 2012)
15 Asa Briggs, *Victorian Cities* (Odhams Press, 1964)
16 Brad Stone & Ashley Vance, 'Facebook's "Next Billion": A Q&A With Mark Zuckerberg', *BloombergBusinessweek* (4 October 2012)
17 Somini Sengupta, 'Zuckerberg Acknowledges "Disappointing" Wall Street', *New York Times* (11 September 2012)

18 Tim Carmody, 'Facebook's "Letter from Zuckerberg": The Annotated Version', *Wired* (2 January 2012)
19 Adi Ignatius, 'Meet the Google guys', *Time* (12 February 2008)
20 Andrew Ross, *No Sweat: Fashion, Free Trade, and the Rights of Garment Workers* (Verso, 1997)
21 Michael James Clancy, 'Sweating the swoosh: Nike, the globalization of sneakers, and the question of sweatshop labor', *Pew case studies in international affairs* (2000)
22 Richard J. Barnet & John Cavanagh, 'Just Undo It: Nike's Exploited Workers', *New York Times* (13 February 1994)
23 Naomi Klein, *No Logo* (Knopf Canada, 1999)
24 Nicholas Ind, 'Beyond Branding: moving beyond abstraction', a paper presented at the conference 'The Role of Humanities in the Formation of New European Elites', Venice (10–12 September 2003)
25 Jodi Heckel, 'Nike, Adidas Officials Discuss Sweatshop Issues at University of Illinois', *Knight Ridder/Tribune Business News* (29 November 2001)
26 Timothy Egan, 'The Swoon of the Swoosh', *New York Times* (13 September 1998)
27 Allen R. Myerson, 'In Principle, A Case For More "Sweatshops"', *New York Times* (22 June 1997)
28 Unicef, 'The State Of The World's Children' (1997)
29 Paul Krugman, 'In Praise of Cheap Labor', *Slate* (21 March 1997)
30 Hannah Jones, 'A Conversation with Hannah Jones, VP of Sustainable Business and Innovation at Nike', Fuqua School of Business, Duke University, http://youtu.be/PToo-HHxRas (uploaded 16 March 2011)
31 Nike, 'Global Manufacturing' (May 2013), http://nikeinc.com/pages/manufacturing-map
32 Jochen Zeitz in 'Puma's Environmental Profit and Loss Account for the year ended 31 December 2010'
33 Oliver Balch & Steven Wilding, 'Analysis: Puma's EP&L', *Ethical Corporation* (6 November 2012)
34 Stephen Gardner, 'Puma's environmental profit and loss innovation', *Ethical Corporation* (5 September 2012)
35 Jo Confino, 'Puma scales up environmental profit and loss reporting to a product level', *The Guardian* (8 October 2012)
36 Colin Harrison, 'The Great East Japan Earthquake', *Proceedings of the 55th Annual Meeting of the International Society for the Systems Sciences* (July 2011)
37 Steve Hamm, 'Reinventing the Modern Corporation', in Kevin Maney, Steve Hamm and Jeffrey M. O'Brien (eds), *Making The World Work Better: The Ideas That Shaped a Century and a Company* (June 2011)
38 P. Hemp and T. A. Stewart, 'Leading Change When Business Is Good: An Interview with Samuel J. Palmisano', *Harvard Business Review* (December 2004)
39 Sam Palmisano, 'The Globally Integrated Enterprise', *Foreign Affairs* (May/June 2006)
40 C. K. Prahalad, *The Fortune at the Bottom of the Pyramid: Eradicating Poverty Through Profits* (Pearson Education, 2006)
41 Unilever Sustainable Living Plan (November 2010)
42 National Institute of Epidemiology, study in Chennai, India, 2005–6, cited in Unilever Sustainable Living Plan
43 Global aerospace and defense industry outlook, Deloitte, 2013

44 Harold Meyerson, op-ed, *Washington Post* (24 November 2010)
45 Brent Radcliffe, 'Why Germany Is The Economic Powerhouse Of The Eurozone', *Investopedia* (7 December 2012)
46 Mark Vachon, 'GE Ecomagination's Mark Vachon in conversation with Marc Gunther', *GreenBiz*, http://youtu.be/rulw5kny2qI (uploaded 15 October 2011)
47 Dianna Games, 'MTN', in Moky Makura (ed.) *Going Global: Insights from South Africa's Top Companies* (University of Pretoria, 2012)
48 Charles Robertson, *The Fastest Billion: The Story Behind Africa's Economic Revolution* (Renaissance Capital, 2012)
49 Committee to Protect Journalists, 'Attacks on the Press in 2012'
50 Ben Elgin & Vernon Silver, 'Syria Disrupts Text Messaging of Protesters With Made-in-Dublin Equipment', *Bloomberg* (15 February 2012)
51 'MTN slated over Iran', *The Times* (South Africa), 2 March 2012
52 Access, 'MTN must stand up for its users, meet international obligations' *Accessnow.org* (November 2012)
53 Robert Neuwirth, *The Stealth of Nations: The Global Rise of the Informal Economy* (Anchor, 2011)
54 Angela Crandall, 'How the Base of the Pyramid in Kenya uses their mobile phone', *iHub* (October 2012)
55 S. Bonini, L. Mendonca & J. Oppenheim, 'When Social Issues Become Strategic', *McKinsey Quarterly*, No. 2 (2006)
56 WWF, 'Belching out copper, gold and waste', http://wwf.panda.org (retrieved July 2013)
57 Sir Robert Wilson, Global Metals and Mining Conference, Toronto (2001)
58 Caroline Rees, Deanna Kemp & Rachel Davis, 'Conflict Management and Corporate Culture in the Extractive Industries: A Study in Peru', Corporate Social Responsibility Initiative Report No. 50, Cambridge, MA: John F. Kennedy School of Government, Harvard University (2012)
59 Goldman Sachs, '190 projects to change the world', *Goldman Sachs Global Investment Research* (April 2008)
60 Richard Wachman, 'The business of fighting AIDS', *The Guardian* (3 November 2011)
61 Greenpeace, 'Guide to Greener Electronics 18', *Greenpeace Magazine* (November 2012)
62 Transparency International, 'Shining a light on the world's biggest companies', http://www.transparency.org/news/feature/shining-a-light-on-the-worlds-biggest-companies
63 John Browne, *Beyond Business: An Inspirational Memoir From a Remarkable Leader* (Weidenfeld & Nicolson, 2011)
64 Blacksmith Institute, 'World's Worst Toxic Pollution Problems' (2012)
65 Global Witness, 'Coming Clean: How supply chain controls can stop Congo's minerals trade fuelling conflict' (May 2012)
66 Shefa Siegel, 'The Missing Ethics of Mining', *Ethics & International Affairs* (February 2013)
67 Andrew Witty, 'Big Pharma as a Catalyst for Change', *Harvard Medical School* (13 February 2009)
68 K. Bluestone, A. Heaton & C. Lewis, 'Beyond Philanthropy: The pharmaceutical industry, corporate social responsibility and the developing world', *Oxfam* (July 2002)

69 'GlaxoSmithKline – A shake-up for Big Pharma', *Ethical Corporation* (2 April 2009)
70 GSK Corporate Responsibility Report (2011)
71 Rachel Cooper, 'Glaxo ventures into fragile markets with Somalian sale', *The Daily Telegraph* (30 April 2011)
72 Golden Agri-Resources Ltd & SMART, 'High Carbon Stock Forest Study Report' in collaboration with The Forest Trust and Greenpeace (June 2012)
73 Felix Dodds, Michael Strauss with Maurice Strong, *Only One Earth: The Long Road via Rio to Sustainable Development* (Routledge, 2012)
74 Suzanne McGee, *Chasing Goldman Sachs* (Crown Publishers, 2010)
75 Douglas Flint, 'Industry Response to the New Regulatory Order', *City Week* (7 February 2012)
76 Matthew Bishop, 'How to make finance socially useful', *Tomorrow's Finance* Lecture (5 December 2012)
77 D. 'Doc' Searls, C. Locke, R. Levine, D. Weinberger, *The Cluetrain Manifesto* (Basic Books, 2000)
78 Christopher Booker, *The Seven Basic Plots: Why We Tell Stories* (Continuum, 2005)
79 United Nations General Assembly (20 March 1987). 'Report of the World Commission on Environment and Development: Our Common Future; Transmitted to the General Assembly as an Annex to document A/42/427 – Development and International Co-operation: Environment; Our Common Future, Chapter 2: Towards Sustainable Development; Paragraph 1'. United Nations General Assembly. Retrieved 1 March 2010
80 Edward O. Wilson, *The Future of Life* (Abacus, 2002)
81 2030 Water Resources Group, 'Charting our water future: Economic frameworks to inform decision-making' (2009)
82 M. E. Porter & M. R. Kramer, 'Creating Shared Value', *Harvard Business Review* (January 2011)
83 Jared Diamond, *Collapse: How Societies Choose to Fail or Succeed* (Penguin, 2005)
84 Marie Jahoda, Paul Lazarsfeld & Hans Zeisel, *Marienthal: The Sociography of an Unemployed Community*, quoted in 'Good Work And Our Times' by Lucy Parker and Stephen Bevan (The Good Work Commission, June 2011)
85 Brief submitted to the Supreme Court of the United States in case 12–307
86 Malcolm P. McNair, in *The Case Method at the Harvard Business School*, (McGraw-Hill, 1954), pp. 15–24 (adapted from a 1953 address given to the first meeting of executives registered for the 23rd Advanced Management Program at the Harvard Business School)

PICTURE CREDITS AND PERMISSIONS

PICTURE CREDITS (IN ORDER OF APPEARANCE)

Uganda Houses – Jon Miller
Sorghum Farming – Jon Miller
Silicon Valley – Michael Marfell
Cottonopolis – William Wylde, "View Of Manchester From Kersal Moor" (1852)
Nike Cartoon – Danziger Cartoons
Nike Flyknit – Jon Miller
Protestors in South Africa – Anna Zieminski Photography/ Getty Images
Andrew Witty – Guardian News And Media Limited
Jet Turbine – Rolls-Royce PLC
Single Crystal Turbine Blade – Rolls-Royce PLC
Oxen – Tristan Savatier Photography
Tractor – Abhijit Bhatlekar Photography
Systems Of Systems – IBM
Smarter Planet – Ogilvy / IBM
India Demonstration – Raveendran Photography / Getty Images
Water Recycling Plant – PepsiCo
Mobile Base Station – MTN
MTN Zoner – Noo Parkinson
Escondida Mine – BHP Billiton PLC
X-ray Of Phone – Kevin Collins Photography
Lifebuoy Soap – Unilever PLC
Lifebuoy Hand-Washing Campaign – Unilever PLC
Rainforest Indonesia – Greenpeace
Bustar Maitar – Greenpeace
Scott Poynton – The Forest Trust
Aida Greenbury – Asian Pulp And Paper

PERMISSIONS

Material from *Off Book* quoted by permission of Public Broadcasting Service (PBS) and Kornhaber Brown.

Material from 'Facebook's "Next Billion": A Q&A with Mark Zuckerberg' by Brad Stone and Ashley Vance used with permission of Bloomberg L.P.

Material from *No Logo* reprinted by permission of ICM Partners, Inc. and Harper Collins Publishers Ltd. Copyright © 2000 by Naomi Klein

Excerpt from 'The Love Song of J. Alfred Prufrock' from *Collected Poems 1909–1962* by T. S. Eliot. Copyright 1936 by Houghton Mifflin Harcourt Publishing Company. Copyright © renewed 1964 by Thomas Stearns Eliot. Reprinted by permission of Houghton Mifflin Harcourt Publishing Company and by permission of Faber and Faber Ltd. All rights reserved.

Material from 'The Globally Integrated Enterprise' by Sam Palmisano reprinted by permission of Tribune Media Services. © 2006 Council on Foreign Relations, publisher of *Foreign Affairs*. All rights reserved. Distributed by Tribune Media Services.

Material from *Only One Earth* by Felix Dodds, Michael Strauss and Maurice F. Strong (Routledge Publishing, 2012) reprinted by permission of Taylor & Francis Books (UK).

Material from *The Cluetrain Manifesto* by Rick Levine, Christopher Locke, Doc Searls and David Weinberger reprinted by permission of Basic Books, a member of Perseus Books Group.

Material from *Collapse: How Societies Choose to Fail or Succeed* by Jared Diamond reprinted by permission of Penguin Group (USA).

Material from *The Case Method* by Malcolm P. McNair reprinted by permission of Harvard Business Publishing.

Material from 'Leading Change When Business is Good' by Paul Hemp and Thomas A. Stewart, *Harvard Business Review*, December 2004 reprinted by permission of Harvard Business Publishing.

BIBLIOGRAPHY

Allen, Robert C., *The British Industrial Revolution in Global Perspective* (Cambridge: Cambridge University Press, 2009).

Attali, Jacques, 'A Brief History of the Future', *New perspectives quarterly* (2007), vol. 24, no. 3, pp. 76–83 (Oxford: Blackwell Publishing, 2007).

Bakan, Joel, *The Corporation: the pathological pursuit of profit and power* (New York: Free Press, 2004).

Bernstein, Ann, *The Case for Business in Developing Economies* (London: Penguin Books, 2010).

Bishop, Matthew, *The Road from Ruin: how to revive capitalism and put America back on top* (New York: Crown Business, 2011).

Blewitt, John, *Understanding Sustainable Development* (London: Earthscan, 2008).

Bragg, Melvyn, *12 Books that Changed the World* (London: Hodder & Stoughton, 2006).

Branson, Richard, *Screw Business As Usual* (London: Virgin, 2011).

Briggs, Asa, *Victorian Cities* (London: Odhams Press, 1964).

Clancy, Michael James, *Sweating the swoosh: Nike, the globalization of sneakers, and the question of sweatshop labor* (Washington DC: Georgetown University School of Foreign Service, 2000).

Crump, Thomas, *How the Industrial Revolution Changed the World* (London: Robinson, 2010).

Diamond, Jared: 'Collapse', *Commentary* (2005), vol. 119, no. 4, pp. 85–8.

Elkington, John, *Cannibals with Forks: The Triple Bottom Line of 21st Century Business* (Oxford: Capstone, 1997).

Elkington, John and Braun, Susie, *Breakthrough, Business Leaders, Market Revolutions* (2013).

Ferguson, Niall, *Civilization: The Six Killer Apps of Western Power* (London: Penguin Books, 2012).

Floud, Roderick and McCloskey, Deirdre, *The economic history of Britain since 1700, Volume 1: 1700–1860* (Cambridge: Cambridge University Press, 1994).

de Geus, Arie, *The Living Company: Growth Learning and Longevity in Business* (London: Nicholas Brealey, 1999).

Goldacre, Ben, *Bad Pharma: How drug companies mislead doctors and harm patients* (London: Fourth Estate, 2012).

Grayson, David and Hodges, Adrian, *Everybody's Business: Managing Risks and Opportunities in Today's Global Society* (Dorling Kindersley Publishers Ltd, 2001).

Grayson, David and Hodges, Adrian, *Corporate Social Opportunity: Seven steps to make Corporate Social Responsibility work for your business* (Greenleaf Publishing, 2004).

Handy, Charles, *The Hungry Spirit: Beyond Capitalism – A Quest for Purpose in the Modern World* (London: Hutchinson, 1997).

Hylton, Stuart, *A History of Manchester* (Andover, Hampshire: Phillimore & Co, 2003).

Kaletsky, Anatole, *Capitalism 4.0* (London: Bloomsbury, 2010).

Katz, Donald, *Just Do It: The Nike Spirit in the Corporate World* (New York: Random House, 1994).

Kay, John, *Truth about markets* (New York: HarperBusiness, 2003).

King, Steven & Timmins, Geoffrey, *Making Sense of the Industrial Revolution, English economy and society, 1700–1850* (Manchester: Manchester University Press, 2001).

Klein, Naomi, *No Logo: Taking Aim at the Brand Bullies* (Toronto: Knopf Canada, 1999).

Levine, Rick, Locke, Christopher, Searls, Doc, & Weinberger, David, *The Cluetrain Manifesto* (Cambridge, Mass.: Perseus, 1999).

Lovins, Amory, Lovins, Hunter & Hawken, Paul, *Natural Capitalism: Creating the Next Industrial Revolution* (London: Earthscan, 2010).

McGee, Suzanne, *Chasing Goldman Sachs* (New York: Crown Publishers, 2010).

Mackey, John and Sisodia, Rajendra, *Conscious Capitalism* (Boston: Harvard Business Review Press, 2013).

McKinsey Quarterly, *A Resource Revolution* (New York: McKinsey Global, 2012).

McKinsey Quarterly, *Government Designed for New Times* (New York: McKinsey Global, 2012).

Maney, Kevin, Hamm, Steve & O'Brien, Jeffrey M. (eds), *Making The World Work Better: The Ideas That Shaped a Century and a Company*, (London: Pearson Education [distributor], 2011).

Mason, Paul, *Why It's Kicking Off Everywhere* (London: Verso, 2012).

Micklethwait, John & Wooldridge, Adrian, *The company: a short history of a revolutionary idea* (New York: Modern Library, 2003).

Moyo, Dambisa, *Winner take all: China's race for resources and what it means for us* (London: Allen Lane, 2012).

National Commission On The Causes Of The Financial And Economic Crisis, *The Financial Crisis Inquiry Report (Authorised)* (United States: Pacific Publishing Studio, 2011).

Porter, M. E. and Kramer, M. R., 'Creating Shared Value', *Harvard Business Review* (January 2011), vol. 89, no. 1/2, pp. 62–77.

Prahalad, C. K., *The Fortune at the Bottom of the Pyramid: Eradicating Poverty Through Profits* (London: Pearson Education, 2006).

Reich, Robert B., *Supercapitalism: The Transformation of Business, Democracy, and Everyday Life* (New York: Alfred A. Knopf, 2007).

Sachs, Jeffrey, *Common wealth: economics for a crowded planet* (New York: Penguin Press, 2008).

Sachs, Jeffrey, *The price of civilization* (London: Bodley Head, 2011).

Stiglitz, Joseph, *Making globalisation work* (London: W. W. Norton & Co., 2006).

Tapscott, Don and Ticoll, David, *The Naked Corporation: How the Age of Transparency Will Revolutionize Business* (New York: Free Press, 2003).

Uglow, Jenny, *The Lunar Men* (London: Faber, 2003).

Weightman, Gavin, *The Industrial Revolutionaries* (London: Atlantic, 2007).

Weiner, Martin, *English Culture and the Decline of the Industrial Spirit 1850–1980* (Cambridge: Cambridge University Press, 1981).

ACKNOWLEDGEMENTS

From the outset, we wanted this book to be filled with the stories of people working to make big business a positive force in the world. Numerous individuals have contributed to making that a reality. Assembled in *Everybody's Business,* they make up an extensive and extraordinary cast of characters. They make the book what it is and we'd like to thank them here.

Many businesses gave us an inside view, as well as a breadth and depth of access. These have included companies we have known as clients, and companies we have met specifically for this book. Some of the people involved are featured in the book, others made the encounters possible. Everyone was generous with their time and experiences, and candid about their own journeys. At **Autodesk**, Carl Bass, Jeff Kowalski, Michael Oldenburg and Christina Schneider. At **Access Bank**, Aigboje Aig-Imoukhuede, Herbert Wigwe, Omobolanle Babatunde and Okey Nwuke. At **Anglo American**, Anik Michaud and Jon Samuels. At **BHP Billiton**, Andrew McKenzie, Caoimhe Buckley, Danie Murray, Samuel Gudo and Osvaldo Urzua, and Chip Goodyear. At **Coca-Cola**, Afzaal Malik and Jennifer Ragland.

At **GSK**, Duncan Learmouth, Dr Mike Strange, Dr Allan Pamba, Katrina Tyson, Nandini Goswami, Hasit Joshipura, Phil Thomson, along with Andrew Witty. At **IBM**, Steve Hamm, Janette Bombardier, Colin Harrison, Alex Aizenburg and Francoise Legoues. At **Nike**, Caroline Whaley, Ben

Gallagher and Kellie Leonard. At **Mahindra**, B. Karthik, Karen Woodin Rodriguez, Partho Chakravarty, Roma Balwani, R. Chandramouli, Sheetal Mehta, R. Balaji, Basant Jain, Sanjeev Goyle, Saurabh Vatsa and Abhijit Page. At **Rolls-Royce**, Steven Halliday, John Brown, Amber Lomax and Hamid Mughal, as well as Peter Morgan, David Howie, Jeff Pasternack and Sir John Rose.

At **McKinsey**, Dominic Barton and Sheila Bonini. At **MTN**, Sifiso Dabengwa, Paul Norman, Karel Pienaar, Themba Khumalo, Christian de Faria, Khumo Sheunyane, Jennifer Roberti, Simo Dabengwa and Serame Taukobong. At **PepsiCo**, Richard Delaney, Jim Wilkinson, Nancy Lintner, Krista Pilot and Dan Bena. At **SABMiller**, Andy Wales, Bianca Shevlin, Nick Jenkinson, Onapito Ekomoloit, Dr Moses Ocen, Fred Balikagira, Julius Biingi, Mayanja R. Omugalanda, Sumin Namaganda, with long-standing support from Catherine May, Sue Clark and Graham Mackay. At **Syngenta**, Kavita Prakash, Aruna Bhinge and Jonathan Seabrook. At **Unilever**, Keith Weed, Stephen Pain, Prasad Pradhan, Madhura Harshey, Sudhir Sitapati, Ashish Rai Deepak Saxena, Vijay Sachdeva, and Paul Polman.

We'd also like to thank Peter Heng at Golden Agri-Resources, Sheryl Sandberg at Facebook, Warren East at ARM, Carl Brancher at Materials Solutions, Gib Bulloch at Accenture, Kaiser Kuo at Baidu, and Monique Villa at the Thomson Reuters Foundation.

Very experienced and insightful people from the NGO community have also made an enormous contribution to this book, helping to ensure we had a rounded picture of how business connects with society. They include Bustar Maitar and Kat Clark from Greenpeace, Nick Conger and Kristin Treier from WWF, Scott Poynton from The Forest Trust, Gunther Faber from One Family Health, Ed Monchen from the Access To Medicines Index, Eddie Rich from the Extractive

Industries Transparency Initiative, and Kulandei Francis from the Integrated Village Development Project.

Our time with TechnoServe in Uganda was especially formative, and we are very grateful to the team there, including Erastus Kibugu, Robert Paul Wamulimah, Rachel Claydon, Nathan Emuron, Juliet Namono, Betty Namono and Deogratius Egeru. Through them we met the inimitable Tukei William Wilberforce, chairman of the Bukedea district, and the farmers and villagers of Nyakoi and Bumwangu in Uganda, whose strength and spirit inspired us to open our book with their story. That's why we decided to dedicate whatever royalties this book may generate to TechnoServe: their work embodies the spirit of our argument, that business can be an engine of positive change in the world.

We would also like to thank Beth Jenkins at Harvard Kennedy School and Tobias Webb at Ethical Corporation, as well as Don Tapscott, Dambisa Moyo, Derek Yach and Robert Zoellick. We owe a special appreciation to a handful of individuals who have dedicated many years to this subject, and helped us shape our thinking, including John Elkington, Jonathon Porritt, Jason Clay and Felix Dodds.

These people have greatly influenced our perspective and enriched our argument. Yet, of course, we readily acknowledge that any faults are entirely our own.

We give heartfelt thanks to our family and friends, numerous collaborators and co-conspirators, as well as colleagues old and new. Mary Miller and Bryan Fisher, Jason Brooks, Kitty and Tom Parker Brooks, all gave us many hours of challenge and debate – and I'm sure will give us many more. Alnoor Ladha, Terry Babcock-Lumish, Marilia Bezerra, Tim Binding, Ilana Bryant, Andrew Roberts, Gail Greengross, Venetia Porter, Benjamin Ward, Stephanie Redlener, James Kydd and Scott Goodson have been great comrades, sharing their thoughts and their contacts. Eleanor Cooksey has been our diligent and creative researcher. Sarah Lloyd and Sarah Patterson showed us the importance of stories. A few brave souls agreed to read the complete manuscript of the book, including Ed Jackson-Young, Catherine Samy, Oliver Parker and Jon Sharpe, as well as Zahid Torres-Rahman from Business Fights Poverty – we really value their time and insights. A special thank-you to Yossi Lemel for letting us use his wonderful image for the cover of our book.

Many people across the Brunswick network have been a source of support and encouragement, especially David Yelland and Maria Figueroa Kupcu, as well as Alastair Morton, Oliver Steeds, Emma Boon, Alex Finnegan, Melissa Ward, Elizabeth Thomas and Nana Eshun and Zoe Sorotos. We owe special recognition to Alan Parker and Susan Gilchrist, who have both been unfailingly enthusiastic about the need to take a new look at the world of business: this book wouldn't have been possible without their support.

To our agent Caroline Michel, thank you for believing in us and in this project, and to our editor Sam Carter for his diligence, patience and encouragement.

If this book has any value, it's because of the stories and perspectives of all those people – as well as the many people we met on the ground during our travels. We hope we've done justice to their energy and goodwill.

INDEX